THE CENTENNIAL EDITION

OF THE WORKS OF

SIDNEY LANIER

GENERAL EDITOR

CHARLES R. ANDERSON

CENTENNIAL EDITION

VOLUME X

SIDNEY LANIER

LETTERS

1878—1881

APPENDICES, CALENDAR, AND INDEX

EDITED BY

CHARLES R. ANDERSON AND AUBREY H. STARKE

BALTIMORE

THE JOHNS HOPKINS PRESS

1945

PRINTED IN THE UNITED STATES OF AMERICA

CONTENTS

ILLUSTRATIONS

LETTERS
1878 — 1881

CHRONOLOGY

1878	Jan.	Living at 33 Denmead St. Ill. Trip to New York. First read Whitman's *Leaves of Grass*.
	Feb.	Began teaching at R. M. Johnston's Pen Lucy School.
	Spring	" Clover," " The Harlequin of Dreams," and " The Dove " published. Bird lectures on literature (Mar. 23–May 11).
	Summer	Wrote " The Marshes of Glynn," and " The Physics of Poetry " (first state of *The Science of English Verse*). Edited *The Boy's Froissart*.
	Oct.	Moved to 180 St. Paul St.
	Nov. 2	Began " Shakspere Course " at Peabody Institute (until May 5, 1879). " The Revenge of Hamish " published. Trip to New York to seek publisher for book on prosody.
	Dec.	" The Marshes of Glynn " published in *A Masque of Poets*.
1879	Jan. 25	Peabody Orchestra season began (until May 3). Ill.
	May–June	Edited *The Boy's King Arthur*. To New York and Boston re: text-books on literature. Wrote " Owl Against Robin."
	July 18	At Rockingham Springs, Va. (until mid-Sept.). Wrote *The Science of English Verse*.
	Sept.	Moved to 435 N. Calvert St. Teaching at private schools.
	Oct. 28– Dec. 19	Lectures at Johns Hopkins University on " English Verse, especially Shakspere's." *The Boy's Froissart* published (Nov.).
1880	Winter– Spring	Seriously ill (Dec.–Jan.). Peabody Orchestra season (Jan. 31–Apr. 23). Class course on Chaucer and Shakespeare at Hopkins (Feb. 8–Mar. 15). Read " Ode to the Johns Hopkins University " (Feb. 23).
	May 12	*The Science of English Verse* published.
	May–June	Ill. Keyser bust modeled. Wrote " The Cloud " and " The Crystal." Futile trip to New York to see publishers.
	July 21– Sept. 9	Seriously ill at West Chester, Pa. R. S. Lanier II born (Aug. 14). " The New South " published (Sept.).
	Autumn	Rejoined by wife in Baltimore (Oct. 7). *The Boy's King Arthur* published (Nov.). Edited *The Boy's Mabinogion.*
	Dec.	Desperately ill. Wrote " A Ballad of Trees and the Master," " Sunrise," and minor Hymns of the Marshes.
1881	Jan. 26– Apr. 15	Lectures at Johns Hopkins on " The English Novel." Seriously ill.
	Apr.–May	Trip to New York re: guide-book on North Carolina.
	May 18	To Asheville, N. C., with brother; joined by wife (May 25). Set up " Camp Robin," Richmond Hill (June 4).
	Summer	Edited *The Boy's Percy*. Visited by father and brother. Moved camp to Lynn, near Tryon Station, N. C. (Aug. 4).
	Sept. 7	Died, 10 A. M.

1878

To Bayard Taylor [1]

33 Denmead St.
Baltimore, Md.
Jany 6th 1878.

My dear Mr. Taylor:

When I tell you that since I saw you I have searched the city of Baltimore for a dwelling suitable to my little flock, have found one, have cajoled the landlord into a hundred repairs and betterments, have painted, whitewashed, weather-stripped and new-locked-and-bolted the entire establishment, have furnished it with all manner of odds and ends purchased from all manner of cheap Johns, have got in my coal and my wood, have provided a lot of oatmeal and hominy against The Wolf, have hired a Cook and General Domestic, have arranged with the daily milkman and all his peripatetic tribe, have done at least a million and sixteen other things, and have finally moved in and settled, —— you will understand why both Xmas and New Year have passed without greetings from me to you.

Though it has been a desperate piece of work, it seems a mere bagatelle when looked back upon from the serene delight with which we all find ourselves at last in something like a Home. I think I could wander about the house – we have nine rooms! – for a month with my hands in my pockets, in supreme content with treading upon my own carpets and gazing at my own furniture. When I am on the street there is a certain burgher-like heaviness in my tread; why should I skip along, like a bladdery Bohemian? I am a man of substance, I am liable, look you, for water-rates, gas-bills, and other im-

---

[1] Previously published, *Atlantic Monthly*, LXXXIV, 137-138 (July, 1899); reprinted, *Letters* (New York, 1899), pp. 205-206.

portant disbursements incident to the possession of two gowns and everything handsome about me.

Let me have some news of yourself, – " yourself " being a term which of course includes Mrs. Taylor and the poem.

I send you part of a Xmas poem which I wrote specially for the purpose of giving an engraver a good chance for four fine woodcuts.[2] Don't you think a sheep-painter could make four lovely pictures by carrying into detail the mere hints given in the poem?

I will probably be in New York before long, and greatly hope to see you. Our new address here is – and, God grant long may be, for we are *so* tired of moving on! – 33 Denmead St. May you write it till your pen, like the mediums', can figure it out alone.

Accept my loving wish for the New Year: thàt it may be full of new creations from your hand; – for this, to the artist, is supreme happiness.

Your friend,

Sidney L.[3]

To Gibson Peacock [4]

33 Demnead St.
Baltimore, Md.
Jany 6th 1878

My dear Mr. Gibson;

The painters, the whitewashers, the plumbers, the locksmiths, the carpenters, the gas-fitters, the stove-put-up-ers, the carmen, the piano-movers, the carpet layers,– all these have I seen, bargained with, reproached for bad jobs, and finally paid off: I have also coaxed my landlord into all

---

[2] The allusion seems to be to " Hard Times in Elfland " (see note 94, 1877), in spite of Taylor's reference to it (see following note) as a " New Year Poem."

[3] In his reply, Jan. 20, 1878 (*Letters*, New York, 1899, pp. 206-208), Taylor wrote: " I think your New Year poem charmingly quaint and fanciful; and so do several persons to whom I have shown it. I wanted to get it into the ' Weekly Tribune,' and the Editor only declined because New Year was 10 days past, and there was a stock of poetry impatiently waiting."

[4] Previously published, *Atlantic Monthly*, LXXIV, 188-189 (Aug., 1894); reprinted, *Letters* (New York, 1899), pp. 49-51.

manner of outlays for damp walls, cold bath-rooms, and other the like matters: I have furthermore bought at least three hundred and twenty seven household utensils which suddenly came to be absolutely necessary to our existence: I have moreover hired a colored gentle woman who is willing to wear out my carpets, burn out my range, freeze out my water-pipes, and be generally useful: I have also moved my family into our new home, have had a Xmas tree for the youngsters, have looked up a cheap school for Henry and Sidney,[5] have discharged my daily duties as first flute of the Peabody Orchestra, have written a couple of poems and part of an essay on " Beethoven and Bismarck ",[6] have accomplished at least a hundred thousand miscellaneous necessary nothings,–and have not, in consequence of all the aforesaid, sent to you and my dear Maria the loving greetings whereof my heart has been full during the whole season.

Maria's cards were duly distributed, and we were all touched with the charming little remembrances.

With how much pleasure do I look forward to the time when I may kiss her hand in my own house! We are in a state of supreme content with our new home: it really seems to me as incredible that myriads of people have been living in their own homes heretofore as to the young couple with a first baby it seems impossible that a great many other couples have had similar prodigies. It is simply too delightful. Good heavens, how I wish that the whole world had a Home!

I confess I *am* a little nervous about the gas-bills, which must come in, in the course of time; and there are the water-rates; and several sorts of imposts and taxes; but then, the dignity of being liable for such things! is a very supporting consideration. No man is a Bohemian who has to pay water-rates and a street-tax. Every day when I sit down in my dining-room—*my* dining-room! I find the wish growing stronger that each poor soul in Baltimore, whether saint or sinner, could come and dine with me. How I would carve out the merry thoughts for the old hags! How I would stuff the big wall-eyed rascals till

[5] Lanier's eldest son, Charles, had by this time been enrolled at R. M. Johnston's Pen Lucy School, at which Lanier himself began to teach about a month later (see note 27, below).

[6] No essay by Lanier bearing this title has been found.

their rags ripped again! There was a knight of old times who built the dining-hall of his castle across the highway, so that every wayfarer must perforce pass through: there the traveller, rich or poor, found always a trencher and wherewithal to fill it. Three times a day, in my own chair at my own table, do I envy that knight and wish that I might do as he did.

Send me some word of you two. I was in Philadelphia for part of a night since I saw you, being on my way to German-town to see Mr. Kirk. I had to make the whole visit between two rehearsals of the Orchestra, and so could only run from train to train, except between twelve P. M. and six, which I consumed in sleeping at the Continental.

We all send you heartfelt wishes for the New Year. May you be as happy as you are dear to

Your faithful

S. L.

TO GIBSON PEACOCK [7]

33 Denmead St.
Bo. Jany 11th 1878

My dear Mr. Gibson:

Tomorrow I will transfer to you by tele-graph one hundred and ten dollars; and the remaining forty I *hope*, on Monday, certainly during the five days following.

I believe it was last Sunday night that I wrote you; on the following morning I awoke with a raging fever, and have been in bed ever since, racked inexpressibly by my old foe, the Pleurodynia. I have crawled out of bed this afternoon, but must go back soon. Will probably be about again on Monday.

Tortured as I was this morning, with a living egg of pain away in under my collar bone, I shook till I was at least uni-formly sore all over, with reading your brilliant critique on the great " artiste " Squirt in his magnificent impersonation of Snooks.[8] The last sentence nearly took the top of my head

---

[7] Previously published, *Atlantic Monthly*, LXXIV, 189 (Aug., 1894); re-printed, *Letters* (New York, 1899), pp. 51-52.

[8] Apparently fictitious characters in a burlesque written by Peacock for the Philadelphia *Evening Bulletin*, no file of which has been discovered for this period.

off. I wish you would keep it up a little while, and fly at the metropolis as well as at the provinces. For example: "The following contribution for our new morning (or Sunday) paper comes accompanied by a note stating that the writer has been long employed as funny editor of the New York (anything, Universe, Age, et cet.) but desires a larger field of usefulness with us": and hereto you might append an imitation of the humorous column of *the World*, for instance, in which any thing under heaven is taken as a caption and the editorial then made up of all the possible old proverbs, quotations, popular sayings, and slang, which have a word, or even a syllable, in common with the text.

Or you might give an exact reproduction (the more exact the more ludicrous) of one of those tranquilly stupid political editorials in *The Nation* which seem as massive as the walls of Troy and are really nothing but condensations of arrogant breath.

—But of course you *won't* do anything of the sort, for why embroil yourself? and I'm only forcasting what might be done in a better world.

We all send our love to you and Maria. May is pretty well fagged with nursing me, plus the housekeeping cares.

Your friend,

S. L.

To Logan E. Bleckley

Address: — 33 Denmead St., Baltimore, Md.
Jany. 15th, 1878.

Dear Judge Bleckley:

I have recently returned to Baltimore with my family, and we now hope to make this our permanent residence. I learn that your son [Paul Bleckley] is in the city preparing to follow the dramatic profession, and am anxious to call on him, but have not been able to discover his address. Please let me know it immediately. I am so charmed at finding a Georgia young man who deliberately leaves the worn highways of the law and politics for the rocky road of Art that

I wish to do everything in my power to help and encourage him. Your own goodness to me in the past makes it also the accomplishment of a grateful duty to carry out my desires in this respect.

I would be very glad to know, from your own hand, something of your welfare, and to share some of your thoughts in these days which seem very strange ones. I am unable to write you a full letter, being just out of a sick bed where I have been suffering great pain for ten days.

I sincerely hope the onerous duties of your Court have not worn your strength overmuch. I remember well what increasing labor they involved when I was in the practice.

Accept my earnest wishes that the New Year may deal royally with you in all that you desire.

Your friend

Sidney Lanier.

To Clifford A. Lanier

33 Denmead St.
Baltimore, Md.
Jany 15th 1878.

My darling Sweet Buddy, You will stop thinking that I am a very extraordinary person when I tell you that my journey to New York— which was to take place soon after my telegram to you, and during which I was to collect the fifty dollars to send you by mail, along with sundry other dollars — was prevented by a stroke of my ancient enemy, the pleurodynia, which has kept me in bed ever since.[9] I would not, if I could, describe to you the tortures of it; suffice it to say I'm up today, and go about my regular business tomorrow. The Peabody rehearsals keep me here the balance of this week. Next week there are none: on Sunday night I expect to go to New York,

---

[9] In a letter to his father, Jan. 10, 1878 (here omitted), Lanier had asked for a loan of $150.00 to be negotiated through Mr. Plant, a Macon banker, saying in explanation: "I had expected to spend this week in New York, and to conclude there an important business arrangement which would have left me comparatively without care for some time."

and very soon thereafter your truant fifty dollars will make its appearance.

It really seems, my dear, that the family would go to pieces without you. What you say about advancing for Aunt Jane surprises me; I thought she was beyond all care in the way of money.[10]

We moved into our house on the Saturday before Xmas and if you only *could* see how snug we are with our cheap John furniture! We have a kitchen—with dumb-waiter to the dining-room above – a parlor, a bath-r[oom] [11] three sleeping-rooms, a study, or den, for me, and a Pandemonium for the boys. It is altogether so charming that in spite of poverty, unlimited work (for something is always to be done), trouble, hard fare, sickness, stupid cooks, and all, I feel that no consideration could induce me to board again. The expense is no greater: and we have good reason to believe that we can make it much less with a little experience. May does work like a Trojan; it is incredible what a lot of severe household drugdery she gets through with every day.

A letter in an Exchange [Hotel] envelope has just arrived for Charley, but the latter has not yet come from school. Did you see my poem to Taylor in SCRIBNER's for Jan'y? I will send you today my Xmas poem in EVERY SATURDAY.[12] I have not forgotten " Two Hundred Bales," which I wish you to cut down by two-thirds, and then send back to me. We will make a good story of it yet. It is now on my desk, waiting till Mary can wrap it up for Expressing.

Charley has just come in, and Wilsie's letter has been read at our little dinner-table amid the admiring plaudits of the family. It is *too* cunning! and makes us want to catch the blessed little fairy up in our arms and kiss her vigourously. Charley beams over it like the new moon.

And now we are all the time hoping that we may soon have you in *our* house, so that we gain a chance to *practice* all the

[10] Lanier's aunt (Jane Lanier Watt Montgomery) had recently lost her second husband (see note 107, 1877).

[11] The MS is torn at this point.

[12] " Under the Cedarcroft Chestnut " and " Hard Times in Elfland." The reference in the following sentence is to Clifford Lanier's MS novel (see note 132, 1874).

love we've been preaching. So many strange and fair things happen to us, that we even hope for this with confidence.

Accept love for all from all; we are continually surrounded with your goodness, walking on it, looking at it, eating it.

Your

S. L.

To John G. James [13]

33 Denmead St.
Baltimore, Md.
Jany 20th 1878.

My dear Sir:

I beg you to believe that your cordial letter would have won an immediate response from me if a severe attack of pleurodynia had not completely interrupted my correspondence.

My friend R. M. Johnston has given me a very attractive portrayal of you and this makes it doubly pleasant for me to find that any of my songs have reached your heart. Although I do not doubt that a manful artist could work without praise all his life, yet I am equally sure that there is a stage in his career when his work will gain an otherwise impossible quality from the knowledge that he has a heartily sympathetic audience, however small. Thus it may bring you a sort of reflex pleasure to know that your generous expressions add not only to my happiness as a man but to my efficiency as a laborer.

I have endeavored to select four of the most characteristic portions of my three longest poems. In order to compress enough of two of them into the requisite length for declamation, I have cut out several passages, leaving such as would preserve the thread of the story or argument.

No. 1.

The Thriftless Farmer.

(From " Corn," &c).

Commence at " Look, thou substantial Spirit of Content," (p.

---

[13] Previously published, *Letters: Sidney Lanier to Col. John G. James* (Austin, Texas, 1942), pp. 1-3. Lanier's letter is in answer to a request by James, Dec. 6, 1877, for permission to use selections from Lanier's poetry in his forthcoming textbook.

15) and go on through the line " And gave to coquette cotton soul and soil." Then omit the next twelve lines: re-commence with the line " Aye, as each year began," and print to the end of the poem. This takes about two and a half minutes to recite.

No. 2.

THE MODERN KNIGHT.

(From THE SYMPHONY &c &c).

Commence with the line "Where's he that craftily hath said " (p. 33) and print to the lines (inclusive)

" At Crime all money-bold
Fair Ladye? "

Then omit the next twenty five lines: re-commence with

" Now by each knight that e'er hath prayed "

and print on through the lines

" To be thy knight until my dying day,
Fair Ladye."

In both No. 1 and No. 2 the hiatus may be indicated by a line of dots.

No. 3.

SOLILOQUY OF COLUMBUS.

(FROM PSALM OF THE WEST &c &c).

Print, for this piece, the last four sonnets of the eight which compose the whole soliloquy: commencing with " Ere we Gomera cleared, a coward cried," on page 56, and continuing to the line " God's, East, mine West: good friends, behold my Land! "

For a boy who will be at the pains to conceive the situation and to avail himself of the dramatic points, I fancy this extract will be most effective of any that might be made from my poems.

No. 4.

THE BATTLE OF LEXINGTON.

(From PSALM OF THE WEST &c &c.)

Commence with the line " Then haste ye, Prescott and Revere," p. 64, and print through to the line " And died at the door of your House of Fame." If you prefer, however (as I now see you probably *do*, on referring to your letter) the Song of The Spirits of June Heat, let that by all means be substituted for The battle-piece. Please exercise your own choice with absolute freedom.[14]

―――――――――――

Perhaps it would be well for you to instruct Barnes & Co. to forward proof-sheets of these (whenever they may be printed) to me, here. This will ensure accuracy, and there may be a word or two I would like to change from the Lippincott book which was very imperfectly revised.

Of course you understand that the headings, or titles, I have given are purely suggestive. Please take the utmost liberty in altering or abolishing them.

In reply to your inquiry for humorous poems, I may mention that about a year before Charlotte Cushman's death my brother (Clifford Lanier) and I wrote a piece of this nature, – using the humor mostly as a veil for the pathos of the piece, – which she intended to read in public. She had previously requested that I would make a poem for recitation by her. She did not appear in public afterwards, and so was unable to carry out her intention: the piece has however been recited by others with great effect, and might suit your purpose. It was printed in SCRIBNER'S for June 1875. I send a newspaper copy taken from that issue.

I hope to have a photograph in a day or two and will be glad to send you one. You are to consider it however strictly in the light of an exchange, and accordingly are to forward one of yourself to me straightway.

I have gotten out of bed to write this, and am now very weary. I will try to fill up the blanks you send with any suggestions that may occur to me, sometime next week.[15]

I heartily wish you triumphant success in your undertaking,

―――――――――――

[14] The four selections here indicated by Lanier, and "The Power of Prayer" (mentioned below), were adopted by James and appeared in *The Southern Student's Hand-Book of Selections for Reading and Oratory* (New York, 1879) on pp. 15, 140, 189, 325, 355, and a brief biographical sketch on p. 18.

[15] James had asked Lanier's advice about other poems by Southern authors to be included.

and will be glad to forward the enterprise in any manner possible to me.

Please let me hear fully of your progress. My address is at head of this letter.

Sincerely yours,

Sidney Lanier.

Col Jno G. James,

Austin. Texas.

To Bayard Taylor [16]

Westminster Hotel,
4. Afternoon.
Wednesday.
[New York, Jan. 23, 1878?]

My dear friend:

I'm going to be in my room here for the balance of the day and evening. If you haven't anything better to do, pray come to me. I wish to see you particularly. Your letter reached me yesterday morning just before I left Baltimore.

My regards to Mrs. Taylor: — which I wd. present in person, but it is too cold for me to venture out.

Your faithful

S. L.

To Robert S. Lanier

N. Y. Jany 26th 1878

My dearest Father:

I have arranged with Charles Lanier to get five hundred dollars for several months. This is in anticipation of the proceeds of some magazine-papers which I am to write; Charles understands all about it. The paper will be in

---

[16] Previously published (out of chronological order), Letters (New York, 1899), p. 179. Conjectural dating from the following evidence: in Lanier's letter of Jan. 15, 1878 (above), he said he was going to New York on Sunday, Jan. 20; the first Wednesday thereafter was Jan. 23.

the form of a draft on you, which please accept when it
arrives. You need give yourself no further thought about it.
It will probably be forwarded from the bank on Monday, for
you to accept and return.

On Wednesday I will send money to meet the Plant draft.

Charles tells me that Mr. Secretary Sherman called on Mr.
J. F. D. Lanier (who is visiting Gen. Dunn in Washington) a
few days ago, and assured him positively that he would very
soon have a position for me in his Department. There have
been difficulties in the way, which are being removed.

I am very much better than when I left home. Am just now
going to dine with Bayard Taylor at his house. The weather
has been very cold, but is like Spring today.

I hope Mama is better. Kiss her for me,

Your son,

S. L.

To John B. Tabb [17]

33 Denmead St.
Bᵒ Jany 30th 1878.

Well you may wonder, my dear John: but I was very ill for a
couple of weeks, and then got strength enough to crawl out of
bed in order to make a much-needed visit to New York. I've
just returned, and hasten to answer your note.

I had a very short interview with Mr. Eggleston,[18] and
wished vainly to meet him again. I made bold to call at his
office; and he took me over to lunch at the Astor House. We
had little chance to talk, however: there were too many people
about, and, for this perfectly sufficient reason! neither of us
dared venture upon anything very sensible in the way of conversation. But I found him thoroughly good, and I hope we
will meet again. It seems his wife is a confirmed invalid, inso-

[17] Previously published, Gordon Blair, *Father Tabb* (Richmond, Va., 1940),
pp. 61-62.

[18] George Cary Eggleston, literary editor of the New York *Evening Post*. (A
surviving note from W. C. Bryant, Jan. 24, 1878, indicates that Lanier apparently
called on him also.)

much that he is obliged to be at home every evening: on this
account he was unable to call.

Don't you need your ms. volume of poems? I am ready to
return it, marked with my preferences, whenever you say so.
Let me know.

I don't believe there is the least hope of my coming to your
College before Spring. In addition to the work which presses
me down every moment, I am compelled to observe a degree of
care against cold which must seem perfectly absurd to any one
unacquainted with the exigencies of consumption. But you
will understand, my dear, that if I *could* get to you, I would.
The sight of your face is good to me. St. Thomas a Kempis
complains : *I went out among men, and I returned home less a*
man than when I went out. This is often my sad experience:
but you redeem the character of our kind, and I love to be
with you.

Come therefore to me, dear friend, whenever you can, sure
of two arms and a welcoming heart and hearth. My house is
out Charles (the *blue* car on Baltimore, or Calvert, street will
bring you within a block of me) beyond Boundary Avenue,
about ten minutes ride from Baltimore street.

And so, God have you in His holy keeping,

Your friend,

S. L.

To Gibson Peacock [19]

33 Denmead St.
Baltimore, Md.
Jany 30th 1878

My dear Mr. Gibson:

It's no use trying to tell you the bitter-
ness with which I found myself a couple of days behindhand
with that hundred. I was in bed, ill, and was depending on a
friend who had promised to come by my house and transact
this, along with some other business for me down town. He
was prevented from coming as expected, and I was without

---

[19] Previously published, *Atlantic Monthly*, LXXIV, 189-190 (Aug., 1894);
reprinted, *Letters* (New York, 1899), pp. 52-53.

remedy. I enclose P. O. order for twenty-five. The balance will go to you soon. Please don't despair of me. My illness was a complete marplot to all my plans for a month or more.

I came through Ph^a. night before last on my way home from New York. I ran round to see you, but you had gone to the theatre. Next morning I was compelled to hurry home without the pleasure of kissing my dear Maria's hand; our Peabody Orchestra meets at five in the afternoon, and I was obliged to reach Baltimore in time for that.

We are all in tolerable condition, greatly enjoying our crude half-furnished home. I have been mainly at work on some unimportant prose matter for pot-boilers; but I get off a short poem occasionally, and in the background of my mind am writing my " Jacquerie ".

It is very thoughtful of you to send the Bulletin. I did not know it was being continued at Chadd's Ford, else I should have had the address changed. Both May and I find a great deal in the paper to interest us.

We send loving messages to you twain. The boys are all at school.

Your friend,

Sidney L.

To Robert S. Lanier

33 Denmead St.
Baltimore, Md.
Jany 30th 1878.

My dear Father:
                I must have expressed my meaning poorly about the New Year's business, for I see from your letter that you have misunderstood me, and I hasten to correct your impression. I did not mean to condemn the New Year *proceedings* at all: on the contrary I think all these friendly and neighborly gatherings are of great value, and I wish they came oftener than once a year. All that I meant to reprehend was the *reporting in a newspaper* of the details of these visits, the dresses of the ladies, the social distinctions of different people – as this one for beauty, that one for wit, another one for

sweetness – and the like.   Any general reference to the unusual observance of the custom, and the heartiness with which it was carried out on this particular occasion would have been perfectly legitimate: but the report, as given, certainly embraced matters which good taste leaves always in the strictest background of privacy.

I have used the money obtained from Charles in paying off some matters which have long been a great burden to me.   I send herein a certificate of deposit in 3rd Nat. Bk. of New York for one hundred dollars against the Plant draft.   If you can manage the remaining fifty of that draft, it will be a great help to me, as I am sorely pushed for a couple of weeks, to keep on good terms with the butcher and the baker.

I am very busy; if the days were forty-eight hours long I would scarcely get through the modicum of work for each.   A good deal of this work, however, is incident to our start in housekeeping, and as soon as we get matters into the grooves of system, it will diminish.   Unless my call to the Treasury comes beforehand, I expect to run South early in April, to write my Scribner papers: [20] when I will have the delight of seeing you.

I get better each day.   We all send love to Mama, with earnest hopes for her speedy recovery.   God bless you all.

Your son,

S. L.

To Bayard Taylor [21]

33 Denmead St.
Baltimore, Md.
Feby. 3rd 1878.

My dear friend:

I was sorry to miss you and Mrs. Taylor when I called on Monday.   My cold had taken such possession of me on Sunday evening that I found it prudent to keep my room.   I delivered your books to the servant.   I read through the three

---

[20] See Lanier's letter of Nov. 14, 1877, and note 98, 1877.

[21] Previously published, *Atlantic Monthly*, LXXXIV, 138-139 (July, 1899); reprinted, *Letters* (New York, 1899), pp. 208-210.

volumes on Sunday: and upon a sober comparison I think Walt Whitman's LEAVES OF GRASS [22] worth at least a million of AMONG MY BOOKS and ATALANTA IN CALYDON. In the two latter I could not find anything which has not been much better said before: but LEAVES OF GRASS was a real refreshment to me – like rude salt spray in your face – in spite of its enormous fundamental error that a thing is good because it is natural, and in spite of the world-wide difference between my own conceptions of art and its author's.

I did not find a fitting moment to mention to you a matter in which I am much interested. – I have an unconquerable longing to stop all work for a few months except the study of Botany, French and German, and the completion of a long poem which I have been meditating. In order to do this, I hoped it might be possible to utilize a tract of timber-land containing about a thousand acres which I own in Georgia. I have somewhere heard that there was an association, or institution of some sort, in New York, for helping literary people: and it occurred to me that such a corporation might take my lands in pledge for a loan of five or six hundred dollars. I should want it for twelve months. The lands lie immediately on a railroad which runs to Savannah, and whose main business is the transportation of lumber and timber to that port. They are in a portion of the state which is now attracting much attention from the North Carolina Turpentine-distillers and lumber-men, and which has recently developed great capacities for sheep-raising. They are also valuable for agricultural purposes, after all the timber is cut off.

Tell me if any such institution exists. I asked Mr. [W. C.] Bryant about it while in New York: he did not know of it at all. He added that if he were now as prosperous as he was five or six years ago he would have offered to advance the money himself on the lands: which was a very kindly thought.

Don't give yourself the least concern about this. Of course it isn't at all probable that any such association exists, if Mr. Bryant does not know of it: and I don't suppose I would mention it to you at all, except for the anxiety with which I long

---

[22] This was apparently Lanier's first serious reading of Whitman (see his letter of May 5, 1878, below). The other two books mentioned were by J. R. Lowell and A. C. Swinburne.

to draw my breath after a hard fight, and to get the ends of my thoughts together – as Carlyle says.

I hope Mrs. Taylor is quite recovered from her cold. As for you – you range over such an enormous compass both of literary and terrestrial ground that I would not be at all surprised to hear at any moment that you were off for

The long wash of Australasian seas [23]

in order to deliver a lecture at Sydney upon Limoges Enamel, thence to Cape Town for the purpose of reading a dissertation on the Elohistic Division of the Book of Genesis, thence home by way of Reikiavik (I deny any obligation to spell this dreadful word correctly) where you were to recite an original poem (in Icelandic) on the Relation of Balder to Pegasus.

Your friend,

Sidney L.

To Bayard Taylor [24]

33 Denmead St.
Bo.Md. Feby, 11th 1878.

My dear friend:

It is long since I have had a keener pleasure than the announcement of your nomination [25] brings me. I have just read it: and without having time for more than a word, I devote that to the practical question, – can I be of any service in the matter of the confirmation by the Senate? Will there be any opposition at all, there? The Senator from Alabama is a dear friend of mine and I can ask *anything* of him: besides, the Senators from Georgia and one from Mississippi – Mr. Lamar – are all gentlemen with whom my relations are very friendly. If there is the least likelihood of necessity for arraying your friends, please let me know, so that I may have the pleasure of telling these senators what I know about you.[26]

---

[23] Tennyson, " The Brook."

[24] Previously published, *Atlantic Monthly*, LXXXIV, 139 (July, 1899); reprinted, *Letters* (New York, 1899), p. 210.

[25] As Minister to Germany.

[26] In his reply, Feb. 19, 1878 (*Letters*, New York, 1899, p. 211), Taylor said: " I heard, indirectly, yesterday, that the Southern Senators are delighted,

God speed your final appointment. Isn't it simply too delightful? I could kiss Mr. Hayes, in behalf of the Fitness of Things, — which was never more graciously worshipped than by this same nomination.

My wife joins me in hearty congratulations to you both.

Your friend,

Sidney L.

To Robert S. Lanier

33 Denmead St.

Bo Feby 24th 1878.

My dear Father:

If the days only had forty eight hours apiece instead of twenty four I could be a much better correspondent: as it is, I find it a difficult matter to get a moment for a letter. During the last two weeks I have been teaching for an hour each day (from 12 to 1 midday) at Col. Johnston's School,[27] and this has added more than at first sight appears to my occupations, by breaking up my working-day into two somewhat inconvenient sections. I get for this service two hundred dollars a session, and hope it may prove the entering wedge to a larger engagement. Col. Johnston — who lives a short distance beyond me — has been unremitting, I might almost say overpowering, in his kindly and thoughtful acts towards us since we moved out to our present residence, and I have conceived a great affection for him.

I had yesterday a very pleasant interview with Mr. Welch, proprietor of the Baltimore GAZETTE, which I hope may lead to some agreeable and profitable employment. He thinks of starting a Sunday edition of his daily, and will want me, I

and will not fail to vote for confirmation. Still, if you could say a word to Lamar, it might be a further assurance; as a Southern man, your endorsement would certainly strengthen me. But pray don't go to any special trouble." (See Lanier's letter of Mar. 4, 1878, and note 30, below.)

[27] Edward Lucas White, a student at the Pen Lucy School in 1877-1880, recalled that Lanier taught classes there in arithmetic, English, and spelling. The boys, he wrote, "admired [Lanier], loved him, and stood in awe of him. He inspired in them deference and fealty. . . . The magic of his demeanor made everyone eager to do and be his best." ("Reminiscences of Sidney Lanier," *Johns Hopkins Alumni Magazine*, XVII, 329-331, June, 1929.)

presume, to take charge of the literary departments suitable to such a publication.

Mary and I attended a charming reception at the house of Mr. Gilman (Pres^t Johns Hopkins University) last night, to meet Mr. [Charles W.] Eliot, President of Harvard University. The wife of Mr. Gilman is the daughter of President [Theodore D.] Woolsey, of Yale: and, as I told May afterwards, it seemed a little overpowering to be calmly conversing with all three of these at a time, – as we were on several occasions. They were all so cordial and friendly to us, however, that it was impossible to feel any sense of aught but the most delightful freedom and absence of stiffness.

The boys are in good condition and appear to prosper in their school business.

We have just parted with Foster Higgins and his wife (Mary's cousins, and only relatives) who stopped in Baltimore to see us and gave us a fine visit of two days. Foster is on his way South, partly for his health and partly to look after various matters of business. I don't know whether we have spoken to you of him, before. He is a man who has made himself a competency by hard work and upright carriage, and has great influence among the best business-men of New York. He came laden with presents for the boys – suits of clothes, overcoats, knives, and what not – and seemed full of affection for us. Please show him all the attention you can when he comes to Macon. (He lived there when a boy). I hope you will be sure to ask him to dinner, or tea, and to take them for a ride through the cemetery and out Vineville. Their hospitality to me when I went to New York first was unbounded. Tell Mama she need not be in the least afraid of entertaining them at meals: they are not in the least snobbish, and Saidee (Foster's wife) is one of the most sensible women in the world. Foster will want to see you about the Brunswick bonds.

I lack forty dollars of an amount of money which I must have ready next week, and if you can send me that by Wednesday or Thursday, it will be a great help.

God bless you both. Mary and the boys are at church while I am writing this.

Your son,

S. L.

P. S.   I am very anxious to write Mr. Day some account of us, and as it would have to be pretty much a repetition of what is herein contained, I will ask you to send this letter to him at Brunswick, with my love.   Mary scarcely ever has time to take up her pen, in her multitudinous engagements with the children.

S. L.

To Clifford A. Lanier

33 Denmead St.
B°. March 3rd 1878.

Dearest Clifford:

I know full well the mood in which such thoughts are conceived as these of your last letter. You do yourself injustice to call this languor of the spirit by such hard names, and to imagine that your day-dreams of unattainable things are nothing more than vain and foolish wastings of time.   One who has such an exacting round of daily duty as yours is entitled, as of right, to these idle moments in which the spirit drifts aimlessly down the great current of being. Although attended with no immediate results, these motions of the soul are far from unproductive.   You will find them leaping to your help, in the shape of half-formed beauty, when you write your next poem, or do your next poetic act of whatever sort.   Years ago I used often to be amazed at myself, sunk in similar depths of apparent laziness.   I would find myself, for months together, seemingly full of poetry, yet held back from the pen by a disinclination which was so unconquerable that it amounted to an imperious command not to write. This would go on until I was filled with morbid self-accusations of the bitterest kind, as being one who knew his artistic duty and yet did it not.   At last however would come a day when the desire to put my thoughts in concrete forms of poetry or of music would be as urgent as it had been lax, and when I *must* write in spite of all the powers of earth.   Then the poem would come, and I would find myself content.

I passed through this alternation so many times that at last I learned, with increasing insight, to see how entirely the artis-

tic instinct *is* an instinct, and how completely it is furnished
with such intuitions as are necessary to its activity. A tree does
not need a meteorologist with barometer and rain-gauge to tell
it when the spring-time has come: it stands quiet during the
winter, – and presently puts forth, in due season.

Thus, both as man of business, and as poet, you need have
no fear of the days and weeks that pass by like a procession of
indistinct and unsubstantial forms, leaving you nothing but
sighs and aspirations.

I do not mean at all to say that a poet cannot work at poetry
every day with as much regularity as you go to your blotter and
ledger. I have often done so, and do. I find that, in whatever unpoetic frame of mind I may be, if I go to my desk and
resolutely take up the pen, in ten minutes the creative mood
comes and I write freely. But I do not believe this is ever the
best work which a poet does. Of course its quality will depend
greatly upon the keenness of his artistic sense and upon the
rigorous fervor of his piety towards his art. But a certain
white heat and rapture which attend the ideal moments of composition I have described are wanting to these more sober and
dutiful labors.

You will be glad to know that I had a very gratifying musical triumph at the seventh Peabody Concert which came off
last night. I had been assigned by the Director to play a concerto by Emil Hartmann (a Danish writer) for violin and
orchestra. The composition was a very difficult one, and many
believed it could not be rendered on the flute at all. The result
however was very satisfactory: the close of the first movement
brought down the house, which was largely composed of
musicians and *dilettanti*: at the same time the orchestra broke
forth in applause and the leader stepped down from his place
and congratulated me. Of course this gave me much pleasure,
and I played the two remaining movements, with even greater
success. The piece occupied twenty-five minutes, and at the
end a wonderful basket of flowers was handed up to me amid
hearty applause.[28] This result was specially pleasant to me,

---

[28] The Baltimore *Gazette*, Mar. 4, 1878, after commenting on this Hartmann
Concerto as being far superior to the average flute music and as making strong
demands upon the technical skill of the performer, said: "The flute part was
admirably executed by Mr. Sidney Lanier; the performance showed not only a

because no such piece had ever been attempted before, with the flute, and the experiment was from the beginning a doubtful one.

My attempts to obtain steady employment still drag themselves along. It has been hard work to maintain a cheerful spirit under the surprising number of defeats, disappointments and delays which have been heaped upon me, and it has really seemed to me sometimes a sober enough truth that I was having more than my share of these. But I have fought off such considerations, with a never-failing sense somewhere inside of me that they could not be right because they were not beautiful, – and meantime have not relaxed my efforts. Mr. Welch, proprietor of the Baltimore GAZETTE, thinks of beginning a Sunday edition of his paper in a couple of weeks, and has very pleasantly encouraged me to believe that he will want me to take charge of the literary department of it, – which would quite set me up in business and relieve me of all immediate care as to the means of livelihood.

– A relief which would not come a moment too soon! for some most unconscionable delays in disposing of my recent magazine work have reduced me to complete destitution for the last two or three weeks. If at any time soon you should be assailed with a sudden draft for forty or fifty dollars, in heaven's name grit your teeth and bear it, long-suffering soul that you are! and hope, with me, that the price of poetry yet may rise and you be re-imbursed some day for all your grievous outlays on my account.

Your tribute to Moses is very manly and beautiful. I had not heard of his death, and was pained to learn that he was no more. I supposed him in the prime of a very vigorous manhood.

How I wish you sat in this third-story den of our dear little home, here, today! I have a great number of steeples in view,

mastery of the instrument, but a refined and cultivated musical intelligence. His concerto was received with great applause." Asger Hamerik wrote of this occasion: "I will never forget the impression he made on me when he played the flute-concerto of Emil Hartmann at a Peabody symphony concert, in 1878: his tall, handsome, manly presence, his flute breathing noble sorrows, noble joys, the orchestra softly responding. The audience was spellbound. Such distinction, such refinement! He stood, the master, the genius." (Quoted in W. H. Ward, "Memorial," Poems, New York, 1884, p. xxxii.)

and afar off a little strip of the Bay down which occasionally a white sail glides slowly. I have this whole room assigned to me by the mistress of the house, and for the first time in my life am the owner of definite places in which to keep my *ms.*, my paper, my pens, my books, and the like. It would be supremely delightful if I had the least basis of security for my rent a month ahead!

This is a long screed, – but I wanted a talk with you.

Send me some account of Aunt Jane's condition. Is she left anything by her husband? I cannot contemplate serenely the prospect of her being dependent for the rest of her life. We want very much to have her here, but are afraid our way of life would be too hard for her. We still have it under advisement, however, and if anything should ameliorate my business prospects we would send for her immediately.

Kiss your Wilsie for me. May is out and does not know that I am writing. We are all in pretty good condition physically. I am better off in the matter of lungs than I have been for a long time.

God bless you, is always the prayer of

Your

S. L.

To Bayard Taylor [29]

33 Denmead St.

Bo. March 4th 1878.

My dear friend:

The enclosed letter from Mr. Lamar [30] came this morning. Its expressions are so cordial towards you that I thought you might care to see it.

With new delight each day I regard the prospect before you. I shall begin to love Mr. Hayes! A man who appoints you Minister to Germany and who vetoes the Silver Bill – – – is a man who goes near to redeem the time. .

– But I can not now do more than send you a violet. I'm

---

[29] Previously published, *Atlantic Monthly*, LXXXIV, 140 (July, 1899); reprinted, *Letters* (New York, 1899), pp. 211-212.

[30] L. Q. C. Lamar's letter of Mar. 1, 1878, has survived; in it he acknowledged receipt of a lost letter by Lanier written in the latter part of February.

making some desperate efforts to get steady work, of any kind: for I find I cannot at all maintain our supplies of daily bread by poetry alone. So far I have failed in getting any constant work; but I keep trying for it, and I do not doubt it will come.

My wife sends hearty messages to you and Mrs. Taylor. As for me, you know how I am always your grateful and affectionate

S. L.

To Robert S. Lanier

33 Denmead St.
Bo. Mch. 10th 1878.

My dear Father:

Your postal card came duly. I hope you are by this time safely returned from the Sumter trip, with success on your brows.

I have received a very flattering invitation to deliver a course of eight lectures on English Literature to a class of twenty cultivated ladies in Baltimore, and am now busy preparing them. There is to be one lecture a week for the next two months. I am to receive a hundred dollars for the course. I have chosen for my special subject " The Sonnet-writers from Surrey to Shakespeare," and have not in a long time had so congenial a task as the research necessary to the accomplishment of the work. There seems every probability that this will be the beginning of a pleasant and profitable business for me. The invitation came without any previous knowledge of such intention on my part. I hope to organize a similar class in Washington.[31]

[31] The plan for the class originated with Mrs. Edgeworth Bird. In reminiscences prepared for Henry W. Lanier some years later (MS Copy, Henry W. Lanier Collection, Johns Hopkins University) she wrote: " As time passed I saw [Lanier's] eagerness for work and felt that I must get something for him to do. I thought of a class of ladies, to whom he might give an hour's talk each week at my house, offering to secure the audience if he would do the work. He asked only a day or two to consider and then agreed. . . . About thirty cultivated women attended. One day I asked Dr. Gilman, President of the J. H. University, to be present. He gladly came, and he, too, was charmed. At the close, he said to me, ' I never heard a more charming lecture,' and with a smile, ' I certainly hear a great many.' " The series consisted of eight lectures at the home of Mrs. Bird, 40 Mt. Vernon Place, delivered on Saturdays at 12:30 P.M.,

A considerable poem of mine called CLOVER is just out in THE INDEPENDENT, a weekly paper of New York.[32] I have not yet seen it, and only know of its appearance through a letter from some enthusiastic gentleman in Pennsylvania who writes thanking me for the poem.[33]

I believe Mary has written you some account of my gratifying success at the Peabody a few nights ago.

A matter which I cannot longer postpone obliges me to draw on you for forty dollars today. I hope to return it to you in a few days. You will certainly know and understand the deep reluctance with which I do it, and will imagine the efforts I have made to avoid it. The necessity is due wholly to vexatious delay in the arrival of receipts which ought to have reached me two weeks ago.

I write with a dozen things pressing for immediate attention. We all hope that Mama improves.

God bless you both.

Your son,
S. L.

TO JOHN B. TABB [34]

33 Denmead St.
Bo. Mch. 11th 1878.

My dear John:

It seems too cruel that I have literally not had the time to finish marking your poems, – an event for which I was waiting before writing you. I hope you will not believe this statement made in the loose sense in which people usually

from Mar. 23 to May 11, 1878 (see Lanier's letter of Apr. 21, 1878, and note 40, below).

This was the beginning of Lanier's career as a lecturer in Baltimore, which ultimately led to his appointment as lecturer in English at the Johns Hopkins University (see III, xii ff.).

[32] " Clover " (I, 84) had been written a year and a half before at West Chester. Lanier was paid $25.00 for it by the *Independent*, where it was published in the issue of Mar. 7, 1878 (see W. H. Ward to Lanier, Mar. 10, 1878).

[33] The letter, from W. C. Rheem, a lawyer of Franklin, Pa., Mar. 8, 1878, read: " Sidney Lanier: I thank you for your gift of ' Clover.' "

[34] Previously published, Gordon Blair, *Father Tabb* (Richmond, Va., 1940), pp. 62-63.

declare they have " not had time " to do things.   It is simply true.   Two extra duties have been recently placed upon me, which are so imperious that I have been in a continuous hurry and rush throughout each day – Sundays and all –, crawling to my bed late each night thoroughly worn to the last ravelling of strength.

Some time ago I was employed by the " Penn Lucy School " to teach mathematics for an hour each day – at an hour, too, which very inconveniently breaks up my day so that I consume a good deal *more* than an hour in getting together again the broken ends of work.

Then I received a very flattering invitation to deliver a course of eight lectures on a special period of English Literature which, although directly in the line of my meditations, yet required a great deal of research in order to enable me to present in an entertaining and profitable way the peculiar views I held upon it.   The teaching, and the preparation of these lectures, in addition to the work I had on hand, have quite usurped me. I was delighted, of course to get both these employments, particularly the lectures, which are not only the most congenial work I have had in a long time but which, once prepared, will probably open the way for other similar engagements that will bring me in enough to admit my dispensing with some of the wearisome and poorly-remunerative work I have so long been doing.   My first lecture is to be delivered next Saturday (the course is before a private association of twenty very cultivated ladies, here, the lectures being delivered in their parlors alternately): and inasmuch as our concert-rehearsals – which now take up two hours of each of my days – will cease after that, I shall have a little more time for you.

I thought it not advisable to send your poem to Scribner's until the other was published.   They would be sure to decline it.   If you will permit me to suggest one or two very slight alterations, I will then be glad to send it to the Editor of Lippincott's: he might accept it, – though of course there is always doubt.

I must therefore bid you farewell until next week when I will write you more satisfactorily, I hope.

I am better in health than usual, and reproach myself that your dear heart should have been troubled by my silence, – yet

I could not help it. Pray come in, if you can, and bless my eyes and my house. It is a great tribulation to me that I am in such a slough of work as holds me fast from you: but many signs appear that my struggle begins to establish me upon the plane I desire to occupy, and that I shall soon be in less desperate case.

Meantime my wife and the boys join me in all affectionate messages to you. Come directly here when you visit the city.

Your faithful

S. L.

To Bayard Taylor [35]

33 Denmead St.
Baltimore, Md.
Mch. 25th 1878.

My dear Mr. Taylor:

Some time when you're riding in a street-car and haven't anything important to think of – or rather *don't want* to think of anything important – won't you be kind enough to read this sonnet (if you can) and find out if it is quite too absurd? [36]

Of course it is merely meant to please a friend, here, – a woman who plays Beethoven with the large conception of a man, and yet nurses her children all day with a noble simplicity of devotion such as I have rarely seen: being withal, in point of pure technic, the greatest piano-player I ever heard.

I have been studying German in the wee minutes allowed by other occupations, without a teacher; and don't want you to

---

[35] Previously published, *Atlantic Monthly*, LXXXIV, 140 (July, 1899); reprinted, *Letters* (New York, 1899), p. 212.

[36] "An Frau Nannette Falk-Auerbach" (I, 117, note). Lanier had known the dedicatee, described in the following paragraph, since his first winter in Baltimore.

In his reply, Apr. 1, 1878, Taylor wrote: "Both my wife and I find your sonnet quite remarkable for a neophyte in the language. It moves stiffly and somewhat awkwardly, but it is anything but absurd—on the contrary, informed with a distinct idea, which, moreover, is German in its nature. You have mastered the secret of the language already: now go on and master its literary treasures."

think I would with malice prepense try to write a poem in that tongue.

I mark a thousand pleasant things about you in the newspapers, and rejoice heartily in them all. God speed you in your whole work.

Your friend,

Sidney L.

To John B. Tabb [87]

33 Denmead St.

Bo. Ap. 2nd 1878.

My dear John: In the whole world you couldn't have found two books that would give me more delight than these do, just at this present stage of my studies.[88]   I have been buried in the *Magister Choralis* for several hours, and find it directly in the line of my thought.   I wish I knew some way to thank you for your kind and thoughtful gift.

— But I am writing this note mainly to ask you if you would allow me to send the poem called " Necros " (in your *ms.* volume) to Lippincott's along with one of the other two? " Necros " is, to me, much the strongest poem you have written, except " The Cloud."

If you answer yea, I will send you the ms. volume immediately by mail, so that you may copy off " Necros " (of course I would copy it myself, but a poem is always best in the author's own handwriting) and enclose it to me.   I have looked over your ms. and have marked with a star the poems that I like best, adding usually some little hint of such change as seems to me desirable.   The freedom of these you will take, as from a brother.

---

[87] Previously published, Gordon Blair, *Father Tabb* (Richmond, Va., 1940), p. 64.

[88] Tabb had sent Lanier Franz Xaver Haberl's *Magister Choralis. A Theoretical and Practical Manual of Gregorian Chant* (translated by N. Donnelly, New York, 1877) and Dominicus Mettenleiter's *Manuale Breve Cantionum ac Precum Liturgicarum Juxta Ritum S. Romanæ Ecclesiæ* (*Ratisbonæ*, 1874).   Both volumes have survived in Lanier's Library, Johns Hopkins University.

The nature of Lanier's studies, here referred to, is indicated in Tabb's letter of Mar. 26, 1878: " Let me know the result of your further investigation as to the Greek accent."

I enclose a Sonnet of mine to Mad. Auerbach (the piano-player) which appeared in the Baltimore Gazette [39] some days ago, and seems to have won much favor.

On further reflection I will send your book immediately, and you may look for it by the mail following this. I write hurriedly: Col. Johnson's wife is very ill, and he has just sent over a request that I will come and teach his school for the rest of the day. This lovely April unearthliness in the atmosphere makes me long for a walk with you among the fields.

Your loving

S. L.

To Logan E. Bleckley

33 Denmead St., Baltimore, Md.
April 15th, 1878.

My dear Judge Bleckley:

I feel sure that I am adding to the pleasure of three men in acquainting you with Mr. Hinckley, of Messrs. Hinckley & Morris, one of the most eminent law-firms of this city. He goes to Atlanta, however, not as a representative of the law of the land, but of the Law of Love, — being a delegate to the Sunday-School Convention about to be held there. I shall feel gratified with any help you may give him towards seeing a little of Atlanta, or — what is much better — a good deal of yourself.

I was very sorry to miss your son when I called, and regret to learn that some trouble of his throat has caused him to return. I beg you will let me know with some detail what his aims and hopes are, and that you will call on me without reserve if I can forward them in any way.

I have asked Mr. Hinckley to take you the accompanying volume of my poems. I have waited some time before sending it, because I wished that it might go with some confirmation of a value beyond the mere popularity of the moment. Your ancient kindness in this behalf makes me sure that you will

---

[39] " To Nannette Falk-Auerbach " (I, 117), the English version of the sonnet mentioned in note 36, above. It was first published in the Baltimore *Gazette*, Mar. 28, 1878.

care to know how the book increases daily in favor with sober and earnest people, so that I have at length found courage to send it to you.

Your friend,

Sidney Lanier.

To CLIFFORD A. LANIER

33 Denmead St.
B⁰ April 21st 1878.

My dearest Clifford:

    I have been wanting to write you of many pleasant things which have happened to me recently, but the time has not presented itself when I could do so. I have never accomplished so much work in the same time, since I commenced to work at all: and have had the rare good fortune of seeing happy results flow almost immediately from every stroke.

  About six weeks ago I was invited to deliver a course of lectures to a private party of ladies, in their own parlors, the class consisting of about a dozen members. The subjects were, for the first four lectures " The Science of Poetry," and for the last four " The Sonnet-makers of Queen Elizabeth's Time."
The labor involved in preparing these was very great: but it was also very congenial, and I have therefore thriven on it. The lectures — or rather " morning-talks," for they are delivered each Saturday at half past twelve — have been delightfully received. After the first one the class increased to twenty members, and by the third had reached thirty-two. Here we had to stop, as a large number was inconvenient for a private parlor: but another class is now forming, and nearly complete. Each member pays five dollars for the course of eight lectures.[40]

---

[40] On Apr. 15, 1878, Mary Day Lanier wrote to R. S. Lanier: " You would be very glad and proud, dear Father, to see for yourself what *choice* and devoted friends, and what number of them, have been *confirmed* and *added to* our fine beloved Soul this Spring. . . . Among the most fortune-spoilt and fastidious of the Baltimore ladies– especially cultured– and with Prest. Gilman and Mr. Tait (the artist), his four lectures have suddenly made a partial revelation of his unexplored powers that has left him seemingly master of the field– and of all hearts. The enthusiasm has been something amazing, and M^rs. Bird's loving

There seems every probability that these will lead to some larger experiments in the same field. President Gilman (of Johns Hopkins University) was at my third lecture,[41] and came up at its close, in the most cordial way, with congratulations and an invitation to deliver it at the University. The project is now mooted of arranging a place in town for the special higher culture of women, where my lectures can be delivered to classes the year round, in conjunction with others on scientific subjects.

I send you a programme of the complimentary concert given me by the Peabody Orchestra and others at the close of the season.[42] The affair was arranged without my knowledge, and was a very pleasant surprise to me. At one of the Peabody Concerts a few weeks ago I played a *Concerto* of Hartmann's (a Danish writer) for Violin and Orchestra, taking the violin-part with my flute. At its close the whole Orchestra applauded, and the leader stepped down and congratulated me. This, it seems, was the immediate occasion of the complimentary concert. The latter was well attended, and netted me, above all expenses, a hundred and sixty-four dollars.

I have tried to get a copy of the New York INDEPENDENT containing my poem " Clover " to send you, but have not succeeded. You will find a poem of mine called " The Dove " in SCRIBNER's for May,[43] just out. Have I sent you a sonnet of mine to Mrs. Auerbach, (a great pianist, living here) which appeared in the Baltimore GAZETTE?

Father will probably forward you an editorial from the

triumph is as irrepressible as an eager child's. You know she projected the class ' of fifteen '; and fully fifty have, later, tried or desired to join. Of course, M^{rs}. B's room and *chairs* have limits— moreover, she thinks it wiser to let people beg awhile until someone requests the course to be repeated. There are indications that this will be done. Lectures in Batimore are as common as paving-stones, but they find his to be unlike anything that has gone before."

[41] The subject of the third lecture, Apr. 6. was announced as " The Melody of Speech."

[42] The concert was given for Lanier by the Peabody Orchestra, Mme. Falk-Auerbach, and Elisa Baraldi at Lehmann's Hall, Baltimore, Sat., Apr. 6, 1878 (program in the Clifford A. Lanier Collection, Johns Hopkins University). For a fuller account of the concert see Mary Day Lanier's letter to R. S. Lanier, Apr. 15, 1878.

[43] On Jan. 14, 1878, *Scribner's Monthly* sent Lanier a check for $20.00 for " The Dove " (I, 99).

N. Y. EVENING POST, containing some auguries of my future as poet which are at least pleasant indications.[44]

I'm glad you liked the sonnet on dreams: [45] you always hear the best that's in a poem, however. May and I wished for you the other night with more than usual intensity: a young professional " reader " of this City has been making a great success of your and my (but very little *my*) " Power of Prayer " before popular audiences, and having learned that I was one of the authors she very kindly proposed to come out to my house and recite it for me. You would be surprised to see what a wealth of dramatic capability there is in the thing: and the young lady did it very well, though I easily saw many points where it would have been possible to make the ideas more effective.

But I must close. We are all a little under the power of spring colds, here; none seriously. My own health is better than for some years past. We send you the most loving messages of loving souls. I have great hope to get south in a month or two, for the purpose of writing my *Scribner* articles, and I will surely then see you.

God bless you all.

Your faithful

S. L.

---

[44] In a review of Edgar Fawcett's volume of poems, *Fantasy and Passion*, in the New York *Evening Post*, Apr. 1, 1878, the critic (probably Geo. C. Eggleston) said that of the very few younger men who seemed qualified to " maintain the poetic succession in this country when the masters who are growing old shall cease to sing . . . Mr. Sidney Lanier and Mr. Fawcett give the fairest promise of succeeding to the high places. Neither of them has won a first place as yet, of course, . . . but both have given proof of the possession of genuine genius – proof which is wanting in the case of nearly all the rest of our younger singers." The reviewer found them somewhat alike in fervor of imagination, luxuriance of fancy, and the apt use of figurative language, but otherwise they were different – especially in their faults: " Mr. Lanier has greater spontaneity – too great we sometimes think – and a stronger tendency to undertake large work . . . to chisel rough full-length figures out of blocks of stone. . . . [But he] mingles good work with rubbish most annoyingly sometimes . . . [and is] audacious and even lawless. . . . They have both made excellent beginnings. They may not win for themselves foremost places in the new generation, but thus far, without doubt, they are well in advance of their fellows in the race."

[45] " The Harlequin of Dreams " (I, 112), published in *Lippincott's*, Apr., 1878.

To Robert S. Lanier

33 Denmead St.
Bo April 28th 1878.

My dearest Father:

I write a line mainly to say that I *can't* write much. My school-duties, the preparation of my lectures, and my magazine-work always press me hard through every week until Sunday, and that day invariably confines me to my desk with a mass of correspondence which I try to dispose of, in some fashion, once in every seven days.

I enclose a pleasant invitation which arrived a couple of days ago to the Congress of Literary Men which is to form one of the solemnities of the French Exhibition. How I wish I *could* run over and mingle for a few weeks with the *Illuminati* of all the world and — better still — shake big old Hugo by the hand! Please send this over to Clifford and ask him to return it to me, – as it is signed by Edmund About whose autograph I would like to preserve.

I enclose also a request to contribute a poem to one of the No-Name series of volumes. The writer of this letter— G. P. Lathrop — married one of Hawthorne's daughters, and is assistant-editor of The Atlantic Monthly.[46]

An unexpected call for money yesterday found me with too little to meet it, and I therefore drew on you for thirty dollars. I hope it will not give you trouble; you know that it was only a last resort.

I am sorry to note the burning of the Brown House, and the death of Boifeuillet.

Mary has written you of my affairs. There is prospect of an invitation to make my lectures one of the regular features of the Peabody Institute for the coming season of 1878-9. No difficulty whatever would be experienced if the Trustees were in funds: but the rascality of the Tennessee Legislature has cut off nearly one-half their income. A large part of Mr. Peabody's bequest to the Institute consisted of Tennessee bonds. These, however, are now not only bringing in no interest, but

---

[46] Lanier's contribution was " The Marshes of Glynn " (see his letter of July 13, 1878, and note 66, below).

are actually in a ticklish situation as to the principal. I hear that the Legislature refused a compromise of fifty cents on the dollar.

But I must stop. We are all pretty well except May whose life is a martyrdom to catarrh. Kiss Mama for us.

Your loving

S.L.

To John R. Tait [47]

33 Denmead St.
B⁰ April 28th 1878.

Dear Mr. Tait:

I hasten to enclose the letter for which you write, and only wish I had some magical key that would unlock the heart of yᵉ grim Editor for all the works you may bring before him.

As soon as you get time in New York, pray let me know how the pictures in the Exhibition are faring. It is possible I may have to visit the great Babylon in the course of the next ten days; so send me your address, there.

I hope you will have met Mr. Peacock under more favorable circumstance than " the Office " before this. I'm too sorry the house is torn up for I really wanted you to experience one of Mrs. Peacock's quiet and simply perfect little dinners.

I've been writing until my pen-arm is quite fagged, and so good-night. I send cordial messages to the Ladye with the small white hands.

Your friend

Sidney L.

[47] Tait, author and artist, though born in Cincinatti (1834), had made his home in Baltimore since 1876.

To James F. D. Lanier

33 Denmead St.
Baltimore, Md.
April 30th 1878.

Dear Mr. Lanier:

In some studies I have lately been prosecuting I have had the good fortune to light upon several very interesting facts connected with a gentleman of our name who was, I make no doubt, a direct ancestor of ours; and, as you share my interest in these matters, I have thought you would care to know what I have found.

It so happens that some weeks ago I received a very pleasant invitation to deliver a course of lectures in this city on the less-known poets of the 16th century: and in preparing these I have been led among many old and curious English books. Early in my investigations I began to come across the name of *Nicholas Lanier*. The name is sometimes spelled as we spell it, at other times "Laneare", and again "Laniere." I finally went to work and, following up one clue after another, managed to get together a considerable number of items about him.[48]

It seems he was of age, certainly, in the year 1617; at any rate there is every probability that he was born before 1600. He was a gentleman, and must have passed through the University of Oxford, as his portrait now hangs (or did hang, fifteen years ago) in one of the public Halls of that institution, among those of its graduates who have rendered themselves famous. This morning I had the pleasure of seeing an engraving taken from this portrait; and, judging therefrom, " Master Nicholas Lanier " (as Ben Jonson calls him) was as handsome a cavalier as one would find in a summer's day. This engraving I found in a copy of Isaac Walton's " Complete Angler ", of an edition of that book printed in London, 1861, (by H. G. Bohn, York St., Covent Garden) edited by Edward Jesse. It seems that after leaving the University Nicholas Lanier

---

[48] Lanier's MS notes have survived (Charles D. Lanier Collection, Johns Hopkins University). For the publication of this genealogical material, see note 23, 1879.

acquired celebrity both as a painter and as a composer of music, particularly the latter. In that time music was the most fashionable of accomplishments for gentlemen, having become so through the passion which several royal persons entertained for that art. Harry VIII, Queen Elizabeth, and the Charleses were all musicians, and the composers of the realm were held in high esteem.

Accordingly I find where Nicholas Lanier was appointed by King Charles to be "Master of The King's Music", and his brother *John Lanier* is mentioned in the same connection. I fell upon a copy of the King's Grant making this appointment and assigning Nicholas Lanier a salary of two hundred pounds yearly for his services in that behalf.

Again: I find that Nicholas was a co-laborer with Ben Jonson in one of the most beautiful of the latter's works. In the year 1617 a Masque (that is, a dramatic poem, like Milton's "Comus" *e.g.*) was acted by a party of noblemen who were friends of Lord Hay, at the latter's house, in the course of a number of festivities given in honor of the French Ambassador. This Masque was written by Ben Jonson, and the music for it was composed by Nicholas Lanier (see Works of B. Jonson, Gifford's Edition, London 1816, pr. by W. Bulmer & Co, page 290, note). Again: he composed the music for a very beautiful Sonnet which was printed in one of the earliest collections of poetry in Queen Elizabeth's time, and the poem and song appear to have been held in great favor thereafter. The first line of this poem "Like to a hermit poor &c" is quoted by several authors, *viz*: Butler, in "Hudibras" part I. Canto 2; Walton, in "the Complete Angler", p. 159, edition already cited; North, in The Life of The Lord Keeper Guildford, and Phineas Fletcher in one of his paraphrases of the Psalms. This song of Nicholas Lanier's is contained in a work published in 1653, called "Select Musical Ayres and Dialogues", which I have not been able to see, and which is not to be found, I think, outside of the great English Libraries.

I find mention (in Sir Egerton Brydges' "British Bibliographer") of another book published in 1659, consisting of various works by "Henry Lawes, William Lawes, *Nicholas Laneare*, and William Web; Gentlemen, and Servants to his late Majesty in his public and private musick".

And lastly, it is mentioned by old Anthony a-Wood, in his great *Athen. Oxonienses,* that Nicholas Lanier composed the music for a funeral hymn to Charles I, the poetry being written by Thomas Pierce, a distinguished graduate of Oxford.

You will laugh when I tell you that I have seized upon all these scattered facts with keen pleasure for the reason that they seem to give some sort of legitimacy to my own passion for music. Hitherto nobody has been able to account for this: it seemed a thing quite out of the family line, so far back as we could look; and I have therefore always had a secret sense of its being a sort of mongrel business — a trait not belonging to the breed — since it equally fails of authority on my Mother's side, which is the [purest?] Scotch. But here [I find it] cropping out nearly three [hundr]ed years ago in the [persons] of King Charles's Music[ians a]nd I therefore feel a sense [of gra]titude to old Nicholas for r[estorin]g me, as it were, to the pure stock of Laniers.[49]

But, seriously, the gentleman seems to have been intrinsically an interesting person, and I shall address myself earnestly to find out some particulars of his birth-place and residence. I do not doubt that any full account of these will give us material for a complete account of the family back to that time, and will throw light upon the history of General Lanier who is mentioned by Macaulay. The old family-name of " John " seems to reappear in the John Lanier, brother of Nicholas. How I should like to see the Oxford portrait ! The engraving taken from it is in one of the books of the Peabody Library, here, and I have not therefore been able to send it to you,- as I should have done if I could have found the book for sale.

I hope your health improves with the charming spring-weather. My own is better than in many years past, and I am able to do a man's full work every day, which makes me very happy.

Please make my regards to Charles and his wife.

Your friend,

[Sidney Lanier]

[49] Words deleted by the excision of the signature on the other side of the sheet have been conjecturally restored.

To Walt Whitman [50]

33 Denmead St.
Baltimore, Md.
May 5th 1878.

My dear Sir:

A short time ago while on a visit to New York I happened one evening to find your LEAVES OF GRASS in Mr. Bayard Taylor's library: and taking it with me to my room at the hotel I spent a night of glory and delight upon it. How it happened that I had never read this book before – – is a story not worth the telling; but, in sending the enclosed bill to purchase a copy (which please mail to the above address) I cannot resist the temptation to tender you also my grateful thanks for such large and substantial thoughts uttered in a time when there are, as you say in another connection, so many " little plentiful mannikins skipping about in collars and tailed coats." Although I entirely disagree with you in all points connected with artistic form, and in so much of the outcome of your doctrine as is involved in those poetic exposures of the person which your pages so unreservedly make, yet I feel sure that I understand you therein, and my dissent in these particulars becomes a very insignificant consideration in the presence of that unbounded delight which I take in the bigness and bravery of all your ways and thoughts. It is not known to me where I can find another modern song at once so large and so naive: and the time needs to be told few things so much as the absolute personality of the person, the sufficiency of the man's manhood *to* the man, which you have propounded in such strong and beautiful rhythms. I beg you to count me among your most earnest lovers, and to believe that it would make me very happy to be of the least humble service to you at any time

Sidney Lanier [51]

[50] Previously published, *Conservator*, VII, 122 (October, 1896); reprinted, Horace Traubel, *With Walt Whitman in Camden* (Boston, 1906), I, 208, and in facsimile on opposite page, from which the present text is taken (MS not found). Lanier quotes, in the middle of the letter, ·from Whitman's " Song of Myself."

[51] Whitman's reply, on a postal card, May 27, 1878, read: " I have to-day

To John G. James [52]

33 Denmead St.
Baltimore, Md.
May 5th 1878.

My dear Col. James:
I feel sure you will believe it has been by no negligence on my part that your last kind letter has remained so long unanswered. A severe attack of illness caught me in the midst of some literary engagements which *had* to be fulfilled, and therefore I was compelled to put myself at double work as soon as I recovered. For the last six weeks I have been either at book or desk from twelve to fourteen hours every day, save scanty allowances for taking my daily bread. I have thought, each week, that the next would leave me freer, and in that belief have postponed writing you. This is the whole story.

I happen to know that our friend Wm Hand Browne is quite busy just at present, and – although he is good enough to quit his business and sit with his feet in the stocks like another Riccabocca for a week if he could oblige anybody he loved by so doing – I determined to look up a magazine article which appeared in Boston about a year ago and which I think contains all the facts you would need for the purpose you mention, in such form as enables you to extract them bodily to whatever extent you may desire.[53] Perhaps the favorable view

sent by mail, same address as this card, my Volume *Leaves of Grass*– Please notify me (by postal card will do) soon as it reaches you safely. Walt Whitman."

[52] Previously published, *Letters: Sidney Lanier to Col. John G. James* (Austin, Texas, 1942), pp. 4-5.

[53] In his letter of Apr. 26, 1878, James had said: "You doubtless have not forgotten the fact that I am dependent upon you for the facts and data for the biog^l. notice of *you* for my Southern Speaker and Reader. . . . Mr. Wm Hand Browne wrote me that if you would give him the *data*, he would take pleasure in preparing a brief notice such as I want."

Lanier instead sent James the issue of *The Cottage Hearth* for June, 1877 (see note 52, 1877) – now preserved in the Mirabeau Lamar Library, University of Texas. One marginal correction in Lanier's handwriting is worthy of record. Where the author had spoken of his ill health incapacitating him for the practice of law, especially for "making its long and laborious pleas," Lanier cancelled the last word and wrote for James's information: "speeches (he means) though you will care to hear that I have now entirely recovered from this disability and have full use of my voice."

therein taken may be all the more available as coming from the Antipodes, where no sectional partiality could have worked any bias *toward* me.

As for the portrait in the article, – my wife grows very indignant over it, and I do not mean it at all as a performance of the promise I made to send you a photograph. This I hope to do in a very few days, when the extraordinary pressure of my work will certainly be over.

Your letters are always read with pleasure here. I beg you to accept my special thanks for your kind expressions in regard to my poems. I feel sure that generous approval of this sort is always helpful to every earnest worker, as aiding him to confirm himself unto himself. Nowadays, – far more than in the time when our sacred master Shakespere wrote that wonderful sonnet – moods must often come to the poet when he does

> . . . with fortune chide,
> The guilty goddess of his harmful deeds,
> That did not better for his life provide
> Than public means which public manners breeds; [54]

and in these moods the intelligent and sympathetic faith of others is particularly grateful. For there are *so* many charlatans: not a street-corner of the time where some glib fellow does not stand and thrive by selling to the unwary by-passers all manner of oroide imitations of statesmanship, or of art, or of all the other useful products which modern cleverness has learned to manufacture in baser metal, at fabulously cheap prices. And so, when one whose fate drives him also to stand at the corner and call out to the people receives some assurance that he has *not* been mistaken for a pinchbeck-vender, at all events, – – – he must needs welcome the voice that brings it. [55]

[54] Sonnet CXI.

[55] In his letter of Dec. 6, 1877, James had written: "Your poems I have read with great delight–. . . indeed, they give me more pleasure than do the poems of any other American writer of today." On Apr. 26, 1878, he had reported: "I know you will be pleased to learn that your Poems have excited great interest in our community. My two copies have been making the rounds of our city for the past three months– with the net result of my ordering this morning from Lippencott *25 copies* for a club of my friends." And on May 14, he added: "I enclose you herewith postal order for ten dollars– it being the very liberal discount allowed me by Lippencott & Co. . . . And as you get *your* copy-right directly from the publishers, I place you under bonds to turn this over at once to Mrs. Lanier as *hers*."

I did not fill out the blank because I saw that I could do nothing more than repeat what Col. Johnston would have already sent you.

Your invitation to Austin is very tempting, and I sincerely wish it were in my power to meet you. For some time, however, I suspect I am to be a fixture here. The matter of boiling the pot, even for so frugal a set as my little household, involves an amount of desperate struggle (when there is nothing but *ms.* to keep up the fire) which no one would credit who has not tried it.

But I hope we may come together somewhere, before long; and whether we do or not, I am always

Your friend,

Sidney Lanier –

To John B. Tabb [56]

33 Denmead St.
Bo May 12th 1878.

My dear John:
 I have been waiting some weeks for Mr. Kirk [57] to send me a final decision as to your verses. I transmitted to him a little collection of your poems – such as I happened to have with me. I suppose he is overwhelmed with work – he usually is – and is taking his time to make a selection. There is no such thing as hurrying a Magazine editor.

Do you know Brother Azarias of Rock Hill College? In the course of my recent work I have had occasion to read his " Philosophy of Literature "; [58] and, whilst I arrive at the goal by a very different road from that which he travels, I find myself in hearty nearness to him as regards the animating purpose and Final Cause of literature.

I hope you are well. The glimpse of green leaves make me

---

[56] Previously published, Gordon Blair, *Father Tabb* (Richmond, Va., 1940), pp. 64-65.

[57] J. F. Kirk, editor of *Lippincott's Magazine.*

[58] Brother Azarias (Patrick Francis Mullany, 1847-1893) was professor of literature at Rock Hill College, Ellicott City, Md., and became its president in 1879. The volume here referred to was *An Essay Contributing to a Philosophy of Literature*, published in 1874.

long for the company of "large amiable trees" where you
live. And then *you* are there: and that makes me long all the
more: for I had *almost* as lief hear you talk, dear John, as a
tree. Don't give up the idea that I will come. When is your
vacation? And what do you do then? And are you not
coming to the Baltimore "Musical Festival" on the 29th of
May? We have sixty instruments in the orchestra, and two
hundred voices in the chorus, with Pappenheim and Remmertz
for the solos.

Have I sent you a copy of my "Dove" in SCRIBNER's, for
May?.

God bless you always, my Jonathan, says

Your

S. L.

To ROBERT S. LANIER

33 Denmead St.

B⁰ May 13th 1878.

My dearest Father:

I am not quite so pushed for time this week,
my lectures being now over for the season; and I am trying to
rest my pen-arm a little, which has had a severe race of it for
the last two months.

The Lecture-Committee of The Peabody Institute met last
Friday and resolved to tender me their lecture-hall for the season of 1878-9. I am to deliver a series of lectures, extending
from the 1st November to 1st April, two each week, under the
auspices of the Peabody. Prest. Gilman (of Johns Hopkins
University) has in the very kindest manner—and at a good
deal of personal trouble — arranged to cooperate with me in
such a manner as to make my course a very attractive one.
During the second half-year of the series, when the progress
of my lectures will have brought me to Shakespere, we are to
have a sort of Shakesperean Revival: parallel with my own
treatment of Shakespere. Prof. Childs of Harvard (who had
been engaged by the Johns Hopkins University for a special
course) will deliver a series of ten readings from Macbeth;
Prof. Gildersleeve, (Greek prof. in Johns Hopkins) will give

two lectures on the relation between the Greek drama and Shakespere's: Mr. Royce (Fellow of Johns Hopkins) will give two lectures on Shakespere in Germany: and two other gentlemen from Johns Hopkins will contribute lectures on their own specialties converging upon the same theme.[59] We hope to wind up the whole with a beautiful spectacular exhibition representing an audience of Shakespere's times assembled on the stage while a play goes on.

It is proposed to sell a hundred subscription tickets to the whole course at twenty dollars each, and this is to be my remuneration.

It would thus seem that my next year's work is thus most delightfully mapped out. My lectures are to consist of ten introductory discourses on Literary Technic, thirty on the less-known poetry of the Elizabeth Period, and ten on subjects connected with Shakespere — fifty in all. These are studies which I take such delight in pursuing that I can not well imagine a pleasanter prospect for my next season in Baltimore.

Meantime: it is necessary for me to devote the entire summer to the preparation of these lectures, and I am going to New York day after tomorrow for the purpose of making such fiscal

[59] A MS outline of the original plan submitted to the Peabody Institute has survived (Charles D. Lanier Collection, Johns Hopkins University). It calls for an elaborate program of eighty lectures—" illustrating the Elizabethan Period with particular reference to the works of Shakespere "— to be delivered at the rate of four a week from Nov. 2, 1878, to Apr. 11, 1879. During the first half of the course, Lanier was to give twenty lectures (eight on the " Technic of Poetry " and twelve on the minor writers of the sixteenth century) ; and twenty supplementary lectures on other features of the period were to be given by Prof. E. G. Daves, R. M. Johnston, and two more unnamed persons. During the second half, Lanier was listed for twenty more lectures (two on pronunciation in Shakespeare's time and eighteen on " The Relation of Shakespere to the Modern English Novel, Drama, Lyric Poem, and Common Speech ") ; and the remaining twenty as follows: ten readings from Shakespeare by Prof. F. J. Child and two by Prof. E. G. Daves, two lectures on science in Shakespeare's time by Prof. Ira G. Remsen, two on Shakespeare in Germany by Josiah Royce or H. C. G. Brandt, two on Shakespeare in France by Prof. Léonce Rabillon (changed to two on unnamed topics by Prof. J. J. Sylvester), and two unassigned— probably the two assigned in the present letter to Prof. Basil L. Gildersleeve. All of Lanier's associate lecturers were connected with the Johns Hopkins faculty except Johnston and Daves; Child was visiting professor from Harvard.

The series as actually given was reduced to only forty lectures and involved a considerable revision in topics and personnel (see Lanier's letter of July 28, 1878, and note 85, below).

arrangements as will enable me to do so. The carrying through of the whole project has been a matter of much work and thought, and the action of the Trustees is regarded as a great compliment to me.

This, together with my current lectures and the school, has kept me from realizing any avails with the magazines for three weeks past, and I am therefore at a small interregnum, just at present, in finances. I will need more than I have about me, when I start to New York, to leave some with Mary and for various household bills. If it should not arrive before day after tomorrow, I wish to draw on you for fifty dollars. Should you be without funds at the time the draft comes, please borrow from Mr. Plant for ten days,– in which time I will arrange to send it back to you if you *should* have to borrow.

I suppose you have seen my " Dove " in the May SCRIBNER'S. I have not been able to get a copy of " Clover " for you.

We all send love to you and Mama. May is still a slave to the chills. The boys are well, and I continue in admirable condition. I hope the Court treats you well: but you have been so long and so uniformly successful that I am always expecting *some* temporary reverses.

Charley asks me to enclose these cards, which he has set up and printed with his own hands on his own printing-press. He wishes you to use them for visiting-cards. He has begun the business, and desires orders from any of your friends who wish cards printed in this style. His charge is eight cents a dozen. He will send you his business-card to put up in your office.

Your loving

S. L.

To RICHARD M. JOHNSTON [60]

Westminster Hotel.
New York, May 21st 1878

My dear and only Richard, I send a hasty line to say that the main person I desired to see is out of town and I have been obliged to follow him, so that I cannot be in place before

[60] Previously published, *Maryland Historical Magazine*, XXXIV, 317 (Dec.,

Thursday next. This gives me a great deal of concern; but my quest here is of such vital importance to my future plans that it seems a duty not to abandon the field until every possibility is exhausted. If I succeed I shall have no more cause of disquiet for a year.

Whenever you have time please run by and cheer up my poor Little Girl, whom I left sadly unstrung by long illness. It is almost more than I can bear,–to be obliged to stay away from home for two days more.

God have you in His holy keeping,

Your faithful

S. L.

To Robert S. Lanier

33 Denmead St.
B^o May 28th 1878.

My dear Father:

Yours of 23rd has just reached me, and I write a line—in the midst of engagements which scarcely leave me time to breathe — to beg that you will reconsider your determination to move out of the house you now occupy. I cannot bear to think of your abandoning all the lovely trees and shrubs and flowers which are now just beginning to reward the affectionate nursing you have given them for so many years. As for the furniture, we can remedy that defect, in the following manner. I gather from your letter that the main articles you will need are: a bed-room set, and a buffet (or its equivalent) for the dining-room. As for the parlor-carpet, that might be dispensed

---

1939). Evidence of the warm relations existing between Lanier and Johnston at this time is found in the latter's letter of May 9, 1878, on the death of Charles Day Lanier's mocking-bird, a family pet for several years. Johnston wrote: "I dont mean this as a letter of condolence, I mean it mostly as a motion to give you both assurance that, if possible, I admire and like you both more than before since I see how you have grieved for this loss."

Lanier's sonnet, "To Our Mocking-Bird. Died, of a Cat, May, 1878 " (I, 117), was published in the *Independent*, Aug. 29, 1878. It was probably at about this same time that Lanier also wrote a prose piece called "Bob: The Story of our Mocking-Bird" (VI, 340), published posthumously in the *Independent*, Aug. 3, 1882.

with until fall, since (*here*, at least) every one takes up carpets at this season. The parlor-floor can be *stained* at very small expense, and will look nicely: that is the universal custom, here. About this I can write you more fully another time. But, for the present, what I started out to say is: that I can get a nice-looking set of bed-room furniture, here, (*imitation* walnut) for thirty six dollars, with the privilege of paying one-third cash, and the balance in three or four months, by monthly instalments. Besides this, your letter mentions "a few other things." I do not know how much these come to, but suppose you do this: let me buy you here (where I doubt not such things are much cheaper than in Macon), say, a hundred dollars worth of things (you to send a list of whatever you need besides the bed-room set). I will myself pay the thirty-three dollars cash — which I can do now — and between us we can certainly make up the balance (about sixteen dollars a month) for the next four months. If you should want a hundred and fifty dollars' worth of things, I can easily arrange it. The furniture men have found me a good customer and are anxious to sell to me, on any terms.

As for the buffet: we have a new sort of refrigerator, in walnut, which answers all ordinary purposes of a small family for *both* these needs, *i.e.* refrigerator *and* buffet. This can be bought for thirty-two dollars, and is a very pleasant-looking article in the dining-room, besides being very convenient for keeping milk, butter &c, and very economical of ice.

Altogether, I cannot at all think of your leaving the Vineville home; [61] and I will be impatient until I hear from you that you have determined to stay in it. Aside from your own behalf, I regard it of great importance for the preservation of the property that a tenant so careful as yourself should remain upon it.

I think you can live there for about the same amount as when boarding; and there is no comparison as to comfort. Indeed I think it a matter of *health*: for you can now get such food as your individual tastes require, and this is often impossible, and always difficult, in a boarding-house.

[61] Apparently the home bought by Gertrude Lanier Shannon before her marriage to Mr. Gibson. Sidney Lanier had lived here during his residence in Macon as a lawyer, and his father seems to have remained in the house thereafter. Vineville was a suburb of Macon.

I have every reason to believe that the time is about at hand when I can be able to help *you* in the way you have for so long been helping *me*. If my health holds, I feel sure I can: and the prospect gives me more pleasure than I can now express.

So, Courage, my dear Father, and tranquillity! There is no telling what the future may bring forth.

I must now break off, for I will be busy until late tonight. Write me that you will remain in the house. All send loving messages, and most of all your

S. L.

I hope my telegram relieved your mind about the draft. I have not now time to explain the mistake by which it was sent south.

S.L.

To Charles Day

33 Denmead St.
B⁰ June 1st 1878.

My dear Father:

We had your letter from Indian Springs yesterday and rejoiced to gather from it that you were improving in health, and that our dear Cubbie [62] is also doing better. The latter's condition gave me much concern, for I feared he might have suffered some internal hurt: but all danger of this sort seems now out of the question, and perhaps the rest which was enforced by the accident was about the best thing for him, as quiet seems to be the main thing he needs.

Mr. Lanier, of New York, a few days ago, in the most cordial and kindly way advanced me some money which I wish to use in a business-undertaking next fall. I wished that he might have some security for it in the event of my death, and to that end I executed in his favor a mortgage on the two Clinch County lots which you deeded to me some time ago. [63] The

[62] Harry Day, Lanier's brother-in-law.

[63] This mortgage survives (Charles D. Lanier Collection, Johns Hopkins University). It is dated May 23, 1878, and covered a loan by J. F. D. Lanier for $2,000 to be repaid in one year. Lanier received the money in two installments, May 23 and Nov. 1, 1878.

opportunity was a sudden one and for this reason I was unable to consult you about the matter beforehand: but I hope the transaction will meet with your approval. The advance relieved me of all present care about a debt which was causing me great anxiety: and I am to receive a further sum on the 1st November next which will enable me to avail myself of what now seems to be a very fine opportunity to establish myself permanently here in my favorite pursuits. All the details of this I will explain when I see you: and I sincerely hope that may be very soon. I will be glad if you can see your way clear to come to us straightway. We all want to see you, and we think we can make you a very useful person about the house.

Our great Musical Festival is just over. In various ways it has kept me very busy, in addition to my other duties. It has been very enjoyable, however, and I have been pleased especially with the delight which Mary took in it. On the last night, Mr. McKee of Washington (Gen. Dunn's son-in-law) came over to Baltimore at our invitation, took tea with us, and escorted Mary to the Academy of Music (my duties taking me into the Orchestra) where they occupied a box with President Gilman and his wife. The proprietors of the Baltimore SUN employed me to write the musical criticism of the Festival for that paper, and you will be glad to know that my contributions, which were upon a somewhat different plan from the usual ones, have been very pleasantly received.[64]
Mary and I paid a flying visit to the Dunns last Tuesday, in Washington, for the main purpose of meeting Mr. [J. F. D.] Lanier who is now staying there. We went over by the 11.20 train in the morning, and returned late in the afternoon in time for me to play at a Concert. We were overwhelmed with all manner of kind attentions: I think May, as usual, made a complete conquest of Mr. Lanier.

My prospects for next fall seem very bright, and I think there is every reason for believing that our long struggle is beginning to tell in our favor. The past winter has sometimes

---

[64] "The Maryland Musical Festival" (II, 316), first published in the Baltimore Sun, May 28-30, 1878. Another prose piece which was apparently written about this time, but which is not mentioned in the letters, was "Mazzini on Music" (II, 307), first published in the Independent, June 27, 1878.

brought me to extremities that I scarcely care to remember, and I fear May has often found me a very dismal companion: but I really believe it is all over now. My health is so fine, as compared with what it has been for five years past, that I can do great quantities of work: and we are gradually getting many little comforts about us which go to make up a home.

Last night I had the first evening I have been able to spare from work for a long time: so after tea we illuminated our cosy little parlor and sat down to — — — a family game of Whist ! You must know that your two youngest grand-children have developed a passion for this amusement which is droll beyond description. Remembering Sidney's flibber-tigibbet ways and nervous restlessness in general, you will ap-preciate the fascination of the game for him when I tell you he sits a-straddle of one end of a trunk (Harry on the other end) and plays for an hour at a time without disturbance. We had, therefore, a great rubber together, Mama and Harry counting as my one partner against Charley and Sidney. If you could have heard the frequent and fervent wishes for you, I think you would be able to free yourself from the captivating spell of Mr. Collier and come straight on to us.

Mary still suffers with the wretched dumb chills, and is now gone down to the Doctor's on errands connected therewith. The boys are pretty well.

You will accept all loving messages from

Your son

S. L.

To Robert S. Lanier

33 Denmead St.

Bo. June 15th 1878.

My dear Father:

In order to write my Southern articles, I wish to prepare my system (as it were) by reading three or four representative southern papers for the next month. Can you send me your CONSTITUTION and the TELEGRAPH & MESSEN-GER every day? You can buy newspaper-wrappers at the P. O. already stamped and thus save trouble in arranging them for the mail.

I am pained to hear of the failure of Cubbedge & H. Are you employed in connection with the case? – for I suppose there will be litigation of some sort.

I write hastily,

Your loving

S. L.

To ROBERT S. LANIER

33 Denmead St.
B⁰.   July 9th 1878.

My dear Father:

One of my curious little interregnums this morning made me obliged to draw a sight draft for fifty dollars on you. I will transfer that amount by telegraph to you on Thursday in time to meet the draft. It isn't worth while explaining how this happens. I'm sure the Treasury of the United States does not require one tithe of the ingenuity in financiering which my small exchequer does. I haven't time to write. The Southern papers arrive regularly and give me much food for thought.   We all send love and kisses to you all.

The proof of a considerable poem of mine called " The Revenge of Hamish " – a Highland Story – has arrived, and I presume it will be out in the July number of APPLETON'S MAGAZINE.[65]

Your loving

Sidney.

To ROBERT S. LANIER

33 Denmead St.
B⁰ July 13th 1878.

My dear Father:

The time when I am to draw my next instalment of funds from Mr. Lanier is a little too far off, and I wish to bridge over the chasm betwixt now and then. For this

---

[65] " The Revenge of Hamish " (I, 112), for which Lanier was paid $30.00, was published in *Appleton's Journal*, Nov., 1878.

purpose I have discounted my note for $200.00 at thirty days, in the National Bank of Baltimore (where I keep my account), and not wishing to ask any one here to do so – though several would be willing – I have made it in the form of a thirty day draft on you.   It will be sent forward today for acceptance, and I write that you may understand, when it is presented to you.   You need give yourself no concern about it.   I will instruct them that it will be paid *here*.   I was gratified with the behavior of the Bank in the matter.

Fearing you might be hard up I sent you fifty dollars by telegraph to meet my sight draft.   I am so desperately busy with my work that matters sometimes come upon me when I cannot spare the time to attend to them except in this summary way.   You must not think me shiftless, or careless.

I have just sent off three poems, hot from the mint.   One of these — called " The Marshes of Glynn," and descriptive of the great salt-marshes on the coast of Georgia — I read to Col. Johnston the other day under the chestnut-trees at his beautiful place near Waverley.   He declares it is the greatest poem written in a hundred years.   It is in tremendous long lines of dactyls.[66]

I am now deep in four articles on " the Physics of Poetry " which I expect to sell to the Popular Science Monthly.[67]   These finished, I will take up the Southern papers.

[66] " The Marshes of Glynn " (I, 118) was the poem accepted by G. P. Lathrop for the anthology in the " No Name " Series published by Roberts Brothers, Boston, in the fall of 1878 under the title *A Masque of Poets*.   In his letter of Apr. 20, 1878, Lathrop had written: " The names of the authors will not appear; but it is intended to make this collection representative of the best poets in this country, with some contributions from England.   Each poem will be paid for out of the profits of the book, after the publishers have sold enough copies simply to pay the expenses of printing, plates, paper, etc.   After a short interval, the contributors will be at liberty to announce the authorship of their pieces. . . .   I should prefer a short piece with some piquant conceit for a basis; something also with Southern coloring.   Please, if you can, send me two or three, with the privilege of choosing."

One of the other two poems mentioned by Lanier as having just been sent off " hot from the mint " was undoubtedly " Remonstrance " (see note 77, below).   The other was probably the unidentified poem submitted to the *North American Review* on Aug. 2, 1878, and returned on the grounds that this magazine did not publish poetry (see *North American Review* to Lanier, Aug. 25, 1878).

[67] For the evolution of these articles into Lanier's volume, *The Science of English Verse* (1880), see II, viii-xvii.

I have not now time to *write* you. Your long letter is
arrived, and I will try to answer it soon. We are in tolerable
conditions, as to health. I am going out into the woods to
shoot bows and arrows with Charley and the other boys this
afternoon, for the benefit of my lung, which suffers a little
under much cramping of work.

God bless you,

Your son,

S. L.

To Daniel C. Gilman

33 Denmead St.
Baltimore, Md.
July 28th 1878.

Dear Mr. Gilman:

I think there will be no difficulty in consum-
mating all the arrangements for " The Shakespere Course "
after the resumption of affairs in the autumn. I happened to
meet Mr. Gildersleeve at the Wednesday Club [68] a short time
before he left town, and was informed by him that he knew
of nothing to interfere with his part of the scheme. Such lectures as are to be delivered by the other gentlemen from the
University can easily be arranged to suit their convenience in
point of time. I feel satisfied that we will find it wise to reduce the number of lectures to two a week during the first
half-year, and this will add to the facility of organizing the
course after the autumn begins, inasmuch as it will give the
lecturers more time for preparing the lectures as they are
wanted.[69]

I desired to call and bid farewell before you left for the
summer; but you looked so tired when I last saw you, and I
was so troubled when I found what inroads upon your time

[68] A club for musical and dramatic amateur performances, which Lanier had
been invited to join as a complimentary member, Feb. 7, 1876 (invitation in the
Charles D. Lanier Collection, Johns Hopkins University). His friends Henry
C. Wysham, Otto Sutro, and George W. Dobbin were on the Board of Gov-
ernors at the time. Basil Gildersleeve was professor of Greek at Johns Hopkins.

[69] See note 59, above, and note 85, below.

had been made by the discussion of my schemes, that I refrained from going.

I hope, now you *are* at leisure, that you will cultivate those arts of repose and of profitable idleness which always improve the quality of a man's work and which we neglect too much in our bustling times.

Please convey my cordial wishes for a pleasant summer to Mrs. Gilman, and believe me always, with the liveliest sense of your good offices,

Sincerely yours,

Sidney Lanier.

To Richard M. Johnston [70]

33 Denmead St.
Saturday Morning.
[Baltimore, Aug. 3, 1878?]

It *is* a " drear interval ", my dear Colonel,

I thought certainly I would be sitting under your trees with you this morning; but my boys, who have for a long time held me in abject servility through an unguarded promise I once made to take them somewhere on a steamboat at sometime — though I appeal to every well-regulated parent if the words " somewhere " and " sometime " have not been held, time out of mind, to deprive all such promises of moral obligation at any particular place or moment — found themselves yesterday arrived at such a pass that life seemed to have reduced itself to the formula " Steamboat or Suicide ": and so, purely to avoid a dark and childless future I bundled 'em all off to Fair Haven.[71]

[70] Previously published, *Maryland Historical Magazine*, XXXIV, 317-318 (Dec., 1939). Conjectural dating from the following evidence: (1) a notation on the reverse of the sheet by Johnston reads: " August 1878 "; (2) the reference in this letter to Mary Day Lanier's health requiring a change of climate places it definitely before the following letter which is written on her " last Sunday at home for a month "; (3) since she left for Rockingham Springs on Aug. 15 (see Lanier's letter to her of Aug. 16, below), the date of Lanier's second letter to Johnston was unquestionably Sunday, Aug. 11; (4) this would place the present letter– dated " Saturday Morning "– on Aug. 3 or Aug. 10, and as the contents of the two letters do not indicate that they were written on consecutive days, the earlier date is assigned to Lanier's first letter.

[71] A small town on the Chesapeake south of Annapolis.

We returned at half-past nine last night, and straightway fell to wondering what horrible and grievous crime we had committed against Heaven, that It should have brought you to our house on that one particular day out of the three hundred and sixty five when we were all absent.

My holiday moreover leaves me with double work today, and I fear I won't be able to get to you until Monday, when, please Heaven, I will write some philosophy under your chestnuts. But meantime *you* might come *here* and smoke.

May is not at all well, and I am trying, in consultation with her this morning, to devise some method — consistent with the extreme attenuation of our purse — to get her into a different air from this.

Sidney has permission to stay until Seven this afternoon, if he isn't in Mrs. Johnston's way. He has taken such a violent fancy to your abode, and to the people in it, that he talks of little else. The other boys would go with him but one is not well — Harry — and Charley has some duties at home.

So, until I see you, God keep you and the chestnuts in such receipt of rain or of sunshine as your spirits may severally desire,– prays

Your faithful

S. L.

To Richard M. Johnston

[Baltimore? Aug. 11, 1878?] [72]

My dear Richard The First (and also The Last, for there are no more like you).

Charley is quite sick this morning, after a very feverish and restless night. We can't exactly tell whether it is indigestion or a chill, but incline strongly to the former theory, remembering a certain birth-day supper at which he " assisted " a couple of days ago. I have given him a bottle of Congress Water, and we await developments.

We won't be able to come out today. May don't like to

---

[72] Evidence for the conjectural dating is given in note 70, above.

leave Charley, and — as it is her last Sunday at home for a month — she don't want me to leave her.

By the middle of the week I shall be alone, and will see you then. Meantime,

God bless you.

Your friend,

S. L.

To Mary Day Lanier [73]

B°   Aug. 16th 1878.

Dearest Soul. After watching the last puff of smoke from your locomotive as it rounded the curve I wandered disconsolately back to town, held high converse with the india-rubber man, returned to – – to – Jane, hailed a passing apple-vender's wagon, helped the apple-vender to load on the silver-box, got up on the seat with him, rode down to the Bank, deposited my precious wares, returned again to Jane, and buried myself in work for the rest of the day. I slept well, and, after a very gorgeous breakfast for a batchelor, have been writing steadily until now, nearly dinner-time.

The weather has been staggering feebly along for twenty four hours, under a great weight of warm and dismal clouds: these have at last found relief, and a torrent of rain has been pouring for a half-hour. Our brook, – nay, our sewer – has become a raging river and the whole basin betwixt us and the Lee's is flooded.

Enclosed is a card from Miss Taliaferro which came this morning with very comfortable news. I have just written her a long letter.

Jane is very tranquil, and marvellously attentive. She has asked twice after Charley; and expressed concern this morning at finding so many musquitoes in my room; besides offering point-blank to iron a shirt for me today. A load of favors like this become embarrassing. I think she is touched by my forlorn condition.

---

[73] Envelope addressed to Rockingham Springs, West Virginia. This resort had been chosen partly because Mary Day Lanier's friend Clare de Graffenried (mentioned in the closing sentence) was spending the summer there.

I have written long letters to my father, thine, Mr. Gilder, Mr. Macdonald, Miss Taliaferro and Wysham.[74]

So now, with such love as I would thou knew'st better by better acts, and with a thousand kisses for my dearest Hal and Sidney, and one for Clare,

Thine

S. L.

To Robert S. Lanier

33 Denmead St.
Bo. Aug. 16th 1878.

My dear Father:

I have in vain ransacked my memory to find some trace of the matter to which you refer. The collocation "Lewis J. Grace, Trustee" has a vaguely familiar sound to me, but in what connection I cannot say. I feel almost sure that I never examined the title for Mrs. Reeves, however: for such examinations used always to cause me a degree of nervous anxiety which usually impressed at least some feature of them very strongly on my memory. I seem to have a shadowy recollection, which becomes firmer the more I think of it, that there was a Petition for Leave to Sell – though I do not know by whom drawn, perhaps by some other firm than ours, on behalf of the Grace parties – and that it was granted in form. Can you not find some record of that on the Minutes of the Court? Your letter only mentions that you find no *charge* for drawing the Petition on our books: which might be accounted for by the circumstance that some other firm drew it for Turpin & Ogden, or for the Graces.

———"———
"

Mr. Wysham, of this place, has occasion to know something of a lady calling herself the widow of an officer in a Georgia Regi-

---

[74] The only one of these letters that has been found is to R. S. Lanier, following. The other addressees were Charles Day, R. W. Gilder (editor of *Scribner's Monthly*), Ronald MacDonald (editorial staff of the New York *Times*), Mary W. Taliaferro (a cousin of the late Janie Taliaferro Lamar Day), and Henry C. Wysham.

ment named Pope, and giving her own maiden name as Mary
A. Calhoun, of Macon, Georgia. Wysham thinks there is some
imposture, and wishes information. Do you know anything of
the parties, or anybody who can tell about them?

———— " ————
"

As to the furniture: I should think thirty-five dollars a large
price for a second-hand bureau, unless it were a very gorgeous
one. If the bedstead is handsome, \$27.00 is not high: a very
pretty Walnut bedroom suit, entire, with marble-top washstand &c. costs here about *forty* dollars. The Refrigerator
about which I wrote you is nothing like so handsome as the
buffet that stood in your dining room, and does not occupy so
much space. It is made of walnut. Mine cost \$32.00 . It is
an absolutely essential article, here, where we have to keep
many things fresh, such as milk, butter, fresh meat &c. A
much larger and handsomer one than mine can be bought for
forty-five dollars, which would answer all the purposes of a
buffet, and add to them the uses of a refrigerator and water-
cooler. The ice placed in the centre compartment furnishes
drinking-water from its own meltings: we never put in any
water. On each side of this centre compartment there are
larger ones, lined with galvanized iron (which has superseded
zinc for such purposes) in which the articles are placed. Ours
works well, and keeps the butter hard and sweet in the hottest
weather.

I am today all alone in my house. Mary had reached such a
degree of emaciation from the chills – she has had one *every
day* for four months – and had become altogether so enfeebled,
though very bravely doing all her household duties daily, that I
became freightened, and packed her off to a quiet sort of big
farm-house in W. Virginia known as Rockingham Springs.
The proprietor agreed to take the whole party – Mary, Sidney,
Harry, and Servant – for fifty dollars a month, which is quite
as cheap as they could live at home. Charley has gone to the
Taliaferros', near Orange Court House, Virginia, to farm it
for a couple of months, his tastes at present being altogether
bucolic. After a couple of days I shall transfer myself to Col.
Johnston's, and then to Dr. Browne's, – both in the country

near Baltimore, – coming in town every morning to spend my day at my own desk, where I have great quantities of work on hand.

In spite of the large amount of writing I have done for many months past, I am in tolerable condition, and am unceasingly grateful for the ability to work. If this will only continue until I get the books printed which I have now on hand, I will feel greatly blest. I have just sent off three long papers on " The Physics of Poetry ", which will be spread into a complete Manual of English Prosody to be published in the Spring. I take great comfort in the principle which underlies the system unfolded in these papers, and which really revolutionizes the whole business of Prosody, solving problems which have worried and divided scholars for ages.[75]

I have a Janis MANUAL OF GEORGIA, and am now about to commence work on my southern articles.

The weather is debilitating, here, but not so warm as represented at the south.

I hope the law will revive before long. What a life we do live! We work all the time and yet store up no money. But we are still better off than those who don't work, or can't.

Kiss Mama for me. How I wish you were here with me for a week or two !

God bless you,

Your son,

S. L.

[75] In reminiscences written for Edwin Mims, probably in 1904, Sophie Bledsoe Herrick wrote: " It was not until the summer of 1878, just before my removal from Baltimore to New York that I learned to know Mr. Lanier very well. . . .

" Mr. Lanier's family were not with him then, and he was busy writing some articles on the Science of Composition [*sic*]– Evening after evening he would bring the Mss. of these articles and read them, and talk them over.

" I was at that time intensely interested in microscopic work. It was curious and interesting to see how Mr. Lanier kindled to the subject; so foreign to his ordinary literary interests. I was too busy with editorial work to go on with my microscopic work, then, and it was a great pleasure to leave my instrument and books on the subject with him for some months. He plunged in with all the ardor of a naturalist, not using the microscope as a mere toy, but doing good hard work with it. I think I can detect in his work after this time,– as well as in his letters, many little touches which show the influence this minute study of nature had upon his mind." (MS, Edwin Mims Collection, Johns Hopkins University.)

To Mary Day Lanier

Bo Aug. 18th 1878.

Today the clouds departed before dawn, and the air has been sweet beyond description. Early after breakfast Col. Dawson came by in his buggy, and would have me drive with him to Towsontown – seven miles – whither he went to see a sick friend. This I did, and the whole world seemed dissolved into a sweet green essence of leaves and clover and sunlight which could be breathed, – as we rolled along.

Returning I stopped at Col. Johnston's, and spent there the rest of my day.

— Becoming, in the course of the same, conclusively satisfied that I cannot pay the visit spoken of, by reason of circumstances not to be mentioned herein but altogther over-whelming.

I am therefore probably in the hands of Jane, until the Mil-lenium.

—"— Tomorrow I will hear of thee, without doubt: but thereafter — write not, at thy peril. I will send the two little tooth brushes also by mail, unless thou mentionest otherwise.

I am doing well in bodily health, and projecting many works, and daily throwing a thousand thoughts to thee and my sweet boys, and hourly growing more entirely — spite of having always been most entirely — thy

lover.

To John F. Kirk [76]

33 Denmead St.
Baltimore, Md.
Aug. 24th 1878.

My dear Mr. Kirk:

I rather expected the poem [77] wouldn't do: though I thought perhaps there might be enough margin of

---

[76] Excerpt previously published, Mims, p. 204; reprinted, Starke, p. 318. Kirk was the editor of *Lippincott's Magazine*.

[77] " Remonstrance " (I, 122), published posthumously as No. 1 of " Street Cries."

obscurity in it to leave Orthodoxy in some doubt as to whether
or not it was being abused.

I send today a paper headed " On Some Old Sonnet-Makers.
I Bartholomew Griffin." [78] This paper, and number II – which
will be a critical account of Nicholas Breton and William
Drummond of Hawthornden, accompanied by numerous specimens of their handiwork – form two chapters in a book which
I wish to offer Messrs. Lippincott & Co. for publication in the
late autumn (or early spring, if they should think better), to be
called " The English Sonneteers, from Surrey to Shakespeare."
The work will make two volumes 8ᵛᵒ of about two hundred pp.
each: and will embrace critical accounts, similar in general tone
to that given in the accompanying paper, of the Sonnets of
Wyatt, Surrey, Griffin, Sidney, Raleigh, Daniel, Drummond,
Watson, Warner, Breton, Constable, Lodge, Peele, Greene,
Barnfield, Barnes, Drayton, Donne, Shakespere, Spenser, and
the anonymous writers in the early collections like *Tottel's
Miscellany*, *The Phenix' Nest*, *The Gorgeous Gallery*, &c. The
book will be arranged with special reference to its becoming a
standard work in the courses of English Literature which are
now becoming so popular in our schools and colleges. It will
present at first hand pretty nearly all the most valuable work of
each author in this particular *genre*; and will really amount to
an expurgated edition of 16ᵗʰ century Sonnets. Some experience leads me to believe that it would soon become a favorite
Reader, or Manual, especially in female schools.[79]

No work of the kind exists, so far as I know. In Leigh
Hunt's " Book of the Sonnet " there is really nothing valuable
except the introductory historical account of the Italian Son-
net. Of the writers I have named above it does not present
any except Shakespere, Sidney, Drummond, Spenser, Raleigh,
Wyatt and Surrey; and of these Wyatt is represented by one
Sonnet (and that one of his poorest), Surrey, Spenser, and
Sidney by four each (wretchedly selected, not by Hunt prob-

---

[78] Rejected by *Lippincott's*, this essay was first published in the *International
Review*, Mar., 1879, as " A Forgotten English Poet " (IV, 273).

[79] This projected textbook was never published. However, four of Lanier's
lectures at the Peabody Institute during the season of 1878-1879 — probably revised and expanded from the earlier lectures given at the home of Mrs. Edgeworth Bird — bore the title: " The Sonnet-Makers from Surrey to Shakspere "
(III, 87-167).

ably, but by his coadjutor, a stupid person named S. Adams Lee), and so on. Hunt's history of the sonnet is good so far as it treats of the Italian period, but wholly insufficient and meagre as to the English sonnet-writers, whom he does not seem to have known at all, not even by name.

As to the paper herewith sent, it introduces a poet to our public of whom probably not a hundred persons in the United States have ever heard, and who is but little better known in England, though he is beyond question worthy of any man's acquaintance. I have found the Peabody Library here a rich mine in collecting materials for my book, especially as affording sources for some presentation of the anonymous poems in the early Collections, which are very interesting.

Please refer this letter to Mr. Lippincott, as soon as you conveniently can. I shall be glad if you and he will make me an offer of a round sum for the two articles in the Magazine, – that is, the accompanying paper and the II described – and the entire copyright of the book: the part due for the articles to be paid as they are sent, and that for the book when the *ms.* is placed in hand. If it should be desired to publish soon, I could have the whole *ms.* complete by the 20th of October.

Mr. [John R.] Tait has some designs for illustrations of some of these sonnets, which I will send you in a day or two. They would make the Magazine articles at least more attractive, and perhaps you might care to have the book illustrated. Please consider that however as a separate matter.

Trusting that Mr. Lippincott may see his way clear to undertake the publication proposed, I am

always sincerely yours,

Sidney Lanier.

To Robert S. Lanier

33 Denmead St.
Bo Aug. 24th 1878.

My dear Father:

Your letter comes with news of perspiration, sweltering, and the like matters which are quite things of the past with us. I have to put on my blanket now every night:

and the breeze in the day-time makes me think very seriously of fall clothing. Since the ten or twelve days of hot weather during the regular heated term, I have not suffered at all.

My health is on the whole better than for a long time. I *am* a little tired with the purely physical labor of writing, of which I do a great deal every day: but this is more than compensated by my satisfaction in being able to work at my chosen affairs and at seeing results growing under my hand.

My book on Prosody will be out D. V. in the Spring. I have just completed a pretty elaborate paper on Bartholomew Griffin — a charming but almost wholly unknown poet of the Elizabethan time — to be followed by others on his contemporaries for which I have collected the materials: and these papers, also, will be made into a book, D. V. by Spring, on " The English Sonnet-makers of the 16th Century ". I am also daily engaged in editing a " Boys' Froissart ", which I hope to get out in the Spring: being an edition of Froissart's Chronicles, with the uninteresting and objectionable parts expurgated, and accompanied by a historical and explanatory introduction, designed specially for boys. This was suggested to me by my own experience in reading your Froissart — which, by the way, I have with me here, and which a second generation, represented by Charley, takes great delight in.[80]

Besides these three books on hand, I am accummulating material for my lectures, about which you ask. These will certainly be given, either at my own house, to a select class of some fifty members, or at The Peabody. Whether at the latter or not, can not be finally determined until about the first of October, when some people will return to town. It is not a matter of much importance *where* they are given: and on sev-

---

[80] This particular copy of *Froissart's Chronicles* (New York, 1849) survives in Lanier's Library, Johns Hopkins University. A fuller account of his edition for boys is given in the following letter.

Referring to Lanier's overwork during this period, Mary Day Lanier wrote to Mrs. Clifford Lanier from Rockingham Springs on Sept. 10, 1878: " As for my poor Sidney, I expect him to die at his desk. He has written enough within five months to kill a stronger man — and it has brought back a very copious lung discharge with other old symptoms. On the other hand, while his precious life holds out we must be too grateful that he has the work to do: that his labor is seldom to be laid aside as hopelessly rejected."

eral accounts it would be much more pleasant for me to deliver them at my own house.

For several reasons, too long to write, I am going to take a house nearer my centres of work in the fall. The rent will be higher: but this will be much more than compensated by my ability to entertain classes and to teach students *there*, as it is impossible to do here on account of my distance from most of those with whom I would deal. I wish to take two young girls, anywhere between ten and sixteen, to board and be taught in my house. We can teach them — Mary and I — French, German, and Music, without extra charge: and could offer some extraordinary inducements in the way of Society, personal attention to their studies (for I shall take *only two*), calisthenics and hygienic care. Please mention this to Uncle Clifford and ask him to speak of it to his friends.

What with getting Mary off, I find my bank-account this morning quite dry: and being obliged to use a small sum I have drawn on you for thirty (30.⁰⁰) dollars, at sight. Please pay it, and I will send it you sometime next week by mail, as the amount is too small to remit by telegraph.

I wish I could send you some satisfactory account of the furniture: but, on reflection, I doubt if anything would be satisfactory except a sight of it with your own eyes. Therefore I think this following plan would be best: suppose you just get whatever is absolutely necessary to sleep on, for yourselves alone, and let the rest wait over until fall. I have a strong desire that you should visit me at that time, and, if my affairs go as they reasonably should, I can accomplish it. You can then see for yourself what is here, and can act after a view of the whole field.

Mary sends a card this morning from which I gather that she is doing well: and they write from Orange that Charley prospers in all ways.

God bless you.

Your son,

S. L.

To CHARLES SCRIBNER'S SONS

33 Denmead St.
Baltimore, Md.
Sep. 1st 1878.

Messrs. Charles Scribner's Sons:
New York:

Dr. Sirs:

I will have soon com-
pleted an edition of Froissart's CHRONICLES OF THE MIDDLE
AGES designed for boys, which I should be glad if you might
feel inclined to undertake.

I find that after sifting out such portions of these Chronicles
as no boy ought to read, and such others as no boy *will* read on
account of their uninteresting nature, a connected story is left
which—as I have found by actual experiment—is in the highest
degree fascinating to boys, while at the same time it combines
so much solid instruction as to the history of the time treated
with so many lively pictures of contemporary manners and customs that there seems fair reason to believe it would constitute
a standard boy's book, with permanent sale.

The work will make an octavo of about four hundred pp.,
and will be called "The Boy's Froissart." It will be prefaced
with an Introduction by myself, historical and explanatory, in
which the attention of the young reader will be specially called
to those persistent remains of Chivalry, and of other features
of 14th Century civilization, which survive in the constitutions
of modern Society.[81]

I could furnish the matter in three weeks from this date, and
would be glad if you might see your way clear to print in time
for a Christmas book.

Asking a reply at your earliest convenience, I am,

Very truly yours,

Sidney Lanier.

[81] Only Lanier's "Introduction" to *The Boy's Froissart* (New York: Charles
Scribner's Sons, 1879) is included in the present edition (IV, 346).

Apparently the Scribners asked to see Lanier's MS at once; for in a letter of
Sept. 13, 1878 (here omitted), which seems to be in answer to a lost letter from
the Scribners, Lanier wrote that he would send the MS soon, adding that it was
suitable for illustration, though this would undoubtedly be impossible if autumn
publication were desired.

TO MARY DAY LANIER

Bo Sep. 3rd 1878.

My dear Soul, I am distressed beyond expression by thine account of the murderous and inexpugnable chills. What must I do with thee ?

Never mind about the two young girls to board. I have quite abandoned that idea.

I am now much on the other tack, *i.e.*, away from the large expensive house. Miss Taliaferro's account of Charley, and the Mr. [S. M.] Maxwell of whom thou wilt read in the enclosed letter, makes me greatly incline to keep Charley there for the winter, employing Mr. M. to teach him. I hope soon to go to Philadelphia on business, and while there should run over to see about Sidney at the Thompsons'. In this connection I went out yesterday to Mount Street to see a new three-story house offered at twenty dollars a month. It is simply charming, and has a glorious outlook over that northwestern part of town which we so much admired in going to visit Letty Young [Wrenschall]. It is much smaller than this house, though admirably arranged, even with back-stairs for the servants. I would most willingly go and be buried out there for a year, and complete, – as I could in that time – the studies which I have been all my life struggling to pursue. With only Harry at home, we might move along very prosperously towards a reunion next July in the mountains.

Do not think or write more about the boarders. I will attend to all the matters thou writest of. Please forward, or see forwarded, a letter which goes herewith to Clare.

The money about which Miss Taliaferro writes was sent her last week. I suppose she had not inquired at Roger's Store where I directed the letter.

Kiss my dear boys, and be kissed by them for thy

husband.

To Robert S. Lanier

33 Denmead St.
Bo Sep. 13th 1878.

My dear Father:

I did not use the draft accepted by you and endorsed by Uncle C. A remittance from Scribner & Co. for my "Physics of Poetry" articles arrived yesterday, and relieved me from the necessity of doing so.[82]

I have been looking each day for your sight-draft on me which I asked you to draw in order to use the proceeds in paying my draft on you at 3 days for $100. The money is in bank to pay your draft whenever it may arrive.

I don't blame you for scolding me. I feel sure I must be the most exasperating creature in the world. The kind of poverty I have to fight, however, and the calls I have to meet, often leave me no resource whatever except these sudden drafts and the subsequent placing of the money by telegraph or in some other way. It is too long a story to tell you how this should be necessary.

I look for May and the two little boys tomorrow night. We have today a tremendous equinoctial storm. Love to Mama, and God bless you.

Your son

S. L.

To Daniel C. Gilman

33 Denmead St.
Bo. Sep. 29th 1878.

Dear Mr. Gilman:

Of course, in view of the series of lectures proposed at the University, it would be folly for me to attempt to carry out my plan,[83] – which was based wholly upon the

[82] *Scribner's Monthly*, in a letter of Sept. 11, 1878, advanced Lanier $300.00 for the three articles.

[83] This plan is apparently the one outlined in a MS "Prospectus" that has survived (Charles D. Lanier Collection, Johns Hopkins University). It was an

supposition that the University course was to be discontinued. The " Shakespere Course " will be given at the Peabody Institute: I have seen Mr. Morison [84] about it and we are to arrange the details early this week.

There is a prospect that I may be able to start a somewhat modified form of my scheme in Washington: and I am making inquiries as to its practicability in Philadelphia. Of course in both these places it would be mainly conducted by others; my own part being merely to visit each city once a week to deliver my lectures.

I beg you to accept my most earnest thanks for your interest in the matter and to believe me always

Sincerely yours,

Sidney Lanier.

To Robert S. Lanier

33 Denmead St.

Bo Oct. 4th 1878.

My dearest Father:

For the past two weeks I have been going my very best pace, and have not found time to send you a line though desiring to do so every day. I enclose an advertisement of my " Shakspere Course " [85] of lectures for which the

ambitious scheme for the establishment of an " Institute," with Lanier as its Director, and Daniel C. Gilman as the Chairman of its Advisory Committee. Declaring that the " educational scheme presented by the various institutions of Baltimore . . . lacks one important branch " — adult education, especially for women — it proposed to fill that lack by instituting four courses of study in general culture: (1) Literature, (2) Art, (3) Science, and (4) the Improvement of Home Life. These were to be conducted by familiar talks, illustrative readings, and practical instruction; and provision was even made for individual research by those " ladies desiring to pursue such studies beyond the limits of merely general culture." The price was $100.00 for the four courses, which could be divided by as many as four subscribers.

The plan was abandoned, as was also the modified scheme mentioned in the following paragraph (see note 92, below).

[84] N. H. Morison, Provost of the Peabody Institute.

[85] Copies of this printed circular have survived (Charles D. Lanier Collection, Johns Hopkins University). Under this revised plan Lanier offered only twenty-four lectures throughout the entire course (five each on the " Technic of English Verse," the " Early English Sonnet," and the " Less-known Writers

Peabody Institute has been kind enough to offer me a nice lecture-room &c. You could have no idea of the amount of trouble involved in getting up this arrangement: but it is now all accomplished, and presents a fair prospect of being not only remunerative in itself but productive of future benefits.

Mary and I have also been on a wild hunt after houses for a long time, – a matter which required a great deal of physical labor and of mental perplexity. We found a large number of places, each possessing advantages and each subject to objections, the balancing of all which was the occasion of great perplexity.

We have finally secured a house with which we are much pleased, and are to move on Wednesday or Thursday next. I'll write you all details as soon as I can get time.

Mr. Day came to us on Tuesday, and we have taken a great deal of pleasure in making him comfortable. It is really affecting to see the delight with which he finds himself in the midst of a home-party, after being lonesome so long.

I enclose the order of Judge Erskine, and will be glad to hear of a full and conclusive receipt being entered on it.

There are many things about which I wish to speak to you, but I must postpone them.   Love to Mama and God bless you all.

Your son,

S. L.

between Surrey and Shakspere "; two each on pronunciation, music, and domestic life in Shakespeare's time; and three on the " Relation of Shakspere to the English Novel and English Common Speech of the Present Day "). The supplementary lectures were reduced to sixteen, beginning on Jan. 8, 1879, as follows: two by Prof. B. L. Gildersleeve comparing *Macbeth* with *Agamemnon* and the *Timon* of Shakespeare with that of Lucian; two by Prof. Ira Remsen on science in Shakespeare's time; two by Edward Spencer on Shakespeare as a political economist and Shakespeare's relations to modern thought; two by Prof. H. B. Adams on religion in Shakespeare's time; five by Prof. E. G. Daves on Marlowe's *Faust* and the Mystery Plays; three by R. M. Johnston on the early English comedy. The lectures were priced at fifty cents each or $15.00 for the series. They were to be delivered at the rate of one a week for the first eight weeks by Lanier alone, and two a week thereafter, Lanier on Saturdays and the others on Wednesdays. But a supplementary circular shows that after Lanier's first lecture, Nov. 2, 1878, he changed his day to Monday. (For other changes in Lanier's lectures as actually given, see III, ix-xi.)

P. S.

The Calhoun-Pope affair is altogether annoying. Wysham has acted very wrongly in procuring this information and using it as he has without telling us in advance exactly what he intended to do with it. I will write the lady and say what I can. The whole business is simply disgusting.[86]

To Bayard Taylor [87]

180 St. Paul St.
Baltimore, Md.
Oct. 20th 1878.

My dearest Minister – always a minister of grace to me –, I have long forborne to write you because I knew your whole mind would be occupied with a thousand new cares and I could not bear to add the burden of a letter thereto. But you must be getting easy in the new saddle by this: and somehow I feel that I can't wait longer before sending you a little love-letter that shall at least carry my longing over the big seas to you. Not long ago I was in New York for some days; but you were in Germany; – and the city seemed depopulated. There were multitudes of what Walt Whitman calls

Little plentiful manikins
Skipping about in collars and tailed coats,

but my Man, my *hæleð a leofost* (as it is in Beówulf), was wanting, and I wandered disconsolately towards 142 E. 18th St., – where I used so often and so ruthlessly to break in upon

[86] See Lanier's letter to his father, Aug. 16, 1878, above. No further light can be thrown on this affair.

[87] Previously published, *Atlantic Monthly*, LXXXIV, 140-141 (July, 1899); reprinted, *Letters* (New York, 1899), pp. 213-214– with facsimile of first and last sheets opposite p. 214 and p. 215. Taylor had sailed in April, 1878, as Minister to Germany.

Lanier's new address, 180 St. Paul St. (now 1022 St. Paul St.), was just a few blocks north of the Peabody Institute, and not far from his original lodgings in Centre St. Explanation for the move is found in Mary Day Lanier's letter to Mrs. Clifford Lanier, Sept. 10, 1878: " We have to move this fall, and it must be either to a cheaper house or to one in the centre of the city where we may avoid the huge drain of car fare. . . . It is no longer a great point with us to be on the edge of town, because this summer's experience shows us that we cannot keep our health in the city, anywhere, during the hot weather."

your labors – as if I could *wish* you back into your chair rolling out the prophecy of Deucalion. Even the Westminster Hotel had new proprietors and I felt a sense of intentional irony in its having changed from the European to the American plan, – as if for pure spite because you had left America and gone to Europe. My dear, when *are* you coming back?

A short time ago I found in a second-hand book-stall a copy of Sir Henry Wotton's works and letters printed in 1685, and bought it, – with about all the money I had; for a joke of old Sir Henry's on a minister carried my mind to you. Having been asked, (he narrates the story himself, being then on a ministerial journey through Germany) to write in an album, he chose to define a Minister, and said: *a Minister is a man sent to lie abroad for the good of his country.*

I have seen your Deucalion announced, but nothing more. Indeed I have been so buried in study for the past six months that I know not news nor gossip of any kind. Such days and nights of glory as I have had! I have been studying Early English, Middle English, and Elizabethan poetry, from Beówulf to Ben Jonson: and the world seems twice as large. I enclose a programme of lectures I am to give before a class of subscribers at the Peabody Institute this winter from which you will see the drift of my work.

You will also care to know that SCRIBNER'S has accepted three papers of mine on " The Physics of Poetry ", in which I have succeded in developing a complete system of prosody for all languages from the physical constitution of sound. It has given me indescribable pleasure to be able, through the principles therein announced, to put formal poetry on a scientific basis which renders all its processes perfectly secure.

If you should see an APPLETON'S JOURNAL for the current month – November – you may be interested in an experiment of mine therein with logaœdic dactyls called " The Revenge of Hamish." Another freer treatment of the same rhythm by me will appear in a book to be issued by Roberts Brothers in the No Name Series (called " The Masque of Poets ") under the heading " The Marshes of Glynn ": – though all this last is as yet a secret and not to be spoken of till the book shall have been out and been cast to the critics for a while. I hope to find a publisher for my book on English Prosody next spring; also for my historical and critical account, in two volumes, of " The English Sonnet-Makers from Surrey to Shakspere "; and I am in treaty with Scribner's Sons for a " Boy's Froissart " which I have proposed to them and which they like the idea of, so far. By next autumn I trust I will have a volume of poetry (" The Songs of Aldhelm ")[88] in print, which is now in a pigeon-hole of my desk half-jotted down.   During the coming week I go to Washington and Philadelphia to arrange, if possible, for delivering my course of lectures before classes in those cities.

There! I have reported progress, up to date. Who better than you – who looked so kindly upon my poor little beginning – has the right to know how far I've gone?

Give me some little account of yourself, if you are not too busy. My wife and I send grateful and affectionate messages to you: adding cordial postcripts for Mrs. Taylor and Miss Lilian.

God bless you and keep you ever in such fair ways as follow the fair wishes of

Your faithful

Sidney L.[89]

To Sarah J. Farley

180 St. Paul St.
Baltimore, Md.
Oct. 27th 1878.

My dearest Sarah,   If I might have an hour's talk with you this morning under the benignant trees of West Chester I would find less to forgive in the firmament. In these days of such a cruel grind of work as I cannot describe to you, I am subject to sudden uprisings of friendly longing after you and the quiet hills there, which are so strong that it sometimes seems as if my thoughts had become infected with the prevalent insubordination of the laborer and were about to strike work for a good holiday off in the fields with you.

---

[88] See the Introduction to vol. I of the present edition.

[89] Taylor died in Berlin, Dec. 19, 1878, a few weeks after this letter reached him.

And then there are continually more timid recollections of you thrusting out above the surface of daily life. Did you ever see a fish pop his head up from the water, and, surprised and disgusted at the more frivolous element of air in which he finds himself, incontinently dart back again into his shadowy depths? So do my thoughts of you. I believe it is the same with my dear Comrade here. In the few brief moments of the day – and alas, even those not coming *every* day – which we get to ourselves, we speak of you, under breath, and as it were clandestinely. You will better understand the deep indignation with which I speak of this flood of cares when I tell you that we have been moving into a new house. I should have written it MOVING INTO A NEW HOUSE. After we determined that the other house would not do for the coming winter – a conclusion which required about three weeks of agonizing discussion and grim deliberation – we set about finding a suitable dwelling, and this consumed another three weeks of more agonizing discussion and grimmer deliberation. And finally when we settled upon a habitation, it took us at least two weeks to get into it and become settled enough to know where to find our clothes in the morning. Thus eight weeks – fifty six good days – six hundred and seventy two delicious and irrecoverable working-hours — nay, thousands of those dear odd minutes which one filches from the sleeping-and-eating half of each day, and which I grudge more than all the balance — have perished, and we seem only to have used some life in saving some life, like the Irishman who cut off one end of his blanket to piece the other end.

I could hate Science for having generalized the universe into modes of Motion: – to think of everything Moving, always, and all together !

And I understand, – since *we* have moved –, with a new and most pathetic insight, that in[s]cription on Shakspere's tomb which always seemed to me a little extravagant in its deprecation of what I had heretofore regarded as a small matter:

> Good friend, for Jesus' sake forbear
> To dig the dust encloséd here:
> Blest be the man that spares these stones,
> AND CURST BE HE THAT MOVES MY BONES.

——"—— I long to know how you are, and that most sweet
lady who is responsible for you. May is better than in the
summer, though not yet free from the daily fever of the old
malarial leaven. I really believe that the supreme necessity of
work has supplied her with a strength to surmount the disease
in great part. How she toils – I cannot tell you. We have
two pretty good servants: yet Mary is driven from seven in the
morning until ten or eleven at night without ever a moments'
intermission. We hope now to settle down into – or rather
to reach upward to – a better life, however: help to pull us up,
my dear, with some news of yourself. The two younger
boys – Charley is still in Virginia – have been talking much of
you and your mother, over the minerals which we have allowed
them to spread out in the library this morning as a great treat.

Perhaps you will be interested in reading the enclosed programme of my " Shakspere Course ". How I should like to
see your face in my audience!

It is not impossible I may have a look at you in a couple of
weeks. Business will probably carry me to Philadelphia in that
time: and, if so, I intend to steal a day purely and simply for
you, having a sort of outraged sense that life owes me that,
and more.

So, now, God have you in His holy keeping. Mary sends
you earnest messages of love by my hand, until she can do so
with her own.

Make also our obeisance to your mother, with our hearty wishes
for her health.

Some morning when you are quite overbrimmed with the
autumn, sit down and write to

Your faithful
S. L.

To Edward Spencer

180 St. Paul St.
[Baltimore,] Nov. 1st 1878.

Dear Mr. Spencer:

        Perhaps you will care to see the enclosed
Syllabus [90] of my first three lectures. These commence to-

[90] Copies of this printed syllabus have survived (Charles D. Lanier Collec-

morrow, Saturday, twelve O'clock, at the Peabody Institute: and inasmuch as I would be glad of any suggestions you might make after hearing one of my discourses — a new business to me ! – I send a line to say that it would be a genuine service to me if you could be present and advise me afterwards.

Sincerely yours,

Sidney L.

To GIBSON PEACOCK [91]

180 St. Paul St.
Baltimore, Md.
Nov. 5th 1878

My dearest Mr. Gibson:

I have been " allowing "– as the southern negroes say – that I would write you, for the last two weeks; but I had a good deal to say and haven't had time to say it.

During my studies for the last six or eight months a thought which was at first vague has slowly crystallized into a purpose, of quite decisive aim. The lectures which I was invited to deliver last winter before a private class met with such an enthusiastic reception as to set me thinking very seriously of the evident delight with which grown people found themselves receiving systematic instruction in a definite study. This again put me upon reviewing the whole business of Lecturing which has risen to such proportions in our country but which, every one must feel, has now reached its climax and must soon give way – like all things – to something better. The fault of the lecture system as at present conducted – a fault which must finally prove fatal to it – is that it is too fragmentary, and presents too miscellaneous a mass – *indigesta moles* – of facts before the hearers. Now if, instead of such a series as that of the popular Star Course (for instance) in Philadelphia, a scheme of lectures should be arranged which would amount to

---

tion, Johns Hopkins University). It indicates that these lectures dealt with poetic form — rhythm, speech-tunes and word-color — but only the first was outlined in any detail (see II, xiii-xv).

[91] Previously published, *Atlantic Monthly*, LXXIV, 190-191 (Aug., 1894); reprinted, *Letters* (New York, 1899), pp. 53-57.

the *systematic presentation* of a *given subject,* then the audience would receive a substantial benefit and would carry away
some genuine possession at the close of the course. The subject thus systematically presented might be either scientific (as
Botany, for example, or Biology popularized, and the like), or
domestic (as detailed in the accompanying printed extract [92]
under the " Household " School), or artistic, or literary.

This stage of the investigation put me to thinking of Schools
for grown people. Men and women leave college nowadays
just at the time when they are really prepared to study with
effect. There is indeed a vague notion of this abroad: but it
remains vague. Any intelligent grown man or woman readily
admits that it would be well – indeed many whom I have met
sincerely desire – to pursue some regular course of thought:
but there is no guidance, no organized means of any sort, by
which people engaged in ordinary avocations can accomplish
such an aim.

Here, then, seem to be, first, a universal admission of the
usefulness of organized intellectual pursuit for business people; secondly, an underlying desire for it by many of the people
themselves; and, thirdly, an existing institution (the lecture
system) which, if the idea were once started, would quickly
adapt itself to the new conditions.

In short, the present miscellaneous lecture courses ought to
die and be born again as *Schools for Grown People.*

It was with the hope of effecting at least the beginning *of* a
beginning of such a movement that I got up the " Shakspere

---

[92] Lanier's scheme for an " Institute " (see note 83, above) reached the stage
of a printed circular (copy in the Charles D. Lanier Collection, Johns Hopkins
University), but did not materialize. It covered the season of Nov., 1878-May,
1879, and was apparently drawn up for possible use in Philadelphia and Washington as well as Baltimore, for the name of the city was left blank. Three of
the " schools " of study announced (" The Household," " Natural Science," and
" Art ") consisted of thirty weekly lectures each, on various topics; the names
of the lecturers were left blank, with one exception: in the last-named Lanier
put himself down for " Four Lectures on the Modern Orchestra, with special
reference to women as orchestral players." The fourth (" School of English
Literature "), consisting of fifty-five lectures, paralleled the " Shakspere Course "
at the Peabody; thirty of the lectures were to be given by Lanier and twenty-five
by lecturers to be selected, the topics being a combination of those listed in
notes 59 and 85 above with one new lecture added on the bibliography of
Shakespeare. The lectures were priced at $20.00 for one school, $35.00 for two,
$45.00 for three, and $55.00 for four.

Course " in Baltimore. I wished to show, to such a class as I could assemble, how much more genuine profit there would be in studying *at first hand*, under the guidance of an enthusiastic interpreter, the writers and conditions of a particular epoch (for instance) than in reading any amount of commentary or in hearing any number of miscellaneous lectures on subjects which range from Palestine to Pottery in the course of a week. With this view I arranged my own part of the Shakspere Course so as to include a quite thorough presentation of the whole *science* of poetry as preparatory to a serious and profitable study of some of the greatest singers in our language.

I wish to make a similar beginning, – with all these ulterior aims – in Philadelphia. I had hoped to interest Mr. Furness in the idea, particularly because I suspected that some local influence would be needed to push forward a matter depending so much *on* ulterior purposes which are at the same time difficult to explain in full and slow in becoming fully comprehended by the average mind of the public. I enclose you Mr. Furness's letter, which I take to be a polite refusal to have anything to do with it: [93] and I may add that Mrs. Wistar has made inquiries which do not give much encouragement from *her* world. But difficulties of this sort always end, with me, – after the first intense sigh has spent itself – in clothing a project with new charms: and I am now determined not to abandon my Philadelphia branch until I shall seem like a fool to pursue it farther. *Apropos* whereof, a very devoted friend of mine,[94] there, having seen some announcement in the papers of my lectures, writes that she once attended a short course of some-

[93] On Oct. 20, 1878, in reply to a lost letter by Lanier, Horace Howard Furness had written: "Your Shakespeare Course interests me much. . . . Should you form a class in this city I should feel highly honoured in having my name joined with yours as a fellow labourer, but, I am afraid, that honour cannot be mine. I have devoted myself to one special work [that] . . . will require every avaiable minute for the next two years. . . .

" Should you come to this city to lecture, pray consider my library as entirely at your service."

[94] Presumably Mrs. C. N. Hawkins, whom the Laniers had met in Florida in 1877, and who with her husband was now living in Philadelphia. In a letter of Nov. 27, 1878 (here omitted), Lanier thanked her for the trouble she had taken in his behalf and sent for distribution among her friends some circulars announcing a series of lectures which he hoped to begin in Philadelphia early in January, 1879 (whether the elaborate " schools " described in note 92, above, or the simpler series of lectures outlined in note 96, below, is not known).

what similar nature in Philadelphia which was very successful. I[t] was conducted, however, by a gentleman of considerable local reputation. I have one or two other friends there who would help the thing forward: and I write you all this long screed for the purpose of giving you an opportunity to meditate on the entire situation and to direct me in making a start when I shall come over for that purpose.

The practical method of beginning is to form a class of grown persons, at (say) eight dollars apiece, to whom I will deliver twenty lectures and readings, one each week, on a suitable day and hour to be agreed on, covering about the ground specified in my twenty-four lectures announced in the accompanying programme of the Shakspere Course.

If a class of only twenty could be made up, I would cheerfully commence; for I feel confident it would be the beginning of better things. I think I know now of *four* who would join and would heartily forward the business by inquiring among their friends and setting forth its aims.

I have good prospect of forming a class in Washington: and thus, with my special poetic work ("The Songs of Aldhelm", which I believe you will like better than anything I have written), you see my life will be delightfully *arrangée*, if things come out properly. Do you think Mr. Henry C. Lea would be interested in such a matter?

— If you write me, after digesting this enormous homily, that you think twenty people could be found, I will come over immediately and make the arrangements to find them. I have, as I said, several friends who at a word would busy themselves enthusiastically in the matter.

May joins me in kisses to you both. I am main happy in hoping to deliver some of them in person erelong.

Faithfully your

S. L.

To Robert S. Lanier

180 St. Paul St.
Bo. Nov. 6th 1878.

My dearest Father:

I have thought many times of you during your " Fair week ", but have had no chance to write. A great many matters have occupied my attention, and continue to do so. We rise in the morning, May and I, and are always astonished, each night, to find ourselves again retiring after a fearful drive and push through the short days.

I hope Uncle C. has had a good fee from Mr. Black, the Terpsichorean partisan. He certainly ought to, – if only for listening to the tedious and disgusting speeches of Mr. Leftwich, at which I glanced in the TELEGRAPH & MESSENGER.

I'm very glad you liked my " Revenge of Hamish." It has been read over to Sidney and Harry a good many times, and I think is the only piece of mine they have ever cared a great deal for. They now read it for themselves: and it is comical enough to hear Harry struggle with the dactyls.

I'll write you about the trunks in a day or two.

We note what you say about the family-gathering for your birthday with the greatest interest. Mary and I are plotting to have the gathering here, in Baltimore, at *our* house, which has never yet been honored with a family meeting. But we will let this lie in abeyance for a month or two, and see what the Fates will bring to us.

I write in much haste. I have just sent a letter to Clifford informing him of a hotel which is for rent in this city, and I sincerely hope he may see his way clear to come on and investigate the matter.

God bless you all.

Your son,

S. L.

To Clifford A. Lanier [95]

180 St. Paul St.
Bo. Nov. 12th 1878.

My dearest Clifford:

Your letter has just arrived. There will be no postponement of the sale of the furniture, I fancy: it is advertised to be offered first in the lump, and if not so disposed of to be sold in small lots. It may easily happen however in this last event that the house will remain unrented, and I will advise you further about it. I do not *urge* the matter because the St. Clair is really not a first-class hotel, and I have thought of it for you more with a view to its leading to something else than as a permanence. If you were once here in that sort of business I make no doubt that opportunities would arise for your entrance into some large establishment like the Carrollton, or perhaps some house in New York. I will pursue further inquiries, however.

I have worked at such a rate for the past year that I wish to get a little relief—at least to the extent of having an occasional evening with my family—during the next twelve months. Under the present *régime* I have to get to my desk – after having been at it all day – as soon as our tea is over; and my little boys, who are away all day at school, are becoming great strangers to me. I do not have time even to pay calls which would advance my projects. As for the strain in matters of wherewithal to get bread, it has been frightful and unceasing.

As I said, I am trying to organize some little regular resources which will make me feel secure at least as to my rent for the next twelve months. Mr. Day is going to remain with us, and insists on contributing such board as he would have to pay elsewhere: – which is a great help. I have written to father asking him to send me twenty-five dollars on a given

---

[95] In a letter to his brother, Nov. 6, 1878 (here omitted), Lanier had written that the St. Clair Hotel on Monument Square, Baltimore, was for rent at $5,300 net annually, and that the furniture would be sold at auction on Nov. 14 unless disposed of sooner at private sale– the asking price being $10,000. He concluded: "I am almost afraid to speak of the delight with which we would welcome you, lest that may make me urge you unduly. But I feel sure that [this is] . . . a chance which might not soon occur again."

date each month. Can you manage to send ten dollars on the
first of each month, during the next year? The sense of this
regular resource would seem like a basis and solid ground to
me. Of course it will tax you: – but I don't dare think in that
direction.

Kiss all your womenkind for your

S. L.

To Daniel C. Gilman

180 St. Paul St.
Bo Nov. 25th 1878.

My dear Sir:

The course of lectures outlined in the accompanying circular has been arranged for a class which I hope to
assemble in Washington. Several friends of mine are moving
in the matter, there: and I write to say that it would add to
my many obligations to you if you would forward the enclosed
circular to any person you may happen to know in Washington
who would likely care for these studies.   The first three,
and the last five, of this series are the same with the corresponding lectures of the Shakspere Course; the rest, different.[96]

The class at the Peabody continues to grow, and there is now
hope that it may prove thoroughly successful.

---

[96] The reference seems to be to a printed circular entitled: " Twenty Studies
in English Poetry," especially since one of the surviving specimens (Charles D.
Lanier Collection, Johns Hopkins University) has a note at the bottom in
Lanier's autograph indicating that 25 copies were sent to Gen. Wm. Dunn and
137 to Miss Sarita Brady, both of Washington, for distribution. The new lectures were as follows: three on Old English Poetry (*Beowulf, The Battle of
Maldon, The Wanderer,* and *The Conversation of a Soul with a Dead Body*);
four on Middle English Poetry (The Metrical Romances, Chaucer, Langland,
Lydgate, etc.); three on 15th Century Scotch Poetry (King James I, Dunbar,
Gawain Douglass, and Lindsay); and apparently two new ones on minor Eliza-
bethans. The price of the twenty lectures was $8.00 (later reduced to $5.00),
and the class limited to fifty members. There is no evidence that any such
course was ever given (in spite of the statement in Lanier's letter of Jan. 8,
1879, below, that they had been " decided upon "); but it is possible that by
this time Lanier had written up the new lectures, the substance of which were
later incorporated in his Johns Hopkin's Lectures in 1879 and in *The Science of
English Verse* in 1880 (III, xii-xiii).

Thanks for the "Rhythmic and Metric" of Schmidt.[97] I have had the German edition for some time, and have found it much the most valuable work of the sort in existence. Perhaps I will review the English translation with some detail in a magazine, and for this purpose I will retain it a week or two unless you need it.

I hope Mrs. Gilman is not ill: I have missed her face at the lecture the last two Mondays.

Sincerely yours,

Sidney Lanier.

To Mary Day Lanier

New York. Nov. 28th. [1878]

My Sweetest Soul: I have stopped at the Post Office building to send thee a little note with a kiss wherein my whole heart is contained. It is just four o'clock: my excursion ticket brought me by the " Bound Brook Route " from Pha to New York,[98] which I have never travelled before. It seems shorter from Pha to New York than by the Pennsylvania R. R.

As soon as thou receivest this, in the morning, please send a note to Mr. Gaul, (thou wilt find his address in the Directory, " Gaul, musician,") telling him that I am unexpectedly in New York (his days for me are Tuesdays and *Fridays*) and that I regret deeply missing my lesson again: [99] but beg him to be sure to come *next Tuesday*, as I want to see him particularly *to get up a Quintette for next* week, when I hope to have Madame Auerbach and to play some of Kuhlau's Quintettes, for Piano, Flute, and three Strings.

Also: here is a gas-bill which ought to be paid on the 30th Nov. to save the discount. If thou canst think of it, please get the $5.40 from Father; or let him pay it and I will hand him the money when I come.

[97] Probably the translation by J. W. White: J. H. Heinrich Schmidt, *An Intro-duction to the Rhythmic and Metric of the Classical Languages* (Boston, 1878).
[98] In a letter to his brother Clifford, Nov. 21, 1878 (here omitted), Lanier had said: " I am writing twelve hours a day, in the hope of carrying my Frois-sart to New York next week and getting some money for it."
[99] Lanier was studying violin with Fritz Gaul.

Let Father send the note to Gaul by a messenger boy that they will call for him at Bean's .

I have rested all day and expect to be bright tomorrow morning.

God be thy guard and thy good comforter, my dear Love, my sweetest Wife, – prays thy

lover.

To J. Blair Scribner

180 St. Paul St.
Baltimore, Md.
Dec. 17th 1878.

Dear Mr. Scribner:

Pray let me know the *status* of the books we discussed.[100] I feel sure you cannot suspect the necessity which makes me urge your decision; and I am so uncomfortable at pressing you in this way that I must beg to explain by mentioning that I have only recently recommenced a literary life which was interrupted for several years. During these the fruits of previous work were pretty well exhausted and I must now live from hand to mouth until I get some more books printed.

Very truly yours,
Sidney Lanier.

To Robert S. Lanier

180 St. Paul St.
B⁰. Dec. 21st 1878

My dearest Father:

Your prompt answer to my letter, with enclosure of check as stated, was in good time, and gave me

[100] During his trip to New York at the end of November, Lanier had conferred with Mr. Scribner about his book on English prosody as well as *The Boy's Froissart*. Scribner's answer, Dec. 20, 1878, said that the former would have to remain in abeyance until the publication of Lanier's articles on " The Physics of Poetry," but that the latter was accepted (for the terms of the contract, see Lanier's letter of Dec. 22, 1878, below).

great relief. I expect to have the money on hand ready to meet the note.

I hope the trunks have not given you trouble and that Lucy attended to all details of packing &c. They contain many things which we will be glad to have.

I believe I have not mentioned that the " Masque of Poets ", in Robert Brothers' " No Name " series, is out.[101] It contains my poem, *The Marshes of Glynn*, which reads well if a man understands the long roll of the dactyls in which it is written. I hope you will like it. Please be careful, however, not to mention yet that I am the author: it would be particularly ungraceful if this should be first heard in Georgia.

I think there is a piece of mine in Lippincott's for January— just out—called *The Story of a Proverb*.

My book to be called " The Boy's Froissart " is to appear next year. The publishers—Messrs. Charles Scribners' Sons— propose to pay me two hundred and fifty dollars for the compilation, and are to add one hundred if the sale should reach twenty five hundred copies in two years.

My work on English Prosody—which I expect to make the monumental book on that subject in our language—is under consideration by the same firm, pending the publication of my three articles on the " Physics of Poetry " in SCRIBNER'S MAGAZINE.

If I could only win a year's time for my own pursuits, and get to England. I could be perfectly sure of a settled professorship for life. I have been studying Anglo-Saxon for some months at such odd minutes as I could snatch, with a passionate delight which I cannot describe.[102] It seems to open up the whole world of English poetry and of the English language to me in a consistent and orderly development. I wonder every

---

[101] In a letter of Nov. 21, 1878 (here omitted) Lanier had written his brother Clifford that a copy had reached him four days previously.

[102] Lanier had been led to the study of Old English by his friend William Hand Browne, with whom he carried on an occasional exchange of notes in Old English during this period (see the surviving undated fragments in the Charles D. Lanier Collection, Johns Hopkins University).

Browne wrote to Henry W. Lanier, Feb. 19, 1903: " I believe I was the first to draw [Lanier's] attention to the Oldest English Poetry, in which he found so much pleasure; but I am not positively sure that I was the first, and therefore will not say so. We often examined difficult passages together.

" I remember also that I called his attention to the Mabinogion."

day that this earliest form of our mother-tongue, in which exists a beautiful literature dating back as far as the fourth century, is practically ignored in our schools, and even in all but the best colleges. Of course it is completely unknown to the great mass of educated people. I have two essays in progress—one on *The Rhythms of Anglo-Saxon Poetry*, and one on *An Anglo-Saxon Job* (describing a very remarkable poem and giving a readable translation of it)—in which I hope to call attention to the study.[103] The Johns Hopkins University wants a Professorship of this sort, and is really at a loss where to find exactly the suitable person to fill it.

I have been wondering if I could not arrange to deliver ten of the lectures outlined in the enclosed circular under the auspices of the Library Association at Macon some time next spring, after my course here is finished, say in May and June. You need not say anything about it: it will be better if the initiative could be taken by others. I will write to Dr. Battle, of Mercer University, about it, and to Mrs. Bird. If the Library people could guarantee me three hundred dollars for ten (*any* ten of those specified in the circulars) lectures—to be delivered at the rate of two each week—I would arrange it. These lectures are not mere literary entertainments but are designed to impart a systematic knowledge of some subjects which are usually wholly neglected in the prevalent system of education.

A class of twenty is about organized for my lectures in Washington, and I hope it will grow. I have long cherished a plan of *Schools for grown people*, and I hope that these lectures may open the way towards its realization.

I will beg you to send this letter over to Clifford, together with the circulars enclosed: I have long wanted to write him some sketch of my plans, but never can get the time.

God bless you, my dear Father, for this and all future Christmas days. If I could send you the amount of my love, in

---

[103] No essays by Lanier bearing these titles have been found. The subject of the former, however, is treated by him in both the Peabody and Hopkins Lectures (III, 9-70, xxiii), in an essay entitled: "The Death of Byrhtnoth" (IV, 290), and in *The Science of English Verse* (II, 111 ff.). No trace of the latter has been found except for the brief treatment of it in *The Science of English Verse* (II, 123).

Treasury notes,—you should quickly stop off your wearisome treadmill there and spend a less lonesome life.

We all send the most loving Christmas greetings to Mama and Pringle, with our devout wishes that another season shall not pass by without finding us all together. Mary is hard at work on a box of goodies to send to poor little Loulie in the Hospital at New York.

Your loving

Sidney.

TO GIBSON PEACOCK [104]

180 St. Paul St.
B⁰. Dec. 21ˢᵗ 1878

My dearest Mr. Gibson:

If love and faithful remembrance were current with the wish-gods I could make you a rare merry Christmas. – I wish I had two millions: I should so like to send you a check for one of 'em, with a request that you make a bonfire of *the Evening Bulletin,* and come over here to spend Christmas – and the rest of your life – with me, – on a private car seventy-seven times more luxurious than Lorne's or Mr. Mapleson's. I really *don't* desire that you should spend your life on this car – as I seem to, on reading over my last sentence – but only that you should *come* on it.

The great advantage of having a poetic imagination is herein displayed: you see how the simple act of enclosing you a check for twenty five dollars – that twenty five which has been due you so long, dear friend! can set a man's thoughts going.

I have a mighty yearning to see you and my well beloved Maria; it seems a long time since; and I've learned so many things, – I almost feel as if I had something new to show you.

Bayard Taylor's death slices a huge cantle out of the world for me. I don't yet *know* it, at all: it only seems that he has gone to some other Germany, a little farther off. How strange it all is: he was such a fine fellow, one almost thinks he might

---

[104] Previously published, *Atlantic Monthly,* LXXIV, 191-192 (Aug., 1894); reprinted, *Letters* (New York, 1899), pp. 57-59.

have talked Death over and made him forego his stroke. Tell me whatever you may know, outside of the newspaper reports, about his end.

Chas. Scribner's Sons have concluded to publish my " Boy's Froissart ", with illustrations. They are holding under advisement my work on English Prosody.

I saw your notice of the " Masque of Poets ". The truth is, it is a distressing, an aggravated, yea, an intolerable collection of mediocrity and mere cleverness. Some of the pieces come so near being good that one is ready to tear one's hair and to beat somebody with a stick from pure exasperation that such narrow misses should after all come to no better net result, – in the way of art – than so many complete failures. I could find only four poems in the book. As for " Guy Vernon " [105] one marvels that a man with any poetic feeling could make so many stanzas of so trivial a thing. It does not even sparkle enough to redeem it as *Vers de société*. This is the kind of poetry that is technically called culture-poetry: yet it is in reality the product of a *want* of culture. If these gentlemen and ladies would read the old English poetry – I mean the poetry before Chaucer, the genuine Anglish utterances, from Cædmon in the 7th century to Langland in the 14th — they could never be content to put forth these little diffuse prettinesses and dandy kickshaws of verse.

I am not quite sure but you misinterpreted whatever I may have said about Mr. Furness's letter. I did not mean in the least to blame him: and his note was I thought, very kind in its terms.

I am in the midst of two essays on Anglo-Saxon poetry which I am very anxious to get in print. These, with the Froissart and my weekly lectures, keep me bound down with work.

God bless you both, and send you many a Christmas, prays

Your faithful

S. L.

---

[105] A long poem by J. T. Trowbridge in *A Masque of Poets*. For a list of contributors to this volume and an account of its reception, see A. H. Starke, " An Omnibus of Poets," *Colophon*, Part XVI (Mar., 1934).

To Charles Scribner's Sons

180 St. Paul St.
Baltimore, Md.
Dec. 22nd 1878.

Messrs. Charles Scribner's Sons:

Dr. Sirs:

Your proposition — to send your check at once for 125.00, another for like amount when the complete ms. of the "Boy's Froissart" is received and accepted if on or before June 1st 1879, and a third for $100.00 provided sales reach twenty five hundred copies within two years from date of publication— is accepted.

I have been so accustomed to treating for books of original matter which carry copyright as of course, that in this first experiment at merely editing it had not occurred to me at all, until your letter mentioned it, that I should have no copyright. It is a matter of which I know nothing, either as to the law or the custom, and I of course unhesitatingly accept your statement as to these.

I will be glad to have the in[i]tial check as soon as it may suit your convenience.

Very truly yours,

Sidney Lanier.

To Robert S. Lanier

180 St. Paul St.
Bo. Dec. 29th 1878

My dear Father:

Mary feels much distressed at having been the occasion of so much anxiety as your letter displays, and really is at some loss to remember what there was in hers to set your mind running so strongly upon our departure from Baltimore.[106] She was only trying, with most loving intent, to

---

[106] Neither Mary Day Lanier's letter nor R. S. Lanier's reply have been found.

give you some details of our daily life, and your apprehensions have probably magnified anything she may have said about my health and prospects. My lectures at the Peabody continue until late in April, and these alone would bar any change of my residence. Besides this I expect to lecture in Washington, where a class is now nearly made up: and there is some movement towards a similar class in Philadelphia. Again, the studies I am prosecuting require books which can not be found south of the Peabody Library: and one of the books I expect to publish next year depends on these studies. A still more controlling consideration is that the climate of Macon has always proved wholly bad for me. Do you not remember how often I had to leave it? How soon I fell sick always after returning to it? And how uniformly fatal it has proved to every Macon consumptive who remained in it? If you could be here for a day – even now when the thermometer is down to 15° — and see how every room and hall in my house is warm, dry and comfortable day and night, you would draw, as I do, a proper contrast with the cold halls, the draughty rooms, and the intermittent fires, of all southern houses.

Should a branch of the State University be established at Thomasville, I would cheerfully go there. I would like a Chair of Anglo-Saxon and English Literature — or perhaps a better title would be the chair of *English*, as contradistinguished from the chair of Latin, of Greek &c — and believe I could carry on such a department so as to render it one of the most important in the University, since I would impart into the work a fervent conviction that the study of the Anglo-Saxon speech and poetry, neglected as it now is, really lies at the bottom of all philosophical conceptions of our modern language and literature.

I should be glad if you would ask Bacon [107] all about the Thomasville movement, and let me know immediately the precise details of the plan. If salary, time, &c, suit, I think I could organize an application so strongly backed as to secure the place. The first thing, however, is to find out exactly what sort of institution the Branch will be, and whether it will require such a chair as I describe.

[107] A. O. Bacon, state senator and a life-long friend of Lanier.

As to my health, you do not take so cheerful a view as the circumstances warrant. I suffer much from sleeplessness, having many details, both literary and financial, to keep in my mind; but, aside from this, and from the natural weariness which any healthy man would feel in sitting as long as I do at the desk, I am as well as I have been in a long time. My old disabilities from continuous writing seem to have passed away. I do an astonishing amount of labor, — for a sick man — and do not take any damage from it which would not be remedied by a month's rest.

I have many works maturing; my connections, both with magazines and book-publishers, are extending; and the most important papers I have ever contributed are to be published in SCRIBNER'S during the next few months. Altogether I have every reason to believe that an established income from literary work – the only work I can do – is near at hand.

And so, I beg you won't be downhearted about me. I need a great deal of help, it is true, and my applications to you, I fear, are quite enough to give you the blues: but *I* am nevertheless full of energy and of work, and have not the least doubt as to the ultimate result of my labors. When my SCRIBNER papers are all published I shall come immediately into possession of a literary field exclusively my own; and my poetry gains ground, at least in dignity if not in popularity, every day.[108]

Pluck up courage, then; and write me all about the Thomasville enterprise.

Perhaps I will compete for the N. O. TIMES's prize; I don't know if the inspiration will come.

As soon as you can communicate with Lucy I will be glad for you to do so, and ship us the trunks at the earliest date after she may have arranged them.

We had a pleasant Christmas here. Charley came up from Virginia and is still with us. He is as fine a fellow as you would care to see: handsome, bold, frank and sweet; and a good scholar withal. His country life is invaluable to him:

---

[108] One more poem written in this period, but not mentioned in the letters and not published until after Lanier's death, was " How Love Looked for Hell " (I, 125).

and I am going to send him back soon. The lady he is staying with is a veritable jewel, and appears to have fallen completely in love with him.

But I must close. Good-night, and God bless you.

S. L.[109]

---

[109] Lanier's engagement with the Peabody Orchestra for this season did not begin until the following month. The series consisted of only eight concerts, beginning Jan 25 and ending May 3, 1879.

1879

To Clifford A. Lanier

180 St. Paul St.
B^o. Jan'y 1st 1879

Dearest Clifford:

Willie's dressing-gown is a perfect symphony in blue and gray. It wraps a man round like two tender arms. I came home from a journey down town with the boys on Christmas-day and found it sitting up on a chair as if it was already at home here, *genius loci.* It is a perfect poem of a dressing-gown; in fact the very first thing I did while wearing it was to write a poem – one of some eighty lines " To Bayard Taylor " [1] — which had the good fortune to be sent off one day and accepted the next, and is to appear in the March number of SCRIBNER'S. Please present the enclosed copy of it to my sweet Will, with my love and blessing: and declare to her that if there is any worthy thing in the poem, it is but a certain distillation and sweet infection from the delicate fingers that made the blue and gray garment.

We have had a pleasant, quiet Christmas, with the boys and no one else. A real pine-tree was set up in my work-room and hung with all the " gifts," besides a great lot of small wax-candles which produced a very gorgeous effect when shining from the dark green recesses of the foliage. I liked the odor and figure of the pine so much that I kept it standing in my study, and it has now become a perpetual joy and inspiration to me. Its scent brings to me most vividly the old hill we used to slide on, by the river, and all the dreams of music and of poetry I used to dream there when I was a boy – dreams which then seemed so far off and which are now so near at hand.

[1] " To Bayard Taylor " (I, 128).

I'm hard at work on an essay concerning "The Rhythms of Anglo-Saxon," to be followed by another on some very fine old Anglo-Saxon poems of the 10th Century, *The Wanderer, The Battle of Maldon, The Address of the departed Soul to the Body*,[2] and the "Rhyming Poem."

I don't know that I ever sent you one of the enclosed circulars in which I have sketched the plan of "Schools for Grown People" which I hope some day to carry out, and for which I am making a far-off beginning in the lectures I am now delivering at the Peabody Institute. I think often of a time when in every town like Macon and Montgomery there might be small associations of people, some desirous to attend one of these schools.

x   x   x   x   x   x   x[3]

To Edward Spencer

180 St. Paul St.
Sunday Night.
[Baltimore, Jan. 5, 1879?][4]

Dear Mr. Spencer:

This is accompanied by an advertisement for The Sun announcing the resumption of the "Shakspere Course" tomorrow afternoon at The Peabody Institute.

This will be the eighth lecture of the course, by me, and will give some account of a very beautiful Anglo-Saxon poem more than a thousand years old, on The Phœnix, or Resurrection, with an alliterative translation. The seven preceding lectures have been attended by a very interesting class of twenty five or

[2] Neither of these essays has been found. For a probable account of the first see note 103, 1878. The second may have been an outgrowth of one of the lectures prepared for delivery in Washington and Philadelphia (see note 96, 1878).

On Apr. 11, (1879?), Mary Day Lanier sent Mrs. S. E. Farley Lanier's translation of the "Address of the Happy Soul to its Body," which, he said, he had made as an Easter present for her.

[3] The rest of this letter is missing. For an account of the circular inclosed see note 92, 1878.

[4] Conjectural dating from the fact that the resumption of the Shakspere Course, referred to in the opening paragraph, took place on Monday, Jan. 6, 1879 (see Lanier's letter to N. H. Morison, Jan. 2; 1879, here omitted).

thirty members, which I am very desirous of increasing if possible, since on next Wednesday the other series of lectures commences and I am anxious for my colleagues to have a larger
audience than my own. Mr. Daves, at four o'clock Wednesday afternoon, gives his lecture on the Oberammergau Passion-
Play — the first of a series of five on the early stage, including
two readings from Marlowe's *Faust*. He will be followed by
Col. Johnston, Prof. Gildersleeve, Prof. Remsen, Dr. Adams
and yourself.[5]

If you can legitimately cause these facts to be mentioned
anywhere in the body of the paper tomorrow morning, as part
of the town news, it will help forward a languishing literary
cause. My own lectures will be delivered for nothing; with
the best help there is not now the least prospect that I will
raise even money enough to pay the expenses of the course
without adding from my own pocket; – which I mention, to
meet any possible suspicion of mercenary motives on my part
in making this request.

Sincerely yours,

Sidney Lanier.

TO CLIFFORD A. LANIER

180 St. Paul St.
B°: Jany 8th 1879

Dearest Clifford:

If you are not using your silver flute will you
loan it to me for a week or two? I have a particular use for
it in my Washington lectures, – which are now decided upon –
and will send it back promptly. I suspect it must be needing
repairs anyhow, by this time. If you can, send it immediately
to my address as above by Express, packing it in long outer
box, – which you can get made by any carpenter, of very thin
white pine or the like wood, for a quarter. Mark " Handle
with Care," on the top.

A very pleasant letter has come from Mr. Longfellow about
my poem " The Marshes of Glynn " in Roberts Bros'. *Masque*

---

[5] For the full names of the lecturers and the titles of their lectures see note
85, 1878.

of Poets, asking permission to insert it, with my name, in one of the volumes of "Poems of Places."

I will not draw on you until tomorrow.[6]

In haste, and with all love,

Your

S. L.

To Henry W. Longfellow [7]

180 St. Paul St.

Baltimore, Md.

Jan. 8th 1879.

My dear Sir:

I am glad you like my poem, and cheerfully consent to the arrangement you propose both as to inserting it in your volume and signing my name to it. I suspect the publishers still control the entire matter, however, and you will doubtless confer with them about it.

I beg you will let me avail myself of this opportunity to send my respectful and cordial wishes that the New Year may bring you all that you desire, in health, wealth and art.

Very truly yours,

Sidney Lanier.

To Robert S. Lanier

180 St. Paul St.

Bo: Feby 1st 1879.

My dearest Father:

The trunks came safely, in due time, several of them with welcome contents. The freight, including drayage, was $10.50 – not so much as I feared.

---

[6] In a letter to Clifford, Jan. 2, 1879 (here omitted), Lanier had asked permission to draw a draft on him to be repaid in thirty days for the purpose of raising money for his quarterly installment of rent.

[7] Previously published in facsimile, Starke, opposite p. 316.

Longfellow had written Lanier, Jan. 3, 1879: "I have read with great pleasure your beautiful 'Marshes of Glynn', in the 'Masque of the Poets', and

We have all been down with the prevailing distemper, which has raged in Baltimore with unexampled severity. The whole city seems to have been sick. I stood it out a long time, but the wave finally struck me, and I have only this morning crawled out of bed, after a week of much suffering. Mary and the boys are all about again, though all laboring under coughs of various kinds.

Do not mind about the foils at present: we will let them lie over till a more convenient season.

" The Marshes of Glynn " has imposed upon some of the Boston Critics in the most delightful manner. Some of their guesses about it are amusing enough. The poem appears to have won most of the honors of the book. The seal of secrecy, I judge, has been removed by the publishers. Several had guessed me as the author of the Marsh poem: others attributed it to Jean Ingelow, one to Tennyson, &c.[8]

I wish you would send me thirty dollars. My week's illness has been a great calamity to me financially, interrupting work which I should have realized on, if in health. A draft at 60 days will go to you from Winslow Lanier & Co.: please accept it: I will provide for the payment of it.

God bless you all.

Your loving

S. L.

To ROBERT S. LANIER

180 St. Paul St.
Bo. Feb'y 5th 1879

My dearest Father:
I am getting back some strength, and managed to take the air in a short walk yesterday which, although it fatigued me, gave me no fresh cold.

---

am very desirous to insert it in the volume of ' Poems of Places ' relating to the South.

" I hope you will not object to this, as the poem so graphically describes one striking aspect of Southern scenery, that I can hardly do without it."

[8] For an account of the contemporary reception of Lanier's poem see A. H. Starke, " An Omnibus of Poets," *Colophon*, Part XVI (Mar., 1934).

I am glad to have a very pleasant piece of news for you. Yesterday a note came from Mr. Gilman, President Johns Hopkins University, informing me that " At a meeting of the Trustees of this institution held yesterday it was unanimously voted to invite you to lecture before this University in the next Academic year, on English Literature, and to offer you for this service the sum of one thousand dollars." [9]

This is all the more charming because I knew nothing of any such intention.   Of course I shall accept: and I hope I can make it the opening wedge towards my favorite Chair.

Mr. Day is in New York visiting Foster Higgins's family.

We are all improving here.   I can not now write more, finding myself tired with this scrawl.

God bless you.

Your son,

S. L.

To Daniel C. Gilman

180 St. Paul St.

Balto: Feb'y 5th 1879.

My dear Sir:

I accept with pleasure the invitation of the Trustees to lecture at Johns Hopkins University during the next Academic year.

I will resume active duties on Friday and will find immediate occasion to confer with you as to details.

I cannot close even this formal acceptance without acknowledging the kindliness of your note, in which – as well as in the invitation itself – I perceive fresh instances of your goodness to

Yours, gratefully and faithfully,

Sidney Lanier.

D. C. Gilman .

President Johns Hopkins University.

---

[9] In his letter of Feb. 4, 1879, Gilman had extended Lanier the formal invitation, adding: " I sincerely hope that we may have the benefit of your cooperation."

To Robert S. Lanier

180 St. Paul St.
Bo; Feby 17th 1879

My dearest Father:

Some months ago I put away a copy of a letter I had written to Mr. J. F. D. Lanier[10] about an old kinsman – as I think – of ours, intending to send it to you. Other matters have continually delayed it until now. I enclose it herewith and hope it will interest you. I have a sketch of Nicholas Lanier, copied from the portrait in Walton's "Complete Angler" for me by my friend John R. Tait, which I design for you. Old Nicholas (born about 1600 and died about 1682) had a visnomy that forms by no means an unpleasant picture for his descendants.

I wish most earnestly that I could see any way to avail myself of your invitation to Macon. I fear it is quite impossible, at least until after April, and perhaps not then. My illness — I have been disabled for well-nigh a month from anything except my lectures which I have managed to deliver, with great care, except a single interruption[11] — has thrown behind a lot of work I had on hand, and thus put me in pressing need both of money and time at present. I am now greatly better, and am plunging vigorously into all my former occupations; but these will bind me to very hard work for some time to come.

My lectures at the University are to be Academic (that is, not "popular") lectures, and will form part of the regular University Courses required for a Degree. They will extend through at least half of the academic year, though I do not yet know *which* half: and the academic year commences during the last week in September 1879, ending in June 1880. I contemplate the series with keen delight. The lectures will not consume more than two hours of my time in each week: and as a large part of the material for them is already accumulated, I shall have a great deal of time to devote to the preparation of my book on Prosody and of my volume of poems, — the publi-

---

[10] Written on Apr. 30, 1878 (see note 23, below).

[11] The one missed was on Feb. 3, 1879 (see Lanier's letter to N. H. Morison, Feb. 2, 1879, here omitted).

cation of which will, there is every reason to believe, secure me a permanent chair and settle my life for a long time.

I *am* — as you say — in need of rest; in such need as I have not been in a long time before.   If I could be wholly idle for a month, I should be very happy.   I wish I could show you the number of pages of original matter — representing too, some of them, arduous research — which I have written in the last twelve months: you would realize how every nerve in me cries out for mercy.   I hope to get a month some time during the summer; but meantime the bread-and-meat pressure must be sustained.

A poem of mine on Bayard Taylor is to be in the forth-coming March SCRIBNER'S, I am informed.   " The Marshes of Glynn " has been attributed to me by several papers, and I believe there is now no further secret about it.

But I must close.   God bless you all.

S. L.

TO CHARLES SCRIBNER [12]

180 St. Paul St.
Baltimore, Md.
Feby 17th 1879.

Dear Sir:

Yours of Feby 15th has reached me.   I had seen in the newspapers that your business would be continued, and my arrangements for work on the Froissart book have not been interrupted.

I will thank you to send me a statement of the number of words on a page of such a volume as you intend printing.   Not knowing either the size, or sort of type, you contemplate, I cannot arrive closely at the relation of my ms. to the book.   If you will be kind enough to determine these two points at once, and to inform me exactly how many words are in the page, I

---

[12] In a letter of Feb. 15, from Charles Scribner's Sons Lanier was informed that the recent death of Mr. Blair Scribner would not in any way affect the business of the firm.   Reasonable conjecture indicates that Lanier's previous correspondence had been with the elder son, J. Blair Scribner, and from this time on with Charles Scribner, Jr., who now became the head of the firm.

can bring the book within the limits you desire without further trouble.

I beg you will allow me to express the earnest regret with which I have learned the death of Mr. Scribner. The one interview to which my acquaintance with him was limited had made me hope for more.

Very truly yours,

Sidney Lanier.

To Robert S. Lanier

180 St. Paul St. B⁰.

Mch. 10th 1879.

My dearest Father:
            I returned on Saturday night from a flying visit to New York, and wished to write to you immediately, but had to work all day yesterday on my lecture for today, which I have just delivered.

I went on to discuss some books for the coming autumn with Mr. Scribner, whereof I will write you more at another time.

I arranged with Charles Lanier to anticipate part of my salary for next year, and the understanding is that at the end of the ninety days the draft (which has probably reached you before now) is to be renewed for another three months so as to bring it up to the time for my stipendium. I wrote you to draw on me at sight for $250 when the other draft is presented for payment.

We are all in tolerable condition. I am very busy. My paper on Bartholomew Griffin ("A Forgotten English Poet" it is called) is in the *International Review* for March, just out, and seems to be, well printed, though in a very hasty review I find some bad misprints of the Sonnets quoted.[13]

God bless you all.

Your loving

S. L.

---

[13] This essay ("A Forgotten English Poet," IV, 273) had been written the previous summer.

To Robert S. Lanier

180 St. Paul St.
Bo: Mch. 13th 1879

My dearest Father:

It is quite necessary to my future prosperity that I should get published by next autumn two books which will have the most important bearing on the permanent chair which I wish to secure at the University. These are (I) The Science of English Verse: A Text-book for Colleges and Universities; and (II) From Cædmon to Chaucer, – a critical series of illustrations of Anglo-Saxon Poetry, including Chaucer, – intended also as a text-book for a University Course of Literature.[14] These two books are representative of my first year's lectures at the University, which will include a series on the Science of Verse and one on the first seven hundred years of English poetry; and I wish to use them as reference-books for the students who will attend my course.   The first book — on the Science of Verse — will be the monumental book on that subject in our language, being based on a principle of classification which for the first time sets the matter of Formal

[14] These are two of the books Lanier had discussed with Charles Scribner's Sons during his trip to New York the previous week. Of the former Scribner's wrote him on Mar. 11, 1879, that it would have to wait until the publication of Lanier's articles on " The Physics of Poetry " created a demand " for a small volume expanding and more thoroughly treating the subject." The latter was one of the series of proposed textbooks of literature which Scribner's turned down with the following explanation: " While we are considerably impressed with the value of the series, we fear that the last four volumes are of too special a character to command a sale large enough to make their publication a success as a business venture."

An undated MS memorandum has survived (Charles Scribner's Sons) which is clearly the one left with Scribner's for consideration during Lanier's visit to New York on Mar. 8. It outlined five projected books, as follows: (1) " The Science of English Verse "; (2) " The First Five Hundred Years of English Poetry," consisting of translations of the most important Old English poems, with a bibliography and historical and critical commentary; (3) " A University Chaucer," consisting of selections " so expurgated as to render them free from objection," with a biographical and critical introduction and " inter column glossary "; (4) " The Scotch Poets of the 15th Century, " similarly treated; and (5) " The English Sonnet-Makers from Wyatt to Milton " — all designed as textbooks for university courses of " pure Literature, as distinct from Literature studied for Philological purposes."

Poetry on a scientific basis. The materials for both books are now in my hands, – collected during my past year's studies; and I could finish them both by next September.

In order to do this I must have my entire time to devote to them. As soon as I get them half-completed, so as to show what stuff they are made of, the publishers will advance me money on them: but, to *get* them half-completed I must abandon the magazine-work which brings in daily income and concentrate myself on them. This I cannot do without help: and my long proëm is to explain what I now wish to ask: can you by any means take care of the $150 draft (the *second* one, I mean due about April 1st. I think: the first one I will pay here, that is, your sight-draft, whenever it arrives). If, when the $150 draft falls due, you could borrow enough from Mr. Plant to pay it, by a draft on me at sixty days, I would be materially helped. Please write me at once what can be done. It is my duty to leave untried no possible resource for getting my two text books into market next autumn. My Froissart for Boys – which is already contracted for and is partly done – will appear about the same time, as well as my three papers on the " Physics of Verse " in SCRIBNER'S.

It pains me to worry you about these matters: but I don't like to drown in sight of shore.

Your loving
S. L.

TO CLIFFORD A. LANIER

180 St. Paul St.
Baltimore, April 7th/79

My dearest Buddy: This beautiful face you have sent me would draw words from stocks and stones, being the very " eye-music " of some Orpheus that wrought for vision rather than for hearing: and you should have had my thoughts about it straightway, – but the last three weeks have been, with me, one desperate struggle for minutes; during four months I have passed my Sundays at my desk, writing from ten o'clock in the morning until twelve at night: and this usually my easiest day, being free from the interruptions which complicated my weekday work. I have had to write twenty-one lectures in twenty-one weeks, except two at Christmas: and each of these lectures has taken at least three days for the merely manual labor of research and of writing, without counting the thought which went to it: so that I have had but four days in a week, using Sundays and all, for the magazine-work and book-work which went to boil the pot. Each night I have thought to write you: but twelve o'clock would come before I knew it, and I would be obliged to stagger to bed, quite blind and worn. I particularly desired to send you some word about your poems: but it has been simply impossible for me to examine them with such care as they deserve, and will be so until my lectures are over, – that is, for three weeks to come. Then, – while I shall be very busy with my " Boy's Froissart " which Chas. Scribner's Sons are to publish in the autumn and which I am bound by contract to send them, complete, on June 1st – I will at least have my Sundays for my own devices, and can write you at large about your sonnets.

As for the photograph, it is a perpetual delight to both of us. Mary, in fact, has raved about it until I feel that it is time for me to stop writing so much and smooth out my wrinkles, else the immortal youth which your countenance preserves in such comely fashion will get the better of me.[15] How much of the " handsome does " must lie behind all this " handsome is "! None but a good man could have such a sweet face at thirty-five. God keep you as good and as sweet-faced always, my dear Soul.

I am just from my afternoon-lecture, where we had a great hubbub of laughter over old John Heywood's Interlude of " The Four P's " (The Palmer, the Pardoner, the Poticary, and the Pedler) which I read in the course of some lectures on Domestic Life in Shakspere's time.

Col. James, of Texas has recently compiled a very pleasant book, — called " Southern Selections," and published by A. S. Barnes & Co. — which contains several extracts from my poems and " The Power of Prayer ", credited to " Sidney and Clifford Lanier." At the end of the first extract is a very enthusiastic little sketch of my life. Have you seen it?[16]

[15] This photograph is reproduced on the opposite page.
[16] See the following letter; also Lanier's letter of Jan. 20, 1878, and note 14.

CLIFFORD ANDERSON LANIER IN 1879

Charles D. Lanier Collection, Johns Hopkins University

Mr. Longfellow's "Poems of Places" devoted to the South is also out, and I see by the papers that my "Marshes of Glynn" is in it. A friend told me the other day of a pleasant allusion in the English SPECTATOR to the "Marshes of Glynn" describing it as one of the few poems in the Masque of Poets which showed signs of original power.[17]

But my time is gone. I wish you would embrace the first opportunity to tell my dear little Sissa how wofully worked I am, and how much – albeit vainly – I have longed to write her.

Go bless you and that most sweet-willed of Wilsies, prays always
Your faithful
S. L.

TO JOHN G. JAMES [18]

180 St. Paul St.
Baltimore, Md.
April 12th 1879.

My dear Col. James:

If there are two sides to everything – as has been said – surely a man's face may plead the common privilege; at any rate the photographer must have had some such thought, I fancy, in despair over my poor fleshless "viznomy", – for when he had gotten me well through the shame and agony of the "full-face" he requested that he might be allowed to take a "profile". In doubt as to which of these is the more mitigated form, I send you both, that you may take warning before lightly asking another man for his photograph.[19]

I had not forgotten my promise of last spring in this behalf;

---

[17] The London *Spectator*, LII, 247-248 (Feb. 22, 1879), said of the volume as a whole: "The poetry is very small poetry, at the best"; and most of the comments on individual poems were unfavorable. With one exception, Lanier's poem fared best; of it the *Spectator* said: "'The Marshes of Glynn' is one of the few poems which show signs of power; it has an air of youth about it, — and we should recommend the writer to beware of adjectives; let his substantives be strong, his adjectives few and quiet, and he will gain in effectiveness."

[18] Previously published, *Letters: Sidney Lanier to Col. John G. James* (Austin, Texas, 1942), pp. 6-7. James had written Lanier on Mar. 25, 1879, that he was sending a copy of his textbook, *The Southern Student's Hand-Book of Selections for Reading and Oratory*, just published.

[19] Lanier apparently sent him the photographs taken by Kuhn and Cummins of Baltimore in 1874, no later ones being known.

your own picture, which we have framed and put in our dining-room, greets me too often for that; but it is one of those things which requires nerve, and an occasion, to carry out, if not done immediately.

And the occasion, this time, was the arrival of your book. I heartily like it, and congratulate you on the successful embodiment of your purpose. Your selections seem to me exceedingly well made, and I have personally drawn many ideas from this collection which offers the largest variety of our native literature at a glance that I have seen. I am much struck with what seems to be a genuine gift for prose-writing displayed in this book. How strongly these men put a thing, how correctly they accentuate the true point and crisis of a story or of a sentence, and what fine prose-rhythms they strike out! I have frequent occasion to be exercised about the prose of the period, and these selections of yours make me hope that with a proper culture the South could do a great deal to better it.

In three weeks from now my lectures will be over, and I wish then to give the book a thorough examination with reference to this point. I have read it but hastily, being in the very depths of a great swamp of work. I hope to be able to print an essay about it with the special aim of calling attention to the prose.

Have you seen my " Marshes of Glynn" in Roberts Bros. *Masque of Poets*, a poem to Bayard Taylor in the March SCRIBNER'S and a paper on " A Forgotten English Poet " (Bartholomew Griffin) in the INTERNATIONAL REVIEW for March? I do not recall anything else of mine, printed since I last wrote you. I mention these only that I may have the pleasure of sending them to you if you have them not already.

I earnestly hope that your book will meet with the recognition it deserves, – in the South particularly, – and that it will bring you some solid testimonial of the people's favor. Let me know how it goes and whether there is anything I can do to help it forward.

With the sincerest thanks for your generous little sketch of me in " Southern Selections ", as well as for all the thoughtful things you are continually doing in my behalf, – I am

> Faithfully yours,
> Sidney Lanier.

To Clifford A. Lanier

180 St. Paul St.
Bo: April 29th 1879

Dearest Clifford:

Yours, with its freight of love, both practical
and theoretical, came to me duly, and I begged Mamie to
answer it for me, in some sort, on your birthday which we
celebrated with much talk of you and many loving waftures
to-you-ward.

This week our last concert is to be given for this season, and
on next Monday my last lecture occurs until the autumn; so
that I hope then to have some time for a good talk with you.
This last I greatly desire; I have some devices of literary nature
which you can help me in carrying out.

I enclose check herewith to pay my draft on you for sixty
dollars. I had some money coming for my Froissart book
which is now in the publishers' hands, but it did not arrive as
soon as I expected and I had to anticipate it by a sight draft
on you.

I am just hurrying down to rehersal, and cannot now say
more.

Your loving

S. L.

To Charles Scribner

180 St. Paul St.
Baltimore, Md.
May 3rd 1879.

Dear Mr. Scribner:

I send you today by express the INTRODUC-
TION and PREFACE to my *Boys' Froissart.* The former is, I believe, one of the most difficult pieces of work I ever had to do.
It was necessary to place some rather profound considerations
before the young readers of the book, and yet to use simple
means; to give a devout tone to it all, and yet to avoid moraliz-

ing; and to state a great number of dry facts without being statistical.

I hope you will find it satisfactory. Apart from all business considerations I have the most earnest hope that it may arouse attention upon some matters which all of us neglect too much nowadays.[20]

This completes the *ms.* of the Froissart book; and I will be glad to have the remaining check for $125 as soon as you can find it convenient.

———————— *"*
"

In the package with the Froissart Introduction I send also ten envelopes containing the complete matter — though not yet edited — of a book in which I feel the liveliest interest, and upon which I have been a good while at work. This is:

" THE
BOYS' KING ARTHUR:
BEING
SIR THOMAS MALORY'S
History of King Arthur and his Knights of The Round Table, Edited for Young Readers,

With an Introduction, Explanations of old Times, and Notes," by myself. The Introduction, Explanations, and Notes are not yet on paper, though I have them all formulated and ready. But I send the book thus partially edited because you will find it referred to in the Froissart INTRODUCTION, and it is such a beautiful companion-book to that one that I hope you may find yourself inclined to print it at the same time and in the same form, with numerous illustrations. The following points seem to recommend it as a business venture.

1. Intrinsically it is— as I find by experience among my own children — the most fascinating boy's book ever made.

2. It is an English Classic, and must remain a good piece of property for many generations. Issued in popular form, with plentiful pictures, —for which it offers an endless list of spirited subjects it could be made to occupy the same place for boys which Mother Goose does for smaller children.

---

[20] The introduction expounded one of Lanier's recurrent themes: the need for " chivalry " in the nineteenth century.

3. It is from Malory's book that Tennyson drew the stories which he has woven into his *magnum opus* — the *Idylls of the King*. In making my selections I have preserved all these stories; and thus the book presents an additional element of popular interest in enabling every one to compare the original tales with Tennyson's redaction of them. One might say it has been already advertised by Tennyson's poems.

4. It is a noble prelude to the Froissart book; for here we have not only the earlier and purer form of knighthood, but its more *personal* form, — when, instead of the armies of Edward and King John, we see the genuine knight-errant riding forth, and striking down, in individual combat; sometimes a wicked knight, sometimes a giant, sometimes a dragon, sometimes the Fiend himself.

5. A further interesting feature is that this is one of the first printed English books. Caxton issued it in 1485.

6. And finally the book itself belongs to the immortal sort. Malory's work has been in esteem for nearly four hundred years, and must continue so, much longer. Indeed those parts of the story which Sir Thomas Malory drew from his own mind show him to have been a great man and a strong writer. The individualization of Sir Lancelot du Lake, the description of his wild insanity in the woods, the gradual mournful tinge which accompanies the movement of the story through the last thirty or forty chapters, the artful plot which underruns the whole tale from beginning to end, and the final dramatic close, — all these are due to Sir Thomas Malory himself, and not to the sources of compilation.

I add a few words as to the plan of my edition, which will enable your reader to get a comprehensive view of it with less trouble.

I have rejected Caxton's division into twenty one books — which was wholly arbitrary — and have arranged mine in five books. Book I treats of King Arthur; II, of Sir Lancelot; III, of Sir Tristram; IV, of the Search for the Saint Graal; and V of the deaths of Arthur, Lancelot and Guenever. I have cut out all the monotonous repetitions of adventure and of combat in the original, and retained those which vary. All the great characters of the original work appear in mine; and I found it possible to reject all the *details* of the relation between Lance-

lot and Guenever and still to carry on the plot to a consistent
development, through the ruin of the state by the treason —
as the original calls it — of the queen. The words of the text
in brackets — thus [   ] — are connecting parts where the
story is greatly abridged; and I shall insert explanations of old
terms immediately after the terms themselves, always putting
the explaining term in brackets and in *italics*. This seems a far
more taking plan than that of foot-notes, at which no boy —
and not every man — cares to look.   .

The complete *ms.* will contain an Introduction similar in
tone and style to that of the Froissart; and a Preface explaining
the plan of the connecting matter, of the notes, &c. I have
indicated the modern spelling up to about the 12th or 13th
page of the copy sent, and no further. Of course this will be
carried through the whole, when finished.

There remains about ten days' work on the book, and I could
furnish it to you complete by the First of June, with a list of
subjects for illustrations.

It will be a very great advantage to me if you will decide the
matter as soon as possible, so that I may lose no time in selling
the book to another publisher if you should find your line full.[21]

Very truly yours,

Sidney Lanier.

To Robert S. Lanier

180 St. Paul St.

B⁰: May 6th 1879.

My dearest Father:

We heard some weeks ago that Uncle Clif-
ford was suffering from one of his old attacks of the heart-
trouble, and, having no word from you since, I fear you must
have been overworked again.

---

[21] In reply Charles Scribner wrote, May 7, 1879, that they could not contract
to publish *The Boy's King Arthur* until the sales of the *Froissart* warranted it,
and that they would consider it unfair if Lanier should submit the former to
another publisher to be issued at the same time and thus become a rival to the
Froissart. Meantime, returning him the MS of his second book with the request
that he hold it in abeyance for them, they asked Lanier to omit all references
to it in his introduction to the *Froissart*.

I have been going, night and day, at an Edition, for boys, of Sir Thomas Malory's *History of King Arthur*, the old English classic from which Tennyson drew the stories which make up his great Arthurian poems. I sent off my Froissart book about three weeks ago, and drove hard at this one in the hope of selling it to the same publishers as a companion-work. It went forward yesterday, and I await its fortune with interest.

If I had not learned to murmur at nothing, I should be inclined to complain at the cruel fate which keeps me editing other men's works to boil the pot, when my head is so full of books of my own that I sometimes have a sense that I must actually fly into fragments if I do not lessen the inward accumulation. If somebody with faith would only lend me two or three thousand dollars for a couple of years !

I have an offer, from a girl's school, of four hundred dollars to teach English literature for one hour each day during the next scholastic year. I shall probably accept; but am waiting a few days before deciding.[22]

A very gratifying invitation was telegraphed me a couple of weeks ago to deliver the annual poem before the Alumni of the Phi Beta Kappa society resident in New York city, at their anniversary exercises in Chickering Hall. Dr. Noah Porter, president of Yale College, delivered the address. I wished very much to accept; but my poverty compelled me to decline, for the writing of the poem would have taken me a week, and a week means fifty dollars. So I gave it up; and saw afterwards that Mr. Edgar Fawcett was chosen.

I send you an account of our old ancestor (as I suppose) Nicholas Lanier, and a lot of his descendants, about whom I had accumulated many notes, and whose history I wished to place before myself in the compact form of print.[23] It is a curious circumstance that I found, only a few days ago, the name of *Nicholas Lanier* among a list of the vestrymen of a church in Brunswick County, Virginia, given by Bishop Meade in his work on the *Old Churches and Families of Virginia.* It

[22] See note 59, below.

[23] Lanier sent his father a literary "letter" addressed to J. F. D. Lanier, dated Apr. 2, 1879, privately printed as a supplement to the second edition of the *Sketch of the Life of J. F. D. Lanier,* the pages numbered in continuation of that book (VI, 361).

seems probable that this Nicholas points back to the elder one
and constitutes the link between him and us.

Have you ever yet seen my " Marshes of Glynn " and my article
on Bartholomew Griffin (called " A Forgotten English Poet ")
in the INTERNATIONAL REVIEW?

Let me hear how you are all faring. The glimpses of green
leaves give me a mighty yearning towards Macon, which I
suspect is now a pleasant grove and a garden of roses.

God bless you.

Your son,

S. L.

To ROBERT S. LANIER

180 St. Paul St.

Bo: May 7th 1879.

My dearest Father:

I wrote you yesterday. This morning I got
yours of 4th and was glad to find that no serious illness had
interrupted Uncle Clifford's work; – as I judge from your
saying nothing of it.

I make better bargains for my books than your letter inti-
mates. I got two hundred and fifty dollars cash for the Froissart book, and am to receive a hundred dollars additional if
the sale reaches three thousand copies. I shall get about five
hundred for the other book. I think there is a growing inclination on the part both of authors and publishers to abolish
the " author's-copyright " arrangement — which is scarcely ever
satisfactory to either party — and to substitute cash purchases.

I have several business matters which call me to New York
tomorrow, and in arranging for them drew on you again at
" one day's sight". When the draft matures, draw on me at
sight for the amount, — $150.00. Your draft will be met.

I'm glad Heindl liked my playing, – and much surprised that
he did, for on the only occasion when he ever heard me I
played under the disadvantage of illness which had taken
nearly all the life out of me.

I return to Baltimore on Saturday, I hope. I want *you* to
come *here*. Baltimore is beautiful now; and I have never had

you in my house. I'll write more about this – which I've had
in my head a long time – next week.

Meantime, God bless you.

Hastily,   Your son,

S. L.

TO ROBERT S. LANIER

180 St. Paul St.
Baltimore, Md.
May 16th 1879.

My dearest Father:

   I send you this morning two copies of my
additional Lanier history, as supplementary to that contained
in Mr. J. F. D.'s book.

I returned from New York on Monday night, and on arriving
here was engaged to go with the orchestra to Philadelphia,
where we gave a highly successful concert on Wednesday. I
dined with my friends the Peacocks that day, and found them
as fine and cordial as ever. My New York visit was pleasant
and successful. I have received four hundred and fifty dollars, part purchase-money and part advance, on my two books, –
The " Boys' Froissart " and " Boys' King Arthur " [24] – and have
the prospect of two hundred and fifty dollars more, condi-
tioned upon the success of the former, which will be issued
next autumn as a Christmas holiday book.

I am now busily engaged in gathering together my poems
written in the last three years, with the idea of printing an
illustrated edition soon.[25] I hope to include herein my two

---

[24] The agreement Lanier had made while in New York is given in a letter
from Scribner, May 14, 1879: " Enclosed you will please find cheque for $200
as agreed upon as an advance toward the $350 which we are to pay you for the
Malory book [*The Boy's King Arthur*] provided, after the publication of the
Froissart, we decide to publish the *Malory*.

" If we do not accept the *Malory*, it is to be considered as a loan." (Lanier
had already received $250.00 for the *Froissart*, with a prospect of another
$100.00 from it and another $150.00 from the Malory.)

[25] In a letter of May 17, 1879 (here omitted), Lanier asked his father to
send him printed copies of eleven of his recent poems, which he listed with
the names of the magazines in which they had appeared.

works " The Symphony" and " Psalm of the West ". I am very anxious to own the copyright of these two poems, and am negotiating with Lippincott for a re-purchase of them. He bought them three years ago, and I think will sell them at a reasonable rate. I expect to get to New York again, and to Boston, in about ten days from now. In the latter place I hope to make arrangements for three works — one a metrical translation and popular description of several Anglo-Saxon poems, another an edition of Chaucer on a new plan I have devised, and a third a similar edition of Langland's *Vision of Piers The Plowman*.[26] I have the keenest desire thus to bring back these great old works into current literature, and there seems good reason to believe that the plans I have hit upon will accomplish that purpose.

In managing these matters — which I strongly hope will result in a larger appointment from the University — I will ask you to continue drawing on me at sight to meet any drafts which may be presented to you, – as you have hitherto done. I hope this gives you no trouble. It is of the greatest importance, often, for me to have a little sum in hand ten days in advance of its arrival from my magazine people or publishers. Your sight-drafts will always be honored; if at any time my own resources should fail I have a friend upon whom I can draw for such amounts as thus become necessary.

Do not, therefore, be surprised at my drafts. These will be made always at one day, so as to carry three days' grace.

How I wish we might talk together! Can you not come here? It is simply impossible for me to leave the North, now. I have a number of matters on hand which I expect to put my future on a secure basis, and these require my presence here.

I wish I could tell you how delightfully my life seems to be expanding, and how completely I am gathering in to myself all that I want for my growth and activity. The way in which

---

[26] The first and third of these books were apparently the same project referred to in later letters as a combined volume entitled: " From Cædmon to Chaucer." No trace of this project has survived except " The Death of Byrhtnoth " (IV, 290). A part of the Chaucer volume has survived, in combination with a study of Shakespeare (IV, 304). None of these were ever published as textbooks, though they are frequently mentioned in subsequent letters (see also note 14, above).

the events of the past year have fitted into my special needs is almost startling: it really looks like a pre-arrangement made Elsewhere.

If you and Clifford could meet at my house between now and the middle of June, it would make a rare completion of the cycle!

Your loving

S. L.

To Mary Day Lanier [27]

180 St. Paul St.
[Baltimore, May 16, 1879?]
Friday.

Dearest Heart of my heart, the house seems quite empty since thou art gone, and there is a certain earnest quiet that broods about, as if thine absence took a form so palpable as that we could feel it.

Sidney is quite well today, though he seemed yesterday to have signs of a coming cold. Harry is as usual. Mr. Rider has just called, intending to say a provisional good-bye. He goes to rejoin his family, but *may* return in ten days.

We are all about as usual. I seem extraordinarily well. I have done but little writing, and the mere laziness of two or three days appears to have put new life into my bones.

The singers get on better and the songs will go very well, except two which I concluded not to present, on account of their great difficulty.

Thy card came this morning. Father has written thee a little note.

Embrace my dearest boy for me. I long to see him.

While as for thee I am never separ[a]te from thee without a certain indignant sense of wrong, as being only a half of thy whole

lover.

---

[27] Mary Day Lanier had gone to Virginia to see her son Charles. The envelope is addressed in care of Mr. Samuel M. Maxwell, Unionville, Va., and post-marked May 16 — hence the conjectural dating.

To Charles Scribner

180 St. Paul St.
Baltimore, Md.
May 22nd 1879

Dear Mr. Scribner:

I should have an uncomfortable sense of monotony, in sending you another book, but this time it is a volume of my poems and offers some contrast to those which have been offered you before.

I forwarded today by express three envelopes, two containing a collection of my poems written since 1876 — about eighty-four *pp.* of copy and *ms.* — and one containing seven *pp.* of " Subjects for Illustration." [28]

The *ms.* will make a convenient volume of about one hundred *pp.*, besides the illustrations which I sincerely wish might be copious. My idea would be to print it in smaller type than customary, for the reason that poetry of this sort never looks well in large letters; it always stares; and should therefore be in the middle of a page with a wide margin. At least this is an impression so strong with me as to make it seem more than a mere fancy. I ask your attention to the illustrations for the last poem in the book — The Story of Christmas Eve — which might be made extremely taking.[29]

All but two of these poems have appeared in one or other of the Magazines; and I suppose it may be safely said that, *as poems*, they have quite passed into the region of success. As a commercial venture, I can say nothing to enlighten you, save that I feel sure of personal friends enough to take up an edition of a thousand copies.

Please make me a cash offer for the book, — if you see any profit in it. I am absolutely obliged to raise ready money.[30]

[28] For an account of this projected volume, which was never published, see the Introduction to vol. I of the present edition.

[29] This was " Hard Times in Elfland" (see note 94, 1877, and Lanier's letter to Bayard Taylor, Jan. 6, 1878, notes 2 and 3).

[30] In a letter returning the MS, May 24, 1879, Scribner wrote: " It would give us pleasure to make you an offer for the poems but for business reasons it is impossible for us to do so.

" The sale of volumes of poems is never large and we could not consider any proposition which involved any advancement of money."

In a letter to his father, May 30, 1879 (here omitted), replying to a lost

Thanks for your check, $200.00.[31] Keep the Malory book as long as you like.

Sincerely yours,

Sidney Lanier.

To Clifford A. Lanier

180 St. Paul St.
B^o: May 27th 1879.

My dearest Clifford:

        I am just getting together a lot of mss. before going to New York and Boston where I hope to make arrangements by which I can write – and edit – the four books on The First Thousand Years of English Poetry which I hope to have in print next winter, and which, as I trust will secure me a permanent place in the University. These four books include a Treatise on the Laws of English Verse, an Account (with specimens and translations) of Anglo-Saxon Poetry, an edition of Chaucer for general readers, and one of Langland.[32]

If it will not trouble you – for I do not know the state of your bank-account, and I am absolutely obliged to raise some money immediately – I would be glad for you to negotiate the enclosed draft @ 60 days. I will have the funds to meet it at maturity.

I have been offered three hundred and fifty dollars to teach English Literature three hours a week, by lecture, during the next term, at a prominent School, and have accepted.[33] I shall begin to feel as if I were on a solid footing for the next year, if this goes on.

A lecture which I delivered some nights ago on " The Music of Shakspere's Time " [34] has had a great success; three

letter from him, Lanier wrote: " You are right about the poems, and I should not have thought of printing them now if I were not so driven for money. The probability is that I shall *not* print."

[31] See note 24, above.

[32] See notes 14 and 26, above.   [33] See note 59, below.

[34] The lecture was delivered at St. Michael's Guild, St. Michael's Hall, Denmead St., Baltimore. A second lecture– " The Doctors of Shakspere's Time " – was delivered before the same group on Dec. 15, 1879. (See IV, 258, and Lanier's letter to his father, Dec. 17, 1879, here omitted.)

other invitations to deliver it in various parts of the city have
come, and I think it will quite set up my Shakspere Course for
next winter. It was originally given before my Shakspere
Class at the Peabody.

May is sick, sick, with the old malarial trouble. I am
hoping to have a week or two in the country with her – for
which I long inexpressibly – after I return from New York.
The Proprietor of Rockingham Springs (Va.) has offered us
board at twenty dollars a month, which is cheaper than we can
live at home.

Don't consider this a letter. I am merely approaching the
point where I can write one.

Your loving

S. L.

To Mary Day Lanier

180 St. Paul St
Alas, no:
Revere House, Boston.
June 4th 1879.

My dearest Heart:

I came over here from New York yesterday,
hoping to do something with my books. I had a talk with
Mr. Osgood this morning, and will have another tomorrow.
Of course he will want time to decide and I can't tell yet what
they will do. I have not offered the poems, but a set of Text-
books: one on The Science of English Poetry, one on Anglo-
Saxon Poetry from Cædmon to Chaucer, and one a "College
Chaucer."

I hope also to see Mr. Niles (of Roberts Bros.) tomorrow
and talk to him about The English Sonnet-Makers book.

As I go back through New York I think to offer the poems to
Putnam, but am not sure whether I will.[35]

I hope to be home by Saturday. It was grievous to send you
such an uncertain telegram from New York, but I couldn't do
better.

[35] There is no evidence that Lanier actually offered his volume of poems to
G. P. Putnam & Sons. Nor did his conferences with Roberts Bros. and with
J. R. Osgood (of Houghton, Osgood & Co.) bear fruit.

I am too lonesome to write you. I do nothing but sigh all day to be back there with you. And then I am so well and strong – in spite of a thousand defeats and disappointments – that I think of you in your tiresome environment with a sense of crime. The travelling rests me: I want it to rest you. Dear Wife. I wish I could kiss you.   Do you have through the day a kind of fanning sense that I am loving-you-from-a-distance? I wish we had one word for these five. Three nights ago I dreamed you were telling me about a great flight of owls over head. The vision was so vivid that I awoke and found high morning: and what between my own sleepy head and your owls a poem came, with such persistence that I had to get up and fall to work on it. It is a monologue of an old owl sitting in the crotch of an oak and complaining bitterly that the robin-songs keep him awake all day.[36]

> Truly and simply
>
> > thine husband .

To Henry W. Longfellow

> Revere House, Boston.
> Wednesday.
> [June 4, 1879?] [37]

My dear Sir:
          A matter of business has called me to Boston for a couple of days, – which will become matter of pleasure if I may see you. Will it trouble you to send a line here saying when I may call, so that I may not be oppressed with the fear of trespass, either as to your mood or occupation ?

> Very truly yours,
>
> > Sidney Lanier.[38]

[36] " Owl Against Robin " (I, 131).

[37] Conjectural dating from the sequence with the preceding letter and from the partial date on the present letter, " Wednesday."

[38] Longfellow replied, June 5, 1879: " I shall be happy to see you this afternoon at 3 o'clock. . . . Or if more convenient for you at 8 in the evening."

To Clifford A. Lanier [39]

180 St. Paul St.
Bº; June 8th 1879.

My dearest Clifford:

I have just returned from a journey to New York and Boston, and find your sweet letter awaiting me, with its enclosure as stated.

I left five books with the publishers for consideration, – two with Roberts Bros. and three with Houghton, Osgood & Co. I am afraid the books are too good for a venture when the market is duller than ever known in the history of the trade, – as the publishers all declare it to be: but I think at least two of them will find favor.

I want *so* much to talk with you. While I have been going about among the publishers, I have been impressed with the most earnest conviction that this ought to be your business. The thought has grown with each recurrence. Nature and circumstance seem to have combined to fit you for a great publisher. More than that, your own literary work – which is going to press you and weigh upon you each year more urgently until you *do* it – demands that you should have familiarity with books. You abound in ideas and you know how to say them; you lack nothing but that subtle result – technic – which can come only from repeated practice and from such familiarity with all the best words of the English language as no man can attain save through the best books and the best company. *Words* do not come by nature, no matter what a man's genius may be; Shakspere had either heard or read all the words he used. Few of us are aware how limited is the speech of ordinary life. I have somewhere seen a declaration by an expert that by learning some four hundred words of any language a man can converse in it with perfect ease upon all matters likely to arise in ordinary life. But when you come to express the matters of *extra*ordinary life — as the poet, the man of letters, has to do — the small vocabulary of everyday use utterly fails. You must enormously enlarge it; and this can be done — as

---

[39] Previously published, Mims, p. 245, 265-267.

I said — only through books or company. Word-craft: that is all you want: and I think the publishing business, which would throw you in contact with a wide variety of literary men and literary works, would give it to you.

Again: I expect to send forth at least two books a year for the next ten years. These are to be works, not of one season, but — if popular at all — increasing in value with each year. Besides these works on language and literature and the science of verse — which I hope will be standard ones — my poems are to be printed. I have enough of these now written to make a volume; and enough, in the form of memoranda hastily scribbled on the backs of letters and odd scraps of paper, to make another volume whenever I could get time to fill out the existing sketches.[40]

If *you* could only be my publisher! Indeed if we could be a firm, together: I have many times thought that

" Lanier Brothers,
Publishers,"

might be a strong house, particularly as to the Southern trade.

The outfit need not be at all large nor expensive. Roberts Bros., who publish extensively, have nothing but a small office on an up-stairs floor. You understand, I mean you only to *publish*, not to *print*, the books: all the printing and binding – the making of the books – is given out on contract by many old publishing houses, such as Roberts Bros, Scribners, Putnams, and others; and the printers are always so eager for a job that they make very accommodating terms. The whole clerical work of the establishment could be done by yourself and a clerk; and a porter would fill out the force.

Practically to accomplish this: I should think the plan would be for you to go to New York and arrange to stay with some publisher for a month or two in order to become familiar with the usual routine of the business. This done we could rent an office in New York and begin business, you residing there and I here. We could be together for three months during the summer, and often during the winter. It is but a six hours' journey from here to New York.

[40] A number of these fragments– some of which were published posthumously as *Poem Outlines*– have survived (see vol. I of the present edition).

And again: I cannot contemplate with any patience your stay in the South. In my soberest moments I can perceive no outlook for that land. Our representatives in Congress have acted with such consummate unwisdom that one may say we have no future there. Mr. Blaine and Mr. Hill – as precious a pair of rascals as ever wrought upon the ignorance of a country – have disgusted all thoughtful men of whatever party; while the shuffling of our better men on the question of public honesty, their folly in allowing such peoples as Blaine and Conkling to taunt them into cheap " hurlings back of defiance " (as the silly Southern newspapers term it), their inconceivable mistake in permitting the Stalwart Republicans to arrange all the issues of the campaign and to bring on the battles not only whenever they wanted but on whatever ground they chose, instead of manfully holding before the people the real issues of the time — the tariff, the prodigious abuses clustered about the Capitol at Washington, the restriction of granting-powers in Congress, the non-interference theory of government — all these things have completely obscured the admitted good intentions of Morgan and Lamar and their fellows and have entirely alienated the feelings of men who at first were quite won over to them.[41] The present extra session has been from the beginning a piece of absurdity such as the world probably never saw before. Our men are such mere politicians, that they have never yet discovered — what the least thoughtful statesmanship ought to have perceived at the close of our war — that the belief in the sacredness and greatness of the American Union among the millions of the North and of the great North-West is really the principle which conquered us. As soon as we invaded the North, and arrayed this sentiment in arms against us, our swift destruction followed. But how soon they have forgotten Gettysburg? That the presence of United States troops at the polls is an abuse, no sober man will deny; but to attempt to remedy it *at this* time, when the war is so lately over, when the North is naturally sensitive as to securing the hard-won results of it, when consequently every squeak of a penny-whistle is easily interpreted into a Rebel yell by the artful devices of

[41] The senators mentioned in this paragraph were James G. Blaine of Maine, Roscoe Conkling of New York, Benjamin H. Hill (or ex-senator Joshua Hill) of Georgia, L. Q. C. Lamar of Mississippi, and John T. Morgan of Alabama.

Mr. Blaine and his crew, – this was simply to invade the North again as we did in '64. And we have met precisely another Gettysburg. The whole Community is uneasy as to the silver bill and the illimitable folly of the Greenbackers; business men anxiously await the adjournment of Congress, that they may be able to lay their plans with some sense of security against a complete reversal of monetary conditions by some silly legislation; and I do not believe there is a quiet man in the republic to whom the whole political corpus at Washington is not a shame and a sorrow.

– And thus, as I said, it really seems as if any prosperity at the South must come long after your prime and mine. Our people have failed to perceive the deeper movements under-running the time; they lie wholly off, out of the stream of thought, and whirl their poor old dead leaves of recollections round and round, in a piteous eddy that has all the wear and tear of motion without any of the rewards of progress. By the best information I can get the country is substantially poorer now than when the war closed; and Southern Securities have become simply a catchword. The looseness of thought upon money-matters among our people, the unspeakable rascality of corporations like Memphis, – how long is it going to take us to remedy these things? Whatever is to be done, you and I can do our part of it far better here than there.

Come away.

Cannot you get here, where we can talk all this over?

A propos, – I was told some days ago that the Westminster Hotel in New York might be obtained on good terms, being now carried on by the proprietor only in the interest of the owners.

We hope to get to Rockingham Springs within three weeks, where we are offered board at the " private " rates (the proprietor putting these on the ground that I am a distinguished person and therefore a possibly profitable guest) of twenty dollars a month grown people, children twelve and a half. It is a wretchedly rough and primitive place, – but the mountains are there, and many trees, and I long for these so pitifully that I hope to wrench myself out of the environment here, for a month anyhow. I expect to keep Mary and the children there the whole summer. Where are you going? And might it not suit you to go there? The regular rates are thirty dollars a month, children half-price; but it is more than likely that the proprietor (who is a very honest and civil Virginia farmer) might extend his reductions to my whole party if we could go together.

Now then! Here are reams of paper written: and nothing is said.

By the way I should have added that the mineral water at Rockingham is good, and that Mary improved greatly during her one month's stay there last summer. It is in, and on, the very mountains; and I think Wilsie would soon be found leaping like a young doe over the mossy boulders.

Mary sends you all manner of loving messages, half for you and t'other for Will; and, whether you come or not, God bless you, my dearest and sweetest boy in the whole world.

Your

S. L.

To Charles Scribner

180 St. Paul St.
Baltimore, Md.
June 13th 1879.

Dear Mr. Scribner:

I send today the Introduction to the Boys' Froissart. On looking over it I found it unsatisfactory, and I therefore remodelled the whole, condensing Preface and Introduction into one, and making many changes. I think its present form will say all I wanted to say and make it much more acceptable to the young readers of the book.

Very truly yours,

Sidney Lanier.

To John G. James [42]

180 St. Paul St.
Bᵒ; June 15ᵗʰ 1879

My dear Col. James:

An absence in Boston, and an illness which has kept me outside of the combat ever since, have combined to prevent me from sending you my own subscription for Mr. Hayne's book which I desired to do immediately. Please put my name down for the $3.⁵⁰ edition. I hope to send you other subscriptions during the week; for I shall take the field tomorrow, in this behalf.

The Provost of the Peabody Institute has gone abroad, but I will speak to him of the matter when he returns in the autumn.

Have you selected your publisher? [43] If you have not, I particularly ask that you will communicate with me before doing so.

As soon as I can get time to write it, you shall have the autograph copy of my " Marshes of Glynn."

I have but time now for this merely business letter, and for a handsqueeze by way of underscoring. God bless you.

Faithfully yours,

Sidney L.

To Edmund C. Stedman [44]

180 St. Paul St.
Baltimore, Md.
June 17ᵗʰ 1879.

Dear Sir:

An absence in Boston has prevented my earlier acknowledgement of your letter.

I send today by mail the volume of poems to which you

[42] Previously published, *Letters: Sidney Lanier to Col. John G. James* (Austin, Texas, 1942), p. 10.

[43] James's project did not materialize until after Lanier's death. The *Poems of Paul Hamilton Hayne. Complete Edition* was published by D. Lothrop & Co., Boston, 1882.

[44] Stedman's letter, to which this is an answer, has not survived. The pre-

refer. Pray permit me to mention that these are only such of my poems as were originally printed in LIPPINCOTT'S MAGA-ZINE: no complete collection of them has been made.   Inas-much as the book was hurriedly made by the publishers, with-out sufficient opportunity on my part to revise the works in it, I should be glad if you would let me know your selection, when it is made, so that I may send you such an amended copy as may present fewer defects.

My Shakspere lectures have not been printed. Pray accept my thanks for your very useful Shakspere Bibliography.

Very truly yours,

Sidney Lanier.

To ROBERT S. LANIER

180 St. Paul St.
Bo: June 25th 1879.

My dear Father:

Yours of 18th is here. I'm sorry to see you are disturbed. The project of letting our house for the summer is not a new one: we wanted to save the rent, if possible, and get off to the mountains where we can live more cheaply than at home. Indeed we should have been getting ready to start by this time, – having given out the idea of a visit from you – but have been delayed by a trouble with Mary's eyes, which required immediate treatment. She had been suffering with her sight for years without knowing exactly what was the matter. On having the eyes examined by an oculist some weeks ago, he pronounced one of them seriously defective, with a structural imperfection, and the other not a great deal better. The tests however were not satisfactory, and subsequent ones have served to modify this opinion so far as to attribute some of the symptoms to spasmodic action of the muscles caused by long-continued sleeplessness during the baby-nursing

sumption, however, is that he wrote requesting data to be used in one of his various literary compilations. His *Poets of America* (Boston, 1885), pp. 449-451, contained a critique of Lanier; and selections from Lanier's poetry were included in both his anthologies — *A Library of American Literature* (Boston, 1889), X, 145-151, and *An American Anthology* (Boston, 1900), pp. 433-440.

days. The oculist is now testing the eyes in order to construct a formula for a suitably-curved glass which he says will entirely remedy the trouble. This however requires time, and we shall not get away for two weeks or more.

I say " we " though I am not quite sure that *I* can go, and it is quite likely I will have to send off my family without me. Some books which I have been earnestly endeavoring to get into print are very much delayed. They are high text-books, or rather literary works which I desire to attain a position as text-books besides their function in general culture. It is hard to find a publisher whose " line " they exactly suit. In fact they are intended to revolutionize the study of English Literature and, being both new and solid, they necessarily make but slow way into the pre-empted tract of publishing work. Roberts Brothers, of Boston, are considering them, and promise me an answer as soon as they can intelligently make up their minds about them.

Thus I am delayed: and thus it is that you are plagued with drafts and re-drafts. This I do not know how to help. I could borrow, here, if I had anything to borrow on or " two good names " to endorse: but I have not the former and cannot ask the latter. In a few days I have two hundred dollars rent to pay.

Is your Life Policy pledged now for anything? If I had that I could probably borrow four or five hundred dollars on it until my next instalment of income arrives which will be in about sixty days. Time is everything to me. I have so many ideas which demand expression, now, imperatively: I have so many books on hand, for which the notes and designs lie in my desk, unprinted purely for lack of time to put them together; – that I awake each day with a mournful sense of indignant protest against the pitiful lack of a pitiful sum of money which would enable me to put in form all the results of my thought and research for the last three years and to take the place which belongs to me. I have five important works which I could get ready for the printer in the next three months. If I could get hold of five hundred dollars to live on during that time, all could be done with ease and repose of mind.

— But I am writing all this only because your letter indicates a wish to know more fully everything about me. I don't

mean to complain, or to seem depressed, at all; and did not
mean so in my other letter which was hastily written and probably stated my plans without giving reasons.

If your Policy is not pledged I would be glad if you should
send it to me immediately. I must gain some time, and raise
funds for my rent.

Pray don't infer that I am downhearted, — as your letter
states. I never get so, and never have time to waste in that
way. I am always at work, day and night, delighted with the
worlds of new thought which open upon me with each acquisition. Although there *is* always stress for money, and will be
until next year when I commence to receive regular pay for
regular work, I do not despond. I must tide over the intervening time somehow: and though it is desperately dark as to
the *how*, I don't doubt it will be done.

I'm glad you have been to the sea-shore, and hope Mama has
found benefit. We all send love to you and her.

Your son,

S. L.

To Daniel C. Gilman

180 St. Paul St.

Bᵒ, June 30ᵗʰ, 1879.

My dear Mr. Gilman:

On sending the enclosed scheme to the
Mount Vernon Hotel yesterday I learned that you had left town
for the summer. I am really grieved to have missed seeing you
and Mrs. Gilman; I somehow got the idea that you were to
remain in Baltimore until July. I had called three times at the
University but failed to find you.

I should be glad to know that the accompanying programme
meets your approval. The *number* of lectures is stated in
accordance with what you told me some weeks ago: of course
you will not hesitate to suggest any increase or diminution that
may seem to you desirable.

You will observe that the Public series is so arranged as to
form an interesting pendant to the Class series: the latter

JOHNS HOPKINS UNIVERSITY, PART OF THE OLD CAMPUS, HOWARD STREET

Lanier lectured in Hopkins Hall (center), 1879-1881

Courtesy of Alumni Office, Johns Hopkins University

giving a view of Shakspere's *moral* development, while the former presents his *artistic* development.

I selected the three Plays which form the burden of the Class Course (1) because they are the three greatest poems in our language, (2) because they are representatives of three striking phases in Shakspere's growth as a man and an artist, and (3) because their wide relations involve commentaries upon, and researches into, the most beautiful works of our own time.

Please make my regards to Mrs. Gilman, and, with my cordial wishes for a happy and restful summer, believe me always

Gratefully and faithfully

yours,

Sidney Lanier.[45]

To Daniel C. Gilman [46]

180 St. Paul St.
Baltimore, Md.
July 13th 1879.

My dear Mr. Gilman:

I see, from your letter, that I did not clearly explain my schemes of lectures.

The Course marked " Class-Lectures " is meant for advanced *students*, and involves the hardest kind of University work on their part. Perhaps you will best understand the scope of the tasks which this course will set before the student by reading the enclosed Theses which I should distribute among the members of the class as soon as I should have discovered their mental leanings and capacities sufficiently, and which I should require to be worked out by the end of the scholastic year. I beg you to read these with some care: I send only seven of them but they will be sufficient to show you the nature of the work which I propose to do with the *University student*. I should like my main efforts to take *that* direction; I wish to get

---

[45] Gilman replied, July 3, 1879: " I like your scheme of lectures very much. The only suggestion which occurs to me is that both series might well be given in Hopkins Hall,– one in the first half year & the other in the second half year."

[46] Previously published, *South Atlantic Quarterly*, IV, 117-119 (Apr., 1905).

some young Americans at hard work in pure literature; and will be glad if the public lectures in Hopkins Hall shall be merely accessory to my main course. With this view, as you look over the accompanying theses please observe

(1) that each of them involves Original research and will — if properly carried out — constitute a genuine contribution to modern literary scholarship;

(2) that they are so arranged as to fall-in with various other studies and extend their range, – for example, the first one being suitable to a student of philology who is pursuing Anglo-Saxon, the II to one who is studying the Transition Period of English, the VI to one who is studying Elizabethan English, and so on;

(3) that each one necessitates diligent study of some great English work, not as a philological collection of words, but as pure literature; and

(4) that they all keep steadily in view, as their ultimate object, that strengthening of manhood, that enlarging of sympathy, that glorifying of moral purpose, which the student unconsciously gains, not from any direct didacticism, but from this constant association with our finest ideals and loftiest souls.

Thus you see that while the Course of " Class-Lectures " submitted to you nominally centers about the three plays of Shakspere therein named, it really takes these for texts, and involves, in the way of commentary and of thesis, the whole range of English poetry.   In fact I have designed it as a thorough preparation for the serious study of the poetic art in its whole outcome, hoping that, if I should carry it out successfully, the Trustees might find it wise next year to create either a Chair of Poetry or a permanent lectureship covering the field above indicated.   It is my fervent belief that to take classes of young men and to preach them the gospel-according-to-Poetry is to fill the most serious gap in our system of higher education; I think one can already perceive a certain narrowing of sympathy and — what is even worse — an unsymmetric development of faculty both intellectual and moral, from a too-exclusive devotion to Science which Science itself would be the first to condemn.

— As to the first six Class-lectures on " The Physics and Metaphysics of Poetry: " they unfold my system of English

Prosody, in which I should thoroughly drill every student until he should be able to note down, in musical signs, the rhythm of any English poem. This drilling would continue through the whole course, inasmuch as I regard a mastery of the principles set forth in those lectures as vitally important to all systematic progress in the understanding and enjoyment of poetry.

I should have added, *àpropos* of this Class-course, that there ought to be one examination each week, to every two lectures.

In the first interview we had, after my appointment, it was your intention to place this study among those required by the University for a Degree. I hope sincerely you have not abandoned this idea; and the course outlined in the " Class-lectures " forwarded to you the other day and in the Theses of which I send the first seven herewith seems to me the best to begin with. If it should be made a part of the " Major Course in English " (where it seems properly to belong), I could easily arrange a simpler and less arduous modification of it for the corresponding " Minor Course." [47]

I am so deeply interested in this matter – of making a finer fibre for all our young American manhood by leading our youth into proper relations with English poetry – that at the risk of consuming your whole vacation with reading this long and unconscionable letter I will mention that I have nearly completed three works which are addressed to the practical accomplishment of the object named, by supplying a wholly different method of study from that mischievous one which has gradually arisen from a wholly mistaken use of the numerous " Manuals " of English literature. These works are my three text-books: (1) " THE SCIENCE OF ENGLISH VERSE ", in which the student's path is cleared of a thousand errors and confusions which have obstructed this study for a long time, by a very simple system founded upon the physical relations of sound; (2) " FROM CÆDMON TO CHAUCER ", in which I pre-

---

[47] An undated MS memorandum by Lanier has survived (Johns Hopkins University), outlining a course of 26 " Class Lectures " as follows: 4 on the Physics of Poetry, 2 on the Metaphysics of Poetry, 6 on *A Midsummer Night's Dream*, 8 on *Hamlet*, and 6 on *The Tempest* — as illustrative of the three periods of Shakespeare's moral and artistic development. But this elaborate course was abandoned. (For the class courses actually given see notes 9 and 19, 1880. For Lanier's public lectures at Johns Hopkins in Nov.-Dec., 1879, see note 63, 1879.)

sent all the most interesting Anglo-Saxon poems remaining to us, in a form which renders their *literary* quality appreciable by *all* students, whether specially pursuing Old English or not, thus placing these poems where they ought always to have stood — as a sort of grand and simple vestibule through which the later mass of English poetry is to be approached; and (3) my " CHAUCER ", which I render immediately enjoyable, without preliminary preparation, by an *interlined* glossarial explanation of the original text, and an indication (with hyphens) of those terminal syllables affecting the rhythm which have decayed out of the modern tongue. I am going to print these books and sell them myself, on the cheap plan which has been so successfully adopted by Edward Arber, lecturer on English Literature in University College, London. I have been working on them for two months; in two more they will be finished; and by the middle of November I hope to have them ready for use as text-books. If they succeed, I shall complete the series next year with (4) a " SPENSER " on the same plan with the Chaucer, (5) " THE MINOR ELIZABETHAN SONG-WRITERS ", and (6) " THE MINOR ELIZABETHAN DRAMATISTS; " [48] the steady aim of the whole being to furnish a working set of books which will familiarize the student with the actual *words* of English poets, rather than with their names or biographies.

Pray forgive this merciless letter. I could not resist the temptation to unfold to you all my hopes and plans connected with my university-work among your young men which I so eagerly anticipate.

I will trouble you to return these notes of Theses when you have examined them at leisure.

Faithfully yours,

Sidney Lanier.[49]

---

[48] None of these three newly projected textbooks materialized.

[49] In his reply, July 16, 1879 (Fabian Franklin, *Life of Daniel Coit Gilman*, New York, 1910, pp. 241-243), Gilman wrote, in addition to a detailed analysis of Lanier's scheme: "You have a high ideal and I certainly hope that your success in striving after it may be all that we anticipate. . . . Now we need among us someone like you, loving literature and poetry and treating it in such a way as to enlist and inspire many students.

"I think your aims and your preparation admirable. I can make no sug-

To Robert S. Lanier

180 St. Paul St.
Baltimore, Md.
July 16th 1879.

My dearest Father:

I completed my arrangements today for the money. I gave, as security, 1st my order on the Johns Hopkins Treasurer for $500 (the amount of the debt) when it shall accrue; 2nd the sixteen blocks (160 lots) which Mr. Day gave me for that purpose; and 3rd the policy; having mind to your possible need of the latter at the time you mention. The party [50] refuses to take any interest; and my friend Lawrence Turnbull, who is practicing law here, after having arranged the whole matter and drawn up all the papers, would have no fee of any sort.

I was relieved of a great load by getting this money. The house we have been living in has proved a heavy elephant on our hands, and we look forward with eagerness to October, when we get rid of it and move into a smaller establishment.[51] On account of the cheapness of board there I am going up to Rockingham Springs with my family day after tomorrow and expect to remain there six weeks. I shall be very hard at work all the time, with my three books which I wish to bring out next autumn; but the air is very invigorating, and I hope to gain some strength and flesh there. I weighed some days ago, and was astonished to find that I could pull down only 118 pounds – the least I remember since I have been grown. Not-

gestions upon these points. I only desire that in the form of presentation, you may be ready to adapt yourself to such circumstances as will develop themselves; and that you will not expect or attempt *too much the first year* lest we all be disappointed."

[50] John W. McCoy. (Numerous papers relating to this loan have survived in the Charles D. Lanier Collection, Johns Hopkins University.)

Lanier had first met Lawrence Turnbull (who arranged the loan for him) in 1870, when he visited Macon as the young editor of the *New Eclectic Magazine*. Though this is the first time his name appears in Lanier's letters since their original meeting, Turnbull was one of his most intimate friends in Baltimore, especially during his last years.

[51] The Laniers had helped to meet expenses during the past winter by taking as a boarder their friend Norah Freeman, but she had now left (see Lanier's letter to his brother Clifford, June 15, 1879, here omitted).

withstanding this lack of flesh, I do a great amount of work daily, and am in average health. But I must pluck up for this winter, which is to be the turning-point in my career.

According to your request I will send you fifty dollars in a day or two, and will *try* to send the additional twenty five within the two weeks mentioned. From now until October I shall be fearfully straitened. If it were not for the relief afforded by getting my family up to Rockingham – where I. have made an arrangement with the proprietor which renders the payments remote and easy – I scarcely know what I should do, until fall finds me with more books ready for the printer.

I hope you will see Clifford; – and I envy you both !

I write hurriedly in the midst of a thousand preparations for leaving.

God bless you.

Your son,

S. L.

Address me:

" Rockingham Mineral Springs
Near   McGaheysville.
Virginia."

To Robert S. Lanier

Rockingham Mineral Springs.
Near
McGaheysville,
Virginia.
July 22nd 1879.

My dearest Father:

We left Baltimore – Mr. Day and all of us, bag and baggage – on Saturday, and reached here at supper-time same day, our journey including a drive of twelve miles through the mountains from Harrisonburg, where we got off the cars.

It seems quite like emigrating into some of the stars; this cool, peaceful, upper story of a fresh cottage, with the wooded ridges running off at all odd angles about us, and the noble Blue Ridge reposing, farther off, in fair view from either window of our room, while the air is invigorating and sweet in all the channels of the breath and the children leap about the brook and hill-side all day like young fawns: – all this, instead of the stifling furnace of Baltimore, and the grim friction of iron wheel and cobble-stone that goes ever therewithal. It is a beautiful enchantment: how I wish the spell included you and Mama !

I have a grand little library, culled from the Mercantile and Johns Hopkins of Baltimore; and the long mornings make my books grow rapidly.   I expect to carry back three, ready for the printer, when I go home on the first of September.   Mary and the children will remain here until October, probably.

I am thoroughly pleased with our location.   The establishment is small; there is no "ball-room", no band, not the least attempt at dress, and no interference with one's privacy or quietude.   We are in a cottage to ourselves.   The fare is tolerable; service thoroughly clean, and water delightful.   Only thirty or forty people have come, so far; indeed, there are not accommodations for more than twice that number; and so the opportunity for hard work and for thorough rest is perfect.

Enclosed is a check for twenty-five dollars.   When I came to pay up, I presently arrived at the end of my resources, for the time being; and though this is but a beggarly third of the seventy five you wrote for, I send it, as the nearest I can come to the mark at present.   I will try to forward some more during the next four weeks.

And now I'll stop writing, for the day.   We all send a thousand messages of love to you both.

Your son,

S. L.

To Clifford A. Lanier

Rockingham Mineral Springs.
Near McGaheysville, Virginia.
July 22nd 1879.

My dearest Clifford:

I postponed our departure from Baltimore for two days, in order to be on hand at the arrival of your draft; but as it did not come, and as our expenses there were much heavier than

here, I left a check for the amount with my friend Lawrence
Turnbull, and furnished the person whom we left in charge of
our house with a written memorandum, to be handed to the
Bank Messenger whenever he should come, directing him to
call on Turnbull and receive the money for the draft at sight.
If I had known through which one of the Bo. banks the draft
would be sent, I could have arranged it there; but this of course
was impossible. I hope it will all come right: but if, in any
way, Mrs. Fleming (our Factotum in charge of the house)
should happen to miss the messenger and the draft be returned,
I will immediately forward a check for the amount, and you
will explain to the banker through whom you drew the precautions I have taken. The money is in bank and will be kept
there to meet the paper.

The sixty day draft I will ask you to renew; and for that
purpose I enclose an undated paper, together with five dollars
to pay discount thereon. I thought I had provided enough
for this also: but when I came to settle all up before moving
here I found myself very short, and so must keep this paper
over until my next accession of funds.

– And now, if you were only here! I don't dare begin on
the still rapture that breathes out of the mountains and is in
me and I in it. I feel the hills about, even while I sleep. It
is a long time since I have had any familiar discourse with the
mountains: indeed since you and I used to fish in Abram's
Creek I can't say that I've had a single word with a big hill.
And then, to intensify this new contact, I have so much more
to bring to the mountains now than ever before – so much
more growth of my own – that I look with new eyes, and my
joy is as great and profound and novel as if I had never seen
them until this moment.

Moreover, to crown all, is the unremitting city-work which
I have done in Baltimore, day and night, for two years past,
amid the infernal grind of wheel against pavement, of buyer
against seller, of sect against sect. Here, the whole morning
goes without a sound, except a distant rapturous shout which
comes occasionally through the woods from the brook where
Sidney and Harry have caught a crayfish; and the mountains,
which are in view from my window through the round-lying
ridges, seem but masses of blue tranquillity.

And so here I work, like a beaver in a dam of delight, (!there!) through the long mornings. I have brought up a whole library of books which I needed in writing my own, furnished me by the liberal kindness of the librarians of the Mercantile and Johns Hopkins Collections in Baltimore: and I expect to go back home on the first of September with three books ready for the printer – my " SCIENCE OF ENGLISH VERSE," my Collection of Anglo-Saxon poems, and my popular Edition of Chaucer.

———"———

We are delightfully situated, in a cottage just built, clean and fresh, with no one else, so far, in the building to disturb our sense of at-home-ness. We occupy three of the four upper rooms; these open upon a balcony, and are altogether fine and breezy. The fare is not for Heliogabalus, but everything is delightfully clean; and the mineral water is very fine. The place is in a nook on the side of the mountain; ridges and spurs zig-zag off in every direction about us and to the east-ward open out to show us the great Blue Ridge bounding the world. The establishment is on a small scale: not more than thirty or forty persons are here; and there is no wretched twang-ing of waltzes and the like, so that we all go to bed at nine o'clock like Christians. I get eight hours' sleep; which I haven't had in a long time.

If you were only here, – again! This is what we say daily: and we please ourselves with locating you in the other rooms of our cottage. Mary and the children expect to stay until October 1st. The air is superb; the sun rises and shines broad upon us straightway, and there is no dampness. Judging from my own sensations, it would be grand for your slender Will. The regular rate for board is thirty dollars a month, but the Proprietor is anxious to bring the place into notice and makes liberal reductions for parties. *We* pay twenty a month for grown people, children twelve. The spot is twelve miles, by carriage, from Harrisonburg, which is on the Valley Branch of the Baltimore and Ohio R.R., about twenty five miles from Staunton (Southern Terminus of the said " Valley Branch ") and about eighty-five miles from Harper's Ferry where the Valley Branch joins the main stem of the B. & O. R. R.

Ann Oh, Oh, Oh – 3 times – *terque quaterque* – if you were only here, you and Will and little you and little she.

But whether here or there, God bless you all four.

I will write to Ginna in a day or two. It has been in my heart to do so a long time, and nothing but pure lack of minutes has prevented.

Address us according to the head of this letter.

Your

S. L.

To John R. Tait

Rockingham Springs.
Near
McGaheysville, Va.
July 28th 1879.

My dear Brother Tait:

I have delayed my letter to you until I could make an excursion to the Shenandoah, in order to see what prospect you would have, in coming here, for a subject.

This afternoon I had a long and delightful stroll-on-horseback among the lovely meadows of the Hopkins Farm which run alongside the river under the protectorate of the all-encompassing mountains. I should think you would find studies and motives in abundance, both of meadow and mountain, within easy range of us, here; and yet I am so distrustful of my untechnical judgment in this matter – so fearful that the views which delight my eye would prove impracticable for the canvas – that I feel the greatest hesitation in urging you to come, so far as artistic purpose goes. The " Springs," as an establishment, is of the most primitive character, yet it exactly fills my need, and I am so comfortably situated that I cannot see how I could have bettered my situation at the most pretentious watering-place. We occupy the upper floor (four rooms) of a two-story cottage. This is of pine, unpainted, and bare enough; yet from our breezy balcony, which runs across the whole front of the cabin, I look off, through a glorious vista of lesser hills leaning to right and left, upon the Blue Ridge, whose gracious inclines of ever-changing blue always slant my thought easily up into the infinite. The rooms have each a bed, with a straw mattress, a table, washstand, open pine shelves, and nails on the door for our dresses and trowsers; but the walls are nicely plastered, the bed-linen is clean, everything about the appointments is perfectly fresh and tidy, the service good, and the proprietor civil and obliging to the last degree. The fare is – – – such as one looks for in the mountains; the bread is *usually* good, the chickens are tender as young love, the milk is drink for the Gods (when they don't let it sour); but, beyond this, pretty much everything requires some forgiveness of one sort or another, either as to the cooking or the quality. Of gayety, or even the usual watering-place sociability, there is none. I believe there are but three men, here, besides my father-in-law and me; and the ladies, who constitute the bulk of the company, while they are exceedingly pleasant at our tri-daily table chats or our after-tea walks, seem mostly like ourselves in pursuit of quiet, and visit little. There is a ten-pin alley, where Sidney and Harry will be delighted to set up the pins as fast as you can knock 'em down, at any time; and you can always get a horse for a ride. The drive here from Harrisonburg – 13 miles– is not interesting; but the whole land is full of beauty, once you are here, and a great variety of 'scape – mountain, meadow, gap, rock, and water – lies within easy distance.[52]

To me, who work all the morning and ride all the afternoon, – home to tea by seven and in bed at half-past eight! – the place is simply heavenly. The air has a tang of new life in it, and breathing and sleeping seem to constitute a sufficient sanction for the complex trouble of existence. The price of a *return-ticket* from Baltimore is $12.65 – which includes the drive from Harrisonburg and is good until the last of October. The terms for board are thirty dollars a month; but I am confident that I can arrange with the proprietor to take you and the dear little lady there at half-rates.

[52] John W. Wayland, in a brochure entitled *Sidney Lanier at Rockingham Springs* (Dayton, Va., 1912), records a tradition that Lanier himself did some sketching this summer– possibly in company with Tait, who shared the Lanier cottage during August (note by Mary Day Lanier, Charles D. Lanier Collection). More authoritative is the account given by Wayland from the *Rockingham Register*, a weekly newspaper, of a " tournament " held at McGaheysville on Aug. 8 at which Lanier delivered the address to the knights.

So! You have all the items I can think of. If you fancy you could stand it – it is perfect isolation and lonesomeness! – you have only to write me, and I will straightway negociate everything with the proprietor. I don't dare urge you to come, because so much of my own content consists in the fitness of the place for the hard work I am doing, and if one came purely for rest, or for entertainment, I doubt whether the environment would be altogether favorable.

Mary joins me in cordial messages for you and Mrs. Tait. Wishing you, – whether you come here or go elsewhere – all the blessings which come to me out of this daily ministration of the mountains, I am

faithfully yours,

Sidney Lanier.

To John R. Tait

Rockingham Springs,
Near
McGaheysville, Va.
Aug. 5th 1879.

My dear Tait:

Your letter is just here, and I scribble a note before the return mail to say that I strongly advise you to bring three or four pounds of good coffee, *parched*, enclosed in tight glass vessel (or otherwise, to preserve the aroma), and a common tin coffee-pot (25cts). We did, and have thanked our stars for it; our coffee is made in our own coffee-pot and brought to us at table. I'm fearfully apprehensive that you and Mrs. Tait will suffer from the fare; we have had a long reign of bad butter; and the bread is good only half the time; and then you two know the Tyrol, and may find the mountains tame enough which ravish *me*.

But, come on; I'm just going to look up the proprietor and arrange for your room &c.

Hastily, yours,

Sidney Lanier.

P.S.

My wife says it may be of service to mention to you that you won't regret bringing some *towels* of your own, and a common *soap-dish*.

To Robert S. Lanier

Rockingham Springs.
Near
McGaheysville, Va.
Aug. 25th 1879.

My dearest Father:

I can scarcely bring myself to believe that it *is* the 25th of August, as I have just written. I have been working on from day to day in such utter absorption – writing each day until about four o'clock afternoon, and then jumping on a horse and cantering about the mountain-roads with Sidney or Harry behind me – that the time has gone by double-winged, and it is incredible that the summer is almost over.

In about ten days I must get back to Baltimore, and prepare for plunging into what will be the busiest, and I hope most successful, year of my life.

I believe we are all improved, more or less. *I* am much better, in strength, and I think I have gained a pound or two of flesh.

Your letter came from Verbena – and we were much concerned for the dear little woman [53] there. We hear since from Clifford that she is quite out of danger. I wrote her soon after your letter arrived.

You will probably receive for re-acceptance a renewal note for the Charles Lanier paper in a few days. This takes it over (by the original arrangement with Charles) until December when it will be paid.

I write in a great haste to catch a mail, – not always an easy thing in this out of the way spot.

We all send our dear love to you and Mama.

Your loving

S. L.

[53] Gertrude Lanier Shannon Gibson.

To John G. James [54]

180 St. Paul St.
Baltimore, Md.
Sep. 15th 1879

My dear friend:

I grew so poorly off for strength soon after writing you last, that we were obliged to betake us to the mountains, where I have been spending the last two months alternating between illnesses and desperate forced-marches of work which had to be done. This will account to you for my failure to send an earlier answer to your last letter, – in part; and when I add that I desired to accompany my answer with the names of some more subscribers to Hayne's book and that this was impossible until the people should return to town from the annual summer-flight, the explanation will be complete.

We have just returned to Baltimore, and I am writing this, in the most uncomfortable way imaginable, sprawling in bed, where I am confined by a villainous boil which has attacked me in a very inconvenient place and has thus subjected me to grievous limitations as concerning posture. This will prevent me from moving about for three or four days and will thus delay my list a little longer.

But meantime I write to say that I have recently become aware of a firm of Quakers in New Hampshire who, as my friend tells me, manufacture books at exceedingly low rates. I believe they are primarily type-manufacturers, but have established a printing and binding department in connection, and thus have extraordinary facilities for doing good and cheap work. These people I am going to see in a couple of weeks, for the purpose of contracting with them to print some books of my own; and it has occurred to me that I might take charge of Hayne's book and save him all the commission which would be charged by any publishers for the *publishing*, over and above the actual price of *making*, the work. That is to say, I could contract with the New Hampshire people for the manu-

[54] Previously published, *Letters: Sidney Lanier to Col. John G. James* (Austin, Texas, 1942), pp. 11-13.

facture of the book; and they could send it to me, when finished, so that I would issue it from my house at Baltimore, by mail and freight, to the subscribers all over the country.

I am beginning a series of text-books of my own, to be " published " in the same manner by myself, on the plan which has been so successfully carried out by Edward Arber, of University College, London. He has issued a number of works, for astonishingly low prices, which are simply invaluable to the English scholar. His saving in expense was effected by editing the works himself, making all his own contracts for printing, paper, binding &c, and issuing the books from his office upon orders received by mail. There are no middle-men; the books are sold by himself only, and the price is the same to everybody.

My " Science of English Verse " is now completed: my " Student's Chaucer " is well on the way; my " From Cædmon to Chaucer " (a presentation of all the most important Anglo-Saxon poems from the 6th century to the 14th, including *The Vision concerning Piers The Plowman*, with a translation into modern English *between each two lines of the text*, and a running commentary in the margin, — the same plan with that of my " Student's Chaucer ") will quickly follow, before the end of the year; and these will be increased next year by " The First English Comedies " (an edition of the Miracle-Play *Noah's Voyage*, old Heywood's Interlude *The Four P's*, and Udall's Ralph Roister Doister) and " The First English Tragedies ", both companion-manuals to " The Modern Study of Shakspere ", which will place before the student, in practicable form, the very remarkable results of the precise methods of inquiry that have formed the modern school of Shakspere Scholarship in Germany and England during the last ten years.

These are all intended as text-books for a college-course of English Literature. Of course, as at present conducted, few colleges would call for so many text-books on this subject: but many more than this are used in the course of Latin or of Greek in every College, and it is a mere relic of a time when there was practically *no* English Literature that we now devote so much more attention to the poetry of dead languages than to that of our own. This relic is already disappearing: and would have disappeared sooner if teachers could have found to their hands any organized Course of such studies. It is a most remarkable circumstance that absolutely no series of text-books exists designed to acquaint the student with even the masters of English Poetry. There are hundreds of Manuals which give the names and birth-days of English authors, with occasionally a brief line or two to show their styles; but this is, at best, the *History* of Literature, and does not in the least help the student to know Literature itself and to reap the gospel it brings to earnest people.[55]

So, write me all about your arrangements for Hayne's book, and we will try to enlarge the returns.

My wife joins me in cordial greetings to you and all yours.

Your friend,

Sidney L.

To Daniel C. Gilman

Bo. Sept. 22nd 1879.

My dear Mr. Gilman:

I have thought it might be perhaps convenient to you if I should send some sort of memorandum which may serve whenever you get ready to take up the subject of my lectures in your own mind.

Your most kind and thoughtful letter gave me an admirable view of the situation, and I quite agree with you that the best plan is to begin with a set of lectures in Hopkins Hall which may develope the aims of Literature in such a way as to attract special students to a more detailed pursuit.

I have thought out a course which I think specially designed to this end, and, whenever you desire, we will discuss it.

As to time: I shall cheerfully work into any appointments you may make. I shall be very glad if the lectures may begin as late as possible in October; and if they can occur on Mondays and Thursdays, at five (or any later hour) in the afternoon. But this is — as I said — personal convenience, and will be yielded to any limitations which may render these days or hours unsuitable to you.

---

[55] Except for Lanier's *Science of English Verse,* none of the plans mentioned in this letter for editing and publishing ever materialized.

The enclosed card contains my new address.[56]

Sincerely yours,

Sidney Lanier.

To Clifford A. Lanier

435 N. Calvert St.
B⁰; Sep. 25th 1879.

Dearest Clifford:

I have been in bed nearly two weeks with a most painful abscess, and got up yesterday for the first time to go out and lecture to two classes of young ladies, – my school engagements having now begun. We have also been moving, and got into our new house last night, though we shall be " fixing " for several days. We are charmed with our new quarters; I, particularly, for I pay only twenty five dollars a month rent, and this makes me feel rich. My total expenses for the coming year will be but about half what they were last year; and I have three school-engagements (for lectures on Eng. Literature) which bring [me eight hundred] dollars, [besides the] Johns Hopkins lectureship.[57] So that altogether the outlook is pleasanter for me than ever before.

I am much better: the Doctor thinks my abscess was a good thing for me; but it was, and still is, very inconvenient, since it effectually prevents me from sitting down, and I have to write lying flat on my back, or otherwise contorted.

[56] The Laniers had moved to 435 (now 1817) North Calvert St., just two blocks south of his first home at 33 Denmead St., on the outskirts of the Baltimore of that day.
[57] Words torn out of this letter have been conjecturally restored from MS notes supplied by Edwin Mims, who made them in 1905 from the original letter, then intact. In a fragmentary letter to his brother, Oct. 16?, 1879 (here omitted), Lanier added: " Were I looking forward to the $1800 as clear money which I will make this year, I could easily do all, for I can live on less than that during the next twelve months. But unfortunately the last year cost me twice as much as this sum; . . . it could not be done at all without spending most part of my Johns Hopkins Salary before it was earned."
For an account of Lanier's teaching engagements for 1879-1880, see his letter of Oct. 9, 1879, and note 59, below. In this connection he wrote to his father in a letter of Sept. 26, 1879 (here omitted), " My Peabody lectures last year were of great service in this regard, and seem to have brought me into much favor."

My Froissart book is now printed, and the publishers have just sent me some lovely engraving specimens of the illustrations. It is to be a very handsome affair, apparently. I believe my three articles on the Physics of Poetry are to appear in SCRIBNER's during the autumn. I have just sold them a poem, written during the summer called "Owl Against Robin," [58] being a complaint of the owl against sundry musical robins for keeping him awake day after day.

I have sent you the two drafts undated, and don't know the time when my last one matures. If you should not hear from me in time for it, please draw on me "*at one day*" for one hundred dollars, and renew for the balance at thirty days with the enclosed note. My abscess – which kept me in indescribable pain for a long time before it could be got to discharge – completely interrupted all my business arrangements, and I am greatly pressed until I can start matters again. I shall still be confined to the house for three or four days. The inability to write – coming from the impossibility of sitting, or of standing more than a few minutes at a time – is a great trial to me.

I'm tired out now, and so send you a kiss.

I don't know exactly where you are, and therefore address this to the Exchange. I suppose some one is there to forward it.

May begs to undertake part of the responsibility of my kiss, and Wilsie must share the same.

S. L.

To CLIFFORD A. LANIER

435 N. Calvert St.
Bo., Oct. 9th 1879.

My dearest Clifford:

Like yourself, – as gathered from your card just received, – I have been quite strained to the highest point with the labor of organizing the manifold interests which I find in my hands for this year. I have planned, and am now carry-

[58] Accepted by *Scribner's Monthly* in a letter of Aug. 14, 1879, with the statement that it had been handed to the artist to see what he could do about illustrations. (It was not published until the issue of July, 1881.)

ing forward, the courses of lectures to my young lady pupils, of which I have four classes. One of these is a class of ladies who have passed college days and are pursuing post-graduate studies for the pure aim of an increase of their culture. I have laid out for them what I think I can call a unique course in philosophico-historico-esthetico-literary studies, and I find it simply delightful to carry these bright and fresh young minds along such paths. Miss Adams – who gets up this class in connection with her school – is having a somewhat detailed programme of the course printed, and I'll send you one as soon as they are finished.[59] My Johns Hopkins lectures commence in a few days.

I am now making such preparations as I can to call the mind of the Trustees to a Chair of Poetry, or to some permanent lectureship in Literature, for me. Of course I shall have no word to say to any of them: I merely mean that I am organizing means to show my enthusiasm in behalf of the poetic teaching of young men, together with such preparation as I hope to bring to such a task. To this end, I earnestly ask your help. I already have the hearty cooperation of Mr. Gilman, who is in thorough understanding with all my plans for the elevation of current views of the literary office and for lifting the poet into his proper place as the great moral teacher of men in all times and over all fleeting forms of belief. With the favorable start which I have, I think nothing more is needed to secure my end than the publication of such works of mine as would illustrate fully my views of such a Chair as I want, the aims to which I would devote it, and the fitness I might have for discharging its duties. This end I propose to accomplish by printing immediately my " Science of English Verse," my " First Course in Chaucer," and my " First Course in Shakspere."

It is in the printing of these three books that I wish your help.

[59] A copy of this printed announcement has survived (Johns Hopkins University). It was issued by " The Misses Adams, 138 West Madison St." Lanier's course of " Readings and Conversational Lectures " consisted of selected works from Chaucer to the present, and were delivered on Mondays and Thursdays at 11 A. M.

The only others of Lanier's teaching engagements for 1879-1880 that can be positively identified were at Mrs. M. C. Singleton's Eutaw Place School, Mrs. Jones's Mount Vernon Institute, and R. M. Johnston's Pen Lucy School.

(1) I have determined to print them, and publish them, myself. The lecturer on Eng. Literature at University College, London, a – Mr. Edward Arber – has adopted this plan, and has sold one hundred and twenty thousand of his reprints at an astonishingly low price, by thus saving all the costs of middlemen and all the complex charges through which publishers have to reimburse themselves out of successful books for their losses on unsuccessful ones. I propose to bargain with a Quaker firm at Claremount, New Hampshire,[60] who are type-founders and do all such work at extremely low rates, to print and manufacture my books for me. They will be sent me here, in quantities of fifty or one hundred at a time, as I order them; and Mary and I will fill orders for them, which are to be addressed to me. I have a room adjoining my library which is admirably fitted for this purpose.

(2) The arrangement is a safe one, inasmuch as I need have but few books printed and bound at a time – not more than a hundred of each, if I desire – and I can then sell off these before ordering more, the publishers keeping the plates. I have nearly enough pupils here of my own to repay the whole investment in a couple of years by their purchases of these books, all three of which will be used in all my classes. Besides this, all whom I have consulted agree that these textbooks supply a growing want. There is indeed nothing like them now before the public; and the study of English Literature is rapidly striding to a front place in all schools and colleges. Col. James, Superintendent of The Texas Military Institute at Austin, writes me enthusiastically on the subject and will at once adopt the books in his college: and I think the State University of Georgia and Mercer University at Macon would immediately do so, with many other institutions, north and south.

(3) I have already raised, with some securities which Mr. Day gave me, about two hundred dollars, and I now desire to mortgage the copyright of the two text-books (The " First

---

[60] There is no surviving evidence that Lanier actually negotiated with this firm, probably the Claremont Manufacturing Co. (See Louis W. Flanders, *Simeon Ide, Yoeman, Freeman, Pioneer Printer*, Rutland, Vt., 1931, and Simeon Ide, *The Industries of Claremont, New Hampshire, Past and Present*, Claremont, Mfg. Co., 1879.)

Course in Chaucer" and "First Course in Shakspere") for five hundred more. Would you be willing to borrow for me, upon any securities of your own, this sum, for one year, and take a mortgage upon said two copyrights for *your* security? If you can do so, I can immediately go forward and carry out my project. I do not believe you would be in any danger; and all present appearances go to show that I would be able to repay the five hundred at the time mentioned from sources independent of the books. Probably you can, by endorsing or otherwise securing my own note which I enclose, undated, arrange the whole matter. This sum will enable me to print, and retain the plates of, my three books, in the cheap way in which I propose to do it.

(4) The investment would be a good one for me if not a dollar ever came from it: for these books would, as I have every reason to believe, procure me the chair which would render me independent for the rest of my life and give me a sphere of influence in the highest degree desirable. Mr. Gilman, in his last letter to me, – written this summer, in corresponding as to the details of my University lectures for next winter, – says, among many pleasant, friendly things; "I think your scheme" (of winter lectures) "may be admirably worked in not only with our major and minor courses in English, but with all our literary courses, French & German, Latin & Greek. The teachers of these subjects pursue chiefly *language* courses, . . . We need among us some one like you, loving literature & poetry, & treating it in such a way as to enlist and inspire many students. . . . I think your aims and your preparation admirable &c &c. . . . I am very glad that you lend us your aid, and you may rely upon all the help I can give to make your work successful." [61]

(5) Such being the situation, my plan is to get my books out *immediately*, so that they may become known before the usual winter elections by the Trustees, which begin to be discussed, I suspect, by the beginning of the year. If therefore you can arrange this five hundred immediately, I can make my bargains for cash and thus get all things much cheaper.

I know that you will do what you can. If the books succeed,

---

[61] See also note 49, above.

I will, I hope, have made an opening for you to become a publisher, – which is a dear dream that I do not relinquish.

– Pray let me know if it gives you any trouble to get one-day drafts on me cashed, to pay mine. Do not be surprised at any such drafts from me, and always draw on me at one day – or, if that is troublesome, at sight – to pay them.

My life is so busy, up to the minute every day, that the privilege of raising these small sums for even five or six days is of the greatest value to me.

God bless you, dear.

Your brother

S. L.

To John G. James [62]

435 N. Calvert St.
Bo: Oct. 16th 1879.

Aha! Do I hear the sound of marriage-bells all the way from the prairies?

Let me give you my hands, — both of them, — my dear friend; for, if she is a good woman, you are about to enter Paradise, — and if she isn't, I am sure you are going to make her so.

You are to write straightway and tell me all about it. Meantime, my Comrade and I have been diligently looking up rings. We are agreed that the most delicate and quaint design we have seen is embodied in a ring at Canfield's which is made on the " lap-pattern " — that is, a pattern in which the two ends of the gold band composing the ring, instead of being brought squarely together and welded, are carried over and " lapped " alongside each other, something like this:

[62] Previously published, *Letters: Sidney Lanier to Col. John G. James* (Austin, Texas, 1942), pp. 14-15.

At the point indicated by the figure 1 is a lovely little pearl, rose-tinted, pear-shaped; and at 2 is a diamond, of about ½ carat weight, just equal in size to the pearl. The band can be made either in dead gold, or in polished gold. The price of the ring we designed upon this pattern – (the original is at Canfield's and we simply suggested one alteration in it, towit, putting a little *larger* diamond in the place of the one already set) is from thirty-five to forty-five dollars. Diamonds are extraordinarily cheap, at present: there was never such a time for making engagements!

Of course you understand that neither of these stones, — the pearl or the diamond — is imposing in size; but they are not so small as to be finical, and I consider them quite large enough for beauty. We both think the ring would be thoroughly charming.

Let me know your thoughts about it.

I write in a great pressure. I have, in addition to my legitimate work, five lectures a week now going, and will shortly have two more.

With all manner of friendly greetings,

faithfully yours,

Sidney L.

To Robert S. Lanier

435 N. Calvert St.
Baltimore, Md.
Oct. 29th 1879.

My dearest Father:

It seems a long time since I have written you, though I cannot now think of any minute when I *could* have done so in the last two or three weeks.

My Johns Hopkins Lectures began yesterday. I had a large and fine audience: indeed the President tells me that twice as many tickets were applied for as could be given out. It is pleasant work, and I hope it may be lasting. I enclose a copy of the "Outline" printed for the use of the students who attend, and send you a copy of the Sun noticing the opening

of the Winter course and giving a tolerable summary of my
lecture.[63]

These lectures — two a week — and the seven which I deliver to the school-classes each week,— keep me pretty busy in
addition to the other work upon which I am engaged.

I think I have mentioned to you that I sent a cordial invitation to Pringle,[64] on receiving his letter, to come and pay us a
visit here. His expectation was, as I gathered, to leave Poughkeepsie about the first of October. I asked him to write and
let me know what day he would arrive so that I could meet
him — or at any rate have some one else to do so — at the
Station. I have heard nothing from him, and fear my letter
must have failed to reach him, though it was carefully directed
according to the address given in his. A letter arrived here
for him two days ago, from Charleston.

I am obliged now to close hastily. Loving messages go to
you from all of us.
                                        Your son,
                                          S. L.

To Robert S. Lanier

                                    435 Calvert St.
                                    B^o. Nov. 12th, 1879.
My dearest Father:

Your letter came yesterday. I have time for
only a note in reply. We hope to see Pringle soon, and I will
do my best to find him a place.

[63] Lanier's first course at the Johns Hopkins University consisted of sixteen
public lectures on "English Verse, especially Shakspere's" (III, 311-410), delivered at Hopkins Hall from Oct. 28 to Dec. 19, 1879, on Tuesdays and
Fridays at 5 P. M. The printed announcement stated: "The object of these
Lectures will be to awaken and develop an interest in modern literary criticism
by special studies in Shakspere. His moral and artistic growth will be compared and the metrical tests recently proposed by scholars will be investigated.
The course will begin with an examination of the Laws of Verse." As actually
given, the first nine lectures dealt with Lanier's theory of English verse; and
the remaining seven were divided between a study of the pre-Shakespearian
drama, the metrical tests as applied to Shakespeare, and a comparison of *A
Midsummer Night's Dream, Hamlet,* and *The Tempest.* Copies of the "Outline" here mentioned have survived (Charles D. Lanier Collection, Johns Hopkins University). The notice in the Baltimore *Sun* here referred to was on
Oct. 29, 1879. The specimen lecture pages (see illustration) show an early form
of material used in *The Science of English Verse* (see II, xx and 201-202).

[64] Pringle Morgan, R. S. Lanier's stepson.

SPECIMEN PAGES, LANIER'S JOHNS HOPKINS LECTURE II, "ENGLISH VERSE," 1879

Manuscript in the Charles D. Lanier Collection, Johns Hopkins University

As to the telegraphic transfer of money: it costs just as much to send the small amount as the large one. Of course, any continuance of such transfers would be expensive. But I have now established a status here as one who meets his engagements promptly; and the few dollars which have been expended for telegraphing, — whenever it has been necessary for me to draw in this way — are a mere trifle when compared with the advantage of a reputation for punctuality. Unfortunately so many literary men have been loose in their ideas about money that the very profession is against one who comes to a new place, — particularly a strictly commercial place such as Baltimore. It has been part of my most earnest work, to do all I could in the way of dissipating such impressions; and, with this view, I have always strained every nerve to be up to the minute in all my dealings. So far I have succeeded.[65]

I will have no occasion to draw on you again, – certainly for some time. It was necessary to do so today; and you will receive the money for the draft ($100, at sight) tomorrow or next day. Pray do not distress yourself about it. I am sure all will come out properly.

My lectures at the Johns Hopkins continue to draw full audiences.[66]

We all send love to all.

Your son,

Sidney L.

To CHARLES SCRIBNER

435 N. Calvert St.
Bo. Nov. 15th 1879.

My dear Mr. Scribner:

The books came day before yesterday, but I have just found time (I have nine lectures a week from now till December) to get a look at them. We all vote them

[65] Charles Scribner wrote to Mary Day Lanier, Sept. 28, 1881, shortly after Lanier's death: " In his business relations Mr. Lanier was always so exact that there is little settlement required."

[66] The average attendance at Lanier's lectures was 170, whereas the average at ten other series was only 113 (see *The Johns Hopkins University Circulars, December 1879-September 1882*, Baltimore, 1882, No. 2, p. 18).

charming, both outside and in; and my nine-year-old has scarcely found time for his meals since they arrived.

You have certainly made a very attractive volume; and, as the book is a classic, it ought to prove a valuable piece of property.

As to advertisement: I suspect you might find it profitable to announce the book in the TELEGRAPH & MESSENGER, published at Macon, Georgia — my old home; in the principal paper of Montgomery, Alabama, where I have also lived; in THE NEWS, of Savannah; THE CHRONICLE AND SENTINEL, of Augusta; and THE CONSTITUTION, of Atlanta. Perhaps, also, an advertisement in THE SUN, of Baltimore, and THE EVENING BULLETIN, of Philadelphia, would be well.

I will avail myself of your kind offer so far as to ask for *three* more copies, in the *red* binding, for my own use.

Besides this: there are a dozen or so people connected in one way or another with the press about the country who would be glad, from friendly motives, to speak of the book in their publications, and who would like a copy from me personally, with my name &c on the fly-leaf; and so, if you think it worth while, you may send a dozen copies, in the red and green bindings, to me for this use. I will forward them to their respective destinations. I am glad to say, in answer to your kind inquiry, that my health is greatly improved, and that I am very hard at work.

I feel the greatest interest in the Froissart book, and shall be glad to know of its assured success at the earliest moment.[67]

Sincerely yours,

Sidney Lanier.

[67] Scribner replied, Nov. 18, 1879: "Your suggestions have all been carried out. . . . The book starts off well and is sure to sell."

In a letter to his father, Nov. 23, 1879 (here omitted), Lanier wrote: "The BOY'S FROISSART is selling finely— so the publishers write me— and I have great hope that it will prove the entering wedge to a series that will profit both the world and me in more ways than one. I hope to run over to New York next Friday, for the purpose of talking over some other books of the same sort with the Scribners and others. (Lanier's letter to Scribner, Dec. 6, 1879, below, seems to indicate that he made the trip to New York, probably on Friday, Nov. 28.)

To Robert S. Lanier

435 N. Calvert St.
B⁰. Nov. 16ᵗʰ 1879

My dearest Father:

We had the pleasure of receiving Uncle Clifford in our house yesterday afternoon, and I have almost begun to feel as if it were not so many miles from here to Macon as before. What a big man he is! We had a good talk last night, and have been together all day. In his honor I suspended the work which I would have been otherwise doing although this *is* Sunday. He bids me tell you that he would have written today but thought my letter would suffice; and asks me to say that he expects his case to come up about two o'clock tomorrow, so as to let him start home Tuesday morning. He returns to Washington tomorrow morning by an early train.

Pringle arrived on Thursday, and we have tried to make him at home. He seems in first-rate condition, and is a fine-looking young man. I will report his qualifications and desires to all the Georgia firms in business here; and we watch THE SUN every morning for advertisements that may offer suitable places.

I sent you the hundred dollars by telegraph on Saturday. I will not have to draw any more drafts, certainly for a good while, and, I sincerely trust, for ever.

I write very hurriedly, in the midst of great pressure. Uncle Clifford will give you a copy of my Boy's Froissart which I have asked him to carry. It is certainly a handsome book. Mr. Scribner writes me that they are confident it will have a wide sale.

My lectures continue to draw full houses.

God bless you.

Your son,

S.L.

To Scribner's Monthly [68]

435 N. Calvert St.
Bo Nov. 23rd 1879.

Eds. Scribners:

I have corrected the accompanying *ms.* so as to make it a fair representation so far as concerns dialect. It may be well to add that the commonest mistake in reproducing the negro's dialect is to make it *too* consistent: and you need not think, therefore, that in allowing the same speaker to say (for example) sometimes "*dat*" and sometimes "*that*", – as I have arranged the dialect here and there – there is any lapsus. The negro, especially since the war, tries hard for the *th* instead of *d* in words such as *the, that,* &c, and thus the same speaker often uses both forms. This remark applies to many other peculiarities.

Very truly yours,

Sidney Lanier

To Charles Scribner

435 N. Calvert St.
Baltimore, Md.
Dec. 4th 1879.

Dear Mr. Scribner:

I have been expecting every day to get the estimate you were to send for the *ms.* of The Science of English Verse, in order that we may make a decisive arrangement for the publication of that book. It is of great importance to me that the work should appear at the earliest possible moment, and every day is of value.

A friend has suggested to me, apropos of my boy's Series of Classic adventure, that if the most wonderful exploits in *Homer* were edited for boys in a lively prose translation, on the same

---

[68] Apparently the editors of *Scribner's Monthly* had written to Lanier asking him to correct the negro dialect in some contribution that had been submitted to the magazine by another author. No composition of Lanier's during this period fits the facts of his letter.

plan with the Froissart, the book might prove a great boon and have a corresponding financial success. The more I think of it the more the idea grows upon me. How does it strike you?

As soon as may be convenient to you, I would be very glad to have the remaining hundred and fifty for the Malory book.

Your very truly,

Sidney Lanier.[69]

To Charles Scribner

435 N. Calvert St.

Bo. Dec. 6th 1879.

My dear Mr. Scribner:

I feel sure that your idea of the necessity for any postponment of THE SCIENCE OF VERSE till after the magazine articles are published is based upon a misapprehension of the nature of the book, and that the following considerations will remove all doubt on that point.

When I was consulting with you at first about the Science of Verse my plan was to endeavor to make a book intended mainly for *the general reader* but capable of being used as a text-book. Upon thinking over the matter more carefully, however, I abandoned this plan; and the book is *purely* a *text-book*, not appealing to the general reader at all.

There is therefore no reason whatever why the *magazine articles* should await the *book*; the whole matter and plan of the book are upon a different scale from that of the articles, and are intended for systematic students in colleges and universities, while the articles are a merely popular exposition of kindred matters. This is easily seen when you reflect that the

---

[69] Scribner replied, Dec. 5, 1879: " As the *Froissart* has only been out a few weeks a decision on the *Malory* book seems a little premature." The suggested book on Homer was rejected since it had already been done several times, as recently as 1878. As for *The Science of English Verse*, Scribner wrote that he was waiting for an exact estimate from the printer, and even then " before taking *definite* steps in regard to the publication of the book, it will be necessary to arrange either for the immediate publication of the magazine articles [" The Physics of Poetry "], or for their non-appearance."

book contains *805* pp. of *ms.*, while the articles contain only about *200* pp.

It *was* desirable, under my first idea, that the articles should appear before the book: but this was because their appearance would have benefited the book, *not* because the book would have damaged the articles. As matters *now* stand, the book addresses only special students, while the articles address only light readers: and there would be as much reason in refraining from publishing a text-book on Geography because the Magazine is printing articles on Brazil.

I make no doubt Dr. Holland will so regard it, as soon as he knows the exact character of the book. For that purpose I will beg that you submit this letter to him and inform me, at your earliest convenience, of his opinion.[70]

I must have quite misinterpreted your reply about the Malory book in New York. When I asked " If the Froissart book had gone far enough to enable you to see your way clear in buying the Malory book," you answered, Oh, yes, and that your idea was to bring it out next Christmas in the same style with the other.

This I only speak of, as explaining why I wrote of it at all. I supposed the whole matter had probably passed out of your mind in the press of business: — and I was hurried by great need of the money.

Very truly yours,

Sidney Lanier.

To Charles Scribner

435 N. Calvert St.

Bo. Dec. 10th 1879.

My dear Mr. Scribner:

        The necessity for early publication of my Science of Verse is now not so great, and I write to say that it will not be worth while to press the question of priority at

---

[70] Scribner replied, Dec. 10, 1879, that the editor of *Scribner's Monthly* (J. G. Holland) had no objection to the immediate publication of the book. But he added that Lanier's letter of Dec. 6 had not increased his own confidence in its sale, and that he thought it " a great mistake to cast the material

present, inasmuch as the magazine articles may possibly still be printed in advance. The purpose which I hoped to forward by printing the book immediately will probably be accomplished without it, and in that event I should much prefer to bring out the book *un*hurriedly for a next autumn publication, — when it would reach its academic audience at a more favorable season than as a spring book.

I note what you say of your pressure during the holiday business, and am sorry to have given you an extra — and useless question — to think of.

Sincerely yours,

Sidney Lanier.

To Daniel C. Gilman [71]

435 N. Calvert St.
Bo., Dec. 17th 1879.

My dear Mr. Gilman:

I was so loth to take up any more of your Sunday evening than I had already occupied that I did not then lay before you — as I much desired to do — some practical suggestions, which I saw from our conversation had not come in your way, regarding a course of English Literature in its special relations to

(1) other literature; and

(2) English linguistic courses.

I here subjoin certain considerations, with an actual outline of a Literary Course based upon them, which I feel sure will place these relations much more clearly before you, as they emerge in the course of the following development. And, in pursuance of your recommendation, I should be glad to embody these fundamental ideas in the preliminary talk which I am to

into *textbook* form " fearing it would thereby " lose much of its freshness and chance of popularity." (See Lanier's letter to his brother Clifford, Dec. 21, 1879, below.)

[71] Previously published, *Independent*, XXXVIII, 325-326 (Mar. 18, 1886). The elaborate program outlined in this letter was never undertaken.

give to such students as may desire to pursue a short course of reading next year.

I.

For obvious reasons, every English-speaking person, of no matter what profession, is more or less directly interested in being able to express ideas in English with clearness, with wealth of illustration, and with beauty. For these ends, it is necessary to acquire :

(1) a working vocabulary of *idiomatic* English words and phrases;

(2) a working stock of illustrative ideas drawn from all those departments of learning, which are within the range of persons of average culture; and

(3) a working acquaintance with those peculiar Forms of modern communication which have evolved themselves out of the special inward needs of our time: as, for example,

(*a*) The Lecture, – Popular, Semi-popular, & Special;

(*b*) The Magazine Paper, – "   "   " ;

(*c*) The Newspaper Leader;

(*d*) The Sermon;

(*e*) The Novel;

(*f*) The Modern Drama;

(*g*) The Address, – Legislative, Forensic, Hustings, &c;

(*h*) The Poem;

and other Forms.

These three aims necessitate three perfectly ditsinct courses of study, as will appear in the following special treatment.

(1): VOCABULARY OF IDIOMATIC ENGLISH WORDS AND PHRASES.

The course for this end should carefully aim to remedy certain evils which inevitably attend the English *Linguistic* Course: *it is indeed precisely opposite to, or complementary of, the philological study.* For: linguistic regards that signification which words of different languages have *in common*, that is, their *un-idiomatic* signification: while the present study has for its paramount search the *idiomatic signification* of English words.

How great is the importance of this distinction no one but the experienced critic or word-craftsman can fully appreciate. But every one, perhaps, can easily recognize that for many purposes, and in many forms, of communication, language is *effective* precisely in the proportion that it is *idiomatic*. In literature this is universally true: and perhaps the most familiar illustration of its truth will be found in recalling the absolute impossibility of translating a great poem from one language to another. Every great poem – as indeed every great literary work – is written in idioms: and idioms are idioms because they are untranslateable. Another illustration may be found in the wretched failure often made by great linguists in attempting to write works of permanent literary value. Dr. Holmes's comic poem, " Dorm on the herb, with none to supervise " [72] &c, is different merely in *degree*, not in *kind*, from the sort of un-idiomatic English to which linguistic studies tend. Without developing this branch farther: the acquisition of such a vocabulary should determine the nature of the English books to be read and the class-lectures to be given, — for this special end. It must be carefully remembered that *every word used by a man in composition or speech is a word which he has either read or heard*. We are apt to think, in a vague way, that our words come to us, *somehow*: but, on the contrary, the proposition just made is strictly true, and therefore the only method of acquiring a rich working outfit of words is either to hear them or read them. With this aim, the class should begin by reading: The minor poems of the Scotch poets of the 15th and early 16th centuries, particularly Henryson, King James I, Dunbar, Gawin Douglas, and Lyndsay: Sir Thomas Malory's History of King Arthur; Roger Ascham's *Toxophilus* and *The Schoolmaster*; Samuel Daniel, minor poems and prose writings; Drayton, minor poems; Stephen Gosson's *School of Abuse*; Nash's *Pierce Penniless*: Gabriel Harvey's *Pierce's Supererogation* and *Four Letters*; Burns; Wiclif's and Tyndale's Bibles; and a selected Chrestomathy from the Ballad-literature of Scotland and England. These readings should never lose sight of their purpose, namely, the gathering of *strong* and *homely English words* and *phrases*: and the exercises and expository

[72] The line occurs in Holmes's poem " Aestivation " (Autocrat Edition, XII, 417).

comments should be so devised as to link together in the pupil's mind idea and word.

Upon the solid foundation thus laid, a further course, extending from Swift to Emerson, should be laid, with the same end.

It may be finally remarked, as to this branch, that such a course is just as necessary to the free and efficient work of every man whose profession hinges upon the use of words as the knowledge of tools to the carpenter or that of nomenclature to the scientist.

(2): STOCK OF ILLUSTRATIVE IDEAS.

The proper expression of thought requires not only the above-described vocabulary of *words and phrases*, but a farther and equally important vocabulary of *ideas* drawn from those systems of thought or of knowledge which have acquired permanency and currency among the ages. In carrying out any presentation, – by lecture, sermon, essay, poem, whatever literary Form, – success will very largely depend on the store of illustrations at the speaker's command, illustrations which relieve the stiffness of elaborate trains of thought and which flash conviction upon the hearer rather by lightning gleams than by steady rays. An extensive acquaintance – general, of course, but precise as far as it goes – with systems of physical science, both ancient and modern, would be found specially useful to this end.

This course should therefore embrace: short but authoritative expositions of Pythagoras, Socrates, Aristotle, Plato, Lucretius, Epictetus, Marcus Aurelius, – expositions presenting the *words* of those thinkers, so far as possible; Bacon, here and there; *Telliamed (de Maillet)*; parts of Leibnitz, of Descartes, of Humboldt; condensed, yet exact, views of modern science, – of Biology, of Theory and Practice of Medicine (both schools), of the general state of physical science and its aims and hopes, with outline sketches of modern Chemistry, Astronomy, Geology, Mathematics; modern theories of Esthetics; and indications of the tendencies of current thought.

The expansion of mental range, as well as of special facilities in expression, attainable by such a course cannot be too highly estimated.

(*3*): ACQUAINTANCE WITH MODERN LITERARY FORMS.

This course would involve the *formal* analysis – *not* verbal – of the best models in each kind of composition mentioned; and it is easily seen that this analysis would necessarily present, in its course, *some* good work of every great author in our language. In this branch, of course, special needs of students intending special professions would be consulted: a student contemplating a professorship would be assigned special work in the analysis of lectures, essays, and the like; one looking forward to law would be assigned special work in the analysis of the Address (see (*g*) above); and so on. But *the main principles of formal criticism* should be impressed upon *all*, as developed from at least *one* analysis of each of these Forms mentioned.

II.

But this three-fold, or three-years', course, arranged thus with a primary view towards the *practical outfit* of every English-speaking man, should, in its last stage, be specially directed towards counteracting that very lamentable narrowness of range which seems peculiarly incident to the absorbed specialist in modern physical science and modern linguistics.

To this end: the spiritual consolation and refreshment of literature when the day's work is over, the delight of sitting down to the favorite poet or essayist at evening, the enlargement of sympathy derivable from powerful individual presentations such as Shakspere's or George Eliot's, the gentle influences of Sir Thomas Browne or Burton or Lamb or Hood, the repose of Wordsworth, the beauty of Keats, the charm of Tennyson, – should be brought out, so as to initiate friendships between special students and particular authors which may be carried on through life.

Although no such course as the foregoing has ever been carried out – or even projected, so far as I know – yet I do not in the least doubt that the time will come when every one will wonder why it has not always been regarded as of quite equal importance with any system of study now in the University programme.

I am always

faithfully yours,
Sidney Lanier.

TO CLIFFORD A. LANIER

435 N. Calvert St.
Bo., Dec. 21st 1879.

My dear Clifford:

A great pressure of duties – most of them public engagements, not to be postponed – has absolutely over-brimmed each day and night of mine for some weeks, and the sad news which Father sends me has added the overflow of tears to the sweat of labor.[73]

Aunt Jane has gone just when I was getting ready to minister to her, and the stroke comes particularly hard to me. Mary and I had discussed the project of asking her to come and stay a long time with us here, where we could cherish her in our own house; but had been so fearful that the comparative luxury in which she has long lived would make our very narrow economies uncomfortable for her that we finally determined to wait a little while, in the faith that some more settled way of life would be granted to us. Meantime, she is departed: and thus the old Too-Late of life, – which we read about and hear of and never believe till it comes, – appears, and gives us the guest's regret instead of the guest.

When your Postal card came, on Monday, I waited all day for news; and, none coming, telegraphed next day to Charleston. James Eason replied; and I learned that she was already gone when your card reached me, and had been buried before I telegraphed.

A letter from Aunt Mina to Mary has arrived, telling us that the poor soul had been suffering with a deadly disease ever since early summer. Of all this no word had ever reached us and we supposed her to be as well as might be after her great loss.

Thus it seems particularly hard – as I said – that she has fled away, in ignorance of our constant thought and loving intent, which were not communicated to her simply because the desperate strain of over-work has not allowed time enough

---

[73] Lanier's aunt, Jane Lanier Montgomery (formerly Mrs. Abram Watt), had died on Dec. 14, 1879.

either for meals or sleep in months to *me*, while my poor Mary has, for a still longer time, been wholly debarred from writing by a disease of the eyes which the physician has worked at in vain and which makes every letter an imminent threat to her eyesight.

I judge from a sentence in Aunt Mina's letter, – and from the fact that although poor Auntie remained conscious to the very last she had not a single word for *me*, – that she died in the belief of my indifference at the very moment when, in the midst of the most cruel weights a man ever bore – weights only known to the pawnbroker and the Lord and me, besides diseases, and secret griefs which I do not believe even the Lord knows I have to bear – I was striving away to bring her to me and to show her how lovingly I remembered her old affection.

– Well. I'll just hitch my pack up a little higher betwixt the shoulders, – for a better centre of gravity, – and trudge on.

The publishing, about which you inquire, is in good train as far as it goes, but has been held back by absorbing engagements which have not even left me time to correspond with the publishers. Scribner has taken a fancy to my SCIENCE OF ENGLISH VERSE and writes that he is " anxious to bring it before the public "; but thinks it would go much better, commercially, as a popular work than as a text-book. I am just now revolving his suggestion in this regard, and will decide in a week from now. In one form or the other the book will be pushed to immediate publication. One of his propositions is that I may pay for the plates – $375, due six months after publication – and thus own the book, receiving from him 15% on the retail price (about $1.50) of all copies sold, he to print, bind, manufacture, advertise, and publish. This is a good offer, and I hope to be able to arrange for accepting it, though it involves more capital than I command.[74]

Scribner writes that the BOY'S FROISSART is selling well,[75]

[74] According to Scribner's estimate, a sale of 1700 copies would be required to return Lanier his investment (see note 70, above).

[75] In a letter to his father, Dec. 17, 1879 (here omitted), Lanier remarked, apropos of not hearing of any review of his book in the Macon *Telegraph and Messenger*: " A special Editor's copy was sent them at my request by the

and I believe he has determined to buy also the other similar work of mine which is already in his hands, the BOY'S KING ARTHUR. I have just laid out in detail two more such books which will keep up the series most captivatingly: the BOY'S MONSTRELET (which takes up the period of French and English history just where Froissart leaves it), and the BOY'S MABINOGION,[76] a lovely collection of stories to be selected from that great Welsh collection which presents us the earliest Celtic legends connected with King Arthur.

Besides these; my FIRST COURSE IN CHAUCER; two volumes of poems, one already put together and the other in the pigeon-holes of my desk; a long study on the *Midsummer Night's Dream* in its connection with Chaucer's *Knight's Tale* and with Gabriel Harvey's *Four Letters* &c; and a work on the Theory of Oppositions in Art and Morality, as displayed in the technical and moral advance of Shakspere's later plays compared with his earlier ones, – for which all the notes, and much of the formal matter, are now in my desk; – are groaning for completion.[77]

With these heavenly visions – and many more purely artistic ones – before my eyes, you may judge of the iron patience with which I have to prepare and deliver ten lectures a week to school girls.

– But I find I am making a selfish Jeremiad in reply to your kind question.

As for your " sight of Mary's hand ", you will see from what I have said of her poor eyes that she cannot write. She has, indeed, a cruel lot, at present: she cannot read either print or music without such pain that the Doctor has interdicted both; she is not strong enough to seek refuge in activity; I am too

Scribners: and I thought surely one or two hundred copies of the book would be sold in Macon."

A favorable review, he said, had just appeared in the *Nation*. This review, appearing in the issue of Dec. 4, 1879 (XXIX, 329), declared the introduction " excellent " and the selections made with good judgment.

[76] The *Mabinogion* was published in 1881, a few months after Lanier's death. The *Monstrelet* was never completed. (IV, 370, 256.)

[77] Fragments of Lanier's scheme for a *First Course in Chaucer* and his comparative study of *The Knight's Tale and A Midsummer Night's Dream* have survived in his " Chaucer and Shakspere " (IV, 304). The " Theory of Oppositions in Art and Morality " was treated in Lectures XIV-XVI of his recently completed public series at Johns Hopkins University (III, 361-410).

busy, and the boys too young, to read to her or help her otherwise; and so she is to be condoled with.

Will you please tell Little Sissa of all these matters? My bitter experience with Aunt Jane makes me fear that some one else will go away in a reproachful silence because we have not written; and my desire never to write any but bright and cheerful letters has, I feel sure, put us in a false light before many of the family who have not the least idea of the struggle which consumption(for I have to fight that all the time in a hundred shapes and with a hundred precautions) and half-blindness and poverty and many unbreathable cares have entailed upon us.[78] If they could but have seen any one day of our common life for the last three years, no reproaches of this kind could ever have been made.

Pray give a Xmas kiss to all who are in kissing-reach of you, for us; and one specially fervent one goes to you

from

me.

To CHARLES SCRIBNER

435 N. Calvert St.
Bᵒ·, Dec. 21st 1879.

My dear Mr. Scribner:

In the course of the next week I will send you the *ms.* of the SCIENCE OF ENGLISH VERSE complete, for examination, as you desire. I note what you say as to its more probable success if cast into the form of a popular treatise than in that of a text-book; and am so distrustful of my inexperience in such matters, as against your larger outlook, that I hardly dare differ with you in opinion, though I am free to confess that I should think the text-book more likely to command a permanent steady role.

It occurs to me, however, that upon reading the *ms.* you may think — as I do, upon examining it with this special view —

[78] In a letter to Mrs. Lawrence Turnbull, Dec. 22, 1879, Mary Day Lanier spoke of her husband's " great distressing feebleness (of fatigue and of business cares) that at present is almost overpowering. . . . He is even dangerously tired– and too anxious to smile."

that a few slight changes, such as the omission of the section-numbers and a recasting of the opening chapter to a more popular form, might adapt the book to *both* purposes. At any rate, I shall be very glad to have the opinion of some other reader than myself about the book as it stands; for I have no friend competent to pronounce upon it whom I would be willing to tax so heavily.

Pray make your report as soon as you can; for in the event you should think it convertible into a popular treatise, — and should hold to that idea — I would be glad to see it published at the earliest moment.

Sincerely yours,

Sidney Lanier.

To Charles Scribner

435 N. Calvert St.
Bo: Dec. 29th 1879.

My dear Mr. Scribner:

I send by todays' Express the *ms.* of The Science of English Verse, in thirteen envelopes, Nos. III to XV inclusive, each containing fifty *pp.* These, together with the three envelopes Nos. I, II, and XVI which you now have, make the book complete.

I shall be glad to know at your earliest convenience precisely how much change in the present form would make it accord with your idea of a popular treatise. These matters have so long been familiar in my own thought that I feel sure I am not a judge of the best mode in which they might appeal to the audience of general readers whom your idea contemplates. I should be apt to assume either more, or less, acquaintance with them than is the fact.

Sincerely yours,

Sidney Lanier.[79]

---

[79] On Dec. 27, 1879, R. S. Lanier wrote to C. A. Lanier that he had recently had his photograph made and would send copies to each of his sons as a New Year's present (see cabinet photograph by J. A. Pugh, Macon, Ga., facing).

ROBERT SAMPSON LANIER IN 1879

Charles D. Lanier Collection, Johns Hopkins University

1880

To Frances L. Turnbull [1]

[Baltimore, Jan. 9, 1880?]

My dear Mrs. Turnbull:

Will you be kind enough to send me, by the bearer, Mr. Turnbull's STUDIES OF SHAKSPERE by Swinburne,[2] — if it can be spared for a short time.

I've been very ill, but am now sitting up in bed, and expect to be at my usual duties on Monday.

With cordial messages from all my household to all yours,

Your friend,

Sidney L.

435 N. Calvert St.
Friday.

[1] Lanier suffered a serious illness of about two weeks at the end of Dec., 1879, and the beginning of Jan., 1880. In a letter begun Jan. 1, 1880 (but not finished and mailed until Apr. 22), Mary Day Lanier wrote to Clifford: "Physically [Sidney] has not entered well upon his New Year,— for the week has been spent in combatting, by patience and caution, one of those frequent haemorrhages which have come but twice before in the last six months." On Jan. 9 (?) she wrote to R. M. Johnston: "Sidney is better, yet very sick; the least draw back might occasion a serious relapse. He is now relieved of the intense excitement of brain which forbade all sleep, and he eats with a fair relish. But the head is *touchy*, off in a moment; and sometimes come sharp lung pains of a flitting nature." (The letter is dated simply "Friday," but a notation thereon by Johnston adds: "Jan., 1880.")

The conjectural datings of the present and the following letters are based upon their references to this illness, and upon their partial dates, "Friday" and "Saturday." During Jan., 1880, Fridays fell upon Jan. 2, 9, 16, 23, and 30. But the evidence given above hardly indicates that he was well enough to be sitting up in bed by Jan. 2; and a subsequent letter (to Clifford Lanier, Jan. 25, 1880, below) shows that he had recovered sufficiently to go to New York by Jan. 19. Hence the date of Jan. 9 has been assigned to the first letter and Jan. 17 to the second (their contents suggesting that they were written at least a week apart rather than on consecutive days).

It was during this illness that Lanier received a Christmas gift that inspired the verses, 'To My Class' (I, 204); and some days later he received from Violet Browne, daughter of his friend W. H. Browne, the gift that inspired the poem "On Violet's Wafers" (I, 205), not mentioned in any of the letters. Her acknowledgement is dated Jan. 10, 1880.

[2] A. C. Swinburne's *A Study of Shakspere* had just been published (1879).

169

To Lawrence Turnbull

435 N. Calvert St.
Saturday.
[Baltimore, Jan. 17, 1880?]

My dear Lawrence:

As I am at my desk my wife has brought me your truly kind and thoughtful note, with the request that I answer it in her name. Your information is conclusive, in suggesting the policy of sending our young applicant [3] to Washington immediately, and I shall do that on Monday.

I am much better today, and at my usual duties: my comrade not so well.

Your lovely New Year's cards found all our hearts " receiving," and were warmly greeted not only by the little ones but by

Your friends

Sidney and Mary Lanier.

To Charles Scribner

435 N. Calvert St.
Bo. Jan'y 22nd 1880.

My dear Mr. Scribner:

(1) It occurs to me that a number of sections in the earlier portion of The Science of Verse ms. are marked in figures, this having been done while I was first arranging the work as a text-book. Under its present *projet*, these will be unnecessary, and I write to ask that you will make some entry on the ms. instructing the printer to δ all such figures.

[3] Pringle Morgan, R. S. Lanier's stepson. After being expelled from Mercer University, Macon, he had attended a business school at Poughkeepsie for a time. Then, about the middle of Nov., 1879, he had come to Baltimore and made his home temporarily with the Sidney Laniers. Several attempts had been made to find employment for him. In a letter to his father, Dec. 17, 1879 (here omitted), Lanier wrote: " He is a bright-looking young man, and I hope a practical acquaintance with working life will bring out his nature which seems to be naturally affectionate and good." After the first of the year an attempt was made to secure him an appointment at Annapolis— the subject of the present reference. (See also Lanier's letter to his father, Jan. 27, 1880, below.)

(2) Can you not arrange to sell the book in England, as with the Boy's Froissart? I think it would find a good market there; much interest upon this subject must have been created by recent kindred discussions in The " New Shakspere Society " at London. The book is a direct and conclusive answer to many questions mooted in those discussions.

(3) I understand that it is to be put immediately in hand, and published at least by the first week in March. Will you announce it in advance? [4]

Sincerely yours,

Sidney Lanier.

To Clifford A. Lanier

435 N. Calvert St.
Bo; Jan'y 25th 1880.

My dear Clifford:
                    I fear I have not written you in a long time: but it is because I have written so much to less dear correspondents. A serious illness, which was good enough to wait until the holidays before quite incapacitating me, kept me in bed during that season, and I have thus had to make up two week's work, besides keeping my regular round.

I ran over to New York last Monday night and gave Tuesday over to negotiations with Publishers and Magazine-editors. I completed the sale of my BOY'S KING ARTHUR to Scribner, which he is to publish next Xmas as companion-book to the BOY'S FROISSART. I also arranged to sell him my BOY'S MABINOGION – a collection of Welsh stories about King Arthur – as a companion-book to the others for the next year.[5]

---

[4] Lanier's letter is a follow-up to his conferences during a trip to New York, Jan. 19-20 (see the following letter). Scribner replied, Jan. 31, 1880, that the printer had been instructed to omit the figures in *The Science of English Verse*, that they would do everything possible about an English publisher, and that the book had already gone to press. He added that it would be announced in the March issue of *Scribner's Monthly*, but would not be ready for publication by the first week in March. The publishing contract (Charles D. Lanier Collection, Johns Hopkins University) was dated Feb. 12, 1880. It provided that Lanier should pay the cost of composition and stereotyping — the plates to be his property. Scribner's agreed to publish the book and bear all other expenses, giving Lanier a royalty of 15% of the retail price ($2.00) on all copies sold.

[5] *The Boy's King Arthur* (IV, 355) was published in Nov., 1880; *The Boy's Mabinogion* (IV, 370), in Nov., 1881.

We completed a bargain for my SCIENCE OF ENGLISH VERSE, and he is to push the book at the utmost possible speed so as to bring it out by the first week in March. I left with him, too, the *ms.* of " How To Read Chaucer," [6] which he is to examine and report upon immediately. I hope he will see his way clear to bring it out at once, upon a ten per cent copyright to me, he assuming all expense.

I have sent my two papers on " The New South " to SCRIB-NER'S MAGAZINE.[7] They will probably appear very soon, being just now very timely to the agricultural passion which is possessing the magazines.

I'm working on an interlinear redaction of THE BRUCE of John Barbour (Scotch poet, 14th century) and of The WAL-LACE of Blind Harry The Minstrel, which I hope to sell to ST. NICHOLAS for illustrated papers.[8]

I send you a Johns Hopkins official circular on p. 18 of which you will find an announcement that will show the nature of my class-work at the university.[9] On the next page is a very gratifying notice of the attendance upon my public lectures, which ended about the middle of last December. The numbers surprised every one.

I think I have not acknowledged yours containing check for $100 which arrived while I was ill.

[6] " How to Read Chaucer " (IV, 304n.) was rejected by Scribner, Jan. 31, 1880; it was not published during Lanier's lifetime.

[7] " The New South " (V, 334) was published in the Oct., 1880, issue of *Scribner's.*

[8] " John Barbour's Bruce " (see IV, 257) was not published during Lanier's lifetime. No trace has been found of the other paper here mentioned.

[9] *The Johns Hopkins University Circulars*, No. 2, p. 18 (Jan., 1880), announced that Lanier would give " ten expository readings of Chaucer's Knight's Tale and Shakspere's Midsummer Night's Dream in connection, beginning in the middle of January. . . . The aim of the lecturer will be to awaken an interest in the poems under review solely as works of art." The course was designed for students not majoring in English literature, and the instructor offered to give three or four preliminary sessions to familiarize them with the language of Chaucer. According to one who attended this course, it was postponed and did not begin until the week of Feb. 8 (Starke, p. 505, note 34).

See note 66, 1879, for an account of the attendance at Lanier's public lectures, referred to in the following sentence. For a fuller treatment of both lectures and class courses, see III, xii-xiv, and VII, xlviii ff.

Have you seen a poem of mine called " Opposition," [10] just out in GOOD COMPANY, a monthly published at Springfield, Mass.?

The Edison electric light is considered a failure by those who know. There has never been any difficulty about the *light*, and many scientific men have devised machinery for making that; but cheapness, and some minor details of construction, have prevented these machines from entering into common use, and it seems clear that Edison has not removed any of those difficulties. Gas stocks are firm, here, and, I believe, in New York. Edison of course advertises – in many ways not ostensibly advertisements – in order to keep up his company's spirits, but their stock is said not to sustain itself.

I am greatly distressed to know that your partner is so infirm. Is he doing better?

Tell me of Wilsie. I long to see her slim-willow figure bending about, once more. Has she quite recovered from her cough? And does she know the virtue of " Valentine's Meat-Juice "?

Your account of your visit to Sissa gives all a great yearning thitherward.

My poor Mary is wholly sick. Nothing is right within her. Her sufferings are scarcely tolerable to witness. I am wholly at a loss to know how to help her, – without money.

All here send love to you. Write me of your home affairs.

Your bro.

S. L.

To ROBERT S. LANIER

435 N. Calvert St.
Bo. Jan'y 27th 1880.

My dearest Father:

I returned a couple of hours ago from Washington, leaving Pringle to come over by a later train when he has spent the afternoon in sight-seeing. I am sorry to write that my mission in his behalf came to grief. The Surgeon

---

[10] " Opposition " (I, 130) was published in the Jan., 1880, issue of *Good Company*.

found him a half-inch shorter than the regulation height; and this seems fatal.[11]

That avenue being closed, Mary and I have been discussing the whole matter, and we are quite agreed upon two points.

(1). That a large city like New York or Baltimore, in which he would be quite away from all supervision of those interested in him, would be an unwise residence for him. In such places a boy can be so completely beyond all keeping-up with, that unless he is of the sort who can go alone he has no safety in them: and from what you write, as well as from our own observations, we judge Pringle not to have reached the autonomous stage yet. He ought therefore to find employment in some place like Savannah, or Montgomery, which is not so large as to allow his being completely lost in the crowd, but which is still large enough to keep him from rusting, – for he likes activity. These things being so, he is wasting his time, here; for, even if he should get a place, this is not a prudent location for him.

(2). We are equally clear that for many reasons he ought *not* to be in Macon.

It therefore occurs to me to suggest that it might be well to see what he could do in Montgomery. Suppose you let Clifford stow him away – as he could easily do – for a month, and try that field. Between Mr. Clopton and all the large family connection there I think it extremely probable he could find something to do.

I've been grieving over my long failure to find him employment here; but on mature thought I am satisfied it is best for him that I *have* failed. This is not the place for him.

I will write to Clifford about it, – if you think well. Meantime, suppose you consult Clifford, and let me know. I hate to see Pringle losing valuable days, here, now that I feel so clear of his course.

Your note about the two drafts is here.

Love to all from all.

Your son,

S. L.[12]

---

[11] The reference is to Pringle Morgan's examination for admission to the U. S. Naval Academy.

[12] Written about this time but not mentioned in the letters was Lanier's music

To Daniel C. Gilman

435 N. Calvert St.
Tuesday, 17th.
[Baltimore, Feb. 17, 1880?] [13]

My dear Sir:

The " complaint " is wholly unjust. The delay, – which was not so great as represented – occurred purely by accident. Near the close of my lecture, after I had been diligently watching the clock as I always do for the concluding twenty minutes, I left my notes and began reciting a conversation which had occurred between Professor Remsen [14] and myself upon the subject in hand during the same day. The suggestions made by Mr. Remsen were of great interest, and it was while absorbed in putting them into shape that the hand passed the hour without my notice. I feel perfectly sure that every one in the audience saw me watching the clock and understood how my attention was temporarily diverted in extemporaneously arranging the thoughts which were not embodied in the written lecture. To make this sure I took the opportunity this afternoon to explain to the audience that such was the case and that the delay was undesigned.

So far as I could judge, the attendance did not seem to be less today than last Friday.

Of course I regret having transgressed the limit: but the occurrence was so manifestly accidental, and the lectures have been so uniformly within bounds, that I must believe any " complaint " in the matter to have been wholly uncalled-for.

critique, "Rubinstein's *Ocean Symphony* and Emil Hartman's *Raid of the Vikings*" (II, 331), first published in the Baltimore *Sun*, Jan. 31, 1880.

The fourteenth season of Peabody Concerts began on Jan. 31, 1880. The eighth and last concert was given on Apr. 23, 1880.

[13] Conjectural dating from the fact that the only "Tuesday" that fell on the "17th" of the month during this period was Tuesday, Feb. 17, 1880, and from the fact that the complaint referred to in the letter would have been more likely to occur in a course of class lectures to students (see note 9, above) than in any of Lanier's series of public lectures.

[14] Ira G. Remsen, Professor of Chemistry at Johns Hopkins University, who had given two lectures on science in Shakespeare's time as a part of Lanier's Peabody course the previous year.

I should be very glad to have the opportunity of saying as much, or more, to the complainant.

Very truly yours,

Sidney Lanier.

To Robert S. Lanier

435 N. Calvert St.
B°. Feb. 25th 1880.

My dearest Father:

My ode went off beautifully at the University on Monday night, and I am sure you would have been gratified with the applause which came loud and long when the reading was finished, and with the individual expressions which followed. I send you a newspaper account. The reporters applied for the poem but I refused to let them have it, knowing how sadly such things lose, when the aroma of the occasion is gone. Mr. Gilman, however, desires to put it into the University Circular, and so it will reach print after all. I'll send you a copy when it appears.[15]

A pleasant commission comes today from the American Cyclopedia (Appleton's) to write an article on Johns Hopkins University.[16] I hope it may lead to others from the same source.

I have just finished correcting proof of an article of mine on The Orchestra which is to appear in Scribner's for April.[17] The proofs of my book are still crowding me for time.

[15] " Ode to the Johns Hopkins University " (I, 133), read on Commemoration Day, Feb. 23, 1880 (since Feb. 22 fell on Sunday this year), and printed in *The Johns Hopkins University Circulars*, No. 4, p. 38 (Apr., 1880).

[16] In a letter to Rossiter Johnson, associate editor of the *American Cyclopædia*, Feb. 25, 1880 (here omitted), Lanier accepted the offer to write this article— having obtained the permission of President Gilman– and said he would forward the MS in ten days. A second letter to Johnson, Mar. 28, 1880 (omitted) said that the article was forwarded " three weeks ago," but that Lanier had received no acknowledgment of its safe arrival.

An article entitled " Johns Hopkins University " (III, 411) appeared in the *American Cyclopædia Supplement* (New York, 1880), pp. 864-867. Though it is without signature and D. Appleton-Century Co. has no surviving verification, it seems beyond question to be the one written by Lanier.

[17] " The Orchestra of Today " (II, 291). It had been written and accepted for publication in the autumn of 1876.

The arrangement you propose for Pringle would never do. There *is* really no chance for him to get work which will support him, here. The salaries are too small. (1) Would *it* not do for him to return to Savannah, and make trial there? He must have come to know a good many people, and our own acquaintance there is pretty large. (2) If he should board at all, he might as well board where there is some chance for him to get work, and there is none here.

I send check for one hundred and sixty dollars, against the two hundred dollar draft. Can you help me with forty? If it is impossible, draw on me for that amount at sight, and I'll try to raise it. I'm quite pushed for some weeks yet.

We send you both our love and blessings.

Your son,

S. L.

To Robert S. Lanier

435 N. Calvert St.
Bo.   March 1st 1880.

My dearest Father:

I send you Scribner's announcement, in the Magazine for March, of my *Science of Verse*.
The ode had very great success. I hear of it often.
I am quite busy, in the lecture-intervals, with the article for the Cyclopedia, and the proof-sheets of the book, together with some negotiations by which I hope to interest the University in a plan for publishing an entire new set of the classic poets of our tongue, expurgated and arranged for use in my classes, the set to be edited by my advanced young men in the University under my supervision. If I succeed in this plan, I will have secured a much easier existence for a year or two so that I can work at a less killing pace.

These matters have kept me so completely up to all my minutes, that I have not had time to get a couple of hundred dollars which is coming to me for work, and which I need. I collected enough to pay your draft, or rather the check I sent to meet it. For this last I kept the amount in bank. I drew on you again today for $150. and will have no trouble in sending you the amount before due. The draft is at one day.

I *so* hope this is the last! I dare not speak of the distress it gives me to be troubling you with these little matters.

I wrote Harry Day yesterday about Pringle, thinking it possible he may have some work for him about the railroad office at Brunswick. I think he needs a messenger.

We hear that the road *is* sold after all.

Love to Mama.

Your

S. L.

To Daniel C. Gilman [18]

435 N. Calvert St.
Bo; Mch. 16th [17?] 1880.

My dear Sir:

It has several times occurred to me to ask if I might not be of further service to you in providing instruction for the *undergraduates* of our Collegiate Department in Rhetoric, Sentence-building, English Composition, Punctuation, and the like, with practical exercises in Essay-writing. I believe this forms part of the " Course " in every College: and I have recently seen some shrewd strokes at Harvard for turning out graduates who could not write a passable English letter.

All the instruction in my special line, so far, has been quite advanced.

Pephaps I should report that I gave the last of my first series of ten readings on Monday night; and that I had a pleasant meeting with the Science-class yesterday afternoon at four in Professor Morris's room.[19]

---

[18] Previously published, *South Atlantic Quarterly*, IV, 120 (Apr., 1905). Conjectural correction to the date from the evidence oft he third paragraph, referring to a " meeting with the Science-class yesterday afternoon." This class met on Saturdays and Tuesdays, beginning Mar. 13, 1880 (see note 19, following) ; and the second meeting would have been on Tuesday, Mar. 16.

[19] The problem of Lanier's student courses at Johns Hopkins University in the winter and spring of 1880 cannot be solved with certainty, but the surviving evidence indicates the following: (1) He definitely gave a series of ten readings from Chaucer and Shakespeare on Tuesdays and Fridays, Feb. 10 to Mar.

The suggestion above made needs no immediate consideration or answer.

Faithfully yours,

Sidney Lanier.

TO CHARLES SCRIBNER

435 N. Calvert St.
Baltimore, Md.
Mch. 26th 1880.

My dear Mr. Scribner:

It is only a few days since I wrote to the
printers asking substantially the same question.[20] You cannot
be as anxious as I am to get the book through. I have asked
them to hasten everything forward at the utmost possible speed.
The proofs are beginning to come more thickly since my letter,
and I see no reason why the book should not be ready in a few
days. I now have my Easter holiday, and can devote as much

15 — the last Friday meeting, Mar. 12, having apparently been postponed
to Monday, Mar. 15 (see note 9, above). (2) The present letter and that of
Apr. 5, 1880, below, seem to suggest that this course was repeated to another
group during March and April; but these references may be to the following
course. (3) He apparently gave a separate and distinct course on the " Art
of Expression " beginning on Mar. 13 (see D. C. Gilman to G. S. Wills, Sept.
27, 1897, MS in the University of North Carolina Library); this course was
announced in *The Johns Hopkins University Circulars*, No. 4, p. 51 (Apr.,
1880) as follows: " Mr. Sidney Lanier, Lecturer in English Literature, has
formed a class (composed of those who are especially devoted to scientific pursuits) for the study of the *Art of Expression*. This class will meet for the
study of Chaucer and Shakspere, in Room 4, on Tuesdays and Saturdays, at 4
P.M."
There is no evidence that Lanier ever taught English composition to the
undergraduates at Johns Hopkins, as mentioned in the opening paragraph of
this letter, though this suggestion was included in later and more elaborate
plans for the academic years 1880-1881 and 1881-1882.
[20] Charles Scribner had written Lanier, Mar. 24, 1880: " I write to inquire
when at the present rate of progress we may expect to issue the ' Science of
English Verse.' It seems to me that it should certainly be brought out by the
middle of April, and I hope you will spare no effort to accomplish this."
Lanier wrote again, Mar. 30, 1880 (letter omitted), saying that he had telegraphed the printers (Messrs. Rand, Avery & Co.) to push the book through
by the end of the week. But Scribner replied, Apr. 1, 1880, cautioning against
too great haste and advising Lanier not to publish without reading " revises."

time as necessary to the proofs, so that each parcel can be examined and sent by return-mail.

I have had no opportunity whatever to submit this book to any expert friend, and have often wished that I might do so before it goes finally forth, in order that I might avail myself of any suggestions which would be likely to occur to another mind, approaching the book from another direction. This being impossible, it has occurred to me that perhaps you had sent the *ms.* to be read by some specialist in these matters, and that possibly some such suggestions might be offered by him. Pray let me know if you think this worth while: and, if you do, put me in communication with your reader for the Science of Verse.[21]

To Robert S. Lanier

435 N. Calvert St.
B°. Mch. 26th 1880.

My dearest Father:

I have just written Mr. Bass.[22] I had held back my answer, hoping that I might be able to see my way clear; but it has finally seemed unquestionably wise to decline. In the first place, I have so much on hand that I could not find time to prepare such an address as I wd. wish to deliver. Again, I do not wish to take up my energies with anything not more directly in my line of thought, at present. I've had to do a great lot of miscellaneous work, lately, which, although miscellaneous, must necessarily be subjected to the criticism of specialists in departments where I am merely an amateur. Not only so, but I have had to do it in a hurry: and I have constantly felt that I might work great injustice to my self and great hurt to my aims unless I could do my work at a slower pace. Again, I should much more enjoy returning to Macon to be prominent on a public occasion at some later day when the works and plans now on foot are further developed and when I can go with more authority. I have some matters which

[21] The signature has been cut out of the MS.

[22] Lanier had been invited by W. S. Bass, President of Wesleyan Female College, Macon, Ga., to give the Commencement Address, June 15, 1880 (see Lanier's letter to his father, Mar. 11, 1880, here omitted).

I wish to set going in Georgia when I come, and I feel that people are not quite recovered from the nonsense that was talked about the Centennial Cantata.   I should like to stamp all that out with some work of universal acceptation, or at least with the weight of aims and plans universally acknowledged, so that I may be able to put forth my ideas when I come without any handicap of previous doubts.   Another year I can do all this, if matters go on: and I make no doubt the invitation will come, either from this or some other quarter.

I am putting up my mouth, as the saying is, to have you with me sometime in the late spring when Baltimore is beautiful and when my immediate pressure of work will be drawing lighter.   I could then see you with a holiday feeling upon me. Can we not arrange it?

Have you seen my article on *The Orchestra* in Scribner's for April?   And the new puff of My *Science of Verse* on the first page and following? [23]   The latter, I fear, is almost too strong.

I have just written and forwarded a little poem on *Ireland* for *The Art Autograph*, a paper to consist of photographic facsimiles of contributions by the chief writers and artists of America, and to be sold for the Irish Relief Fund under the auspices of the New York HERALD.[24]

[23] No copy of Scribner's for Apr., 1880, containing the advertisements has been located.   But the squib here referred to was undoubtedly identical with that in the issue of June, 1880, which read: "Mr. Sidney Lanier's Science of English Verse is certain to excite the widest attention and discussion.   Mr. Lanier's previous work and the thoroughness of his special study have made him a place among the first authorities to students of English literature; and the publication, by a scholar of his rank, of an entirely new theory of English prosody would be of great importance in itself.   His book is, however, more than this.   It includes critical studies of the older English poetry, which bring out admirably Mr. Lanier's accurate learning and keen appreciation of his subject, and have all the charm of his particularly attractive style.   Finally, with its strikingly suggestive review of the relations of music and verse, it opens a line of thought so original as to make this volume, if its conclusions are accepted, the pioneer of a new science and new methods."

[24] "Ireland" (I, 136).   In a letter to Arthur B. Turnure, editor of the project, Mar. 18, 1880 (here omitted), Lanier had signified his willingness to write the poem.   When the *Art Autograph* appeared in May, 1880, Lanier presented a copy to Joanna, the Irish cook of Mrs. Edgeworth Bird, who had frequently made soups for him in his illness.   Mrs. Bird wrote in her reminiscences: "he sent a marked copy of his poem for Joanna ' With the regards of her friend S. L.'   I can see her now, with tears of joy in her eyes, as she said, ' And sure, it is himself that is the gentleman.' "   (Copy, Henry W. Lanier Collection, Johns Hopkins University.)

Clare de Graffenried is here, staying with us for the few days of her Easter holiday. Did you receive all my checks for the drafts? They were sent in time to meet each one.

With great love to you and Mama.

Your

S. L.

To Virginia Hankins [25]

435 N. Calvert St.
B⁰. April 5ᵗʰ 1880.

My dear Ginna:

How long it is since I have written your name, or seen your strong up-and-down pen-strokes! To begin a letter to you makes me feel as if I had been on a protracted scout far down into Nansemond County, and were approaching your dear old Castle on the return. I do not feel any farther away from you than an hour's ride: and I do not suppose there is any possibility of setting more distance between us than this. But it is as if I were on picket duty in sight of your house: I know you are there, yet cannot leave, just now, to get to you.

I long to have something fresh from your hand, with details of you. Clifford never writes more than generalities about you,— wretched hotel-keeper that he is, who ought by virtue of his profession and surroundings to gossip like a running brook. What are you doing, and how, and where? I read with pleasure your article on Chaucer some time ago. I am now lecturing on some comparative views of Chaucer and Shakspere, at the University, and carrying a class of advanced students through a critical reading of *the Knight's Tale* and *the Midsummer Night's Dream* in connection.[26] I often think of you during these lectures.

My book on The Science of English Verse will contain some studies of Chaucer's rhythm that may interest you, and

---

[25] Excerpt previously published, *Southern Bivouac*, II, 760 (May, 1887). Virginia Hankins was still teaching school in Montgomery.

[26] See note 19, above.

I'll send you a copy. It should be out in about two weeks from now.

Mary has gone this morning to visit our son Charley in Virginia, and, I hope, to get a little strength, whereof she is sadly in need.

Write me, dear friend, of *your* Mary, and your brothers; look upon this scrawl as the merest out-cry from the midst of an indescribable whirl of work; and hold me always

Your faithful

S. L.

To Mary Day Lanier [27]

435 N. Calvert St.

Bo. April 6th 1880

Dearest Soul:

I'm just starting down to the P. O. with a load of proofs, after a very busy day, and send you this line in a monstrous hurry.

I concluded after all not to go to Boston,[28] and so will be here all the week.

Harry still has fever at night, and it seems pretty hot, but he keeps up, and is now playing cards with Father, Sidney and Miss Maggie. The latter is very pronounced in protestations of devotion to him, and begs me to convey these to you, wh. I now do. Nothing important by mail. We do *not* play the Heroic Symphony this week, but Schubert's Symphony in C.

The house is all one Great Sahara without you,— to all, and specially to

me.

[27] This letter is addressed to Rapidan Station, Culpepper Co., Va.

[28] Lanier had thought of going to Boston to be near the printers, Rand, Avery & Co., in order to speed up the publication of *The Science of English Verse* (see Charles Scribner to Lanier, Apr. 1, 1880).

To Charles Scribner

435 N. Calvert St.
Baltimore, Md.
April 21st, 1880.

My dear Mr. Scribner:

I have just sent off the last page-proof of the Science of Verse.

The Table of Contents seems to look very bare to me. Do you think it would be worth while to arrange a more minute Table, consisting of the Chapter-headings in large print, with the page-headings (which can be all obtained from the plate-proofs) attached, in smaller type? Thus

"Chapter I.   Investigation of Sound &c   21
     Verse a Phenomenon of Sound, 23; Four pos-
     sible Sound-relations, 25; Duration, Intensity,
     Pitch, Tone-color, 29; Indefinite Comparison of
     Sounds, 33; Definite Comparison, 35; Examples
     of exact co-ordination, &c &c &c.   "

If you think well, this could be prepared at your office (but of course at my expense) in an hour or two, and forwarded to the printers, who could send me proof and receive it back before the book is all printed.[29]   It gives a much more attractive outlook at the beginning of the book; and would be thankfully hailed, as an abstract of the work (which every such treatise *should* have) by librarians, reviewers, and others whose business compels them to know the general drift and argument of books which they cannot possibly read minutely.

I hope you have selected a binding with some attractive figure or other on the front cover; even a plain band or line relieves the dead blank of the otherwise unbroken surface.

I write hastily to catch this mail.

Sincerely yrs.

Sidney Lanier.

[29] Lanier's analytical table of contents was included in *The Science of English Verse* and is reproduced in the present edition (H, 13-19).

P.S. I enclose the Table of Contents. If the plan proposed causes delay, or seems otherwise inadvisable to you for reasons not occuring to me, please forward this corrected proof to the printers.

S. L.

To Robert S. Lanier

435 N. Calvert St.
Baltimore, Md.
April 22nd 1880.

My dearest Father:

I am just getting through with the final part of my long and tiresome job of proof-reading, and hope for the last batch of " plate-proofs " of my SCIENCE OF VERSE to-morrow. The book has been a very troublesome one to print, requiring type of a kind not ordinarily in the font, for the musical demonstrations in connection with rhythm &c.

Mary came from Virginia last Tuesday and reports our Charley to be a great-limbed and great-souled fellow.

I have been expecting to run over to New York and Boston for several days but have not been able to get away. I have many matters in both places needing attention.

I want to make a loan of two hundred dollars for sixty days, payable *here.* I enclose a draft, accepted by me, undated. Will you sign as drawer and endorser, and date, and ask Mr. Plant to discount it, forwarding proceeds to me as soon as possible? I thought of sending the draft directly to Mr. Plant,– in order to save you the trouble of seeing him,– and would have done so but it occurred to me that might seem strange to him.

I am hoping for some comparative rest in May. God bless you. I write hastily —

Your loving

S. L.

To Robert S. Lanier

435 N. Calvert St.
Bᵒ.   May 1ˢᵗ 1880.

My dearest father:

Your letter brings great delight to all here, with the prospect of seeing you at an early date. I shall be ready for you any time this month. My journey to the north has been postponed, mainly for the reason that my engagements here are such as to render only a flying trip possible, and this is so unsatisfactory, as compared with what I might accomplish if I had a week or two in Boston and New York, that I have decided to wait until after the 15ᵗʰ June, when my schools all close. The proofs of my *Science of English Verse* are now all corrected, and Table of Contents drawn up; and the book should be out within a week from this date. It has been a tedious work, to get so many complex musical diagrams, with all manner of minute points to be watched, correctly through the press: and no one would believe the labor of reading these proofs, without trying it. I am quite prepared for a little relaxation.

Little Sidney says he wishes you could bring your garden with you! The poor boy longs for some out-door life and greenery. By the first of June I expect to deposit him and Harry with Charley in Virginia, for a whole summer on the Taliaferro farm.

And now for some directions which may facilitate your journey here. There are two roads from Washington to Baltimore; the Baltimore & Ohio (on the Tickets " B. & O."), and the Baltimore & Potomac (" B. & P."). When you buy your ticket, observe whether it brings you by the B. & O., or the B. & P., and let me hear, so that I may know at which station to meet you. The " Charles Street Station " (also sometimes called the " Union Depot "), on the B. & P. Road, is but four minutes' walk from my house. The B. & O. station, though not so near, has a convenient street-car line a short way off. For fifty cents you can send a night-telegram after buying your ticket stating *hour of your departure* from Macon, and whether ticket brings you by B. & P. or B. & O.

I am sorry Mama cannot come.   But perhaps she will enjoy being alone with Pringle, after his long absence.

How I yearn to see you, my dearest father!   You must not be shocked at seeing a very hatchet-faced cadaver, with a grey beard and hair, when you arrive: [30] spite of appearances there seems a fund of strength in me which will likely turn out many a book yet.

We all send love and speeding wishes.   Your enclosure, check 199.²⁵, safe, and arrangements very acceptable.

Your loving

S. L.

To Clifford A. Lanier

435 N. Calvert St.
B⁰. May 1ˢᵗ 1880.

Dearest Clifford:

Have you ever thought of the infidelity and irreligion of dyspepsia?   This suffering which begins every morning a few minutes after breakfast – is it not the Day of Judgment, does it not come for the ungodliness of the stomach which has broken the law of the Lord, is the stomach exempt from the process by which the wise man's " *delight* is in the law of the Lord " (see Psalm I) and when it sins is it not one of the " ungodly " who, it is declared, " shall not stand in the judgment " (*ibid.*, verse 5) ?   To find out the law of the Lord so far as it concerns the plan of digestion in general and of one's own digestion in particular is a condition-requisite to all religion; for a man cannot properly perform a single one of the Ten Commandments, – no, nor even understand the Eleventh – until he has done it.

It has always been the most inscrutable, – as it is certainly the most dreadful, – fact in the world's economy to me, that throughout the whole round of nature's operations there is absolutely no relaxation in favor of the most innocent ignorance.   If a baby whom Nature has never given the least chance

---

[30] R. S. Lanier's visit to Baltimore was called off (see Lanier's letter to his father, May 15, 1880, here omitted).

to learn the properties of fire puts a finger in the flame, it will be unhesitatingly, quietly, remorselessly, burnt off; and a man may be praying for his worst enemy, but if he kneels in a draft to do it nature has not a whit more regard for his bronchial tubes than if he were feeling for the enemy's heart to stab it, and will take him off with a galloping consumption as debonairly as if he were an assassin.

The unpardonable Sin, which Nature never forgives, is ignorance of her laws.

If I had not preached this sermon to myself, I could not to you. None so vigorous as he who has lately awaked!

And now for the personal application.

(1) It is an inexorable law of nature to all stomachs except those which differ very greatly from yours, that a cup of coffee in the morning at breakfast followed by a glass of milk is as if a man should tie a Guelph and a Ghibelline, or two cats, together in a bag, and look for peace. The keen pains in the heart are well-known results of this compound. A man might as well hope to reverse time by turning the hour-glass as to fight this with liver-pills.

Therefore:

If you take coffee in the morning, take no milk, either with the coffee or as a separate beverage. And if you take milk, leave off the coffee. But there are many conditions of the stomach in which milk is not tolerable. If experiment reveals such a condition, stick to the coffee. Do you know " Alke-threpta," a preparation of cocoa without the oily trouble? It is a delightful drink when made of just *half* the strength given in the printed directions, and is very sustaining, with none of the nervous complications of coffee. Ask for a package of it at your grocer's, and get Willie to see it made for you, at least by way of experiment for a few meals. What a quantity of work these slim muscles of mine have done on it, in the last six months! Instead of the water in the printed directions, use milk *and* water, half and half.

(2) Fried sweet potatoes are as so much leather to the ordinary stomach. To yours, they are wholly obstructive and unmanageable. Cast them utterly away. Instead thereof, eat every morning an egg—two eggs, if possible—boiled one minute, or, at most, two.

(3) Cultivate brains, first boiled, then browned with the yellow of egg; and, in general, phosphoric foods. Bacon is certainly the worst meat you could take, for breakfast or any other meal. The work of digesting it is so great as to make even negro-laborers " lazy "; this so-called laziness being simply the lack of energy beyond what is being exerted in disposing of the food eaten. Broiled beefsteak, mutton, or brains (either hog-brains or beef-brains), is the food for you..

(4) Thus, of the five articles you mention as constituting your breakfast, four are certainly sinful; and as for the fifth – " bread " –, if it is made with the " Baking Powders " in ordinary use it is in all probability worse than the other four combined.

(5) Your dinner needs to have both its head and tail lopped off before you can consider it even scotched. For a man with weak digestion, soup is as hurtful at the beginning as " rich pastery " at the end. Look upon both, for the present, my dear boy, as you look upon stealing and cheating. I have not time to enlarge upon the effect of liquids taken at the beginning, or rich sweets at the end, of a meal: but any modern work on digestion will show you how they are hurtful.

(6) On the other hand you *should* take some supper; for no man with nervous strain upon him should pass so long an interval as from your dinner-time until breakfast next morning without support. It must be fifteen or sixteen hours: a huge overtax of the system, and sure to make you rise with a sense of great fatigue in the morning.

(7) Anything less than eight hour's sleep, for a worried man, is a crime.

(8) A walk of " three or four blocks at dusk," as the daily quantum of a grown man's exercise month in and month out, is simply insult and flat blasphemy to the Lord. The law of vigorous exercise as the inexorable condition-requisite to every function of every organ in the body is a law which every man of ordinary experiences comes to know clearly by the time he is thirty. To break it is indefensible by any arguments which would not also justify suicide.

These considerations result in urging upon you the following, or some similar, regimen.

BREAKFAST. Either " Alkethrepta," as above, or Coffee, with

sugar, but without milk; two eggs, dropped into boiling water a minute, not more than *two* minutes at most; brains cooked with yellow of egg, or beefsteak, or mutton; dry toast, not hard nor too dry, made of bread guiltless of all patent baking-powder; with a very small pat of butter. (Bacon, sweet potatoes, milk —three Deadly Sins.)

DINNER. Fish,*without* Worcester or any like sauce; poultry only rarely; but for steady work, roast beef, or mutton; vegetables, but no turnips, no cabbage, no " greens "; along with dinner, milk, if it agrees with you at all; no ice-water, and very little water of any sort; at the end, apples, or pears, or peaches, or any available fruit (except strawberries, for *me*, at least, and, I suspect, for you also) by all means, but never any pastry whatever. No stimulants before, during, or after, dinner, for *you.*

TEA. Toast, a little butter, and either Oolong, or English Breakfast, or some good Black Tea. Never Green tea. If you take the tea, no glass of milk afterwards. Try milk instead of tea, occasionally.

SLEEP. From 11 to 7 if possible. At whatever limits, eight continuous hours.

EXERCISE. Nothing will do for you save to go to your livery-stable keeper and bargain with him for a saddle-horse two hours a day by the month. Do not dream, my dear Clifford, of expense in this matter: you might as well eat your own flesh to reduce your butcher's-bill. Get your horse, and a good one, and canter freely, every day, as a religious duty, beginning with an hour, increasing to an hour and a half, then to two hours. Walking is wholly insufficient for your purpose.

And now, finally: try this for one month only. Try it, not perfunctorily, but as a repentant devotee, who has wounded his Lord with many sins and would be more tender hereafter. If, in the prescribed month, you do not come to have a new life, a healthier heart as well as body, and muscles such as a man should have, together with entire absence of heart-disease and unconsciousness of stomach or liver, – I will agree to eat bacon and fried sweet potatoes for the balance of my life. And as for the Tutt's Liver Pills and the White's Iron and Liver Tonic —medicines which can no more substitute good food and exercise than swearing at the blue skies can bring rain—you will wish that the respective patentees thereof were submerged each in a butt of his own decoction until he learned the sin of deluding men into the belief that any arrangement is possible for breaking the Law and avoiding the Penalty. When will we learn that for the physical sinner there is absolutely no sanctuary of refuge? Even the plan of salvation does not profess to whiten a man from these transgressions; and no amount of sanctification will help the liver and stomach of a man who sleeps too little, exercises none, and eats indigestible food.

Try it, Clifford. Ask Willie if this isn't all true. Her affection for Tutt will make it a struggle: but she is a woman of unlimited good sense and reasonableness (ahem: if I don't get a kiss for this some day, there is no justice in the female economy) and will, I doubt not, take charge of the programme and see it carried out. If she would ride with you, in the afternoons! though, I – ah – – I don't know exactly – ah – how a lady of her – of her – ah – size would appear on the ordinary horse; the horse is an animal of great though limited, powers, and is regarded as trying to the figure of corpulent persons. You might put her aboard the train, and canter alongside.

Whatever you do, dear Clifford, God bless you and her, says always

Bro. S. L.

To Charles Scribner

435 N. Calvert St.
Baltimore, Md.
May 6th 1880.

My dear Mr. Scribner:

An article of mine on " The Orchestra to Today " in the April SCRIBNER s has excited wide interest, and I am asked from several quarters to write another paper giving information for practically carrying out the recommendations in the first, particularly those urging that women should abandon the exclusive cultivation of the piano and learn the purely orchestral instruments. In meditating upon this paper thus asked for, I find the matter growing quite beyond all possible bounds of a magazine article, for any useful treatment; and many ideas which I have long cherished, growing out of my own experience in the Orchestra, cluster about the subject; until what seems to me a most useful and profitable hand-book has taken definite shape.

I have drawn off a synopsis of its Chapters, in their main topics, which I herewith enclose.

Will you be kind enough to read it carefully over, as a *projet* for a next-autumn book, and give me your ideas? So far as I know, nothing of the sort exists, and I believe it might have a wide sale and permanent value.[31]

Sincerely yours,

Sidney Lanier.

To Charles Scribner

435 N. Calvert St.
Baltimore, Md.
May 11th 1880.

Dear Mr. Scribner:

(1) Several editors &c. would like to have my name in their copies of The Science of Verse, and if you will therefore send me twenty (20) copies I will distribute them advantageously to the book's interest.[32] I enclose also a list of other editor's copies which may be sent by you.

---

[31] A six-page MS entitled "The Orchestra" has survived (Charles D. Lanier Collection, Johns Hopkins University) which seems to be connected with the project here referred to. (See II, 333.)

On May 7, 1880, Scribner replied that the "Handbook for Orchestras" seemed like a formidable undertaking, but they would give it careful consideration. He added that *The Science of English Verse* would be published on May 12, and that they would be glad to have suggestions for review copies. (In a letter to his father, May 15, 1880, here omitted, Lanier gave the actual publication date as May 13.)

[32] Among others, Lanier sent copies to the following: G. H. Calvert (now in the Redwood Library, Newport, R. I.), Salem Dutcher (see Starke, p. 501), D. C. Gilman (Johns Hopkins University Library), P. H. Hayne (Duke University Library), O. W. Holmes (see Holmes to Lanier, July 24, 1880, below), R. M. Johnston (Enoch Pratt Free Library, Baltimore), Clifford Lanier (see Lanier's letter of May 20, 1880, here omitted), R. S. Lanier (see Lanier's letter of May 15, 1880, here omitted), Joseph LeConte (see his letter to Lanier, Nov. 6, 1880), H. W. Longfellow (Craigie House, Cambridge), T. R. Lounsbury (see Lanier's letter of May 18, 1880, below), J. W. McCoy (Johns Hopkins

(2) Please forward the King Arthur *ms.* to me, so that I may edit the remainder and prepare the introduction. If you will name a day by which the copy must be in your hands complete, I will work up to it. Please make it as late as will consist with leaving you ample time for printing. The *ms.* will be returned to you ready for the press punctually at the appointed date.

(3) The Handbook for Orchestras &c would be a small work, of say 250 pp., and not at all a " formidable undertaking." My idea of the specimens of music accompanying it was to print them in the form of an unfolding map, the separate parts for instruments to be detached by cutting them off at the creasing of the pages, if desired. This latter however is mere matter of detail. The book would be about the size of the Science of Verse, all complete.

Sincerely yours,

Sidney Lanier.

To Edmund C. Stedman [33]

435 N. Calvert St.
Baltimore, Md.
May 14th 1880.

My dear Mr. Stedman:

Some days ago in searching for a special letter of our beloved Bayard Taylor I came upon one which dwelt on *you* so much and so tenderly that I felt myself moved to snatch a moment from the frightful bread-and-meat work which has owned me so long, for the purpose of sending a line that might bring me some little word of your health and personal concerns.

Herewith goes to you a copy of my *Science of English Verse,* just published by Messrs. Scribner's Sons, which may interest you, since, in finding physical principles of classification for

University Library), J. L. Spedding (see note 105, below), Herbert Spencer (see Spencer to Lanier, Nov. 29, 1880), and E. C. Stedman (see Lanier's letter of May 14, 1880, below).

[33] Previously published, *Critic*, I, 293 (Nov., 1881.)

all possible phenomena of verse, it seems to place those phenomena in their true relations, – for the first time, so far as I know. I hope you may find the book a sound one, – all the more because it was so indescribably irksome to write. To go back, and interrogate one's own artistic procedure, and formulate in cold propositions for the general mind processes which are so swift and instinctive as those of the poet's technic: none but the artist knows the appalling constraint of this task. Indeed I could never have found courage to endure it, save from the fact that in all directions the poetic art seemed suffering from the shameful circumstances that criticism was without a scientific basis for even the most elementary of its judgments, and I had some poems which I hope soon to print but which I could not hope to get understood generally, without educating their audience.

I will be very glad to know of your work and your welfare, and am always

Sincerely yours,

Sidney Lanier [34]

TO CHARLES SCRIBNER

435 N. Calvert St.
Bo. May 16th 1880.

My dear Mr. Scribner:

Please send me the outline of the Orchestral Handbook.[35] I think I will submit the possible pros-

---

[34] Stedman replied, May 17, 1880 (Laura Stedman and G. M. Gould, *Life and Letters of Edmund Clarence Stedman*, New York, 1910, II, 154-155): "I always have borne you most tenderly in mind, and am now doubly indebted to you– for your letter and for the early copy of your volume. . . .

" Let me congratulate you, & all of us, upon the heroic industry, & the profound rhythmical analysis, which have enabled you to render so complete this most scientific– this wholly unique work."

But he added: " I should much prefer recognizing the truth of your novel and wonderful analysis, in my own works, after having written them by instinct, than to attempt, *a priori*, to sing in accordance with laws which govern the poet willy-nilly "– thus indicating the same misunderstanding that was to annoy Lanier from all sides: the assumption that *The Science of English Verse* was a handbook of rules for writing poetry.

[35] Scribner had written, May 14, 1880, that the Orchestra Book seemed admirably planned, but they could not accept it because they saw no market for it. The outline was returned in his letter of May 17.

pects of it to some music-publisher, who would have direct connections with its audience and would know its chance for a market. I suspect, myself, it is a doubtful book: but the subject-matter has such a fine parallelism with that of *The Science of Verse*, and would enable me to develop so many principles hinted at therein, that I should like to write the work, if I can possibly make it pay only expenses.

As to the *Science of Verse*: the printing and make-up seem to me admirably suited to the book. The size of type selected is perfect, and the pages are particularly pleasant, I think, to the eye, besides having a purely *visual* attractiveness in the light and varied sensation produced by the musical diagrams. I see nothing to suggest, in this matter of general make-up, — unless possibly in the direction of darker bindings, and of this I am not sure. The *Socrates*,[36] published by you last year, in black with slight gilt relief, is, I think, the most taking book I have ever seen in external appearance, — of inexpensive publications.

A glance over the *Science of Verse* in its compact form shows me several points where I should like to modify the form of expression, and two at least where I could impart great interest to the matter by a considerable development into directions hitherto unexplored. What chance will there be for this? If not immediately *here,* how in England? And have you yet made any definite arrangement with the publisher to whom your letter referred? [37]

The book, altogether, pleases me, and I am perfectly sure that while sales will probably be slow at first it will soon take its place as the standard work on the whole subject and be a marketable book for a long time.

Very truly yours,

Sidney Lanier.

[36] Probably W. W. Goodwin's *Apology of Socrates*.

[37] Scribner had written, May 7 (in reply to Lanier's inquiry of May 5, 1880, here omitted), that he had already interested a London publisher in *The Science of English Verse* and had sent him a set of the sheets.

In answer to the present inquiry, Scribner replied, May 17, 1880, that all improvements should be reserved for a possible second edition: " It would not pay, I think, to *improve* the plates simply for the English edition, and might cause dissatisfaction among American purchasers of the book." (See also Lanier's letter to Scribner, Aug. 13, 1880, and note 65, below.)

P.S. I have not had the time to examine the contract; but I expect to spend several days in New York, within the next three weeks, and we will then arrange it.

S. L.

To Charles Scribner

435 N. Calvert St.
B⁰. May 18th 1880.

My dear Mr. Scribner:

Please send me twenty more copies of *The Science of Verse.* I wish to use some ten more in sending to specialists in this country and England and Germany. The other ten should be charged to my account, as I shall present them to personal friends.[38]

My desire to enrich future editions with any suggestions of reviewers that may be worthy causes me to ask also that you will send me such notices and reviews of the work as fall under your eye. Of course many of these will be silly; there are really very few persons in the world whose studies have led them into such directions as would entitle them to " review " the book, yet every newspaper reporter will of course consider himself amply qualified, and many of these have old scores to pay off for the beating they received about the Centennial business.

Still, a good suggestion sometimes crops out from a silly notice, and it seems my duty to look for such.

Sincerely yours,

Sidney Lanier.

---

[38] (See note 32, above.) Scribner replied, May 19, 1880, that since " an unusually large number of free copies " had already been sent out, he hesitated to send any more for distribution unless they were of special importance. He added that very few notices of *The Science of English Verse* had appeared so far; when enough accumulated, he would forward them.

To Thomas R. Lounsbury

435 N. Calvert St.
Baltimore, Md.
May 18th, 1880.

My dear Sir:

I was particularly pleased with some passages in the Introduction to your charming edition of *The Parlament of Foules*. Will you regard as a slight manifestation of this pleasure the copy of my *Science of English Verse* which I have ventured to send you by this mail? On pp. 147 *et seq.* I have reduced some Anglo-Saxon rhythms to musical notation, which, with the treatment of Chaucer's rhythm, may have a special interest for you; and I should feel genuinely obliged by any suggestions which might occur to you upon examining the general system developed in the earlier pages.[39]

Of course the incidental explanations as to Anglo-Saxon sounds &c. are to be considered mere compromises in favor of the brevity and simplicity necessary for a work meant — as the Preface explains — to be at once a popular treatise and a general student's handbook.

Very respectfully,

Sidney Lanier.

To Charles Scribner

435 N. Calvert St.
Bo. May 20 / 80.

Dear Mr. Scribner:

I understand from the two items of the enclosed bill[40] that the *only* charges made for " alterations and

[39] In his reply, May 29, 1880, Lounsbury said: " I was especially interested in what you said about the Anglo-Saxon versification, which is indeed the only part of your book I have yet had time to examine with any care. I recognize myself as having been one of that numerous host who have ben making the statements in regard to it which you criticise. I am inclined to think that you are right, & that Everybody else has been wrong: but revolutionary opinions must fight their way to acceptance. I don't propose to give up any of my ancient prejudices without a battle for them with myself."

[40] On May 18, 1880, Scribner sent Lanier a bill for the plates of *The Science*

corrections" are the $5.50 for music and $15 for "Altns &
Plates" &c. To these I should not object, though I do not
exactly comprehend all the particulars of them. The two items
immediately preceding — " 205 Hours – – 50 – – 102.50," and
" Comp. Music 150 hours – – 60 – –90 "— appear to be *additional* to the general cost of composition & electrotyping embraced in the first four items, and I do not understand them:
but of course you *do*, and I confidently leave the whole to you.

As to the letter you enclose, and herewith returned: the assertion that the book was " delayed in consequence " of the " fearful slaughter " of my alterations is untrue, and would be
impertinent if it were not stupid. Nothing is easier than to
test it by comparing the *ms.* with the printed book. With the
exception of the Preface, and of the first thirty pages, —
wherein I did find some changes advisable and ordered second
revises, — the alterations made by me were few and not extensive, and need not have delayed the book at all.

The sentence on p. 2 of the letter beginning "He said of
his own accord " is a deliberate perversion of a remark made
in another connection, so as to give it the very opposite effect
to what was really meant. When the first chapters were being
corrected, I saw that time could be *saved* by instructing the
compositors to disregard certain italics and capital letters which
I had employed for the purpose of calling the attention of
younger students to certain words and phrases worthy of memo-
rizing or otherwise prominent: — the book having been written, as you remember, upon the idea of making it a text-book,
and only afterwards judged by you as suitable for a popular
treatise also. I therefore wrote the printers to instruct the
compositors accordingly, in order *to preclude the necessity of
alterations* in proof; and this was done. Yet the very remark
which I added in explaining to them *why* these instructions
should be given the compositors, is here adduced " as if in
apology " for new alterations which delayed the book! It was
made in explaining a course which was to save, and which *did*
save, alterations in proof.

of English Verse and a letter from Rand, Avery & Co., the printers, to whom
Scribner had written asking a reduction in their bill. This statement has not
been found, but a later one has (see note 2, 1881).

You will understand how strenuously I worked at getting back the proof as quickly as possible, when I tell you that a good part of it was carried by me personally at three o'clock each afternoon — having been received at nine o'clock the morning of the same day, and corrected — to the railway station, where I placed it in the hands of the postal agent on the fast mail reaching Boston the next morning. The proof thus sent, being mailed to me in the afternoon of the day before it reached me, really did nearly all its travelling by night; and thus not only have my corrections and alterations *not* delayed the book, but even my distance from the printers delayed it very little. The second revises ordered in the early part of the proof-reading came before the music-part of the work was reached, and before the use of the same sorts of music-type became necessary. They did not, in point of fact, delay the next proofs, for after this galley-proofs began to be sent.

This is too small a business to merit so much talk: but it seems proper that I should not be placed in the position of having needlessly delayed the book, when the fact is that nearly the whole delay arose from the inadequacy of the printers' resources, and that I was making the whole of my other work bend to the sole aim of getting the book out as early as possible.

Although the bill is more than one-third larger than the original estimate, yet I leave it entirely to you, and, if you find it just, will accept it. Whatever amount you decide upon will be paid when due.

I expect to be in New York next week, and will bring the contracts with me for execution. There are some details whose force, on a hasty glance, I do not understand, but which I doubt not a few minutes' talk will enlighten me upon. I am very much occupied, and may be delayed here until the school-year closes, — June 10th — , after which I am quite free, and shall be in New York for some weeks.

Very truly yours,

Sidney Lanier.

To Lawrence Turnbull

[Baltimore, May 25, 1880?] [41]

My dear Lawrence:

I have drawn up a note and mortgage in favor of Mr. McCoy for the additional sum offered by him last March to forward the publication of my "THREE COMPARATIVE STUDIES OF CHAUCER AND SHAKSPERE."

The copyright, herein mortgaged, entitles me to fifteen per cent on the retail price (two dollars) of each copy of *the Science of Verse*, sold, for the next fourteen years; and is probably worth many times the amount secured.

I have written Mr. McCoy that this note and mortgage are deposited at your office, and have asked, – if the arrangement is entirely satisfactory to him, – to send the check to you, for delivery to me upon the final execution of the documents.

Will you be kind enough to look over my mortgage and see if it is a good one under your Maryland laws? I drew it up in advance because I knew you *would*, and I didn't want to trouble you. It is such a one as I would draw in Georgia.

With all good wishes,

Your friend,

Sidney Lanier.

45 Lexington St.
Tuesday morning.

---

[41] Conjectural dating from the evidence of the surviving mortgage here referred to (Charles D. Lanier Collection, Johns Hopkins University), covering a loan from J. W. McCoy for $250.00, payable Mar. 15, 1881. It was executed May 27, 1880, and May 25 was the "Tuesday" immediately preceding.

A letter to an unnamed publisher — probably J. B. Lippincott & Co. — dated Feb. 10, 1880 (omitted from this edition), seems to be concerned with negotiations for the publication of the projected volume mentioned in the present letter as the purpose of this loan (see also note 51, below).

To Charles Scribner

435 N. Calvert St.
Baltimore, Md.
May 30th 1880.

Dear Mr. Scribner:

A letter comes to me from Messrs. Rand Avery & Co. inquiring as to some missing proofs from their file — which they seem to have supposed I might have — and adding: " The publishers have called for the proofs to verify our charge for alterations " &c.

This gives me real distress, with the fear that I am the occasion of embroiling you with your printers; and I write to beg that, unless the sum in dispute is quite large, you will let it go. I should very much prefer to give them the benefit of any doubt, and pay any reasonable amount, to causing any trouble of this kind.

I begin, too, to fear that my last letter may have been needlessly harsh in expression, for I remember that I was indignant at the idea of being made a scape-goat for the delay after my extraordinary efforts to prevent it. If I said anything unjust, I will be equally quick in making amends.

I will not be able to get to New York until my duties end here, — on the 10th June. I hope to be there on the 11th.

Sincerely yours,

Sidney Lanier.

To Annie A. Fields [42]

435 N. Calvert St.
Baltimore, Md.
May 30th 1880.

My dear Mrs. Fields:

Your invitation to Gambrel Cottage is very pleasant and tempting, but – remembering other possible guests – I ought to send you word immediately that my visit to

[42] Excerpt previously published, Starke, p. 348. It is not clear when Lanier

Boston cannot be very definitely fixed, and that even when I come I can't hope to do more than dine with you, or some· thing of that sort, as I shall be working like a beaver, – and ought therefore naturally to be in a dam, – which is certainly an expressive synonym for a hotel.

Don't therefore make any allowance for more than a pop-call from me, unhappy ghost as I am and must be for yet many days.

I am astonished – and, I confess, a little taken aback – that you, and several others who have written me about my book, find it abstruse. Almost every one refers to the " patient scholarship " of it; – and you can fancy that this is perplexing, when I add that the book was planned and written from beginning to end during the five weeks of my last summer's vacation, in the mountains of Virginia, where I had no works of reference save what I carried in my trunk. I have no more claim to " scholarship " than to the throne of England, and you cannot imagine how it embarrasses me to find newspaper notices thus shoving upon me responsibilities I can never hope to support and am even unambitious to deserve. To be an artist, and preach the gospel of poetry: that is the breath of *my* life.

Mrs. Lanier sends you cordial messages, and we both hope for more meetings, and longer.

Faithfully yours,

Sidney Lanier.

became acquainted with James T. Fields, the Boston publisher, and his wife, the author of occasional verse and a famous literary hostess. On Mar. 9, 1880, Mrs. Fields had written Lanier: "I have a room ready for you here which I trust you will occupy when you come to Boston. Then perchance we can have some music too! As well as talk about the divine art of poetry– Mr. Fields has not been well and we are seeing no ' company ' but we are all the more grateful for a friendly visit now and then. . . . Pray tell Mrs. Lanier that I cannot forget her!'' Lanier's letter is in answer to a second from her, not found.)

To Gibson Peacock [43]

435 N. Calvert St.
B^o., June 1st 1880

My dear Mr. Gibson:

I have just read your notice of the Science of English Verse, and cannot help sending a line to say how much it pleases me. It seems a model of the way in which a newspaper should deal with a work of this sort which in the nature of things cannot be fairly described without more space than any ordinary journal can allow.[44]

I was all the more pleased because I had just read a long notice sent me by the *Evening Post's* " critic " which, with the best intentions in the world, surely capped the climax of silly misrepresentation. It is perfectly sober to say that if this " critic " had represented Professor Huxley's late treatise on the Crayfish as a cookery-book containing new and ingenious methods of preparing shellfish for the table, and had proceeded to object earnestly that the book was a dangerous one, as stimulating over-nicety in eating, – he would have been every whit as near the truth. Indeed, on thinking of it, I find this is a perfect parallel: for he " objected " to the Science of Verse on the ground that it had a " tendency . . . to exaggerate . . . the undue attention already given to . . . the pretty fripperies of ingenious verse-making "! If the book has one tendency beyond another in this respect, it surely is, as you sensibly say

---

[43] Previously published, *Atlantic Monthly*, LXXIV, 192-193 (Aug., 1894); reprinted, *Letters* (New York, 1899), pp. 59-61.

[44] No file of Peacock's newspaper, the Philadelphia *Evening Bulletin*, has been found for this period. The review in the New York *Evening Post*, mentioned following, appeared in the issue of May 24, 1880. The critic completely misunderstood the book and was guilty of the " silly misrepresentations " cited by Lanier, though his comments were well intended, as the following excerpts will show: " As a masterly critical analysis, we do not undervalue the work either for its worth or for its interest, and we are full of admiration for the patient scholarship which has produced it; but it is a book for the delectation of scholarly readers, rather than for the education of anybody to the appreciation of abstruse meters. . . . [It is] the work of a scholar whose learning embraces both a mastery of the science of music and a loving familiarity with the poetic literature of the language." (For a further account of the contemporary reception of *The Science of English Verse*, see II, xxxi ff.)

in your last paragraph but one, to make real artists out of those who study it, and to warn off all scribblers from this holy and arduous ground.

But this is the least offense. Although three of the very mottoes on the Title-page (namely, those of Sir Philip Sidney, of King James, and of Dante) set up the sharpest distinction between Verse and Poetry — between mere Technic and Inspiration, and although the preface presents an ideal of the *poet's* (as distinct from the *versifier's*) mission which culminates in declaring the likeness of all worthy poets to David (who wrote much poetry but *no verse*), – while, further, the very first ten lines of Chapter I carry on this distinction to what one would think a point infinitely beyond mistake, – in spite of all, the " critic " gravely makes, and as gravely discusses, the assertion that " in Mr. Lanier's book, . . . *poetry* . . . is a mere matter of pleasing sounds and pleasing arrangements of sounds "!

This would be a curiosity of woodenness, if it were not still obscured by another assertion: that this Science of Verse originates in " a suggestion " made by Edgar Poe as to the " division into long and short syllables ", – which suggestion, he says, " is the key to Mr. Lanier's system "!

It would be quite as accurate to say that Professor Huxley's argument from the transition-forms of the horse in proof of the evolution of species was suggested by King Richard the Third's exclamation of " a horse, a horse, my kingdom for a horse ".

— The Easter-card with the lovely design of Corn has been in my work-room's most prominent niche, and is the constant admiration of my visitors who always quickly recognize its propriety. Tell Maria, – between two kisses, – that nothing but outrageous absorption could have made me fail so long to acknowledge what has given us all so much pleasure.

—But this letter will make you perspire, with the very sight of its five pages; and so, God bless you.

Your friend,

Sidney L.

To John F. Kirk [45]

[Baltimore, June 15, 1880]

x   x   x   x   x   x   x

I have been studying science, biology, chemistry, evolution, and all. It pieces on, perfectly, to those dreams which one has when one is a boy and wanders alone by a strong running river, on a day when the wind is high but the sky clear. These enormous modern generalizations fill me with such dreams again.

But it is precisely at the beginning of that phenomenon which is the underlying subject of this poem, "Individuality," [46] that the largest of such generalizations must begin, and the doctrine of evolution when pushed beyond this point appears to me, after the most careful examination of the evidence, to fail. It is pushed beyond this point in its current application to the genesis of species, and I think Mr. Huxley's last sweeping declaration is clearly parallel to that of an enthusiastic dissecter who, forgetting that his observations are upon dead bodies, should build a physiological conclusion upon purely anatomical facts.

For whatever can be proved to have been evolved, evolution seems to me a noble and beautiful and true theory. But a careful search has not shown me a single instance in which such proof as would stand the first shot of a boy lawyer in a moot court, has been brought forward in support of an actual case of species differentiation.

A cloud (see the poem) *may* be evolved; but not an artist; and I find, in looking over my poem, that it has made itself into a passionate reaffirmation of the artist's autonomy, threatened alike from the direction of the scientific fanatic and the pantheistic devotee.

x   x   x   x   x   x   x

[45] Previously published, Mims, pp. 316-317, from which the present text and date are taken (MS not found). In addition to this fragment a surviving note (Edwin Mims Collection, Johns Hopkins University) contains a further extract from this letter: "With inexpressible delight I have got a singing-pen in my hand again, after eight months of bookmaking and lecture making and teach— x x x"

[46] "Individuality" (I, 139, "The Cloud"), rejected by Kirk, editor of *Lippincott's Magazine*, was not published until after Lanier's death.

To Robert S. Lanier

B⁰·, June 19th 1880.

My dearest Father:

I have had a considerable attack of fever, which has quite disabled me for ten days past and has sadly interfered with my work. I am better today, and expect to start to New York tomorrow night, but may be delayed until Monday. A manuscript, which I hope to sell, had to be finished, and I have been working at it pretty steadily in spite of the fever, though it has been up hill indeed. It will be done, however, by tomorrow night.

I enclose a notice of the *Science of Verse* from the Boston *Courier*,[47] just sent me by a friend. I do not know the author. My expectations have not been at all for any immediate recognition of the book. Newspaper Critics in general will of course be completely in the dark: and there are really very few persons living who happen to have made any studies in this direction far enough to qualify them for really advancing an opinion about it. But, that the book will slowly make its way, no one can doubt. It sets at rest, upon a basis of pure physical fact, a large number of questions which have hitherto rested upon bases of mere moonshine.

I have received an official letter from President Gilman announcing my re-appointment as " Lecturer in English Literature " for 1880-81, at a salary of one thousand dollars. The prospect of a professorship is completely clouded by the fact that one of the Associates already has a department of English,[48] and there is really not full work for two, – under the present system. I could soon *make* work enough for more

---

[47] The review in the Boston *Courier*, June 6, 1880, was highly favorable. It began: " Mr. Sidney Lanier has written an epochal book. Whether or not it at once attracts all the attention it deserves and even if all that it contains be not immediately accepted or require modification, the laws which he lays down will have to be received as the only adequate and intelligent ones possible in these premises." And concluded: " The whole work, in fact, abounds in evidences of a fine erudition. . . . It is a fresh source for pride in American literary scholarship."

[48] A. S. Cook was giving regular classes in Anglo-Saxon and Shakespeare (see *The Johns Hopkins University Circulars, December 1879-September 1882,* Baltimore, Md., 1882, *passim*).

than two, if I were in charge; but my ideas are all revolutionary, while the Board are all cautious and slow-going.

I had hoped to be able to break off entirely from work for a week or two: but cannot take a single day. The need of money interferes.

I am glad to see a movement to make Uncle Clifford Senator. But has not Bacon all under-hold with the Legislature? He seems the most popular man in Georgia with that body; while I fear that Uncle Clifford is personally unknown to a great number of the members, in the quietness of his life. I shall hear any items of the combat with great interest.[49]

Col. Johnston has ridden by, bringing Aleck. Stephens, with whom I had a little chat. We are asked to dine with them tomorrow.

I must get back to my *mss.*   God bless you.

Your

S. L.

To CHARLES SCRIBNER

[New York, June 26, 1880?] [50]

My dear Mr. Scribner:

I am feeling so unwell this morning that I have determined to go immediately down to Coney Island for a breath of fresh air; and therefore write to ask that you

---

[49] A political scandal was precipitated in Georgia when in May, 1880, Gen. John B. Gordon suddenly resigned from the U. S. Senate, and the charge was made that he had resigned to accept the presidency of the state-owned railroad, then controlled by the unpopular ex-Gov. Joe E. Brown. Neither Lanier's uncle. Clifford Anderson, nor his friend, A. O. Bacon, was appointed to fill the unexpired term of Senator Gordon. Instead, Gov. A. H. Colquitt appointed Brown, and the cry of corruption was raised. In the ensuing State Democratic Convention Bacon presided and Anderson led the opposition to Colquitt's renomination. The name of Lanier's uncle was even offered for governor, but he refused to split the party and instead was nominated and elected Attorney General of the state. Lanier's references in this and ensuing letters to his senatorial campaign are somewhat misleading.

A. H. Stephens (mentioned in the following sentence), formerly Vice-President of the Confederate States of America, was a close personal friend of R. M. Johnston.

[50] Conjectural dating from the evidence of the following letter, which indicates that Lanier was in New York from Wednesday, June 23, to Monday, June 28; and from the partial date, "Saturday morning."

will retain the *mss.* left with you until Monday, when I will call, — probably about 11 A.M.

I was too ill the other day, when I saw you, to be able to give you any idea of the plan of this book — the " Three Comparative Studies of Chaucer and Shakspere." [51] That is, in brief: to bring it out in as cheap form as may be consistent with attractive appearance — say not over $1.⁵⁰ or $2.⁰⁰ —, looking for a *general* market (1) among all that large class of persons now interested in the new views of modern Shakspere scholars and (2) among all academic students pursuing English Literary courses — to which latter class this book offers several matters and facilities not elsewhere found —, and, for a special audience, (3) to those whom I shall have occasion to address, in lectures on a number of subjects developed from these six works of Chaucer and Shakspere, and who will comprise audiences in several parts of the United States. At the beginning of each of these series of lectures, I shall request each of the audience to buy this book and come with it in hand to each lecture. I am now making arrangements for extended lecture-courses like this in help of some struggling Library Societies of Georgia.

This last use of course precludes me from owning any share of the copyright; for, necessarily, I would seem like a charlatan, — to begin a course of lectures with asking people to buy a book in the sale of which I was interested. Thus I do not wish to make any profit from it; I will be obliged only to get some sort of return for the time actually spent in writing the book; and, with these views, I am willing to sell the entire work for three hundred dollars.

Sincerely yrs.

Sidney Lanier.

St. Denis Hotel.
    Saturday morning.

----

[51] See " Chaucer and Shakspere " (IV, 304) for the preface — dated Oct., 1880 — and the introduction to this textbook which was never published. Scribner's rejection was probably given orally. Lanier also tried, unsuccessfully, to place his book with D. Appleton & Co. and with another publisher not indentified (see his letters of July 17 and Nov. 12, 1880, below).

To Robert S. Lanier

435 N. Calvert St.
Bᵒ. June 29, 1880.

My dearest father:

I went to New York on Wednesday last, but was taken anew with a villainous fever on my arrival, and, after fighting this desperately until Monday — five very lonesome and struggling days — I was driven by fear of serious evil to crawl out of bed and get me home. I arrived last night, and, what with May's good tendance and my homoeopathic doctor's skill I'm greatly better this morning, – though not yet free from my enemy. I am enjoined to rest profoundly for some days.

I fear we shall be driven out of Baltimore by the frightful heat and malarious air. A friend has written us of a lucky vacancy just happened at West Chester where we can get board at six dollars a week apiece for Mr. Day and Mary and me. West Chester is a fine climate, and would help us both. I think it very likely I will write and engage the place tomorrow.

I'm glad you are going to Sister's, and only wish we could have a happy meeting with you there. I shall be greatly distressed if you have any trouble in arranging the Plant note. Let me know.

We both send love to you both. How does Uncle Clifford's senatorship look, as time progresses?

S. L.

To Ephraim Keyser [52]

[Baltimore, July 3, 1880?]

My dear Mr. Keyser:

I want at least two copies of the bust; and a sudden occasion has arisen for me to get *one* of them in the greatest haste, for a friend who is leaving to go abroad on the

---

[52] Conjectural dating from the fact that July 3 was the first Saturday after Lanier's return from New York (mentioned in the second paragraph).

Keyser's bust of Lanier had been made during May and June, 1880. A para-

15th of this month. Would this be possible? It would add greatly to my already great obligations. Please let me know, immediately.

I've been very ill. I went to New York, fell sick – or rather *more* sick, for I had been in bed before starting, for some time — staid 'five days, getting worse every day, and had finally to crawl home, without accomplishing anything whatever. I'm still confined to the house.

I suppose Tait is gone, by this time.

With cordial messages,

faithfully yours,

Sidney Lanier.

435 N. Calvert St.
Saturday.

To Charles Scribner

435 N. Calvert St.
Baltimore, Md.
July 15th, 1880.

Dear Mr. Scribner:

I send today by Express the entire copy of *The Boy's King Arthur*, ready for the printer.

(1) I have directed that the dialogue, instead of being run in solid as in the text used, should be paragraphed as in the *ms.* at page 5. Please examine this, and see if you do not agree

graph in the Baltimore *Sun*, June 10, 1880, announced that it was complete and on exhibition at Meyers and Hedian's, and described it as a great advance in the sculptor's work: " The execution is almost perfect – the broad, simple lines having the genuine character of an antique, which, while perfect in bringing out the portrait and expression, avoids every unnecessary detail. . . . Besides being an excellent portrait [it] is highly idealized and full of poetry."

Ephraim Keyser (1850-1937) was a Baltimore sculptor who had recently returned from Rome to execute some commissions. To his studio Lanier was brought one day by his friend John R. Tait. In a reminiscent letter to J. A. Fisher, Sept. 13, 1883, Keyser told the sequel: " The noble cast of his features, the soulful expression of his eye led me to express a wish to model his bust ere I was personally acquainted. . . . I had the pleasure of a number of sittings, during which he expressed many a noble sentiment & and charmed me by his eloquent & polished conversation. . . . I was only able to see him during the 7 or 8 sittings he gave me & the couple of times I called on him when he was unable to be out."

with me. The method of running it in solid gives the book a heavy appearance; and a boy, particularly, is always attracted by the look of a page broken with question and reply &c. If you should think otherwise please change the direction on p. 4, accordingly, and also that marked (4) in the instructions "to the foreman of composing room" sent outside the first envelope.

(2) I found, on making a somewhat closer calculation, that the book would be too long. It should be shorter, if possible, than the Froissart. I therefore cut out some twenty six pages from the earlier part, and about the same number here and there from the succeeding parts. It should now make a little over 400 pp. of the Froissart size. But I ought to add that I have no means of making this estimate very exact, and would be glad to have it verified by your more precise methods.

(3) I have remodelled the book, and brought the whole work together in various ways, so that the *ensemble* is now, I think, much more striking.

(4) The notes have been given, as often as possible, in brackets containing the explanatory word in italics and inserted along in the body of the text, thus reducing the number of footnotes to the minimum. I have confined the annotation almost entirely to explanations of old terms; upon the principle that the fewer notes in a boy's book the better.

(5) The INTRODUCTION will be sent some time in the course of the next four weeks, unless wanted earlier.

(6) It will be best to send me galley-proofs of the book, at least for the first hundred or two pages, until I get all the proper names and other minute items fairly straight with the compositors. The proof will be returned always on the following day.

(7) I place in the Express package the envelope of notices of *The Science of Verse*, which I forgot to return.

Very truly yours,

Sidney Lanier.

To Clifford A. Lanier

435 N. Calvert St.
Bo. Md. July 17/80

My dearest Clifford:

I have been buried in work ever since your letter (with enclosure as stated) came. I had contracted with Messrs. Chas. Scribners Sons to let them have at least half the ms. of the " Boys King Arthur " wh they are bringing out as a holiday work for next Christmas, companion book to the Boys Froissart – by the middle of this month, in condition for the printer. Although sorely beset with fever, I could not bear the idea of being behind time & thus of breaking the good record for promptness I have so long enjoyed. So I went at it, and in spite of the fever, & of the thermometer capering about 95 to 98, I got it ready in time & triumphantly expressed it to them at the appointed day.

Upon the heels of this came a somewhat elaborate paper of mine on the " New South " wh. is to appear in the Sept. Scribners, & wh., at my request, was condensed from the two papers I had written on this subject into one. The condensation was a troublesome job: but I have managed to finish that also.[53]

And upon the heels of this I had to formulate & write down a very comprehensive scheme of a course in Eng. Lit. involving a number of my text-books, wh. I am trying to interest Appleton & Co. in publishing.

This is just finished, & I am taking the earliest moment afterward to send you a kiss for your good & brotherly response to my letter.

We have sent all our boys to the house of our friends, the Taliaferros in Va. and they have already toughened into hard little mountain men, – we hear, – as well as gotten rid of their distressing sore throats and other ills.

I wish with all my heart that I cd come & meet you & Father & Sissa & all the rest. But this is on second accounts

[53] Two versions of " The New South " have survived (see V, lvii). For the negotiations with D. Appleton & Co., mentioned in the next paragraph, see the following letter.

impossible, & I must turn away from it. On Tuesday next
Mary & Mr. Day will go to W. Chester, Pa, – the only spot
within our means – for a two mo's stay. The place has suited
us before, & we hope for great accessions of strength there. I
am expecting to be idle for the first time in a couple of years:
& the prospect is simply ravishing. My muscles & nerves seem
to have been completely overworked, & to have lain down, like
an omnibus horse in the street, saying dumbly, Beat me if you
choose, – but I simply cannot go another step. The D^{r.}, says
that this rest is absolutely necessary: & I have found a means
of accomplishing it Address me here, until further notice.
As I cannot write much, pl. send this letter to Father, if he is
not with you. I am sure you will both be glad to know that
for the next mo. I am to be wholly idle & free from care. God
bless you all.

S. L.

To D. Appleton & Co.

435 N. Calvert St.
Baltimore, Md.
July 17th 1880

Messrs. D. Appleton & Co:

Dear Sirs:
Your letter of the 10th, signed " D. A. & Co. by
J. M. ", in relation to the *ms.* entitled " Three Comparative
Studies of Chaucer and Shakspere ", is evidently written in
ignorance of the arrangement under which the *ms.* was left
with Mr. [A. B.] Bunce. That was: that I should write off in
detail the plan of a course in English Literature, of which these
" Comparative Studies " &c form one of the text-books, so that
this *ms.* might be examined with reference to its place in the
general scheme. A letter containing the outline of such a plan
would have been sent you immediately, to accompany the *ms.*
into the hands of your reader, but has been delayed by a severe
illness, from which indeed I was suffering at the time of my
interview with Mr. Bunce.
I send herewith the plan referred to. Permit me to ask with

some earnestness that you will closely examine the principles therein set forth, with a view to publishing the entire series of text-books which, if those principles are sound, ought to be issued. After long and mature thought upon the matter, I feel satisfied that this course of study, if properly brought forward, would soon become simply indispensable in the education of every American youth; and this judgment, though originally based upon *a priori* reasoning, I find amply supported by recent experience with advanced students in Johns Hopkins University.

Very respectfully yours,

Sidney Lanier.

P. S. I will ask you to preserve the accompanying òutline; I shall make it the basis of a magazine-paper in a short time.[54]

S. L.

---

[54] The " outline " appended to this letter (18 MS pages) was entitled: " A COURSE IN APPLIED LITERATURE." The aim was to teach the " art of English expression " by providing the student with the best possible stock of (1) idiomatic English words, (2) general illustrative facts, and (3) literary forms. For this purpose Lanier proposed a series of textbooks. For (1): the volume on Chaucer and Shakespeare now under consideration; and a similar collection of " typic 15th and 16th century prose," including Sir Thomas Malory, Lord Berners, Roger Ascham, and others. For (2): six " primers " in Biology, Botany, Chemistry, Physiography, Astronomy and Philosophy — to be written by specialists. For (3): a further textbook to be written by Lanier " (indeed already partly provided for among my notes) which shall set forth, analyse, and in various ways discuss. . . The Editorial; the Scientific Essay; the Popular Magazine Article; the Lecture . . . ; the Address; the State Paper; the Sermon; the Play; the Poem, — Ode, Sonnet, Drama, Epos, &c, . . . each discussion being illustrated with specimens of the most perfect English work in that kind."

No part of this elaborate scheme ever materialized except the Chaucer and Shakespeare text, and even that was not published during Lanier's lifetime. (See IV, 000. For related schemes see his letters to Gilman, July 13 and Dec. 17, 1879; to James, Sept. 15, 1879; to Clifford Lanier, Dec. 21, 1879; to Scribner, June 26, 1880; to a publisher, Nov. 12, 1880.) Appleton's answer has not survived.

To Waldo S. Pratt [55]

435 N. Calvert St.
Bo; July 19, 1880.

My dear Mr. Pratt:

It is a genuine pleasure to have a word from you, and particularly to know that you have been looking for me.

It is now nearly six weeks that I've had a villainous fever, which has finally become the disgust of my doctor and the opprobrium of all medicine. Nothing seems to have the least effect on it. If it goes on it must result in overturning the most fundamental concepts of philosophy: for it is apparently without cause and without end, – though it certainly had a beginning, – and it is self-existent, – though a parasite.

Day and night it remains, calm, inexpugnable. I am satisfied that nothing ever acquired a state of existence so wholly imperturbable and elevated beyond the powers or the prayers of men, – except perhaps one of the grand gods of Lucretius, whose nature

> Ipsa suis pollens opibus, nihil indiga nostri,
> Nec bene promeritis capitur nec tangitur ira. [56]

In truth this last line seems almost allegorical, in this connection; for *bene promeritis* may well enough symbolize the mild homoeopathic suasives with which my Fever has been appealed to; while *ira* admirably represents the heroic doses of allopathic truculence with which it has been fought; but with the former *nec capitur*, with the latter *nec tangitur*.

Seriously, I've been ill enough; and your imagination is all I can rely on – for words are here simply exasperating – when I

---

[55] Excerpt previously published, Starke, pp. 403-404. Waldo Selden Pratt, a fellow in æsthetics and the history of art at Johns Hokins University, had attended Lanier's lectures in Hopkins Hall in the autumn of 1879 and his classes on Chaucer and Shakespeare in the spring of 1880. Several times during this period he was a guest in the Lanier home, occasionally joining in duets for flute and piano. In June Pratt went to the Metropolitan Museum of Art as an assistant curator. He later distinguished himself as an author and professor of music history.

[56] *De Rerum Natura*, Book II, 650-651 — inaccurately quoted.

tell you that about three weeks ago, thinking a change might help me, I managed to crawl down to Charles Street Station and *went* to New York, – and took to bed as soon as I reached the hotel, there, – and tossed thereon for four days with a fairly flaming fever, – and finally had to crawl back to Baltimore, without having accomplished a single stroke of business, without having seen a single picture or friend, without having heard a single crash of the horns and violins, – for which I longed unspeakably.

Since I reached home, I've been very hard at work. I had promised the Scribners to have ready for the printer by July 15, the *ms.* of my " Boy's King Arthur " – an edition, for boys, of old Sir Thomas Malory's *Morte d'Arthur*, which they are bringing out for the next Xmas holidays as a companion book to my " Boy's Froissart " of last year. I could not bear to be behind time, and so in spite of the fever I buried myself in the work and triumphantly forwarded it on the appointed day.

But the doctor has decisively ordered no more of this; and so on Wednesday, 21st, my wife and Mr. Day and I are to leave for West Chester, Pennsylvania, a pretty little town about thirty miles from Philadelphia, where we will spend a couple of months.

But I keenly wish to run again to New York, – largely drawn thereto by you and your wonders fair at the Museum; and you need not be surprised at seeing me, any day in a couple of weeks from now. It depends entirely on the disappearance of my fever, which today seems to be flickering a little as if it *might* go out.

The boys were sent to Virginia three weeks ago, and appear to have become a sort of combination of monkey and centaur already; for, by all accounts, they live either in the tops of trees or on the backs of horses. They are at a farm-house, among the mountains; and declare that they are in Paradise.

Mrs. Lanier enjoyed your letter with me, and sends you all manner of cordial messages. To us both, Baltimore seems to have lost a great many inhabitants since you left. Pray send us something about your goings-on, often: although we saw much less of you than we desired, when you were here, still it was a comfort to know that you *were* here; and we find it a great *dis*comfort now that you are gone.

Letters will reach us addressed to "West Chester. Pa." I am sure the boys would send you affectionate messages; whereto pray add those of

Your faithfully,

Sidney Lanier.

FROM OLIVER W. HOLMES [57]

Beverly Farms Mass. July 24th 1880

My dear Sir,

I thank you very cordially for your kindness in sending me your interesting and original Essay on English Verse. I have everything to learn from it, for though I have been writing verse all my life, as M. Jourdain had been talking prose, – not exactly without knowing it, but certainly without studying the mechanism beforehand of what I was going to write – I know precious little of the technicalities of metrical construction. As your Essay must be studied and not merely skimmed over, like so many of the books I receive, you will not expect me to write critically about it before having had time to "weigh and consider," as Lord Bacon tells us to, all that is new and distinctive in a work which has every appearance of being a patient and exhaustive study of the subject.

I am tempted to mention two small incidents in my own experience suggested by your Treatise. — I have a copy of one of my own poems in the handwriting of Edgar Poe, with some pleasant comment I think on its metre.[58] I do not know why it was not printed with other criticisms of his – all I know is that it was given to me by the late Mr. Robert Carter. The poem is one entitled " The Last Leaf " which you may have met with, as it is often reprinted.

[57] Lanier's letter accompanying the copy of *The Science of English Verse* here acknowledged has not been found. Two of his letters to Holmes have survived (Aug. 3 and Nov. 7, 1880) among the papers of the late Justice O. W. Holmes, deposited in the Library of Congress, but they were not accessible for the present edition because of the war. The contents of Lanier's lost letter and that of Aug. 3, however, are indicated by Holmes's replies (July 24 and Aug. 11, 1880), here printed.

[58] See Holmes's note on the history of the poem in the special illustrated edition of *The Last Leaf*, published by Houghton Mifflin & Co., 1895, p. [56].

The other fact is that I printed a short article a few years ago on the relation of the length of verse to the natural rhythm of respiration.[59] I traced the " fatal facility " of the octosyllabic verse to the circumstance that each time, in reading it, consumed one natural expiration. Even in unarticulated – or rather mentally articulated-reading, we follow something of the movement of audible reading. All other verses but the octosyllabic will interfere with the ordinary rhythm of respiration in average individuals – so my experiments indicated.

I hope to be able to appreciate your conscientious labor more thoroughly hereafter, but I have too little leisure to follow out many subjects which interest me and which deserve more time than I can give them.

I am, dear Sir,

Yours very truly

O. W. Holmes.

To Francis F. Browne [60]

West Chester, Pa.

July 31, 1880.

My dear Sir:

I have been prevented by illness from sooner acknowledging your letter, with its accompanying copy of *The Dial*.

I think there can be no doubt whatever that nearly all the phenomena of verse would necessarily be wholly inappreciable by a person always deaf. In determining such a question, the four possible sound-relations enable us to arrive at very clear results. For example, it is manifest that a person always deaf could not conceive differences in the (1) Intensity, or in the (2) Pitch, or in the (3) Tone-Color, of sounds, any more than a person always blind could conceive differences of a

---

[59] " The Physiology of Versification," published in the *Boston Medical and Surgical Journal*, XCII, 6-9 (Jan. 7, 1875).

[60] Previously published, *Ex Libris*, V, No. 3 (Johns Hopkins Univ., Mar., 1936). Francis Fisher Browne, journalist and author, had formerly edited the *Lakeside Monthly* (1869-1874), then the *Alliance*, and in 1880 founded the *Dial*.

corresponding nature in colors. This being so, all those verse-effects which are referable to Intensity, Pitch, and Tone-Color – namely, (1) the higher orders of rhythm, (2) tune, and (3) rhyme, alliterative and the like — would seem to be *ultra vires* here. The other sound-relation, – Length, or Duration – might be approximately conveyed to a deaf person through parallel conceptions of sight: the person might, for instance, be taught to associate definite portions of time with each *printed word* in a poem, by beating the actual rhythmic movement with a finger or baton before his eye, appropriating a definite beat to each syllable and conveying to him that he is to *see* (rather than to hear) *that* syllable during *that* beat, and so on. Thus conceptions of "primary rhythm" might be impressed upon him through the sense of *sight*.   I believe I have somewhere mentioned in the ' *Science of Eng. Verse* ' that we can receive rhythmic impressions through any of the senses.

This is quite analogous to the conception of a complex painting by a man always blind. He could obtain some primary ideas of the *forms* in the painting; but of the different hues, the lights and shades, the values, the effects of related colors, he could not by any possibility have the least conception, in the absence of that sense which is the prime originator, or at least channel, of such ideas.

I thank you for your notice [61] of my book, and am very glad to be in communication with every one interested in these matters. The work on *The Science of Verse* was indeed wrung out of me: I have no desire ever to write anything but poetry, and keenly feel that I go to all else with only half my heart: but the reference of all verse-phenomena to three physical principles of classification seemed to be a discovery from which a genuine scientific theory of Verse could be developed, for the first time in the history of man; and of course a possession of this sort always burns the pocket of one's conscience until it is fairly given forth to one's fellows.

Very truly yours,

Sidney Lanier.

[61] The review appeared in the Chicago *Dial*, I, 55-58 (July, 1880). For excerpts from this long and favorable critique, see II, xxxii, n. 30.

To Robert S. Lanier

West Chester, Pa.

Aug. 10, 1880

My dearest Father:

Your letter of Aug. 7 is just arrived, and I
hasten to assure you that in a hasty reading of Mary's letter –
which was probably written, indeed, under some momentary
lowness of spirits — you have received an impression of our
state of health much more dark than the facts warrant. It is
true that I have not succeeded in breaking the singular fever
which has caused me such daily distress for two months past;
and the necessity, or rather the desire, of nursing me has
added a very heavy weight to Mary's condition, which will
soon require all her attention to be given in other directions;
yet a quiet view of the whole situation does not present anything more than reasonable ground for some regret that both
of us should be under the weather at once. My fever holds on;
yet I am up at my usual hour every day, have as much appetite
as ever, am apparently as strong as ever except in the periods
of exacerbation, and show not the least sign of any more
trouble in the lung than has existed for five years past. My
doctor thinks the fever a result of overwork, not of *mental*
overwork but simply of the continued strain of muscle and
nerve involved in sitting at the desk for a great number of
hours a day through a long period; and he declares that with
absolute rest he has no doubt of my pulling through. My own
belief is nearly the same; but I am aware of an element which
I feel sure has a great influence in the matter, indeed I would
not be surprised if it were not the cause of my woe. This is
the nervous strain of *waiting*. For two years past – since I
have become in health to study at all – I have had such a rush
and storm of ideas demanding immediate expression, and have
had to put aside such an enormous proportion of them in
favor of small daily duties which physically limited me to a
book or two a year, that I have been continually jarred and
shaken with ever-recurrent shock and resistance, like a steamboat's frame with the pull and push of the walking-beam.
Especially wearing has it been, to do the work for which I care

least, and to be continually crushing back poem after poem –
I have several volumes of poems in the form of memoranda
on the backs of envelopes, odd slips of paper, and the like!
while I addressed myself to such work as seemed to offer more
immediate return in the way of money. This may seem intan-
gible; but an amount of nervous strength is given out in mere
dumb endurance of this sort which far exceeds that lost in
physical labor. If I could write nothing but poetry for the
next two years — which means if I had five thousand dollars —
I would be in vigorous health by October next !
— But the chances are strong that I will be, anyhow. While,
as I have said, my fever still gives me great distress — it is
attended with a peculiar *malaise*, a misery in every bone — yet
I seem to have lost no ground, but on the contrary am a little
better than a month ago. I have had three or four horseback
rides within a week past, though of course short and easy
ones. As soon as Mary is safely past her crisis, which should
occur now at any day, I expect to run over to New York and
consult the best physician I can find there, – unless, of course, I
should be then decidedly better. I went to Philadelphia last
week, and gave Dr. Lippe a full account of my case. He is
the physician, you remember, who treated me when I was so
ill at the Peacocks' in '76, and who sent me to Florida from
there. I am taking his medicines daily, and the *malaise* seems
on the whole somewhat lessened.

Thus there is no reason to feel mournful about me. I assure
you I have many a year's work in me still. As for May, she
has borne her trying situation with a fortitude not to be described. You would be surprised to see the quantity of daily
labor she has been doing, since we have had our own establishment; and this has never ceased during the days she has had
to nurse me and to carry her own burden. She has been wonderfully free from the troubles usually incident to her situation; but her old enemies, the chills, have proven perfectly
inexorable, and the very inexorableness of them is enough to
wear out the strongest spirit. She is seldom depressed, and
generally shows the brightest of faces. Her " mournful " tone,
in the letter you mention, doubtless was more in the nature of
a lament over her coming inability to nurse me, than anything
else.

Do not think of coming on before October. Then we shall probably be cosily esconced in our house at Baltimore, and should hope for you to see our great lovely boys; moreover the climate will be favorable. *Now*, Baltimore is unendurable: the heat, the dust, the musquitoes, and the malaria, contend for victims, there. I do not expect to return before the last week in September, and will not, then, unless my duties call me. We should take such delight in having you at our own house! and have been all the time looking forward to next autumn for our reunion. I am glad you went to Alabama; it was much more enjoyable than any possible journey this way at the present season. So I beg you arrange, if possible, to get away in the fall, and husband all energies and resources during the rest of the summer to that end.

The proof-sheets of my " Boy's King Arthur ", which The Scribners will bring out as a Christmas book and companion volume to the Boy's Froissart, are now coming to me, and give me a little anchorage of work every day. My article on " The New South " is to be in the next Scribner's Magazine, I believe.

But I must now stop. I look with great interest upon Uncle Clifford's campaign. God bless you all,

Your son,

S. L.

FROM OLIVER W. HOLMES

Beverly Farms, Mass.
August 11th 1880

My dear Sir,

       Your letter was not one word too long – I hope mine will not be too short. I could not fail to be much interested in what you wrote and gratified with the pleasant way in which you spoke of my metrical compositions.

I can not lay my hand on the number of the " Boston Medical and Surgical Journal " in which my article referred to was printed, – being at the seashore for the summer and rarely visiting Boston. I will write, however, and try to obtain the number of the Librarian of of our Boston Medical Library, or of Dr J. C. Warren one of the Editors. As soon as I can get a copy I will send it to you.[62]

With many thanks for your polite letter, I am, my dear Sir,

Yours very truly

O. W. Holmes.

To LAWRENCE TURNBULL

West Chester, Pa.
Aug. 11, 1880.

My dear Lawrence:

Your letter brought us most welcome tidings of people about whom we longed to hear. I should indeed have written specially to evoke some account of you all, but since we came here I've been too good-for-nothing to set pen to paper save under the direst necessity. The curious fever which seems to have taken such a fancy to my house of clay still lingers, in spite of all the actions of ejectment which several learned counsel have brought against it. The fatal defect in all the proceedings apparently is the difficulty of serving process; and the right party does not seem yet to have been brought into court. In short, the physicians cannot name, or account for, the things. One certainty, however, emerges clearly: that it is nothing serious. I go about as usual every day, eat with customary appetite, have no lung-symptoms indicating trouble there, and seem in average health otherwise.[63]

[62] On Aug. 20, 1880, Holmes wrote that he was sending a copy of his article (see note 59, above).

[63] With reference to Lanier's account of his illness in this letter, Mary Day Lanier wrote to Frances (Mrs. Lawrence) Turnbull, Aug. 27, 1880:

" I am quite certain he did not tell Mr. Turnbull how absolutely unimproved was his condition.

" The joy of Baby's coming [R. S. Lanier, II, born Aug. 14], of my safety, and of the tender new treasure (which he enjoys with a fervor & gentleness which few *women*, even, feel for such unconscious infancy) stimulated him for a day or two. Since, I have watched him, as he has moved around in his unwearying care of me, with my heart so strained that it has been hard to avoid hurting what I was longing to bless. He is too ill for me to dare to talk to you, *now*, of what I see & feel regarding him. I hardly think he was worse four years ago, before we went to Florida. I live— only by saying to myself

My poor May is still struggling with her old-time chills, though she moves actively about and keeps up a bright face. She has been free from many of the ills commonly incident to this trying time. We look every day for the little him or her who is to come out of the Far Country.

The proofs of my " Boys King Arthur " – the companion work to the Boy's Froissart, which Charles Scribner's Sons are to bring out for a Xmas book – are now coming to me, and give me a little daily modicum of work. Beyond attending to these, I do almost nothing.

— Your trouble with the poem [64] came from an initial misconception of the sense in which I use the word " forgive." The Lord's Prayer, for example, runs: " Forgive us our sins as WE *forgive* those who sin against us." In my poem, Shakspere and Socrates and the rest are " those who sin against us "; and it becomes thus not only our right but our duty to " forgive " them. Your mind, at the start, took the forgiveness to be as from Above, not as between equals.

But, going beyond this, my meditations long ago brought me to a point of view from which " forgiveness " becomes a term that can be used in the most reverent sense as from man to the Lord. We are so constituted that by our very natures when a keen blow falls the first result is a quick feeling of resentment. It seems to be a perfect spiritual analogue to the physical reflex action which makes the frame *jump*, at any sudden sting. Now this instinctive resentment asks not – indeed has no time to ask – who is the author of the blow which arouses it. That author may be man or God. In the case of the latter, the separate steps of (1) the first vengeful feeling, (2) the inquiry who dealt the stroke, (3) the discovery that

---

' The worse he is, the quicker must be your recovery; you cannot nurse him if your spirit fails *now.'* . . . And I try to . . . thrust back the fearful forecasting of the day of wo. O friends! I read it all in the Sculptor's moulding of his likeness– it was too strong a revelation for my shrinking Soul– But, no more.

" He is to-day almost in bed from acute bronchitis. We fear he cannot remain in this climate & possibly he may return to the empty house in Bo. where, altho if warmer, other risks, of lonely illness & irresponsible attendance, will meet him. . . .

" *Of course* I do not let Sidney know how ill *I* find him."

[64] " The Crystal " (I, 136), published in the *Independent*, July 15, 1880. Lanier had been paid $20.00 for this poem. (See W. H. Ward to Lanier, July 23, 1880.)

it came from the Lord, (4) the conquering and crushing away of the sense of wrong when one is conscious that one deserved no such pain, — these constitute, I think, a true act of " forgiveness " from the lower to the higher being.

In truth, I am not sure but this is the only " forgiveness " which can properly be called a virtue.

Without pursuing this idea, however, I think your difficulty with the poem will certainly disappear if in beginning to read it you recall the sense of the word " forgive " in " as we forgive those who sin against us."

—   I will ask you to execute a little commission for me. I send by express today to the Receiving Teller of The National Bank of Baltimore a check for deposit, together with my bankbook. Will you please call for the bank-book and keep it for me? I shall be sending other funds soon.

May joins me in all affectionate messages to you and your wife and the little fairies. We long to see you, and hope always for a day when we may be as near you in daily communications as we are in spirit. Write me when you can, and know me to be always

faithfully yours,
Sidney L.

To Charles Scribner

West Chester, Pa.
Aug. 13, 1880.

My dear Mr. Scribner:

(1) A long illness, from which I am recovering slowly, has prevented me from doing any except immediately pressing work, and for this reason I have failed to make any move at all towards pushing the *Science of Eng. Verse* in England. I write therefore to ask if your correspondent is doing anything to this end, and if the matter has yet been brought to the attention of any publishers besides the one you mentioned. I should be very glad if some arrangement for sale of plates could be made.[65]

---

[65] Scribner replied, Aug. 16, 1880, that he had not secured an English publisher and indeed had not pushed the matter " as you seemed confident that you

(2) Will you be kind enough to inquire whether any copies of Lady Charlotte Guest's *Mabinogion* are in your English department, and if so at what price I can get two.

(3) I am making notes for a magazine article which I shall offer to the INTERNATIONAL REVIEW, to be called " The Function of Technic in Poetry," [66] in which I wish to discuss some matters upon which the notices of my book in THE EVENING POST, THE TIMES, and some other papers have betrayed the most surprising ignorance; which I can do all the more easily, since the ignorance is revealed mostly in the praises they give the work, and I am thus freed from all suspicion of tirade and resentment. For this purpose, I will ask you to send me any notices of the book worthy of attention since the batch I have already seen and returned to you. I observe that THE NATION has had nothing to say in the matter; is this probably intentional, or merely because the work has not been reached?

Very truly yrs.
Sidney Lanier.

TO ROBERT S. LANIER

West Chester, Pa.
Aug. 14, 1880.

My dearest Father:

Robert Sampson Lanier Jr. — for so we had from the first called him, if it should be a him — arrived this morning at three o'clock, and, with a consideration which augurs well in one so young, gave his mother as little trouble as any boy of his size could reasonably be expected to give. He is as proper a man as you would find in a summer's day,

could secure the cooperation of one of the old English publication societies." He added that he had ordered from London the two copies of *The Mabinogion*, requested in the following paragraph.

[66] No such article by Lanier has been found. The substance of it was probably included in his " Letter to the Editor of *The Nation*," which was itself never published (see II, xxvii-xxx).

The review in the New York *Times*, mentioned following, appeared in the issue of June 18, 1880. (For excerpts from this long and sharply unfavorable review, see II, xxxi, n. 29. For the review in the New York *Evening Post*, see note 44, above; in the *Nation*, note 106, below.)

perfect in limb, wind and looks; and I think you would not object to be perpetuated by him, if you could see him. The nurse says he weighs ten pounds; and I have an unusual feeling that he is going to be a man that will do credit to the race some of these days.

Mary is doing well at this writing — 11 A. M. — and everything goes on normally. Our hosts of the hotel [67] — the establishment is conducted solely by two young and comely sisters, the Misses Kenney – are all kindly attention, and we lack for nothing. The nurse is a faithful old Scotch soul, not long from Glasgow, with a burr in her speech that makes every *r* sound like the beginning of a locust's song in among the leaves, and with all manner of odd and kindly ways.

I am feeling somewhat better today, and have hope that my daily fever will soon wear off. I await some account of the political situation in your neighborhood with eagerness.

The morning telegrams bring word that an opposition candidate – Mr. Norwood – has been put forward against Colquitt. How will this affect Uncle C'.s nomination as Attorney General? And how will *that* affect his senatorial hopes?

Did you receive a copy of THE INDEPENDENT, with my poem *The Crystal* therein? I must stop, as there are many things to do.

Love to Mama, in which May begs to join heartily. I sent you a long letter on Tuesday last.

Your loving

S. L.

TO CHARLES D. LANIER [68]

West Chester, Pa.
Aug. 15, 1880.

My dear Charley:

A young man came to our house yesterday morning who claims that he is a brother of yours and Sidney's and Harry's, and that he is entitled to all the rights and privi-

---

[67] The Turk's Head Hotel (see Lanier to Sarah Farley, Aug. 14, 1880, here omitted).

[68] The text of this letter is taken from a surviving MS first draft, apparently

leges appertaining unto that honorable connection. You will be surprised to learn that both your mother and I are disposed to allow his pretensions, from the fact that he looks a great deal like Sidney, — and from several other circumstances which I need not detail. Indeed your mother has already gone so far as to take him on her breast and nurse him exactly as she did you three young scamps somewhere between twelve and seven years ago. I write therefore to ask whether you and Sidney and Harry are willing to accept our opinion of this young person's genuine kinship to you, or whether you will require him to employ a number of lawyers, like the Tichborne Claimant in England, to assert his rights in due form before the courts of the United States. If the latter, you had best give him early notice of your intention: for the fact is he has taken such a hold upon our affections here, by the quietness and modesty of his demeanor and by the beauty of his person, that if we were summoned into Court as witnesses in the case of

Robert Sampson Lanier Jr (so called), Plaintiff,

Versus

Charles Day Lanier
Sidney   "   Jr.
and   } Defendants
Henry   "

Action on a Bond (of brotherhood),

we would be obliged to testify that we feel almost as sure — if not quite — that he is your brother as that you are our son.

As I have said, he is a most exemplary young man. He never stays out late at night; neither chews, smokes, nor uses snuff; abstains from all intoxicating liquors, and does not touch even tea or coffee; however much preserves and fruit-cake there may be on the supper-table, he never asks for any; he does no kind of work on the Sabbath; he honors his father and mother,

retained by Lanier. Of the letter as actually sent only a fragment has been preserved — pp. 1 and 3, mutilated. The date and salutation have been supplied from the latter source.

The allusion to the "Tichborne Claimant" is to the famous case of Roger Tichborne, young heir to a large estate, who was lost at sea in 1854. One Arthur Orton was the "claimant" who, in a famous trial in 1872, lost his suit and was sentenced to prison for perjury.

particularly his mother; he plays no games of hazard, not even marbles for winnance; and I am positively certain that in the whole course of his life he has never uttered a single angry or ungentlemanly word. I am bound to admit that he has his shortcomings: he *isn't* as particular about his clothes as I would like to see him; he has a way of trying to get both fists in his mouth which certainly does look odd in company; and he wants his breakfast in the morning at four o'clock — an hour at which it is very inconvenient, with *our* household arrangements, to furnish it to him. But we hope that perhaps he will amend in these particulars, as time rolls on, and that he will become as perfect a gentleman as his three brothers. In fact we attribute these little faults of his to the fact that he appears to have been in a Far Country — like the Tichborne Claimant —, and the manners and customs of peoples are so different that we really don't know whether it may not be considered a sign of good breeding *There* to cram one's fists into one's mouth, and perhaps the very highest circles of the nobility and gentry in that Region take their breakfasts before daylight.

Earnestly hoping that this lovely little (for I omitted to mention that he is small of stature) brother Rob may find a good warm place in your three hearts without being obliged to resort to extreme measures, and with a hundred embraces for you, my dear big Charley,

I am

Your &c &c &c.

To Isabel L. Dobbin [69]

West Chester, Pa.
Aug. 18, 1880.

My dear Mrs. Dobbin:

Here is come a young man so lovely in his person, and so gentle and high-born in his manners, that in the course of some three days he has managed to make himself as necessary to *our* world as the sun, moon, and stars; at

---

[69] Excerpt previously published, Mims, pp. 325-326. Mrs. George W. Dobbin and her husband were intimate Baltimore friends of the Laniers, though they appear infrequently in the letters.

any rate, these would seem quite obscured without him. It just so happens that he is very vividly associated with *you* for among the few treasures we allowed ourselves to bring away from home is the photograph you gave us, and this stands in the most honorable coign of vantage in Mary's room. Thus your face lent the welcome grace of a friend's presence among the strangers who "assisted" at my boy's arrival; and whenever I go in to steal a look at his heavenly little face I find yours not far off.

You will be glad to know that my dear Comrade is doing well, — better in all respects than ever before. She has escaped all the more serious ills incident to the time, and seems altogether bright and prosperous. The three critical days are now happily over, and we have reason to expect a speedy sight of our dear invalid moving about her accustomed ways again. "If you could see the Boy asleep by her side! The tranquility of his slumber, and the shine of his mother's eyes thereover, seem to melt up and mysteriously absorb the great debates of the agnostic, of science, of politics, and to dissolve them into that pellucid Faith long ago re-affirmed by the Son of Man. Looking upon the child, this term seems to acquire a new meaning, as if Christ were in some sort reproduced in every infant." [70]

Send us some word of yourself, dear friend. Your letter was most welcome, save that we grieved over your fruitless journey to our outlying habitation. Mary joins me in all manner of friendly messages to you and I am always

Faithfully yours,

Sidney Lanier

To Epes Sargent [71]

West Chester, Pa.
Aug. 19, 1880.

My dear Sir:

If the following answers to your inquiries are either too full or too meagre, please attribute the defect to my ignorance of the scope of your work.

---

[70] This quotation has not been identified.

[71] Epes Sargent (1813-1880) had written Lanier Aug. 18, 1880, to ask per-

(1) I was born at Macon, Georgia, February 3, 1842.

(2) My residence is at Baltimore, Md., where I am lecturer on English Literature in the Johns Hopkins University, and a member of the Peabody Orchestra — an organization for rendering classic music, maintained in connexion with the Peabody Institute.

(3) No general collection of my poems has been made; but in 1876 Messrs. Lippincott published a small volume made up of such poems only as had appeared in LIPPINCOTT'S MAGAZINE during the preceding years, – where I suppose it may be said my literary career began. I have two volumes of new poems which I am just now about to offer for publication,[72] besides a volume of pieces which have already appeared in other magazines.

(4) My prose works consist of a book called *Florida*, published by Lippincott, Ph^a. 1875; and *The Science of English Verse*, Chas. Scribner's Sons, New York, 1880. Perhaps also I may mention my editions of classics for boys, which began with *The Boy's Froissart*, Chas. Scribner's Sons, N. Y. 1879, and is to be followed by a redaction (now in press) of old Sir Thomas Malory's *History of King Arthur* &c., for this year, and so on: each containing a historical introduction and specimens of English in the 15th and early 16th centuries. I have made many prose contributions also to magazines in the last three years.

Inasmuch as the Lippincott volume consists of early, and comparatively crude, works which are scarcely representative: and as my later magazine poems have been printed without an opportunity on my part even to correct proof: I cannot think it will be indelicate if I enclose three or four of the latter which may increase your range of selection.

The "Marshes of Glynn" was first printed in Roberts' Bros *Masque of Poets*, without my name. "Glynn" is a county on the sea-coast of Georgia, near Savannah, and the picture is a

---

mission to copy several of his shorter poems in a cyclopedia of poetry which he was editing for Harper & Bros. He also asked for biographical information.

[72] For these three uncompleted volumes of poetry ("Clover and Other Poems," "Songs of Aldhelm" and "Credo and Other Poems"), see the Introduction to vol. I of the present edition.

strictly local one. The other poems sent have all appeared in magazines.[73]

Please let me thank you for your kindly message about the *Science of English Verse*.[74] The book has been so widely misunderstood that, although I have long ago learned to work very equably without recognition, I enjoy intelligent sympathy very greatly. Most persons have taken the book to be an insidious attempt to make versifying easy; but it is really a purely scientific study of certain subtle phenomena of audition, aiming to filiate all those curious facts connoted under the term "Verse" by referring them to a common physical origin in the relations of sound. It is purely theoretical, and has no more necessary reference to verse-making than Prof. Huxley's work on *The Crayfish* has to preparing lobsters for the table. Each teaches the anatomy of its subject: readers, of course, can apply the knowledge therein gained to any practical end desired.

Very truly yours,

Sidney Lanier.

To Epes Sargent

West Chester, Pa.
Aug. 26, 1880

My dear Sir:

I have found a copy of the Lippincott volume, which I beg you will accept. Suppose that instead of "The Waving of the Corn" — which takes up considerable space — you insert the little song on p. 93 which I have headed "A Rose-Moral". It is much shorter, and represents an artistic

---

[73] On Aug. 21 Sargent replied that for his *Cyclopedia of British and American Poetry* he had chosen the following poems: "Evening Song," "From the Flats," "The Harlequin of Dreams," "The Waving of the Corn," and "The Dove." When the volume appeared, in 1881, it included the first three here named, but the last two had been dropped in favor of "Rose-Morals" (see the following letter).

[74] Sargent had written on Aug. 18, from Boston: "Happening in at Williams's bookstore today, one of the clerks told me that your book on English verse &c was highly praised by my friend Dr. O. W. Holmes; — also by J. T. Fields."

mood perhaps more fervent. I would not find boldness enough to make this suggestion but for the fact that it will save your pages considerable room.

Very truly yours,

Sidney Lanier.

Mr. Epes Sargent.
Boston

To Henry W. Lanier [75]

West Chester, Pa.
Aug. 27, 1880.

My dear brother Harry:

As the weather is such, to-day, that I can't go out for a horseback ride, — nor climb into the top of an apple-tree,— nor walk down a peacock and pull out his tail-feathers,— nor go to the Archery Club with my bow and arrows, — I thought I would send you a line, particularly as I want to ask your advice on some points that puzzle me beyond my capacity. You are so much older and wiser than I am, however, that I do not doubt you can enlighten me: you are, if I am not mistaken, seven years and two months of age, and as this makes you just seven years and six weeks older than me, you are a very venerable person indeed, to *my* thinking.

In the first place, I'm bound to say this is a very strange country I've come to. I think there's something in the atmosphere that is stupefying: for I have done scarcely anything but sleep and sleep ever since I came here; and,— what is still more odd,— although I have been here but thirteen days, I can't for the life of me remember the name of the Land I came from.

But there are worse troubles, here, than that. This is certainly the hardest country to get enough to eat in, that ever *I* saw. I am not a very large person; and I take only eight meals a day; but when I wake up and ask if dinner is on the table, I *do* think people are longer in getting things ready than any folks *ever* were before. I wish you would write me if you

[75] The signature on this letter from Lanier to his son Harry is, of course, assumed.

know of any hotel where they are more prompt with the victuals.

All this is bad enough; but it's *nothing* to another difficulty which sometimes completely upsets my dignity, and thus pains me all the more because I have been trying to set a good example to these people in the way of gravity of behavior ever since I arrived.

The matter is this: pretty nearly every afternoon, just after I get through my supper, I have the most remarkable sensations just under the waistband of my trousers: my stomach begins to twist and turn and tumble and jerk and roll and swell and squeeze as if it was insane, and then it aches until I positively cannot stand the anguish of it. If this sort of thing is what I am to expect in this country, I want to go *Somewhere* else. If you know anything that is good for this curious trouble, please write me straightway; in fact, I would like you to send me word by telegraph. I have tried all the remedies I could think of: I have rammed both fists into my mouth and shaken them at my stomach, but without much effect; and I have resorted to opening my mouth very wide and telling my stomach candidly just what I thought of it; but my voice isn't very loud yet, and I don't think I have made myself heard down there. Please let me hear fully from you on this point: though it is such a long while since you were a little boy that I am afraid you have forgotten what you used to do for troubles like this. I should think grown people would be ashamed of themselves, — to have been living and living ever so many years, and bragging about their science and philosophy and progress and the rights of man and all that stuff, and yet never to have found out a way to keep a little baby like me from having the colic.

— I am obliged to break off rather suddenly, for I think it's coming on now. If I could only hold my eyes open, and get my food quickly, and *not* suffer with the colic, I think I would be " having a very nice time."

Please tell Charley that his letter came to-day, and two from Mrs. Maxwell.

Your loving brother

Rob.

To Francis F. Browne [76]

West Chester, Pa.
Aug. 28, 1880.

My dear Sir:

The letter is entirely at your service. I ought to add, however, that I cannot say I have fully thought out the matter, and I wish you would closely examine any principle you may quote, – particularly as my letter was written hastily.[77] It will give me pleasure if you find anything of service to your contemplated article.

The pitiless effacement of one's work, such as you mention, is indeed tragic. And when, in addition, it leaves behind — as I grieve to learn that it has done, in your own case — an enfeebled body and a diminished capacity for labor, it brings a man sheer up against the very hardest question of life. For one asks why should such gentle service be requited as if it were the most hideous of rebellions ? It is even hard to pardon an English king who in defeating a rebel lord not only scatters his forces but puts out his eyes, against future conspiracy; and, if so, what would men think of a king who should thus treat his most devoted servant and faithful defender ? I suppose every man of letters comes soon to feel a sense of consecration and priesthood : and it must seem astounding when in the very midst of service the Deity smites down His bishop and leaves that servant a cripple forever.

But perhaps it is here that the significance of The Individual, and of The Spirit of Man, comes in and solves life for us. I am conscious of a certain sense of exultation in the very bigness and pitilessness of these blows; looking upon Moral Greatness as a Miranda who cannot be attained except by shipwreck and suffering, I have a feeling, when Prospero (I believe in God) sets me to carrying logs by way of testing my love for her, that I would at any rate like my logs to be – not straws and trifles – but such as only a *man* could stand up under. It is by this

[76] Previously published, *Ex Libris*, IV, No. 4 (Johns Hopkins Univ., May, 1935).
[77] The reference is to Lanier's previous letter to Browne, July 31, 1880 (above), in which he had discussed some matters related to his theory of verse.

terrific process — so all the facts of current nature seem to demonstrate — that the evolution of the individual goes on. After such a stroke, the man who rises, – or who, if too much maimed, still shows some front like Widdrington in the old ballad who when both legs were cut off in combat yet

" kneeled and fought on the stumps," [78]

– or who perhaps is deprived of every thing else save mere endurance, – feels that his self has been somehow confirmed and that he has won a sort of right to a really separate existence, as against that frightful merger into voidness and uniformity which seems to be the terrifying part of the idea of death.

I find infinite food in reflecting on the manful conduct of Christ, in these connections. Perhaps you will care to see a poem of mine which has just appeared in THE INDEPENDENT and which is not without relation to this matter.

Accept my thanks for your pleasant expressions. Perhaps it is only he who has learned to do without sympathy who can really permit himself to enjoy it without stint when it comes; and I was taught, in the very beginning of my literary career, that a certain essential non-conformity which seems to beat in the blood of all reformers and preachers like myself could result in nothing but misunderstanding and ridicule as my portion, at least for several years. This is, of course not to be complained of; it ceases, as soon as people find out that a man is genuine; and it appears to be a test of genuineness, usefully fixed in the very constitution of things.

I sincerely trust you will get stronger and redeem THE LAKESIDE [79] with THE DIAL.

Very truly yours,

Sidney Lanier.

Mr. F. F. Browne.

---

[78] " The Ballad of Chevy Chase " (included in Lanier's *The Boy's Percy*, New York, 1882).
[79] An earlier magazine, edited by Browne, that had failed.

To Richard M. Johnston [80]

West Chester, Pa., August 28, 1880.

My dear and sweet Richard,— It has just occurred to me that you were *obliged* to be as sweet as you are, in order to redeem your name; for the other three Richards in history were very far from being satisfactory persons, and something had to be done. Richard I, though a man of muscle, was but a loose sort of a swashbuckler after all; and Richard II, though handsome in person, was " redeless," and ministered much occasion to Wat Tyler and his gross following; while Richard III, though a wise man, allowed his wisdom to ferment into cunning and applied the same unto villainy.

But now comes Richard IV, to wit, you,—and, by means of gentle loveliness and a story or two, subdues a realm which I foresee will be far more intelligent than that of Richard I, far less turbulent than that of Richard II, and far more legitimate than that of Richard III, while it will own more, and more true loving subjects than all of those three put together.

I suppose my thoughts have been carried into these details of nomenclature by your reference to my own young Samson, who, I devoutly trust with you, shall yet give many a shrewd buffet and upsetting to the Philistines. Is it not wonderful how quickly these young fledgelings impress us with a sense of their individuality? This fellow is two weeks old to-day, and every one of us, from mother to nurse, appears to have a perfectly clear conception of his character. This conception is simply enchanting. In fact, the young man has already made himself absolutely indispensable to us, and my comrade and I wonder how we ever got along with *only* three boys.

I rejoice that the editor of " Harper's " has discrimination enough to see the quality of your stories, and I long to see these two appear, so that you may quickly follow them with a

[80] Previously published, Mims, pp. 322-325, from which the present text is taken (MS not found) ; excerpts reprinted, Starke, p. 404; reprinted in full, *Maryland Historical Magazine,* XXXIV, 320-321 (Dec., 1939). The last source identifies Johnston's stories, mentioned at the end of this letter, as " The Expensive Treat of Colonel Moses Grice " and " Puss Tanner's Defense " — both included in the third edition of *The Dukesborough Tales* (New York, 1883).

volume. When that appears, it shall have a review that will draw three souls out of one weaver—if this pen have not lost her cunning.

I'm sorry I can't send a very satisfactory answer to your health inquiries, as far as regards myself. The mean, pusillanimous fever which took under-hold of me two months ago is still *there*, as impregnably fixed as a cockle-burr in a sheep's tail. I have tried idleness, but (naturally) it won't *work*. I do no labor except works of necessity—such as kissing Mary, who is a more ravishing angel than ever—and works of mercy —such as letting off the world from any more of my poetry for a while. But it's all one to my master the fever. I get up every day and drag around in a pitiful kind of shambling existence. I fancy it has come to be purely a go-as-you-please match between me and the disease, to see which will wear out first, and I think I will manage to take the belt, yet.

Give my love to the chestnut trees and all the rest of your family.

Your letter gave us great delight. God bless you for it, my best and only Richard, as well as for all your other benefactions to

Your faithful friend,

S. L.

To Mary Day Lanier

St. Denis Hotel, N. Y.

Sep. 2, 1880.

Dearest Mutterchen:

I arrived here yesterday afternoon, in no worse condition than when I left.

Just as I was sitting down to my Graham-bread and cream, in came Mr. Pratt, and we had a hearty reunion.[81] After my supper, I felt that if I could only hear the melodious storm of

[81] Mary Day Lanier had written to W. S. Pratt, Aug. 31, 1880: "If not too feeble to travel, Mr. Lanier will start for N. Y. tomorrow A. M. to consult there the most eminent student (in Homæopathy) of lung diseases. . . . He is very ill; his fever has never relaxed for three months, and the loss of flesh is continuous, as is increase of debility. I encourage the journey, but with a fear that is unutterable. . . . He has told me he wd. be willing, if ill, to send for you. I ask you, without his knowledge, to seek him."

the horns and violins and reeds, though even in an ignoble waltz, my poor nerves would vibrate to some different rhythm; so, as the night was perfectly dry and clear, I bundled up and sallied forth to the Metropolitan Garden, a structure recently built for summer night concerts on Broadway near 41st St. Here we found a charming concert-room, and a moderately good orchestra of fifty musicians; whereupon we settled ourselves, and spent the evening. The music was mostly light; but here and there a nobler piece was played: and, as for me, all I wanted was the breeding of dreams, and the forcible new rhythms. I really think it changed the habit of my own feverish movement, at least for the night. I came home, and slept better than in a long time before.

This morning I found Dr. Marcy,[82] in very gorgeous quarters, at 307 Fifth Avenue. I was the sole patient, and had a free interview. He urges in the strongest manner that I stay here a week, and says that if I do so he can then make up a course of medicine for me in an intelligent way, after watching the effect of his remedies during that time. He examined my lungs, and said the recent attack of bronchitis had affected the upper part of both lobes; but added that he could remedy it. I could get nothing further from him, as to old damages. He then mixed a lot of his medicines, in his unique way, and requested me to see him again tomorrow morning. I am taking the remedies every hour.

My morning was very bright, and I felt extraordinarily well. Towards afternoon the fever has risen; but I do not seem so completely cast down by it as usual.

I think I will give Dr. Marcy his chance, and stay out the week; but will make it depend on my daily improvement entirely. The weather is simply perfect.

Forward proofs and letters (after reading all the latter, of course) until you hear otherwise. I telegraphed you today, having failed to get the card in before the mail closed yesterday. Love to dear Father: how I wish for him these bright days !

As for thee: it is mere suspension of life till I see thee again, and I am simply thy

husband.

---

[82] Dr. E. E. Marcy, a Swedish physician, to whom Lanier had first gone for treatment in 1870.

To Waldo S. Pratt [83]

West Chester, Pa.
Sep. 5, 1880.

My dear Mr. Pratt:

I was filled with regret at finding, from your card, that I had missed you. I waited until nearly eight, thinking you might come; and then fared forth to another " garden " – Koster and Biol's, 23rd. St. near 6th Av. – where I heard some noble music most beautifully played by a remnant of Thomas's old orchestra. Pray go there when you feel like spending an hour in that way. You will be glad to know that smoking is allowed *everywhere* in the premises.

I had planned to feed my soul with some of your fine things at the Museum on Saturday; but the rise in the external temperature appeared to stir my own internal flame to greater intensity, and I seemed so near consuming that I thought best to flee to this place, where the atmosphere is cooler.

I was so ill during the time we were together on Wednesday evening – I really thought I would fall on the floor, and busied myself with picturing the scene, detailing the curious faces and so on, and regretting in advance the trouble it was going to give you – that I postponed until a better time many questions I wanted to ask about this same lady who is going to complete your existence. What is she like, is she tall or short, dark or fair, musical or architectural, Aristotelian or Platonist; and is she really such that your married life will be, as Sainte Beuve (I believe) calls it, an *égoisme à deux?* I have told my own adorable comrade of your new happiness, and she heartily joins me in friendly congratulations.

I shall return to Baltimore in about ten days, and will look after your little commissions. Is there not something else I can do for you there?

I have many things to say to you, but my sword-arm has given out, now, and I must wait.

With all good wishes,

Sincerely yours,

Sidney Lanier.

[83] Excerpt previously published, Starke, p. 404.

To Ephraim Keyser

West Chester, Pa.
Sep. 7, 1880.

My dear Sir:

Please make two casts of the bust for me. I expect
to be at home in four days from now, and would be very glad
to have one of the casts at the earliest moment after I arrive.
The other can be finished at your leisure. I will esteem it a
great favor to have the first one immediately.

I will report to you when I reach Baltimore; and meantime,
with cordial messages, am

Very truly yrs,

Sidney Lanier.

Mr. E. Keyser.
Baltimore.

To Mary Day Lanier

435 N. Calvert St.
Bo., Sep. 10, 1880.

So many things, my sweet angel, come crowding to the point
of my pen that one jostles t'other off; for indeed there is room
now only to tell thee that I am here, in this abode which I
cannot call home until thou art in it.

I lunched with the Peacocks, and we had a pleasant reunion.
Then I went to Boericke & Tafel's, and got some codeine,– in
powder which does not bring the effect of the other, I find.   I
came on the 3.50 express which is a fast train to Baltimore:
another train, leaving Pha at four (ten minutes after) is a very
slow accommodation: all of which I mention if perchance thou
shouldst come to be taking any such trains.

I found Mrs. Fleming, and a bright fire burning in my
room.[84]   The floor thereof has been painted, and a parlous

---

[84] In a letter of Sept. 7, 1880, thanking the Lawrence Turnbulls for their
invitation to Lanier to stay with them on his return to Baltimore, Mary Day
Lanier wrote that Mrs. Fleming, "my devoted good nurse," had agreed to go
to their own house and take care of him.

odor of linseed oil seemed to fill the universe. I got to bed at nine, and slept more than for several nights past. Breakfast this morning was late — everything was to find &c &c &c &c &c &c — but enjoyable, and after a thousanod puttings-up and gettings-out &c&c&c&c&c&c&c&c&c&c&c&c &c &c I became dressed, accomplished some work on the King Arthur, wrote Charley a birth-day letter (enclosing three dollars), sent Mrs. Fleming down to express the arrows, &c&c&c&c&c ———————— until now it is growing late in the afternoon. Fatsy is crowing a kind of come-home crow somewhere off among the lots, and thy man is very tired and ready for bed.

Thy letter came duly this morning, and Mrs. Fleming, who is now out for a little while, will straightway look into the matter of the flannel. The meat-juice was brought in and taken according to thy commands, and I do not now remember that I have left anything undone which thou orderedst to be done. Thou wilt kiss sweet heavenly-minded Sarah [Farley] for me, and say that she will be answered.

Is it but one day yet that thou hast been out of reach of thy

husband ?

To Mary Day Lanier

Bo. Sunday, Sep. 12, 1880.

Dearest Comrade, I send a little line to say that I seem to be doing well. I think the lung is better: the possibility of a long breath does not appear so absurd as some days ago. Yesterday the expectoration was very great, but comparatively easy; and I feel some relief, in consequence. This apparent clearing-away would seem to be fairly attributable to the Sanguinaria and phosphoric Acid, which I began to take, according to Dr. Marcy's directions, on Friday, and have continued regularly. The pulse is still much too fast; but there appears to be a distinct period of exacerbation of this symptom, and I think this period is shorter today than yesterday.

I have been absolutely idle for two days, and have not seen a soul but Mrs. F. She does as well as can be expected, and I will wear away very well until thou art ready to come.

I have not yet been able to get hold of Isaac, nor to see Mr. Appold. Tomorrow I must finish up the King Arthur addition,[85] and make a start towards several matters.

Mrs. Fleming thinks the flannel must have gone to Rapidan. She has searched the trunks, but is unable to find it.

Father's note with its parcel of letters came safely. I will write him tomorrow or next day. THE NATION also arrived.

I have made a frightful vacuity in one jar of thy cherry preserves. I get a couple of perfectly fresh eggs every morning for breakfast. We have had a chicken baked, which is now *pendente lite.* Of our coffee, I will not speak: wouldst thou have me abuse the feeble? Yet its weakness is so profound, that my own strength seems by comparison gigantic; and its atrocity is so monstrous, that my own guilty soul shows like an angel of light by the side thereof; so that it is very excellent *moral* coffee, though physically indifferent. Thou art to take none of thy wild actions anent this: I am to have a new tin coffee-pot tomorrow, and also some new coffee, and we will see what comes therefrom.

My arm is very intolerant of the pen, somehow; and so, with nothing said, I must stop, and send thee a direct kiss which thou mayst transmit secondarily to all the loved ones of thy

husband.

To MARY DAY LANIER [86]

Bo., Sep. 14, 1880.

Dearest Mutterchen,   I have just gotten off the package of *King Arthur* matter, after some day's of hard work, and, having written, beside, a letter to Rand Avery & Co. and two notes to advertising nurses &c, there is nothing left in me wherewith to tell thee more than that Turnbull and Tabb have come, that

[85] Charles Scribner's Sons had written Lanier, Sept. 1, 1880, to suggest that he restore passages excised from his *King Arthur* to make the book equal in length to the *Froissart.*

[86] The friends mentioned in this letter were Lawrence Turnbull, John B. Tabb, and Dr. Thomas Shearer. "Isaac" and "Emma" were probably domestics.

Mrs. Turnbull hath kept me supplied with great loaves of good home-made bread, that I have not put my nose out of doors since I came here, that I expect to go down town tomorrow, that I am about as yesterday in health, my main difficulty being to sleep, that I will see Dr. Shearer soon, that Isaac hath been here and we have talked over matters whereof he will speak further on Saturday, that Emma has also called (Emma " Jack ") and I fancy wanteth a place, that thou must have no fear about me, that I will now go with lighter heart about my *King Arthur* Introduction which I hope to finish in three days, and that thou art the sun and the weather wherein grow all the thoughts and desires of thy

husband.

To Mary Day Lanier

B⁰. Sep. 15, 1880.

I was just making ready, at five P. M., to get off a good long letter to thee when Mrs. Singleton came; and we were then discussing school arrangements for the next year a while, when, just as she departed, came Dr. Brown , and so my time is gone.[87]

I went into the town this morning and attended to several matters that needed me; reaching home, not more tired than usual, about four. Another great loaf of bread, and a lot of rolls &c have come from Mrs. Turnbull.

I can scarcely say how I do, seeing no change. I have great trouble to sleep; but I have been today taking some codine, and hope for a better night. My strength is as when I left thee: but a good symptom is the disappearance of the shortness of breath upon exertion; I certainly breathe better, and more fully. My appetite is good, and digestion fine.

Please tell father I had set apart this afternoon to write him and return him Harry's letter, but have been prevented as aforesaid. I sent his overcoat this morning by Express. There is now just time to get this into the box.

---

[87] Mrs. M. C. Singleton was the proprietress of the Eutaw Place School, at which Lanier had taught the previous year. W. H. Browne, an old friend, had recently been appointed Librarian at Johns Hopkins University.

I am one day longer from thee, and, blessed thought! one day nearer to thee; but thou art to be in no hurry, for all the thee-want that now maketh thy

husband.

To Mary Day Lanier

Bo, Sep. 16, 1880,

Thou only *me* that I love, and in comparison whereof I hate the other one,

I think I have found the nurse we want. I have been diligently perusing " Situations Wanted " and all similar literature recently, and having seen an advertisement that sounded well, I wrote begging the party to call here. She came this morning, and after a good long talk I take mightily to her. She is about forty, small and slender, with a face and eyes that suggest Josephine Seaton's— the eye being particularly good, blue, faithful, and steady— Irish, has had three children who are still young and are disposed of in various orphan " asylums " and " homes," was dressed in decent black, has not been in service for fifteen years, refers me to Father McCoy, of St. Mary's Star of the Sea Church, has supported herself by washing for Mrs. Park Fisher of 259 St. Paul St. during the last thirteen months, greatly wishes a home, blue eyes filled with tears when she spoke of putting out her last child in a certain home to kape him out o' the strates, is very quiet and open in manner, homely at first view but growing in attractiveness each moment as to her face provided you look more at her eyes and less at her large Milesian mouth, is willing to,— and can — turn her hand to many things, makes beds, sew, general work &c besides the baby, and in short impressed me altogether as a person we might look long to find the like of.

I am sending Father McCoy a note today, by Mrs. Fleming, and she is to call tomorrow at eleven for a final answer.

If it is favorable, I shall make some arrangement with her, at least to secure a trial. Wouldst like her to come to thee? Or would it not be better to keep her here? Thou wilt exercise thy free judgment about this, and whatsoever thou desirest shall be done.

The Morgan's sister,[88] I feel sure, is not the person for us: what Mrs. Fleming tells me gives me the idea of a flighty and wholly unsuitable person.

I have been down town at work in settling school-matters all day, and am dreadfully tired. I dodge thine imaginary rebuke when I tell thee that I walked home from the Peabody. But the weather was simply divine, and the gracious air felt like heavenly balm to my lungs. The tired is only a good tired. I must surely be stronger.

I enclose father's letter from Harry, which I fear he has wanted ere now. Please tell father that if Mr. Lamb will (1) give immediately one note which can be discounted in bank, for $500, due October 15, and (2) another for $300, due at some convenient time not more than two months thereafter, and (3) make satisfactory arrangements for an inspector in *father's* interest who may report to father the exact amount of timber taken,— I should say accept his offer.

Here must I close, with snatching

a kiss.

To Mary Day Lanier

Bo., Sep. 17, 1880.

Dearest Soul,   It happens oddly enough, that Mrs. Turnbull had answered the same advertisement I did, and upon seeing the party was so favorably impressed that she sent me word about her this morning. A few minutes afterward the party herself called; and at the same time came a note from Father McCoy earnestly recommending her; so that it was like the end of a play, all the characters coming on the stage and taking hands around the bag of gold just found, bowing back and curtain down.

            (1)   (2)   (3)
Upon such concatenation of confirmation I had no hesitation
      (4)   (5)   (6)
at my conversation in the acceptation of her application, with
  (7)
the compensation of ten dollars a month.

---

[88] Ellen Morgan, sister-in-law of Mrs. Bridget Morgan, in whose charge the

In short I have hired Mistress Quigley,– bedad; and if we could now only find a Mrs. O'Shaughnessy or O'Flanagan to cook for us, who should be the very moral of her, I think our household mayht consider itself on a good honest Keltic basis.

She will go to thee or not, just as thou desirest. Meantime, she boards herself, on half wages. I feel so puffed up with pride over this business that I am going a-cook hunting in all possible ways.

I would grieve over the news thy letter brings me of thine old-time infirmity; but if I should grieve, then that would grieve thee, and therefore I will not grieve, – which is a clean abandonment of the dearest right of man.

The weather's very warm. I went down to see Mr. Gilman, and had a short talk, settling that my public lectures there shall not commence before November 1, which gives me still six weeks' respite. Miss Adams will want no assistance this year: I have therefore only the two hours a week at Mrs. Jones's and one and a half at Mrs. Singleton's.[89] These I have stipulated not to begin before October 1st.

My fever is considerable today; yet my appetite is good, my strength certainly greater, no right-sweats, and a better condition of lung. I begin Winchester's Hypophosphites tomorrow, according to Dr. Marcy's directions. Tait called last night. Sarah's rose-letter followed her mother's roses. It must be thou that inspirest these lovely thoughts of theirs toward thy

husband.

Great love to dear father, whom it seems I can never write to. Mrs. Plant's letter is most charming. My father's dismal enough: – and life is too short for me to go after Pringle at present. I suspect it to be all a sham, at last.

Laniers had left their house during their summer absence (see Mary Day Lanier's letter to Mrs. Lawrence Turnbull, Sept. 7, 1880).

[89] Lanier had taught at all three of these schools the previous year (see note 59, 1879).

To Mary Day Lanier

Balt⁰. Sep. 20, 1880.

Dear Soul, After much meditation I am wondering if several advantages would not result from getting thy present English nurse to come with thee as far as to Perryville, – when thou comest, ah me, – whence she could return to West Chester, and where either Mrs. Quigley or I would meet thee. This seems to present the following advantages:

(1) it saves thee the trouble of breaking-in a third nurse to the ways of the hotel and thine own, which would be considerable;

(2) it saves the possibility that Mrs. Quigley — who, I suspect, is no traveller, and who, being Irish, is liable to error — might, should she set out alone for West Chester, fetch up in Terra del Fuego or Candahar;

(3) I do not know whether the poor soul has precisely such garments as thou would'st like her to attend thee in, at a public place; she was very respectable in a black dress and black bonnet, here, but I know not of her home-gowns whether they be lovely, and if they should happen not to be, it would possibly give thee an awkwardness to overcome.

If thy nurse could haply not travel with thee to Perryville, some one else would doubtless do it, just for the little trip: maybe Mrs. Stewart.

Mrs. Dodge's letter came, and I accepted.[90] I today sent the portrait-bust to Dr. Shearer, with my inscription on the back of it.[91] I have been down in the city this morning, though with much fever after noon. My condition is altogether curious: I am certainly stronger, with more lung-room and less heart-trouble: yet for the past three days the fever has been

[90] Mary Mapes Dodge (1831-1905), editor of *St. Nicholas*, had written Lanier on Sept. 17, 1880, asking for "a short paper . . . introducing . . . readers to the story of ' King Arthur and his Knights ' . . . to call attention to the book." "King Arthur and his Knights of the Round Table" was published in the Dec., 1880, issue of *St. Nicholas* (see IV, 257).

[91] This plaster model of Keyser's bust (now owned by Mr. Walter Buck, Baltimore) has inscribed on the back in Lanier's autograph his poem " To Dr. Thomas Shearer" (I, 207). Lanier had paid Keyser " Fifty Dollars for 2 copies of his bust in plaster." (See MS receipt, Charles Day Lanier Collection.)

excessively hot and long-continued, lasting entirely through the night.

My " New South " is in the SCRIBNER'S just out. I cannot describe the amazement with which I read it: did I write it, and if so, when ? HARPER's for October has a pleasant notice of the *Science of Verse*.[92] I expect to see Dr. Shearer tomorrow or next day. Fruit from Mrs. Brown, and bread from Mrs. Turnbull have come; and so has Col. Johnston with all manner of love.

And now, farewell, lovely Soul that exhaustest grace in loving

me.

Sarah's notes are too delightful ![93] Tell her I think of her, and the silver-haired lady, every day.

To Mary Day Lanier

[Baltimore, Sept. 22, 1880?][94]

Dearest Maker of Vacancies and longings,

There is but time to say there is *not* time. Yesterday, at the hour I write to thee, Dr. Shearer came and staid a long time, to him succeeding Mrs. Egerton and Mrs. Tom Dotterer of Charleston.[95]

Dr. S. made a careful examination of my chest. He believes there is no degeneration of the lung, and was bold enough to say, this is *not* consumption: as the result of his examination, supported by the circumstances (1) that I am even now able, by the exercise of some will, to pump my lungs quite normally full of air, and to maintain a full equable breathing for some time if the will be concentrated thereon, (2) that although very thin I am not in the state called emacia-

---

[92] The review appeared in *Harper's*, LXI, 796-797 (October, 1880). (Excerpts from this brief but favorable review are given in II, xxxii, n. 34.)

[93] Four notes from Sarah J. Farley written to Lanier during this period have survived. Her mother is referred to in the following sentence.

[94] Conjectural dating from the reference to Dr. Shearer's visit at the close of the preceding letter and the opening of this one.

[95] Mrs. T. D. Dotterer was the wife of an old Charleston friend of Lanier's (see Appendix C, vol. X). Mrs. Egerton was an intimate Baltimore friend.

tion, (3) that the fever is unlike the characteristic " hectic " of consumption, (4) that there are no night-sweats.

But he roundly confesses that the exact nature of the fever puzzles him; whilst he *thinks* it is certainly due, directly or indirectly, to the inflammation of the mucuous membrane of the lung. The fever is fairly fierce, for three days gone: it seizes me like a tiger about twelve, and dominates me and burns me and laughs me to scorn. The heart-symptoms are decidedly better; and the shortness of breath upon exertion has nearly disappeared.

Thine, enclosing Mrs. Dodge's, came this morning. It is heavenly to hear thy bright news of health. Embrace thy father and our dear friends for thy

husband.

The Dr. comes again today.

To Clifford A. Lanier [96]

435 N. Calvert St.
Bo., Sep. 24, 1880.

My dearest Clifford, I have been longing for some news of you. Willie's letter to Mary gave but a doleful account of your physical welfare. But you were then about to go away for some rest, and I hope you have stored up some supply for the winter.

As for me, I have for three months been waging the most desperate struggle with a fever which has been as baffling and as savage as the Knight Garlon in *King Arthur*, who fought invisible. The New York doctor, the Philadelphia doctor, fought it in vain; and so, a few days ago I left Mary at West Chester, – which was getting too cold for me, – and crawled home, where I have been camping, *en garçon*, working at my ` Introduction to *The Boys' King Arthur* (which is now nearly all in print) and at an article on King Arthur which St. Nicholas has asked me to write for it, what time I puff away the consuming heat of my daily fever. This has brought me to a mere bag of bones, and as for my strength it is nought. However, my

[96] Excerpt previously published, Mims, p. 294.

good doctor Shearer, here – a heart of gold and a skilfull leech – gave me yesterday a medicine which shows some sign today of making head against the enemy, and we are in great spirits about it.

My article on the New South is in the October SCRIBNER'S just out, and appears to have made a very strong impression. The current HARPER'S too has a pleasant notice of THE SCIENCE OF VERSE. I send you a copy of the Bo. AMERICAN – a Republican paper, which four years ago was fond of abusing me – in which the leading editorial is on my New South article. Its concluding third is simply a mass of error: not a word in the article claims that the *Southern* small farmer is *alone* to save the spirit of independence; and the increase of bonanza farming in the Northwest is not my " speculation " but a fact, stated and supported with great detail, by two recent authors after a personal inspection of the country; and the land-owners of England in the 16th century were *not* " the law-making power," – for if they were, how could the statutes which I cite in the article ever have been passed – statutes which struck directly at the most privileges of the landlords? – But this is newspaper writing.[97]

I have six books in preparation continuing the Boys Froissart series, – which has been a tremendous success. I hope to be able to retain a copyright upon some of them.

Can you by any possibility raise me another hundred dollars, and charge it against the legacy? My long illness has been the cruelest stroke to me, financially. My work is in demand, in every quarter, and is well paid: but I have been too profoundly sick to do anything save correct the proofs of the King Arthur, which I did at great cost of strength and which seemed to me a Herculean labor.

THE NATION of today gives what it considers a very good notice of the New South article.[98]

[97] The editorial on Lanier's " New South " appeared in the Baltimore *American*, Sept. 22, 1880. Lanier wrote a letter to the editor in answer (elaborating the three points made in this letter) which has survived in MS. But a search of the files of the *American* fails to reveal it, and there is no evidence that it was ever sent. (Both editorial and answer are treated in V, lviii, n. 113.)

[98] The *Nation* of Sept. 23, 1880, contained a favorable notice of Lanier's article, declaring: " This writer's poetic fancy . . . and nice literary taste have invested an economic topic with a palatable husk of philosophy and history."

Have you read Cable's book, *The Grandissimes?* It is a work of art, and he has a fervent and rare soul. Do you know him? [99]

I have written too much. God keep you, my dear Buddy — how many thousand years is it since I called you that? — and your sweet Other one.

Your

S. L.

To Mary Day Lanier

B⁰. Sep. 24, 1880.

Dearest Soul,   The Dr. began giving me Cactus last night, and the indications are today that it has modified the fever. In so doing, however, it has made me very weak and nervous, and I can write but little without fatigue. I am overjoyed at the prospect of delivery from this fearful haunter. Night before last, in order to get a conclusive proof as to my fever being the " hectic " of consumption, the Dr. left his registering thermometer for me to try at bed-time.

I did so, and found $99\frac{1}{2}°$. This, he pronounced conclusive against hectic, which calls for 101 to 102 or 3 &c. It was then determined to work against malarial poison complicated with bronchial catarrh and for this purpose Cactus seemed the remedy. I really believe it has worked: the doctor was sure it would at least relax the constriction from which I was suffering in lung and abdomen.

I made the inclosed check payable to father, for convenience of cashing.

Canst do aught with fifteen dollars ? I am in the greatest straits until the first of October. Oh, to have no money for thee, is more than too much

for thy poor

husband.

---

[99] George W. Cable and Lanier never met, but the admiration was mutual (see Starke, p. 451). Lanier included *The Grandissimes* in the scheme of his lectures on the English novel at Johns Hopkins University in the winter of 1881 (IV, vii).

To Mary Day Lanier

Bo, Sep. 26, 1880.

My sweetest Soul, one thing and another have kept my pen from thee today until now there is but time, as usual, for the least little line, to say that things seem to go on with me; the doctor has just left me, and says my condition is better. For three days something like a wee chill has seemed to come on about 12 M., and on learning this last night he put me on quinine-beans and lachesis. Today my head is ringing, and there really seems much less fever than at this usual hot time. He seems altogether confident about the matter, and is as good as ever.

The publishers have hurried me as to the Malory *Introduction*, and tomorrow that will keep me busy.[100]
I have almost made up my mind to decline the school-engagements, being now wholly unfit to begin them, and feeling loth to bind myself to anything which will run me, in all weathers, as these did last year.

I cannot bear to hear of thy head and thy sweet eyes.

I wrote to Mrs. Maxwell yesterday, affirming thee as to the continued stay of the boys.

Sarah's letter is floating about my heart like a soft pink cloud about the west: and, better, fades into no gray. Pray tell her that my sword-point has now to be in a great many words at once, and that as soon as the environment relaxes a little, — which will be when thou comest home, – I will have somewhat to say to her.

Meantime I am, not so much thine, as a thought of

thee .

---

[100] In a letter the next day (Sept. 27, 1880, here omitted) Lanier wrote to Charles Scribner's Sons saying that he was forwarding the Introduction to *The Boy's King Arthur*: " I have endeavored to correct some faults in the Froissart Introduction, which was, I think, in some passages too clearly written down."

To Daniel C. Gilman

435 N. Calvert St.,
Bo.   Sep. 28, 1880.

My dear Sir:

I send a line to express my regret that severe illness prevents me from attending our reunion tonight.

While I am writing, let me add that an exhausting fever, — which has for three months baffled the skill of physicians in New York and Philadelphia as well as here, and which has quite disabled me from work during that time, — seems just now to have come to a crisis, and my physician believes he has found a controlling remedy for it; but its departure has left me in a state of great feebleness, and the medical gentlemen urge that, after being so long overworked, I must rest. For this purpose, I have given up all my school-engagements for the following year; and, with the same view, I beg that before causing my public lectures to be announced you will inquire whether any of the other lecturers would as lief begin their series in November, so as to throw mine over until after the Xmas holidays. This would be a great help towards — what now seems possible — a complete restoration of health for me.

If the lectures have been announced, I will deliver them as appointed: any postponement of *that* sort would be painful to me: but all I mean now to say is, that if any one else can be conveniently found to begin, – in the absence of any announcement – I should be very glad to wait. After the first of January, I should be entirely at your service for lectures and class-work for the rest of the school-year.

Pray do not take any trouble in this behalf. I will be glad to know some time within the next two weeks if any arrangement is possible.

I send Mrs. Gilman my article on " The New South ", in Scribner's, which seems to have awakened great interest.

Very sincerely yours,

Sidney Lanier.

To Mary Day Lanier

[Baltimore,] Sep. 29, 1880.

Dear Past and Future, whose absence maketh the present a thing of naught,

I have failed twice to get thee a letter written, by reason of calls at the last hour; to which, indeed, I should not have postponed thee, save for great pressure of work. I have finished and sent off the long-burdening Introduction to King Arthur; and pending this four great packages of proofs, embracing all the additional matter I had sent, had accumulated. These also I have finally dispatched; and am now upon the St. Nicholas article.

I have given up the school-engagements. Mrs. Singleton has just called, to make a despairing final appeal, but I have told her that profound rest has become absolutely necessary to me. I have written Mr. Gilman to put off my public lectures there until after December, if possible: and so, when the St. Nicholas paper is done,[101] and the last few odds and ends of the King Arthur finished, I propose to rest me, under thy nursing.

I was almost, if not quite, free from fever yesterday. Today, I have a little: but nothing like last week's flame. My lung is certainly greatly better: *Lachesis* appears to have worked wonders in that behalf.

Pray inquire me the amount of Dr. Jones's bill, immediately, and give me a hint as to how much beside will be needed to clear thee in all directions there. I have sent Mrs. Maxwell seventy five dollars,

God have thee in good keeping, prayeth thy

husband .

---

[101] In a letter to his wife, Oct. 2, 1880 (here omitted), Lanier wrote: " I sent off the St. Nicholas article complete last night." (See note 90, above.)

To Mary Day Lanier

Bo. Sep. 30, 1880.

Dear Soul. my spirit groaneth and travaileth upon the matter of a cook. I have not yet found a satisfactory person. And, the time growing short, I am wondering if after all it would not be a severe matter for thee to start housekeeping with *two* new servants, and if – in that view – it might not be well enough to put up with foul Fanny for a few weeks while we are slyly looking about. Herein Mrs. Turnbull could help us: and you cd. appoint interviews at her house, to keep Fanny from turning off applicants.

Or again. Emma is here: might it not be somewhat better to engage *her* temporarily as cook?

Of course, whether with her or Fanny officiating, Mrs. Quigley could eat in the dining-room after us, and not in the kitchen with them.

I wd. be glad to have the amount necessary to pay all thy bills as soon as possible, that I may straightway arrange for it.

I am better today than yesterday. Enclosed is a cordial note just come from Mr. Gilman, which gives me great relief.

It is one week from this day until thou comest to thy

husband.

To Mary Day Lanier

Bo. Oct. 4, 1880.

Dearest Soul, in preparing to receive thee I find a little solace by way of anticipation.

Yesterday afternoon came Mr. and Mrs. Gilman, who sat an hour: also Mrs. Bird, and Dr. Brown. The publishers write pleasantly of my Introduction, and I am just sending off proofs of it today which came yesterday morning.

I have engaged Emma, at $2.^{50} per week, to cook and do all else required; and she has begun bright and early this morning. The kitchen looks like another place, already. So thou wilt

not need to bring Mrs. Ouseley.   The beds and trunk will be
attended to as directed; the carpets are being put down; and
the stoves will be arranged.

I send three checks, thinking they will be in convenient
lumps for thee to pay with.   The $49. one thou wilt hand to
Dr. Jones: $48.⁰⁰ one to thy hosts: and the 45.⁰⁰, which is
a dollar or two over the sum thou specifiest for all other needs,
Father can have cashed at the bank for thee, to which end I
have made it payable to his order.

Now must I close, with perfect

love.

To Ephraim Keyser

435 N. Calvert St.
Bo.   Oct. 5, 1880.

Dear Mr. Keyser:

It will give me pleasure to speak to Mr.
Gilman about the matter you mention.

Please let me know immediately for what sum you will make
a bust of Prof. Sylvester,[102] so that I can begin my subscription-
list at the University without delay.

My house is all upturned with whitewashers, paperers, car-
pet-layers, &c. and I must get you to keep the other copy of my
bust until I can make a place here for it.   This will be in a few
days.

I've been desperately ill, and for this reason have not called;
but am much better today, and will be out by the end of the
week.[103]

Truly yours,

Sidney Lanier.

---

[102] J. J. Sylvester (1814-1897), professor of mathematics at Johns Hopkins
University and also the author of *The Laws of Verse* (1870).   He seems to
have been a close friend of Lanier.

[103] Mary Day Lanier returned to Baltimore on Oct. 7.   No letters by Lanier
between Oct. 5 and 29 have been found, but his illness during this period is
recounted in his wife's letter to J. B. Tabb, Nov. 5, 1880, below.

To CHARLES SCRIBNER

435 N. Calvert St.
Baltimore, Oct. 29, 1880.

Dear Mr. Scribner:

While my mind was freshly full of King
Arthur studies I desired to finish my work on that subject-
matter; and so, when the Malory book was finished I began
The Boy's Mabinogion. This I have now completed, except
some notes which I had better reserve until nearer the time of
printing; and I send you the work today by Express. The
pages run pretty uniformly 400 words each, and the book in
print will be about 350 pp., with the paragraphing of the
dialogue.

I send with it a list of subjects for illustration. You will
perceive on reading it what a field is here for grotesque and
spirited pictures. With the experience of the two preceding
works before me, and after looking over some current books
of Cassell, Petter . . & Co, let me earnestly renew my recommendation to you to consider the policy of illustrating this book
with a great many dashing woodcuts, of cheap but effective
style, like, for instance, those of " Chatterbox ".[104] I am satisfied
that the present work, which appeals very strongly to the local
pride of Welshmen and of Englishmen, can be made to have a
great sale abroad as well as at home by popularizing this edition.
If the engravings should present actual scenery of the spots in
Wales where these adventures occurred — which spots in many
cases are easily identified — the book might be rendered still
more taking.

Will you be kind enough to consider the matter at your
earliest convenience. I sincerely hope that the great success of
the Froissart may enable you to see your way clear for offering
a much larger sum in buying this book. For four months of
the spring and summer a desperate fever, which baffled all the
skill I could find in New York and Philadelphia, kept me from
all work, save the proofs of *The Boy's King Arthur* which I

---

[104] The popular series of cheap juveniles published by Donohue & Co. of
Chicago.

corrected under such circumstances of difficulty as make me
wonder, now that it is over. From this illness I have but lately
begun to recover, and the long enforced idleness has left me
in want of money.

I suspect, too, — from your silence about the matter, — that
I shall have some balance to pay on the Science of Verse enterprise; and I should be glad to adjust this — if my fear be
true —, as well as the advance of one hundred and fifty dollars
kindly made by you, out of the proceeds of The *Mabinogion.*
Among many inconveniences, my illness has wholly prevented
me from actively introducing my Science of Verse in England,
where it is already privately appreciated by some scholars.[105]
This I propose to do, immediately. The doctrines, though
meeting with much opposition and wide misunderstanding by
reason of their novelty, are daily gaining ground among those
whose opinion is of value. Many letters bring me evidence of
new friends the book is making.

Very truly yours,

Sidney Lanier.

To Clifford A. Lanier

435 N. Calvert St.
Bo; Oct. 30, 1880.

Dear Clifford:

Your letter, as rich in its enclosing as its
enclosed, came duly, and some loving reply would have been
sent you straightway but for illness and the double work that
follows thereupon. My fever, though abating, and even intermitting for two or three days, has never quite left me. I seem,
however, to be fairly mending, and have been able to do good
work for a week past.

I've been making up my " Boy's Mabinogion " – a companion
to the *Boy's King Arthur* now just coming out – and hope some

---

[105] One of these was probably James Spedding (1808-1881), the editor of
Bacon. Lanier's letters to him have not been found; but two letters from
Spedding have survived– Aug. 24 and Dec. 17, 1880– and are discussed elsewhere in the present edition (II, xxx, n. 27). (For Lanier's account with Scribner
re: *The Science of English Verse,* see note 2, 1881.)

good things from it. This finished I'm going at *The Girl's Paston Letters*, and *The Boy's Monstrelet*, with the hope of boiling our pot. Then if Heaven please, I will sing some of the multitude of songs which have accumulated within my heart.

I hope your fall business opens well, and health abounds. How are you? I liked not the last report we had of your physical welfare. Mary has been very bright since getting home again, but is under the weather today. My boy Robin is in admirable condition, and my three young men in Virginia are said to be sons of Anak for strength and size. These latter prosper so finely in the hill-country that we are minded to keep them there until Xmas at any rate, and longer if possible.

Dear soul, I crave a sight of you most grievously; will I never have it?

THE NATION of this week has a review of my *Science of English Verse* which, even in *my* experience, is unequalled for placid misrepresentation and Dryasdust stupidity. I have noted fourteen easily provable misstatements of fact in it, which I will send to the editors for publication, next week. I doubt they'll print my letter, however.[106]

Do you notice how gas-stocks are "booming" here and in New York? And would you not be wise to sell, if possible, on such a market?

I have four or five letters from various parts of the United States brought out by my New South article in the last SCRIBNER'S, inquiring the price of lands and many like things in the South, with a view to emigration there. They seem to be from substantial people. Is there any thoroughly sober-talking and reliable real-estate dealer in Montgomery who would send lists of actual farms for sale, with descriptions &c, to these people if I should forward their addresses?[107]

---

[106] An unfavorable review of *The Science of English Verse* appeared in the *Nation*, XXXI, 310-311 (Oct. 28, 1880). On reconsideration, Lanier decided not to send his answer (see his letter of Nov. 15?, 1880, below); but two drafts of his letter to the editor have survived, dated Nov. 11, 1880. (Both the review and Lanier's unsent reply are treated in II, xxvii-xxx.)

[107] Inquiries came to Lanier from Illinois, Michigan, Minnesota, Vermont, and England; and there were possibly others that have not survived. Apparently Lanier went to considerable pains to gather information for all of his correspondents (see V, lviii-lix, n.).

Here must I close, with kisses for you and t'other you, from both of

us.

To Daniel C. Gilman

[Balimore, Oct. 30, 1880?] [108]

Dear Mr. Gilman:

Please send me by bearer the English trans- lation of Schmidt's work on Greek Rhythm and Metre which you loaned me some months ago.[109] The messenger will pro- tect the book under his cloak.

A reviewer of my *Science of English Verse* in this week's NATION *hints* that I *may* have stolen from Schmidt, and *de- clares* that I *have* acknowledged my obligations to Helmholtz. Fortunately, abundant facts exist to prove both the hint and the assertion not only untrue but stupid; and I'm putting these together in a note to THE NATION.

Sincerely yours,

Sidney Lanier.

435 N. Calvert St.
Saturday.

From Mary Day Lanier to John B. Tabb

435 N. Calvert Street
Nov. 5th, 1880.

My good friend:

I do feel very guilty towards you – imagining myself at your point of view – but I am sure that you will trust me when I say that the neglect has been all my misfortune, not my fault. I appreciate the loving anxiety which prompted your inquiry and appreciated especially that thoughtful tenderness

---

[108] Conjectural dating from the reference to the composition of his reply to the reviewer in the *Nation* in this and the preceding letter, and from the partial date " Saturday."

[109] Actually borrowed two years before (see Lanier's letter of Nov. 25, 1878, and note 97).

for Sidney which directed the inquiry to me. For it is true that
he has needed absolute freedom from the pen, and this has
not been possible to him whose pen is his one implement. I re-
joined him in the lonely home on Oct. 7th and found that he
had made a little progress toward convalescence during the
month of our separation. The fever was lulled, the breathing
freer, and a little exercise possible.

But those fever flames arose too soon again, with only a week's
intermission; and I doubt that they have entirely spared him
for any day since then. During his holiday of one week he
gained two pounds. This looks as if he *would* rally quickly if
once freed from the consuming enemy. It has wasted him
since last May, continuously, although he failed to recognize
its nature and periodicity until June.

While the lung is seriously affected we entertain, more
strongly now than in the late summer, the hope that the root of
this attack is malarial and not hectic. There are times still
when in cherishing this hope we appear to be deluding ourselves; but we have our good physician's constant encouragement. He has never confessed to believing the illness original
with the lungs while he has avowed his repeated disappointment in determining its precise nature. It was his firm conviction that a few weeks of profound rest from both work and
business cares would reinstate the dear patient. But the experience of three idle months has not verified this prediction.

As to the present, Sidney eats well and sleeps tolerably;
what is to me, most encouraging is that he also *drinks* well:
for he has in past years made wonderful improvement whenever he could take whiskey freely. Dr– Shearer sent him some
famous old whiskey which was the first thing of the kind he
succeeded in taking without after suffering. Later we have
found a chemically pure native wine, simple grape-juice from
the Catawba and Concord grapes. This he drinks freely with
water and finds it altogether wholesome: the only wine that
gives him no suffering. He goes down town occasionally and
has worked (rather too much) at his books and business letters
daily for two weeks.

Another " boy's book " is ready: the " Mabinogion" Welsh
legends – and the " Paston Letters " are on the way. The
" New South " article in Scribner's October number brings him

about two letters weekly, ranging from Michigan to England, filled with questions relative to colonizing in or emigrating to various parts of the South. Perhaps you know that Sidney was compelled to give up all the school lectures arranged for this winter. He is still hoping to recover sufficiently to undertake the University lectures in January, and was sketching their outline to-day. Before I leave you let me tell you that I have taken your " Keats " sonnet into my heart — as has another, a West Chester friend, whose appreciation is worth far more than mine. I'm so very glad that you are a poet. But in fact " you " would not be " you " with the poet left out and, so I may instead rejoice, simply, *that you are*. This – for Sidney's sake, primarily, and also, for

Your faithful friend

Mary Day Lanier.

— I suppose *you know* that Sidney's love is herein !

To DANIEL C. GILMAN

435 N. Calvert St.,

Bo.   Nov. 5, 1880.

My dear Sir:

I suppose you will be soon desiring announcements for the Circular giving information as to the lectures of 1881, and I therefore enclose an outline of my own, leaving blanks for the details of date and hour.[110] I expect to be

---

[110] A memorandum has survived (MS, Johns Hopkins University) outlining twelve lectures on the English novel which differs only in wording from the course as actually announced and given in the winter of 1881 (see note 127, below).

Another surviving memorandum (MS, Johns Hopkins University), dated May 9, 1880, containing an elaborate program of courses for the year 1880-1881, was probably submitted earlier in the year. It offered a Minor Course in English Literature divided into four parts: (1) The Science of English Prose– a nine months' course in composition meeting twice a week; (2) The Science of English Verse– a month of lectures, twice a week, with Lanier's own book as the text; (3) The History of English Literature– lectures with textbook, three times a week throughout the year; and (4) Readings in the Greatest Writers– including Caedmon, Chaucer, Shakespeare, Milton, Pope, Keats, and Tennyson, with lesser writers of their periods, three times a week throughout

present at Prof. Morris's lecture tomorrow morning at ten, and will call as soon as it is over, to receive any suggestions you may wish to offer. I should be glad, too, to speak to you of my very instructive experience with the two classes I taught last winter,[111] as determining the nature of further courses of the same kind.

Faithfully yrs.

Sidney Lanier.

To Daniel C. Gilman [112]

[Baltimore,] Nov. 6. [1880]

My dear Sir:

I had been meditating, as a second course of public lectures during next term — if you should want them, — twelve studies on " The English Satirists ;" [113] and on my visit to the University today I observed from the bulletin-board that Mr. Rabillon is now lecturing on " The French Satirists." It occurs to me therefore that perhaps some additional interest in the subject might be excited if my course on The English Satirists should follow the completion of Mr. Rabillon's — which I suppose will not be before the holidays — and should be given in January and February, instead of the course mentioned in my note to you this morning. I may add that if some other gentlemen would offer courses on

the year. For a Major Course, the above program constituted the first year, and the second year was divided into four parts as follows: (1) General Philosophy of Literature– lectures; (2) Special Development of English Literature– lectures and textbook; (3) The Art of Expression– lectures, readings, and exercises on the acquisition of words, ideas, and forms; (4) Historic Study of English Criticism– from 1553 to the birth of the Chaucer and New Shakspere Societies in 1880 (all to be given two or three times a week throughout the year). No correspondence relative to this proposed program has been found (but see note 38, 1881).

Charles D. Morris (mentioned in the following sentence) was Collegiate Professor of Latin and Greek at Johns Hopkins University.

[111] See notes 9 and 19, above.

[112] Previously published, Mims, pp. 257-258.

[113] This course was never given. Prof. Léonce Rabillon, mentioned following, held a position as Lecturer at Johns Hopkins University similar to that held by Lanier.

the Greek and Latin Satirists we might all together make a cyclus of it.

Faithfully yours,

Sidney Lanier.

435 N. Calvert St.
  Saturday evening.

To SIDNEY LANIER, JR.

435 N. Calvert St.
Baltimore, Md.
Nov. 12, 1880.

My dearest Sidney:

What a long time has passed since I have been able to write you ! And, mercy upon us, what an age it is since I have seen my dear slender tall boy! It seems so long that I am wondering if you have had time to grow as tall and as slim as my long-legged friend Dr. Cockey who has to stoop in order to walk under our parlor chandeliers. I suppose it is a very good thing to have long legs when one is riding a horse. A great French writer named Dumas tells a terribly wild story of his father, who was a great horseman, and who – as Dumas says – could break a horse's ribs merely by the pressure of his legs. Have you learned to jump your horse over ditches and fences yet?

I expected to send you a text-book in Latin several days ago, but have not been able to find the one I wanted you to study. I hope to get it soon, and I feel sure you will enjoy learning to speak a little of this wonderful old language. I am going to ask you to find out who the people were that spoke Latin, and what language of the present day is most like it, so that you can tell me when you come home.

It gives me great pain to tell you that Fatsy [114] is dead. He suddenly grew sick, some weeks ago, and we did what we could for him. But, poor fellow, he couldn't tell us where he felt badly; and we were not able to discover any symptoms that would enable us to treat his disease. We have missed him,

---

[114] A neighbor's rooster (see Lanier's letter of Sept. 10, 1880, above).

sadly, and the back-lots around us seem quite desolate without his very striking figure.

I have just received your letter, and am glad to know you liked the ST. NICHOLAS. The next one will have an article by me on King Arthur.

Mother and I are indulging in many a fine dream of the week before Christmas, when we expect to bring you and our other two men home. You must caper about, and grow as fat and strong as possible before that time, so that we may be able to hug a great deal of you at once and thus make up for the time when our arms have been empty.[115]

Please tell Miss Mary that the letter to which she refers has reached me.

I send Charley a copy of the last SCRIBNER's today, and write him by the same mail. I wish I could tell you how much love goes with it ! to him, and to my little man Hal, and to you, from

Your father,

S. L.

TO A PUBLISHER [116]

435 N. Calvert St.
Baltimore, Md.
Nov. 12, 1880.

Dear Sir:

If you can see your way clear to print the handbook entitled " Chaucer and Shakspere, Three Comparative Studies &c," the *ms.* of which I send you today by express, I will be glad to see it brought out under your auspices.

---

[115] In a letter to S. M. Maxwell, Nov. 3, 1880 (here omitted), Lanier had written that his son Sidney had been sickly from birth, and that out-of-doors exercise should be emphasized even at the expense of his studies. Maxwell, at whose farm the Lanier boys were staying, was the husband of the former Mary Taliaferro, referred to in the following sentence.

[116] The MS from which this letter is printed seems to be a first draft, retained by Lanier. The publisher to whom it is addressed has not been identified, nor is there any positive evidence that the letter was actually sent.

The textbook here described had been previously submitted to other publishers (see note 51, above).

You will find in the Preface, bottom of p. 5 to the end, a statement of the special classes of readers for whose needs I have prepared this book. To that statement I may add that I have been brought in contact with many persons during some years past who have neither time nor desire to read Chaucer or Shakspere thoroughly but who would gladly welcome any book which would enable them to learn enough of both these masters to base at least the sense of a fair acquaintance on.

Again: in giving systematic courses of lectures upon Chaucer and Shakspere to parties of thirty or forty ladies and gentlemen, – during which I require each person to have the text in hand, so as to *see* as well as hear the words and passages commented on, — the difficulty I have found in procuring the books needed for this purpose — especially the Chaucers – has been incredible. Not one family-library in a hundred seems to have any Chaucer at all; and those persons who *could* bring one, would bring old editions of defective text, or, at best, unexpurgated editions containing passages which no man *can* read to a woman (I hope it is not prudish, but *I* can not read them to *myself*) and yet to skip which, in the course of the reading, was simply to accentuate the trouble. Oppressed more and more each year with this difficulty, I finally resolved to put together the present work, which contains the three masterpieces of Chaucer, made (I hope) additionally interesting by connecting them with the three masterpieces of Shakspere. These six works are a sort of education to any person who should master them. I have scrupulously cleaned them of grossness; and have given a short method of learning to read the original text of Chaucer (by a brief study of a few lines from Wycliffe's Bible) which I do not remember to have seen used elsewhere, and which has met with great success in my own experience.

You will observe that the notes are not yet appended to the texts of the plays and tales. They are all ready; being indeed mostly the substance of lectures given at the Johns Hopkins University and elsewhere, upon these topics: but I did not write them out because I happen to be oppressed with a cruel amount of work just at present, and do not care to spend any more time upon this book until I am sure that it can find a good publisher.

I am of the opinion that if this work were printed in moderately cheap form so as to bring it within popular reach, it might sell largely, and for a long time. – But my opinion in such matters is not of great value, I fancy.

I ought to add that inasmuch as, upon the commencement of future courses, I should request each hearer to come provided with a copy of this book (if it should be printed); and inasmuch as, further, I could not do this, of course, if I had any pecuniary interest in the sale of it — a scholar can not tout for his own books: — I should be obliged to part with the copyright at the outset. Since, if printed, the book would be *indirectly* very profitable to me, by enabling me to take large audiences through the courses which now are possible only to small parties of persons, for lack of such a book; I would be quite willing to sell the work outright for just what might compensate me for the time spent on it — which was about a month (or would be, when the notes should be appended, which will add about fifty printed pages to the book as it stands) and which might be valued at (say) three hundred dollars.

Very truly yrs,

Sidney Lanier.

To Charles Scribner [117]

435 N. Calvert St.
Baltimore, Md.
Nov. 12, 1880.

My dear Mr. Scribner:

You have certainly made a beautiful book of the *King Arthur*, and I heartily congratulate you on achieving what seems to me a real marvel of book-making art. The binding seems even richer than that of The *Froissart*; and the type and printing leave a new impression of graciousness upon the eye with each reading.

I suspect there are few books in our language which lead a

---

[117] Excerpt previously published, Mims, pp. 326-328. Scribner had written, Nov. 1, 1880: "We are expecting to publish the *Arthur* Oct.. [Nov.] 9th."

reader — whether young or old — on from one paragraph to another with such strong and yet quiet seduction as this. Familiar as I am with it after having digested the whole work before editing it and again reading it in proof — some parts twice over — I yet cannot open at any page of your volumes without reading on for awhile; and I have observed the same effect with other grown persons who have opened the book in my library since your package came a couple of days ago. It seems difficult to believe otherwise than that you have only to make the book well-known in order to secure it a great sale not only for the present year but for several years to come. Perhaps I may be of service in reminding you — of what the rush of winter business might cause you to overlook — that it would seem wise to make a much more extensive outlay in the way of special advertisement, here, than was necessary with the *Froissart*. It is probably quite safe to say that a thousand persons are familiar with at least the name of Froissart to one who ever heard of Malory; and the facts (1) that this book is an English classic written in the 15th century, (2) that it is the very first piece of melodious English prose ever written, though melodious English *poetry* had been common for seven hundred years before, — a fact which seems astonishing to those who are not familiar with the circumstance that all nations appear to have produced good poetry a long time before good prose, usually a long time before *any* prose — (3) that it arrays a number of the most splendid ideals of energetic manhood in all literature, and (4) that the stories which it brings together and arranges, for the first time, have furnished themes for the thought, the talk, the poems, the operas, of the most civilized peoples of the earth during more than seven hundred years, — ought to be diligently circulated. I regretted exceedingly that I could not, with appropriateness to youthful readers, bring out in the Introduction the strange melody of Malory's sentences, by reducing their movement to musical notation. No one who has not heard it would believe the effect of some of his passages upon the ear when read by any one who has through sympathetic study learned the rhythm in which he *thought* his phrases.

Speaking of rhythm reminds me that on reading the review of my *Science of Verse* in THE NATION of two weeks ago I counted fifteen errors of fact, embracing (and nullifying) every discussed allegation in the article. I have quite a little museum of curiosities of criticism; but this makes my previous collection very tame. I don't think any one would accuse me of *finicalness* in such matters, after an experience of newspaper follies during my short career which I sincerely believe to be wider than that of any American writer of my age; and, *with* this experience, I must say, in all soberness, that for pretentious ignorance and constitutional wrongmindedness this article is unique. Of course such a charge as this would be silly unless supported by specifications of line and paragraph, and detailed proof. These I have prepared, in the form of a letter to THE NATION, simply stating the facts without comment.

But, meantime, the hint of my indebtedness to Schmidt in the first paragraph of the review, and the extraordinary assertion in the second paragraph that I have " acknowledged obligations " to Helmholtz &c, occur to me as matters which ought immediately to be disproved to *you*, as publisher of the book. To this end: (1) will you be kind enough to read the specifications numbered (8), (9) and (10) contained in the accompanying *ms*,[118] whenever you have leisure; (2) then to open the translation (which you probably have in your own store) of Schmidt's *Leitfaden* &c, printed, under the title of " Schmidt's Introduction to The Rhythmic and Metric of the Classical Languages," by Ginn & Heath, Boston, 1878, and, comparing it with my book, see whether the " principles " are " the same " or whether the two works anywhere " move parallel "; (3) and finally examine the foot-note to p. 27 and the top of p. 32 of my book — the only places where Helmholtz's name is mentioned in the chapter cited — and note whether anything but the most nervous anxiety to find me indebted to somebody, combined with the vaguest hearsay knowledge as to Helmholtz, could find in them anything approaching an acknowledgement of indebtedness for the fundamental applications of physics to verse (Helmholtz's achievements and theories, so far as they regard art, relate to *music*) in my first chapter. With these compare the first two paragraphs of the review in the NATION.

---

[118] The MS inclosed was a copy of the letter which Lanier had addressed to the editor of the *Nation*, but which he never sent (see the following letter and note 106, above).

As showing, too, the ease with which the reviewer's ignorance is exposed, I send with the *ms.* the first three pages concerning his treatment of Anglo-Saxon verse.

— All this, of course, in the event that you think the matter worth bothering with. You will at any rate recognize that the reviewer's hint, in his first paragraph, as to Schmidt &c is one which *must* give me discomfort until I know that you have satisfied yourself about it.[119] I shall not send my letter to THE NATION for several weeks: since every day makes my book stronger with scholars.

Sincerely yours,

Sidney Lanier.

To Daniel C. Gilman

[Baltimore, Nov. 15, 1880?][120]

My dear Mr. Gilman:

A Sunday's sober thought quite decides me *not* to send the NATION letter: I think it *sounds* truculent and unscholarly, in some places. Perhaps I may send a communication, simply pointing out the errors of fact, entirely without comment; but I'll think it over. Please send me the letter, by bearer. I'm sorry to have troubled you with reading it.

After you have thought at your leisure upon the lecture matters, send me a card appointing an hour, and I will call, to get your suggestions.

Faithfully yours,

Sidney Lanier.

435 N. Calvert St.
Monday morning.

[119] Scribner replied, Nov. 24, 1880, that Lanier's letter proved the "entire dishonesty of the criticism" and added that it was "out of the question for the 'Nation' to confess that anything is original." He hoped they would publish his letter as it might "excite some discussion and so help to advertise the book," but doubted they would print it in full.

[120] Conjectural dating from the fact that the surviving draft of Lanier's letter to the editor of the *Nation* is dated Nov. 11, 1880, and that the first Monday thereafter was Nov. 15.

To Charles Scribner

435 N. Calvert St.
Baltimore, Md.
Nov. 17, 1880.

Dear Mr. Scribner:

President Gilman is at once so thoughtful
and so practically wise in his sayings and doings that I fancied
you would care to see the enclosed note from him about the
King Arthur,[121] the earnest commendation of which represents
the universal opinion I have heard expressed about it hitherto.
You can return it whenever you may happen to be writing.

Very truly yrs.

Sidney Lanier.

Mr. Chas. Scribner.
New York.

To Paul H. Hayne [122]

435 N. Calvert St.
Baltimore, Md.
Nov. 19, 1880.

My dear Mr. Hayne:

I have been wishing to write you a long
time, and have *thought* several letters to you. But I could
never tell you the extremity of illness, of poverty, and of un-

---

[121] In a letter of Nov. 15, 1880, thanking Lanier for a copy of *The Boy's
King Arthur*, Gilman wrote: "You are doing a right good service by suggesting such old, sound stories to the readers of our younger generation,— and you
seem to me yourself a valiant knight, fighting against ill health and other
opponents, a fight for all that is noble and inspiring. It is a wonder to me
perpetually that you can complete so many good undertakings, and I hope you
will have a life as long as you wish for, to devise and execute fresh enterprises."
(Fabian Franklin, *The Life of Daniel Coit Gilman*, New York, 1910, pp.
243-244.)

[122] Previously published, *Critic*, VIII [o.s.], 90 (Feb. 20, 1886). No letters from Lanier to Hayne between Oct. 16, 1875, and the present one have
been found. In spite of the long silence here referred to, there were undoubtedly other letters written during this period that have not survived (as indicated
in eight surviving letters from Hayne, including one of Oct. 19, 1880, thanking
Lanier for a copy of *The Science of English Verse*).

ceasing work, in which I have spent the last three years; and you would need only once to see the weariness with which I crawl to bed after a long day's work, – and often a long night's work at the heel of it, – and Sundays just as well as other days, – in order to find in your heart a full warrant for my silence. It seems incredible that I have printed such an unchristian quantity of matter, – all, too, tolerably successful, – and earned so little money; and the wife and the four boys – who are so lovely that I would not think a palace good enough for them if I had it – make one's earnings seem all the less.

This leads me to think of *your* fervent ascription of praise in the October *Scribner's* which several of my friends admire with me.[128] I will get the November *Harper's* – to which your note alludes – and read your poem there. A couple of songs by you, which I read in a news-store a short time ago while rapidly turning over the leaves of *The South Atlantic*, gave me much pleasure. I fancy that I perceive a *clarified* quality in your later verse which shows a distinct growth in you. The plane of the art seems higher and quieter, and the air purer.

I send you by this mail a copy of my *Boy's King Arthur*, which the publishers have brought out in sumptuous style as a companion-book to my *Boy's Froissart* which was so successful last year. I hope you will like the Introduction; as for the matter, – it is old Sir Thomas Malory's, and I doubt not you already know him well for one of the sweetest, cunningest, simplest, and skillfullest writers of English, as well as story-tellers, that ever lived. I'm greatly interested in the sale of this book: not directly, for being in narrow straits I sold the copyright for cash several months ago; but because the price of another book I've just sent on, to continue the series with, next Christmas, depends on it.

For six months past a ghastly fever has been taking possession of me each day at about twelve M., and holding my head under the surface of indescribable distress for the next twenty hours, subsiding only enough each morning to let me get on my working-harness, but never intermitting. A number of tests show it not to be the "hectic" so well known in con-

---

[128] Hayne's poem to his wife, "Love's Autumn," appeared in *Scribner's*, Oct., 1880. His poem in the Nov., 1880, *Harper's* (referred to in the following sentence), was "The Battle of King's Mountain."

sumption; and to this day it has baffled all the skill I could find in New York, in Philadelphia, and here. I have myself been disposed to think it arose purely from the bitterness of having to spend my time in making academic lectures and boy's-books – pot-boilers all – when a thousand songs are singing in my heart that will certainly kill me if I do not utter them soon. But I don't think this diagnosis has found favor with any practical physicians; and meantime I work day after day in such suffering as is piteous to see.

– I hope all this does not read like a Jeremiad; I mention these matters only in the strong rebellion against what I fear might be your thought – namely, forgetfulness of you – if you did not know the causes which keep me from sending you more frequent messages. I do not, and will not, forget the early encouragements which used to come from you when I was just daring to think of making verses.

I am glad to see, from your letter, that your illness abates. I protest against your sick terrapin, floating down a muddy current; and substitute a soul sweeping down a stream bank'd with marvels, whose duty is to keep all eyes open, and report, in poems, from time to time.

Please thank Mrs. Hayne for her card, and believe me always

sincerely yours

Sidney Lanier.

To William H. Ward

435 N. Calvert St.
Baltimore, Md.
Dec. 6, 1880.

Dear Sir:

Perhaps the enclosed [124] will be more suitable to you than either of the two little Songs just sent.

I hope this one is intelligible without its context. It is a song in one of my *Hymns of The Marshes*, – a volume of

---

[124] The poem sent with this letter, "A Ballad of Trees and the Master" (I, 144), had been written during the illness of Nov.-Dec., 1880. Lanier was paid $15.00 for it by the *Independent* (see W. H. Ward to Lanier, Dec. 24, 1880), where it was published, Dec. 23, 1880. William Hayes Ward (1835-

EARLY DRAFT OF LANIER'S "SUNRISE," PAGES 1 AND 6, DECEMBER, 1880

Including " A Ballad of Trees and the Master" as an intercalary song

Manuscript in the Clifford A. Lanier Collection, Johns Hopkins University

poems I have nearly completed, which I hope to print soon.[125]

While I am writing, let me acknowledge – as I should have done sooner but for continued illness – your kind expressions in regard to my work, accompanying your request for more of it. These tempt me to be so personal as to add that I've been trying a long while – with " Boy's Froissart " and " Boy's King Arthur " and the like bread-winning books – to win a little respite from the fierce distractions of daily necessity, in which I could merely reduce to form a volume or two out of a great number of poems that lie about me in memorandum. It seems slow work: but I do not despair of a time – indeed I do not look forward to any possibility of life other wise – when my only business will be to sing.

– Pray pardon this : a sympathetic word makes one forget conventions.

Very truly yours,

Sidney Lanier.

Mr. William Hayes Ward,
New York.

1916), the editor, became Lanier's first biographer and a champion of his fame, though they never met. The " two little Songs just sent " were probabaly " A Sunrise Song " (I, 143) and " A Song of Eternity in Time " (12), both published in the *Independent* in 1881. Other possibilities are " Between Dawn and Sunrise," " To the Sun," and " Marsh Song—At Sunset "—the first two being intercalary songs for " Sunrise," the third published in the *Independent*, 1891.

In a reminiscent letter to Mrs. Charlotte Ware, Sept. 13, 1910, Mary Day Lanier has left a detailed account of the composition of " A Ballad of Trees and the Master," one of Lanier's best known poems. A Mrs. F. Q. Ogden, who is described as devoting herself " to musical interests and earnest study of philosophy of religions," had become an ardent friend of the Laniers and, in spite of suffering from " a prolonged and terrible illness " herself, was constantly solicitous of Lanier during Nov., 1880, when he was passing through " a critical battle for life." Finally, " one stormy morning," she sent an urgent call for Mary Day Lanier, to lay before her a new course of treatment for her husband. Lanier insisted that she go. " After meeting his routine wants and turning to change my nurse's dress for storm outfit, he asked me to first attach to his bedside a swinging writing-stand, gift of . . . Lawrence Turnbull, and to give him pen and ink and paper. Fifteen or twenty minutes later, as I came ready to start, he turned over to me a leaf bearing the poem, saying: ' Take this to her, Maydie, and tell her it is fresh from the mint.' . . .

" A month later the first autograph of *Sunrise* incorporated this ballad within itself. . . . " (See the manuscript pages opposite, including both poems.) Mrs. Ogden's letter of thanks for the poem is dated Dec. 2, 1880.

[125] For an account of this projected volume, which was never published, see the Introduction to vol. I and note 7, Letters of 1881.

To Nicholas Murray? [126]

435 N. Calvert St.
Bo·, Dec. 10, 1880

My dear Sir:

I return proof corrected.

I am greatly your debtor for calling my attention to the *lapsus* concerning Collins and *The Moonstone*.[127] The outline was made up in the midst of a burning fever which rendered me very absent-minded. It will add to my obiligations if you will carefully see that the substitution is made, as per proof.

It occurs to me to ask if you wished to state the *hour*, as well as the dates, of the lectures. I find the latter only are given. There is room in the third line to add, " at 5 P. M. ", — or such hour as is determined on.

Very truly yrs,

Sidney Lanier [128]

From Mary Day Lanier to Clifford A. Lanier

Baltimore. Dec. 10th 1880.

Dearest Clifford:

Our loved one has long been a very ill man — and your Maydie's letter of last August was made to spare the hearts that cherish him *all it could.* To leave you quite igno-

---

[126] This letter was probably addressed to Nicholas Murray, who in 1880 was assistant to Pres. D. C. Gilman, and as such superintended the publication of the Johns Hopkins University Circulars.

[127] The MS memorandum (Johns Hopkins University) announcing Lanier's lectures for the winter of 1881 names Trollope rather than Wilkie Collins as the author of *The Moonstone*.

The announcement in *The Johns Hopkins University Circulars*, No. 8, p. 99 (Jan., 1881), states that Lanier will lecture in Hopkins Hall on Wednesdays at 5 P. M. from Jan. 12 to Mar. 26, 1881, on the subject: " From Aeschylus to George Eliot: Twelve studies in the Modern English Novel as a Development of the Greek Drama." (See IV, vii, for differences in dates of lectures as announced and as actually given.)

[128] In a note of Dec. 11, 1880 (here omitted), Lanier asked C. J. Meyer, Treasurer of Johns Hopkins University, to send a check for half his salary ($500.00) by the Librarian, W. H. Browne, " who lives near me."

rant, seemed wrong.   He rallied during the first, ten days, of
October; the fever almost disappearing for a week.   With that
exception his course has certainly been — from one fortnight
to another — steadily downward ever since the first of May.
His last letter to you, upon business, was written in bed.   He
has been sitting up about one fourth of the time during the
last month.   Until then his appetite continued good and he
had found a pure red wine he could drink freely, also taking
some of his good, *blessèd* doctor's old whiskey at night, in a
glass of rich cream, daily cream, daily sent to him by Mrs. Wm.
Hand Browne, from her Alderney cow.   During these four
weeks all stimulants have been stopped, as increasing the spasmodic cough to an intolerable point.   There is no appetite,
though kind, anxious friends are daily sending in every kind of
delicacy to him.   He swallows Cream, Meat Juice, an egg,
Malt Extract a few bites of solid food, and thus supplies fuel
for this wild flame of fever that wd. soon consume him without the concentrated & generous nourishment.   The last three
days have been uncommonly severe — temperature ranging
from 100 to 104¾ — pulse from 95 to 130.   This goes on
without intermitting.   The fever fluctuates but never goes off.
   He has still done some snatches of work this fall, even when
unable to be propped up in bed.   The lecture classes had to be
given up.   The University still waits for him – in hope.   I, too,
wait in hope, my darling.   Often through the silent and de-
fenceless *nights* dark possibilities possess me as certainties, and
in stillness and tension of soul I meet it all.   But the days have
their armor — of work for him, — of the blessed light, of the
sight of his face; and I find nothing without hope while I can
look in his eyes.
   We cannot say how far the doctor is candid with us: at least,
he is careful to tell our friends the same encouragements.   He
confesses to finding it a very difficult case – and it *has* been
baffling, contradictory, inexplicable, in several particulars.   But
he has assured me lately, in private, that while Sidney is " seriously ill " he does expect to see him up and at work again.   I
replied " I believe there is a chance "; when he emphatically
said – " there are *several* chances."   I had the interview because I needed guidance about writing to poor Father, who
would suffer so much from alarm, and to you, my darling, and

I told the doctor what my responsibilities were: Sidney having always concealed his illness. This opinion was given upon the belief that the lungs were the main trouble, together with over-taxed nervous system. A few days later, on the 8th, finding that his expectations were not being realized he brought a consulting physician, Dr. [Marbury] Brewer. They have decided *the heart* to be responsible for the fever. Its condition is given *to us*, as with " slight hypertrophy — not considerable: *dilatation* causing *thinness of the walls*." It is " the opposite of fatty degeneration of the heart." The lung, with tuberculous deposit and a pleuritic adhesion; but no cavity as yet. The report of the lungs was better than I had thought possible, having laid to them so much of his suffering that likely belongs to the heart. Our boys were to come home to us for six weeks on Dec. 18th.[129] I still think of allowing it – tho' all is now indefinite. He is too ill for them *not* to come: yet too ill for any noise or excitement. Please communicate as much as is best to Sister, but *let us speak to Papa*. We will do so to-morrow – You can have no idea how hard for me to find a chance to write carefully, and to him I dare not write in this direct and hasty way. Am too sorry to do it to you. I have been very ill for ten days – an abscess at root of tooth & ulcerated throat – and cd. neither eat nor sleep — nor, for two days wait on Sidney beyond an hour or two. The anguish in eyes and head disabled me from thinking, or I should have written sooner. My brother dear, write cheerfully *for him*, I entreat you. Do not show either grief or alarm, or it may be dangerous. I promise you he never sees either from me. Send him a love-word when you can, and, of course, having told you his danger I will now send a postal or more every two or three days until we are in smooth waters.

Blessings to Willie & little ones,

Maydie.

[129] On Dec. 18, 1880, Mary Day Lanier wrote to their three sons in Virginia a frank account of their father's serious illness, saying that ten day ago his life had been despaired of: " He lives, and gains a little strength each day, this week, so that now he is sitting up. But still we have a long hard battle to fight for his recovery. His heart calls for the sight of you;– he has been so near to leaving you that he needs to look into your dear eyes and to hear your words of love and to press your dear rough little hands in his. It will help him to get well if you will come awhile and help me nurse him. . . . I am sure you will

To FRANCIS F. BROWNE

435 N. Calvert St. Balto.
Dec. 13th, 1880.

My dear Mr Browne:

For several weeks a shrewd wrestle between me and that old Champion who has so long held the belt against all comers — that same John Death — has completely occupied my powers, both physical and mental. Your letter came to me in the midst of it and I was so touched by your friendly appeal that as I lay in bed I wrote reply after reply to you, though I was obliged to content myself merely with the longing desire that one of these warm responses might go to you in palpable form immediately. I could not write, and those about me were too busy with momentary cares for my safety to write for me. It is a real distress to me that another kind letter comes from you to-day before I have been able to testify my sympathy with the suffering which you were good enough to show me in your previous letter, and my grateful pride that you should have thought of relief in my direction. I should like greatly to dwell upon some parts of your letter, but my ability to dictate is extremely limited and I must postpone all that.

You will care to know that the physicians' opinion points to a functional disturbance (not organic) of the heart as the immediate cause of my present crisis, and to a favorable termination. As for my own opinion: I doubt the accuracy of the heart diagnosis, in detail, at least, and am satisfied I shall write many another poem.

I will ask you to say nothing of *this* illness in print. You will not consider this as implying the least objection to your former kindly notice which met with my full approval.[130]

believe that it is not to make ourselves comforted at your expense that we bring you from a merry country Christmas to a Christmas in a house of illness and in the city's restraints."

[130] In a letter of Oct. 30, 1880 (here omitted), Lanier had thanked Browne for "the pleasant expressions of our very agreeable DIAL." The notice appeared in the Chicago *Dial*, I, 139 (Nov., 1880), under Personal Mention: "Mr. Sidney Lanier has been quite ill since midsummer, and has been barely able to perform the labor of correcting the proofs of his 'Boy's King Arthur,' which the Scribners have in press. He is, however, recovering."

Special reasons, not then existing, render this advisable at present.

I return your slips with many thanks for your wish in the matter. I *would* be glad of a chance to say something about Mʳ. Tennyson whose work is just now at that stage where a few quiet words — words which "hear the roll of the ages" — would be of service to its proper appreciation by many doubting Souls.[131] But I can hardly hope to do any work before the first of January, and I shall then be crowded beyond my capacity.

Let me hear from you whenever you feel like writing: your letters are always of interest to me, — and, may I add? to my wife, who writes this for me.

Sincerely yours,

Sidney Lanier.

per M. D. L.

To Frances L. Turnbull [132]

[Baltimore, Dec. 18, 1880.]

My dear friend:

After a glittering preamble of smiles and tears and fair sayings, my wife has just told me of this wonderful and beautiful piece of forethought in my behalf.

I cannot conceive it as the product of anything but true love, and all the lessons of my life have converged in teaching me to follow without hesitation where love leads: and so, in spite of a struggle whose bitterness any man will understand, I am able to say, out of a heart somewhat cleared by that tempest, that I accept your help as freely as it has been given.

It will remove some grievous burdens imposed on me by a half-year of almost complete disability for work. Of course all understand that I am to have the additional pleasure of sometime repaying, when health and strength return: of which latter I have never doubted.

---

[131] In a letter of Dec. 9, 1880, Browne had asked Lanier to review Tennyson's latest volume, or to write "an article on 'Recent Poetry', devoted mostly to Tennyson, but saying something of them all."

[132] This letter is addressed to "Mr. or Mrs. Lawrence Turnbull, 414 Beethoven Terrace."

As an arm clothed in white samite, mystic, wonderful,[188]
which has reached up suddenly out of my lake of trouble and
has handed me a helpful Excalibur: it is thus, dear Mrs. Turnbull and all the unknown others, that I will think of your
friendliness in this action.

I turn with complete dissatisfaction from all forms of thanks
to you, save the single one of making a future which shall be
more worthy of this beautiful sanction you have set on the past:
appealing to that by anticipation, and shrinking from all words,
I am

gratefully and faithfully

your friend

Sidney Lanier.[184]

435 N. Calvert St.
Saturday, Dec. 18, 1880.

To Sarah J. Farley

Bo. Dec. 31st, 1880.

Your words come, my dear Sarah, and run out along all my
affections and meditations to the very end of them: have you
seen the Southern " Yellow Jessamine," which grows alongside
a great live-oak, and winds its curling vines about each twig
and bough until the whole great globe of the tree-top is one

---

[188] The phrase is quoted from Tennyson's " Morte D'Arthur."

[184] On the same day (Dec. 18, 1880) Mary Day Lanier wrote to R. S. Lanier
that her husband had been sitting up since noon for the second time and was
stronger than yesterday, but urged him to come to Baltimore for Christmas,
which he did. On Dec. 24, he wrote to his son Clifford from Baltimore:
" Sidney rested pretty well last night & stood our long talks yesterday better
than expected. Talking much makes him cough more, & he raises a good deal
of matter. I believe a few months rest would build him up greatly & yet he
talks of resuming his lectures at John Hopkins about the middle of Jany.

" One does not have to be in his home long to find out that he is greatly
esteemed and loved by many good people here, & elsewhere. This is shown not
only in words but in substantial tokens. And I do not wonder at it– he is so
charming & sweet even in his illness.

" . . . Our dear boy sits about dressed, looking feeble enough, tho' not greatly
reduced in flesh, & talks brightly and hopefully. My stay here will depend
on his improvement."

mass of heavenly gold bloom, – in bloom-time? My Mary feels this same effect, and we have exclaimed simultaneously over the wonder of your loving utterances to us. You give us great comfort, friend.

I seem surely to have turned the corner. Pulse and temperature have fallen steadily each day for three days, and my growth in strength is great. We will not go to New York, or anywhere, for the present. I expect to deliver my University lectures, according to appointment, beginning January 12. Our boys are to be with us Monday. Mary is out, shopping, – for blankets. This is written in the dark, a messenger waiting to get it in the mail.

My very heart is herein.

S. L.

1881[1]

To Charles Scribner

435 N. Calvert St.
Baltimore, Md.
Jany 7, 1881.

My dear Mr. Scribner:

A long and severe illness has prevented me from sooner acknowledging the kindness of your last letter in deferring settlements &c. in order to enable me to avail myself of the *Mabinogion*[2] — a kindness which I particularly appreciated.

It occurs to me to make two suggestions about *the Mabinogion* for your consideration whenever you take up the *ms.*, — which I beg you will do entirely at your leisure, since my main motive in hastening forward the book was my desire to meet my obligations to you promptly.

(1) " Mabinogion " is at once so outlandish and so little known that I incline to think it might be well to call the book " The Boy's King Arthur Number Two, *Or* Mabinogion," espe-

[1] R. S. Lanier left Baltimore Jan. 6, 1881. On Jan. 10 he wrote to Clifford Lanier from Macon: " I left Sidney still affected with his fever. By the Postal of Mary rec'd this morning, enclosed, it appears he remains in bed to try to abate the fever. He was very desirous of being able to sit up, as he feared he might get more feeble by remaining in bed."

[2] On Nov. 24, 1880, Scribner had written that he had not yet found an opportunity to look over the MS of *The Boy's Mabinogion*, but added: " With regard to the payment for the new book and your account on ' Science of Verse ' I can only write also that I will, after making some estimates, soon make you some proposition. The sale of the ' Science of Verse ' will, I fear, prove a disappointment to you and will certainly not be large enough to cancel your indebtedness for the plates. But rest content about that matter until you hear from me. I will meet your views as far as I can."

A statement of Lanier's account as of Feb. 1, 1881, submitted by Charles Scribner's Sons (in Scribner's letter of Apr. 13, 1881), showed that the cost of *The Science of English Verse* had been $529.02. To this was added interest since May, 1880, bringing the total to $551.77. The amount of Lanier's royalties on 405 copies sold, at .30 each, was subtracted, leaving a balance due by him of $430.27.

cially in view of the great success of the *King Arthur*, whereof many accounts have come from enthusiastic friends and others in all parts of the country.

(2) Would not the very remarkable passages in the book involving color make it worth while to reproduce them in a few illuminations of medieval style? What a taking picture, for example, could be made of the scene in the first tale where King Arthur is shown, robed in bright-colored (I have forgotten the exact color, but it is given) satin, resting on *green* rushes covered with *red* silk, while Queen Guenever and her attendant ladies, gorgeously attired, occupy the other end of the apartment. I should think that two or three illuminations of this sort, for which the book offers rich material, would amply pay for themselves.[3]

I think I have made a great " find " in a book which I will soon complete — " The Girl's Paston Letters " — and which, as giving a charming contemporary picture of English *domestic* life in the otherwise dark 15th century, would be an admirable book to print in connection with my " Boy's Monstrelet," which gives the *political* life of England during the same period. I presume you know the history, and the fascination, of " The Paston Letters," which, though published about a hundred years ago, have hitherto been mainly known only to scholars. I happened to observe that they were largely written — particularly the most naive and interesting of them — by the female members of the family, and was struck with the idea that, by selecting and popularly editing these ladies' letters mostly, a beautiful and classic girl's-book could be made, which would have the additional value of presenting the same period (from a purely domestic and social point of view) with that treated in Monstrelet's *Chronicles*. In the course of a month or two I will send the *mss.* of these two books — " The Girl's Paston Letters," and " The Boy's Monstrelet " — complete.

With cordial messages for the New Year, I am

Very sincerely yours,

Sidney Lanier.

[3] Scribner wrote on Apr. 13, 1881, that he had decided to illustrate the *Mabinogion* in the same manner as the preceding volumes. (For the new titles suggested in the following paragraph see Lanier's letter of Feb. 12, 1881, and note 7, below.)

To Daniel C. Gilman

[Baltimore, Jan. 7, 1881.]

My dear Sir:

I had entertained no other thought than that of appearing in my place on the 12th according to appointment, and had prepared myself to that end; but a few minutes after the arrival of Dr. Browne's note containing your kind suggestion of postponement, my physician called, and upon mentioning the matter to him he urged my agreement so strongly that it seems a duty to comply. And so – although I have a nervous horror of "postponement" which regards it as a sort of crime — I will ask that the date for my first lecture be fixed in accordance with your suggestion as January 26, being two weeks from January 12 as first appointed.

I cannot help adding, however, that if any public announcement has been made of the original arrangement I am confident I can lecture on the 12th, and that if it is of importance to adhere to that plan I beg you will let me do so.

With the most grateful acknowledgements of your kindly forethought in the matter, I am

faithfully yours,

Sidney Lanier.

435 N. Calvert St.
Friday, Jany 7. '81 .

To Daniel C. Gilman

[Baltimore, Jan. 19, 1881.]

My dear Sir:

I send a line to say that I was out yesterday, and transacted some business in the city, not only without bad consequences but with a sense of benefit from the open air exercise; so that you may feel no doubt as to my entire ability to begin lecturing next Wednesday according to appointment.

I expected to call at the University this morning and report in person, but am detained at home by some work.

Faithfully yours,

Sidney Lanier.

435 N. Calvert St.
Wednesday, Jan. 19th, 1881.

To Sarah J. Farley

435 N. Calvert St.
Bo., Jany 28, 1881.

Dearest Sarah, I wish they had appointed you Old Probs, instead of Gen. Hazen who seems able to get us nothing but ice and snow. A letter of yours always makes fair weather in our house: your words come veritably like the sweet South breathing o'er a bank of violets: [4] and such a bank your love is, indeed, to my Self and me. If you had eyes and hands enough to write us every hour !

You — you summer-maker ! – make me think of the world's general summer which will also come: for several days I have found myself looking forward to some peaceful and warm hours which I mean to spend by you next summer, unless all the heavens and the earth say nay. After eight months of fever, the term " repose " comes to have a quite new significance. It is *so* long since I have been able to repose, physically ! But a great change has come, and I begin to feel a sense of the *possibility* of physical rest which is itself delightful. When I think of flâner-ing all a-stretch in a great chair, perhaps under a tree, with a bird about, and the sky above and you in voice-reach below, — I try not to think of anything else for a long time. Of course we will arrange this. Let me alone for arranging ! particularly with May to help; and still more particularly when she knows that the me under the tree includes her.

My great easy-chair, bought with that " message " of your mother's, receives me every day with a certain graciousness and

---

[4] The phrase is quoted from Shakespeare's *Twelfth Night*.

amplitude of welcome that remind me of her, and I take great comfort in this little far-away resemblance.

I mourn over those eyes. Do not you think the weakness is merely part of your general feebleness? The latter is often known to produce what seems actual local disability of the eye, in one form or another, which disappears entirely with the return of general strength.

Mary has sent you a card, to let you know how cleverly my lecture went off. It was simply a miracle! I could scarcely speak a dozen loud words at home — before going to the lecture-room — without coughing, a special attack of influenza having irritated my vocal apparatus some days ago: but I read, so as to be heard clearly to the end of the hall, for exactly fifty five minutes, without a break ! I feel sure that some one of the angels whose patience is tested with the charge of me is a good throat-doctor, and that I am a living example of the skill thereof.

I wish I could stop writing you, dear: but I can't: I shall be going on, — though I now close this visible tablet to send it to you; — and I think I surely indite a thousand pages to you a day. 'Tis a vile age, and a stupid: with all the -graphs, to have no psychograph, or cardigraph, to take down thoughts and feelings at some kind of tolerable speed.

And as this is merely part, what is the use of the formula of closing? as if my letter were ended. I've just begun: and haven't said anything yet but " dear Sarah ".

FROM MARY DAY LANIER TO LAWRENCE TURNBULL [5]

[Baltimore, Feb. 2, 1881.]

Dear Mr. Turnbull:

Your note is so good and kind and shows me so plainly that we have thoughtlessly (in our haste) caused you some trouble of mind that could have been avoided, that I am tempted to let regret for that usurp the main place in my

---

[5] On Feb. 1, 1881, Mary Day Lanier sent a note to Lawrence Turnbull asking him to be godfather to Robin (Robert Sampson Lanier II), who was to be baptized on his father's birthday. In a reply written the same day Turnbull declined her request, saying that he did not consider himself an orthodox Christian. The present letter is her answer to his note. After he had declined

thoughts. And I wish, good friend, that I could see you, because I am too unwell to write out in form what I have to say.

I think I had already surmised that you were not in exact accord with any of the established forms of worship. Neither is Robin's own dear father, whom I pray to keep as his best and wisest earthly teacher; still, he finds himself able sometimes to join in our church worship by using what seem to him larger interpretations of the same general truths. For myself — I was differently taught in childhood — but I have learned, through much anguish, to believe in many ways of reaching the Truth, the Light and the Life. I think orthodox people are very peaceful and enviable but *we* have no prospect of bringing up an orthodox family ! You would not bring in one disturbing element.

It is enough to receive Christ as *the Master* and *the Saviour*. All lesser details we can trust with Him. I wished to take no unwarrantable responsibility and had a moment's talk about it with Mr. Kirkus. It was pleasant to find him heartily of our way of thinking. He says, in conclusion, "Why — if your friend could not impart to his godson *all* of the teachings of the Church — let him take so much as he can " — in the infrequent event of such ministration being necessary.

I love my church, dear Mr. Turnbull, but I do not feel sure that it is without error. I have the trust that it holds more power to bless its children than any other – if they understand their privileges – – – – –

– – – – – Just here comes the enclosed note from my dear pastor. Sidney has read it with great satisfaction and joins me in begging you to accept its message just as we do. It enables me to dispense with more blundering attempts at expression.

You see we cannot give you up easily. Cannot conscience and love go together this time?

Sidney begs you to be with us at, (or soon after) 4 o'clock

a second time, she wrote again on Feb. 3 apologizing for having urged him. The sequence of notes reveals the sympathetic understanding that existed between them.

Lanier's fourth son was baptized Feb. 3, 1881, by the Rev. William Kirkus, rector of the Church of St. Michael and All Angels. The Parish Register carries the names of Mary Day Lanier and Charles Day Lanier as the only witnesses.

tomorrow; no matter what your decision is. But it will be hard to make us yield to any decision but the one we want.

My fondest love to dear Mrs. Turnbull and regrets, the heartiest, that she is not strong enough to smile on us with you.

If it suits you to do so please direct the bearer, Charley, to call back for the briefest line of reply – either at your house or office, at the hour you find best.

Very truly your friend,

Mary D. Lanier

Feb. 2nd
1881.

To Sarah J. Farley [6]

Ibid. [Baltimore]
Feb. 12, 1881.

Ah-ha, you subtlest of Sarahs, – " no writing inside," eh ? " none whatever ", indeed la, now, the idea ! But if the poor deluded Post Office Department of your wronged country should charge up the proper postage upon this communication of endless meaning — nay, even upon what the Smilax alone did say to these eyes of mine, which, longing for some green thing, suddenly found it and found it infused with *you* — you were beggared, my child, to pay these postal dues.

The flowers came early, and were almost the first thing I saw on awakening from a late tired sleep. Before they were taken out, I, with my long nose thrust deep down into the cool mass, was full happy a long time; the odor, the moisture, the color, all seemed to come three-in-one by some single sense.

———" My lectures take all my time, and I cannot write you. I had not thought they would be so laborious: but I find the numerous illustrations of antique thought and habit require a great deal of research, and each lecture is a good week's work for a well man.

And when I contemplate the other things I am waiting to do, many of them half-done, towit:

[6] Excerpt previously published, W. M. Baskerville, *Southern Writers* (Nashville, Tenn., 1899), I, 220-222.

(1) My *Hymns of The Marshes*, nearly complete, (whereof you have seen *The Marshes of Glynn* and the little Song of *Trees and The Master*);

(2) my *Clover And Other Poems*, now quite ready for the press;

(3) my *Credo And Other Poems*, a thick volume, all in memoranda ready to be written out in a few weeks;

(4) my *Choral Symphony*, for chorus and Orchestra, being my *Psalm of The West*, with music;

(5) my Symphony *Life*, in four movements, 1st, Childhood, 2nd Youth, 3rd Manhood, 4th Old Age;

(6) my *Symphony of The Plantation*, being the old and new life of the negro, in music;

(7) my *Symphony of The Woods*, – all these symphonies lying in chaos now about my musical memorandum-books;

(8) my *Girls' Paston Letters*) now in my desk, half prepared;

(9) my *Boys' Monstrelet*, also in desk, ready to arrange;

(10) my *Boy's Gesta Romanorum*; [7]

---

[7] Lanier's catalogue of work in progress would lead one to suppose that at his death he left more finished work than the state of his MSS indicates, for much that he lists here was far less than " half-done."

" Credo and Other Poems " was never carried beyond the stage of " poem outlines," written on scraps of paper, backs of letters, envelopes, etc. " Clover and Other Poems " was planned as a collection of the bulk of Lanier's previously published poetry (see Printer's Copy, Henry W. Lanier Collection, Johns Hopkins University). " The Hymns of the Marshes " was apparently to include " The Marshes of Glynn," " The Cloud " " A Ballad of Trees and the Master," and four other poems composed in 1880-1881 but not mentioned in any of the letters: " Sunrise " (I, 144), the long poem which according to Mary Day Lanier was written in Dec., 1880, and put into final form shortly after New Year's, 1881; " A Sunrise Song " (I, 143); " Between Dawn and Sunrise " (I, 142); and " Marsh Song—At Sunset " (I, 142). These three projected volumes of poetry are discussed more fully in the Introduction to vol. I of the present edition.

Of the musical compositions listed no trace has been found of the orchestration of " The Psalm of the West," but the other three are represented by the following surviving fragments: " Symphony Life," " The Southern Suite. The Corn-Shucking. / The Breakdown," and " Mem. Symphony. / The Woods " (MSS, Charles D. Lanier Collection, Johns Hopkins University).

As for the juveniles, a letter from Scribner's to Clifford Lanier, Sept. 29, 1884, acknowledges receipt of his proposed introduction to the *Monstrelet*. Lanier's copy of *The Chronicles of Enguerrand de Monstrelet* (London, 1877), translated by Thos. Johnnes, has survived, with a bill indicating it was purchased on Oct. 22, 1880. There are no markings in it, but it may have been turned over to

— when I contemplate these, now lying upon my hands in actual form of one sort or another, – without daring to think of books merely projected; – I fall to wondering whether I have any business or right to wait, whether I had not better go and borrow a lot of money, five thousand, ten thousand, dollars, — which could be so easily repaid in five years (the copyrights of the Boys' *Froissart* and *King Arthur* would have done it, if I had not been obliged to sell them), — and put myself in heaven at once with nothing but poetry to write, and two years of freedom from slavery to butcher and baker !

— I wonder that I should be talking to you of such things; is it that I feel a dim urgence to see how a thing will look in plain words which I have only dreamed of in inarticulate desires ? But I find, dear Sarah, that I can talk to you of more things and nearer things than any friend I have ever had.

I am not very well: some fresh cold troubles me; but withal I have given three lectures, and the voice reaches the farthest listeners without strain. A special exposition of strength appears to come Down for each effort.

I wish you to have, dear friend, such blessing as you *are* to

your friend

S. L.

To LAWRENCE TURNBULL

[Baltimore, Feb. 21, 1881?] [8]

My dear Lawrence:

You are like the fairy godmother: as soon as I want anything, you wave your wand and it appears.

I have marked Geo. MacDonald's *Paul Faber* and *Robert Falconer*, Reade's *Hard Cash*, and Disraeli's *Endymion*. The others are very tempting: but I'm obliged to confine my treat-

---

Clifford Lanier for posthumous editing, a project that never materialized. Lanier's copy of the Bohn Library edition of the *Paston Letters* (London, 1859), has also survived. Vol. I, pp. 1-159, contains marginalia in his hand for editorial matter and markings indicating his selection of 91 out of the first 202 letters. No trace has been found of his work on the *Gesta Romanorum*.

[8] Conjectural dating from the evidence of Mary Day Lanier's letter to Frances Turnbull, Feb. 23, 1881, saying that the one ticket (mentioned at the close of the present letter) would admit them both; and from the partial date " Monday."

ment to the *English* novels, – which are indeed much more than
I can give any account of.[9]

I enclose one ticket to the course, and will send another.

Faithfully yrs,

Sidney L.

435 N. Calvert
Monday.

To Sarah C. Bird

[Baltimore, Feb.-Mar., 1881?][10]

My dear friend:

I find that Mary has a copy of " The Crystal,"
and beg you will give it with my compliments to Mrs. Harwood.

In looking over the poem, I am inclined to believe that it is
a better work when the little poem is struck out, so as to make it
begin with

" The companies of governor-spirits grave,
Bards &c, &c "[11]

What a comfort your good face is after one has disgraced
one's self with a lecture dreary enough for a speech among the
gray ghosts that huddle by the Stygian stream!

Your friend

S. L.

435 N. Calvert St.
Thursday.

---

[9] Lanier seems to have intended discussing these books in his lectures on the English novel, but they were not included in the course as actually given. The reference here may be to a list which Turnbull offered to lend him from his Library or to a catalogue of books for sale by Turnbull Bros., booksellers, etc. – from whom a list of Lanier's purchases in 1879 has survived (Charles D. Lanier Collection, Johns Hopkins University).

[10] Conjectural dating from the mention of a copy of " The Crystal," which Mary Day Lanier's postscript to her husband's letter to J. B. Tabb, Mar. 19, 1881 (below), indicates had been recently given away.

[11] As originally published in the *Independent*, July 15, 1880 (and in subsequent reprints), " The Crystal " was introduced by twelve lines which provided a setting for the rest of the poem (see I, 136).

To Clifford A. Lanier

435 N. Calvert St.
Bo; Mch. 7, 1881.

My dearest Clifford:

To take my pen in hand has been for many weeks an enterprise requiring as much stoutness of heart and concentration of muscular fibre as would have sufficed Sir Launcelot to seize a great spear and unhorse six knights in one sally. Although my immediately-dangerous symptoms abated months ago, yet the amount of unceasing pain seems to have increased, and I've been working for the last two months particularly under such a load of physical distress that I have several times found myself *almost* at the point where one throws up one's hands and cries My sufferings are more than I can bear. The suffering is most peculiar and baffling: I cannot locate it in any limb or organ, just as one cannot locate thirst which is a lack in the whole blood; a severe fever comes – or rather stays, it never goes – and therewith a general discomfort under which I can scarcely refrain from such groans and shrieks as a wounded dog gives, crawling off with a broken back and hind-legs dragging. To lie spread out and *repose* for one hour – that is my dream; not old Aeschylus' Io, stung through the world by the unreachable gad-fly, ever longed so for a moment's surcease of misery.[12]

Some infringement of heart upon lung, or contrariwise, seems to have occurred: I can lie but in one position, poised on my right hip and shoulder; and each morning finds me properly tired.

To fall-to, each week, and begin the writing of a lecture wherewith I am bound (or else lose my place) to amuse and instruct some two hundred people in developing a continuous line of systematic thought – is, you may fancy, forlorn enough: particularly when I give a longing glance toward my desk where lie two volumes of poems and some half dozen other books in various stages of completion.

[12] The allusion is to Aeschylus, *Prometheus Bound*, which Lanier had discussed in the fourth lecture of his series, Feb. 16, 1881.

Yet, thanks to the great God of strength, I have never yet *quite* lost heart; and have written and delivered six lectures, of my twelve, which have been received with many pleasant tokens of satisfaction. Moreover, amid all the distress, it seems clear I am better and stronger; no lesion of the lung appears to have occurred, and the inflammation is still in the curable state; I abound in plans and new books; and admit no ground-tone but hope. It seems a miracle that I have weathered such a savage winter as we have had, in which ice, snow, wind, sleet, and rain have kept us whirling in one eddy of danger; and I look forward with joyful longing to the warm days when I can taste some un-furnaced air and relax this tension of continuous resistence to cold which we must all keep up through these unfriendly blasts.

Meantime ways and means has been, as you may imagine, a most perplexing question, and in fact my solution of it has been little less than a series of miracles.

In which connection: is anything farther available from the gas-stock? I have received four hundred dollars from you on that a/c; and, whilst I *think* the arrangement you proposed was to pay $50 a month for twelve months. My recollection is not in the least clear and I may very well have gotten the idea of $600, as the whole amount, from some other source. At any rate, about the middle of this month I must discharge a considerable obligation, for which I have been able to provide enough temporarily except about two hundred dollars. For this I am obliged to turn towards you; and, if the stock is not worth so much (though Edison seems now completely in the dark and gas-stocks are very high here), I must beg you to arrange that sum for me.

I am anxious for more news of Wilsie. She was coughing, and otherwise misbehaving, when we last heard. My poor May is turned out such a worker as the world never saw; it is a marvel how she goes, goes, from early morning until late at night, caring for the baby (our Robin, who is a wonder of milk-and-roses skin, and heavenly-blue eyes, and perfect Cupid-anatomy), for me — who am endless trouble, and have to be rubbed with olive-oil every night from head to foot, for example — for the three ever-wanting-something boys, and the trying housekeeper's business; and she is ever struggling beside with the daily chill.

We learn from Clifford's letter to Harry that you are painting the Exchange: but this gratifying news he sets off with the painful intelligence that you lost two window-glasses by careless snowballing.

I have been dreaming a little of Southern air in the spring: but it is only a dream. Tell me if you prosper in the new single-handed venture; keep out of speculation; and hold me always

Your loving

S. L.

To Lawrence Turnbull

435 N. Calvert St.
[Baltimore,] Mch. 15, 1881.

My dear Lawrence:

I wrote Mr. McCoy last week asking if it would give him the slightest inconvenience to receive $350 today and to let the balance of my obligation to him remain until January 1st. 1882.

I enclose his reply, which displays his usual goodness.

I am going to avail myself of his kindness so far as to pay $200 now,– instead of $350,– and for that purpose I enclose my check to his order for $200. Will you be kind enough (1) to credit same on the $500 note, (2) to file his letter with the papers, and (3) to transmit the check to Mr. McCoy.[13]

– You will fancy without any description from me, the grief of asking postponements in such a case. I made up my new boy's book (The Mabinogion) months ago, under great stress of fever, and sent it to Scribner with the express hope that I had provided for this whole matter, to which I intended applying the purchase-money of that book; and I have never yet been able to get an answer from them as to price; they are going to

---

[13] A surviving receipt dated Mar. 15, 1881, credits Lanier's debt to J. W. McCoy with a payment of $200.00. Lanier had borrowed $500.00 from him in July, 1879, and $250.00 in May, 1880. A memorandum dated Jan. 14, 1882, shows that $550.00 remained unpaid at Lanier's death; the final settlement is dated Feb. 18, 1882 (documents in the Charles D. Lanier Collection, Johns Hopkins University).

buy, they say, but have been too crushed with business of the New Year to give a full consideration to the matter of engravings &c., which is a troublesome business and has much to do with profits. Of course I can't hurry them;– and so I've had to let this wave roll over me, with such endurance as I can muster.– However, it will come right.

With all loving messages from my comrade and me to you and Mrs. Turnbull,

Your friend,

S. L.

To John B. Tabb [14]

435 N. Calvert St. Baltimore.
March 19th 1881.

My dear Jonathan:

The more I am in your debt for your blessed letters the less I seem to put you in mine by answering them; much as Charles Lamb, when reproached with reaching the office late in the morning, replied that he would try to make up for it by going away early in the afternoon.

I did not send your long poem to the editor of THE INDEpendent because I felt perfectly sure he would not accept that and I feared that the Sonnet would share its fate. I knew the latter would suit him and am glad to see that he was similarly wise. Your little sprig from Shelley's grave is a delicious breath of Rome and Spring to me. It is only a few days since I was lecturing on the *Prometheus Unbound* at the University. This — from a great press of work, and bodily pain not to be described — is not offered as more than a mere waving of the hand in your direction. Here is a poem of mine just printed in the INDEPENDENT,[15] which appears to have won some favor and may have that grace with you.

Your friend,

S. L.

—— by his wife.

---

[14] Previously published, Gordon Blair, *Father Tabb* (Richmond, Va., 1940), p. 65. Tabb's poems mentioned in this letter have not been identified.

[15] " A Song of Eternity in Time " (I, 12), published in the *Independent,*

— And his wife must take another moment to tell you that she was long holding for you a last copy of *the Crystal*, without finding even ten minutes leisure for the message that was to go with it; until, at last, it was begged from Sidney by a lady who had some special use for it. You will wish to hear that he is better – but I cannot tell you so. His sufferings increase and multiply, and all manual work must now be done through this "broken reed" which has been too long bent. The acute crisis of December is not here – but there is a hard battle for the dear life and he is worsted by the effort to work. Thanks for your good letter of long ago.

Your friend

Mary D. Lanier.

To Clifford A. Lanier

435 N. Calvert St. Balt°
[Mar. 19, 1881?] [16]

My dearest Clifford:

Enclosed I send your receipt and also the transfer of stock. You will observe that I have not filled the blanks in the latter. Please do so as you see proper. I sincerely trust the stock may have appreciated; but be sure and save yourself from loss.

How I wish that a thousandth part of the sweetness of your words were really my due. For they are so sweet that the least fraction of them is precious.

I delight to think of you and Wilsie playing the *Adelaide*, and in response to your enquiry for more songs of this nature, suitable to flute and piano, I charge you to get straightway the *Schubert-Album* in which there are a large number of Schu-

---

Mar. 3, 1881. (This was a revised version of "Eternity in Time," originally published in the *XIX Century*, Feb., 1870.)

[16] This letter was signed by Lanier, but dictated to his wife. Conjectural dating from a pencil notation on the MS in another handwriting. The reference to "transfer of stock" in the opening paragraph places it after Lanier's letter to his brother of Mar. 7, 1881 (above); and the project of the southern lecture tour, discussed in the fourth paragraph, places it before his letter of Apr. 8 (below).

bert's Songs; some of these are among the most intense and satisfactory of all musical aspirations. Be sure, specially, to play " *Du Bist Die Ruh,*" " *Jägers Abendlied* ", " *Ave Maria* ": though there are twenty others almost equally beautiful. You will find, too, in the *Schumann Album* of Songs a number of lovely pieces.

A few days ago I received a letter from the lecture committee of the Macon Public Library as to the feasibility of a lecture by me before that body. I send you a copy of my reply, desiring that you will consider the practicability of carrying out in Montgomery, — during late May and early June after the Macon series, — a like course upon a like plan. If there is in Montgomery any such institution as a public library, with influence among the people, the thing might be done; otherwise it cannot. I had hoped to be able to make arrangements for three such courses during April, May, June and part of July, in Macon, Montgomery and Atlanta. But do not make any public mention of the matter; I cannot at all be sure yet that my health would permit anything of the sort; and I merely wish to ascertain if it would be feasible, so that I could make all arrangements speedily as soon as any certainty comes.

We are truly sorry to hear of Sister's illness and beg you will transmit our joint love and sympathy to her. Keep us apprised of her condition: we feel very anxious.

Longing for music to convey all further messages,

S. L.

per M. D. L.

To Clifford A. Lanier

435 N. Calvert St.

Bo. April 8, 1881.

Dearest Clifford:

I find there will be no possible chance of my getting South this spring, and I scrawl a line to ask that you will close any inquiries &c in the matter of lectures which you may have started.

Several reasons concur to render the journey impossible, the main one being health. My next – and, heaven be praised, last – lecture [17] occurs next Wednesday, and I hope soon thereafter to crawl over to New York, for a thorough examination of my heart (which continues to give me great physical distress), and for a business-talk with the publishers, before whom I have a fearsome lot of books to lay.

I am trying very hard to settle my summer. I'm infinitely tired; and I found such possibilities of repose at Rockingham Springs, (near Harrisonburg, Va.), when we were there two years ago, that I am greatly tempted to steal thither about the middle of May, and rest, rest, until October. I can do light work on my pending boy's books as well there as anywhere. (1) Is sister coming to Virginia this summer- (2) Where is her place? (3) Who lives there when she is not there? Please answer these questions categorically, and at once; we wish to know what chance we may have to see her, during the summer.

I am about to send my boys back to Rapidan, for some months. I need Mary's care, and even their merriment is often trying, so as to involve further resistance.

What is Ginna Hankins doing, and does she get well paid for it?

I will write you about the politico-economic article another time. Will I never see you? Surely we must try to arrange it this summer or fall.

God bless you, dear, and those whom you bless, prays always

Yr.

S. L.

[17] Frances E. Willard, "Notes of Southern Literary Men & Women," *Independent*, XXXIII, 3-4 (Sept. 1, 1881), tells of meeting Lanier in Baltimore and attending his lectures on the English Novel, which she praised. She described him as follows: "In personal appearance Sidney Lanier is of medium height, exceedingly slight figure, closely buttoned in a black suit; face very pale and delicate, with finely-chiseled features, dark, clustering hair, parted in the middle, and beard after the manner of the Italian school of art. Altogether, he has a countenance unique and pleasing as his verse."

To Sarah J. Farley

435 N. Calvert St.
B⁰· April 15, 1881.

Dearest Sarah, this is the most doleful picture— this of your
" 4: 14 : 81 "— that ever I looked on, and if the wind were
but a single degree less raw, or my poor flaccid body a single
degree more resistive, I would start for you by next train, if
haply I might mitigate your loneliness with a little true love. –
But surely it will grow better with you, there: the start is a bad
one, – so bad indeed that you have the dismal consolation of
feeling pretty sure you can't have anything worse to come.
Dear soul, how fervently I hope you *may* find some alleviation
of these dreadful ills of the flesh which are so contagious to
the spirit. There's where *my* rub comes: to keep my soul from
having the consumption and the heart-disease.

I feel as if we would meet you this summer, though I do not
see the *place* definitely outlined yet. My lectures are over: and
you will be glad to know that though written in such extremities of bodily distress as made my whole existence one groan,
and though delivered under such weight of disadvantage —
wretched dyspnœa, lung inflamed to preternatural sensitiveness,
weakness so great that to rise from my chair (I sat while lecturing) and write a word on the blackboard would completely
exhaust my strength, and a hundred smaller ills — they were
fully attended throughout by an audience which gave every
sign of appreciative interest.

I hope to go to New York about ten days from now; and a
great number of summer-arrangements, as well as of future
movements, will be determined by the visit. If I am strong
enough for the excursion, I will stop at Philadelphia, and look
you up. This is not likely, however: and most probably will
be postponed until by return-trip from New-York, where I
think to stay ten days or maybe two weeks.

My comrade and I have kissed each other for you, and I
wish I might send you both caresses, dear, for the morning-
greeting of yr. faithful friend

S. L.

To Charles Scribner

435 N. Calvert St.
Baltimore, Md.
April 19, 1881.

My dear Sir:

I do you so much justice as to feel sure that upon my statement of the two following facts you will materially change your views as to the proper share of profits from *the Mabinogion* which should fall to me.[18]

(1) At $350 each, neither the *Froissart*, the King Arthur, nor *The Mabinogion*, would pay my expenses during the actual time of my manual labor upon them; leaving out of view all question of return for (a) the *idea* of the series — which has certainly so far been successful — and (b) for the patient studies involved in the scholarship which was necessary to edit the books. If, therefore, I should receive but $350 for *the Mabinogion*, I shall have realized less money on the whole set of " successful " books than it cost me to put them on paper, *i.e.*, I shall have paid out a considerable sum for the privilege of presenting them to the public.

I was willing to accept such a price for the other two books because, in the first place, I believed in the series heartily and felt sure of better offers for future works, and, in the second place, I was under such pressure that I was obliged to sell at any price and too unwell for further negotiations.

(2) But if you reflect further that I have already collected materials for, and partly completed some of, the following

[18] On Apr. 13, 1881, Scribner had written that Lanier's account (see note 2, above) had been credited with $200.00 more on the *Mabinogion*, making the total paid for that book $350.00: " As ' *King Arthur* ' has not proved quite as successful as the ' *Froissart* ' we think that this sum (the same as paid for the first two books) is as much as the prospect of sale for the new book warrants.

" There is still a balance against you [$230.27], but you need give yourself no anxiety about it, and I trust it will even be diminished by the sale of the ' Science of Verse.' If you could succeed in selling a set of plates or an edition in England you would probably cancel the debit balance at once."

No letter from Scribner has survived in reply to Lanier's request in the present letter for a larger share of the profits of the *Mabinogion* (see also note 24, below). His answer was probably given orally, and in the negative, during Lanier's trip to New York at the end of April.

works, towit: *The Girls' Paston Letters* } [19]: two companion
              The Boy's Monstrelet

works, the former showing, from the actual correspondence of
the Paston family, the most vivid and naive pictures of English
domestic life during the dark period of the Wars of the Roses,
while the latter gives similar pictures of English and French
political life, during the same period, and longer, extending
from the moment when Froissart's Chronicles end, down to the
latter part of the 15th century, embracing the romantic adventures of Henry V, of the Queen of Henry VI, of Joan of Arc,
Richard III, and so on:

The Boy's Utopia } [20]: two companion volumes, the former
The Girl's Arcadia   being Sir Thomas More's world-cele-
brated (but how little read!) *Utopia* edited upon the same
principles with the Froissart &c, and the latter Sir Philip
Sidney's work similarly redacted for girls, — both giving the
most delightful insight into English thought from the early
part of the 16th century to the last part;

"*The Boys Percy's Reliques*," (or, perhaps "*The Boy's
Percy*"): [21] being a redaction for boys, made since the original
Percy folio has been placed within reach of scholars by the
reprint of Messrs. Hales and Furnivall, who succeeded a short
time ago, mainly at the instigation (and largely with the money-
help) of our own Prof. Child, in purchasing the original ms.
of this charming classic. I recently discovered my three boy's
reading this book with the utmost avidity, — even in the
old form — and had much grief in finding myself obliged to
hide it from them, because it contained so much matter which
no one, boy or man, should read.

  In addition to these I have found in The Peabody Library a
collection of French Chronicles, never translated into English,
more curious and amusing, as well as historically instructive,
than any I have seen in a long time, and I have simply postponed details of bringing them before the public, in this same
series, until I get more time. I have also under consideration

---

[19] See note 7, above.

[20] No evidence has survived to indicate that Lanier's project for these two
volumes ever went beyond the selection of the titles.

[21] This volume was completed (IV, 382) and is the subject of several letters
in June, 1881, below.

three girl's-books representing later centuries, from which I shall select one.[22]

— Here, then, you observe, are at least six books with which I have hoped to make — in addition to those already issued — a first-class foundation for future household English literature, and in the selection of which I have been enabled to apply the practical test of my own children's preferences. It has been my most cherished wish to lift up the plane of youth's reading with these books so that nothing less good would be hereafter acceptable, and I have already gone to considerable expense in collecting materials, in preliminary studies, and in actual work upon them. I have perfect faith in the series, and would be entirely willing to print it at my own expense, if possible.

Under these circumstances, you see immediately that to sell the *Mabinogion* at a price which makes the book fail even to feed me while I was getting it up not only renders the whole business most disastrous to *me* so far, but overturns my whole future project as to this series, — for, of course, I must abandon it if I fail to make even my bread at it.

I have been waiting until the close of my lectures at the University, — which have kept me under some pressure of work, — in order to confer with you as to these matters. I expect to be in New York, for a visit of several weeks, about the 25th of this month. I ask you to take these matters into consideration, and find if you cannot see your way clear to a better offer. I will let you know when I arrive in the city.

Pray accept my thanks for your kind wishes as to my health, — which is greatly better, and bids fair to be entirely restored with warmer weather.

I note what you say as to the Harper controversy,[23] for which I am truly sorry.

Sincerely yours,

Sidney Lanier.[24]

Mr. Charles Scribner,
New York.

---

[22] The projected volumes mentioned in this paragraph have not been identified.

[23] The controversy apparently concerned the reprinting by Harper's of certain titles claimed by Scribners, including Carlyle's *Reminiscences*, Froude's *Caesar*, and Stanley's *Christian Institutions* (see Charles Scribner's letter to Lanier, Apr. 13, 1881).

[24] Accompanying this letter was a memorandum (here omitted) drafting the

To Mary Day Lanier

St. Denis Hotel, N. Y.
April 26, 1881.

It has seemed, dearest Soul, as if I could never reach the exact hour to write thee. What between business and the consequent exhaustion, I had to content myself with telegrams. The pen is unspeakably tiresome to me, as well as hurtful, I find: and so thou wilt take a few words today understandingly.

I got through Saturday by many miracles, being hard at work all day, and in great distress from dyspnœa .

Sunday I devoted to rest, but found towards night a heavy attack of pleuritic trouble in the lower lung-region, and had to give up Monday to fighting that, with Dr. Marcy's assistance. I had a good night last night, and am so much better today that I have made a call at Scribner's. Charles Scribner is out of town, I find, but expected home today; and I hope to meet him tomorrow.

Pope [25] offers me the round sum of fifteen hundred dollars

title page for the *Mabinogion* (here called *The Girl's Mabinogion*) and the *Percy*, with the request that the former cover Lanier's present indebtedness to the firm— thus constituting a total payment of $580.37— and that he be paid not less than $500.00 for the latter. Scribner's reply to this letter has not been found. But a letter from him to Mary Day Lanier many years after her husband's death, May 31, 1899, in final settlement of the account for the juvenile series, makes it clear that Lanier was paid only $350.00 for the *Percy* – which would imply a similar price for the *Mabinogion*. However, he was also advanced $175.00 each for the *Monstrelet* and the *Paston Letters*, half their purchase price. This advance was cancelled off against the further amount due Lanier in 1899 on the *Mabinogion* and the *Percy* ($150.00 each), by virtue of the sale of over 3000 copies.

[25] A. Pope (formerly agent of the Atlantic Coast Line Railway, for whom Lanier had written *Florida*) had become General Passenger and Ticket Agent of the Associated Railways of Virginia and the Carolinas. On Mar. 21, 1881, attracted by " The New South," he had written Lanier about a projected book on the territory served by the railways with which he was connected. According to Pope this volume, which was designed primarily to attract European immigration, should be an " absolutely *accurate complete* (and yet not verbose) description of climate, soils, products of mines, fields, forests, and animals, scenery, sanitary advantages, contiguity to markets— adaptabilities for creating attractive homes &c &c &c—

" I recognize your ability as an author and have faith in your love for your

to write a book on his summer resorts, I to bear all expenses (save railway tickets) out of that sum, and the book to be ready in October. I have not yet replied — he has gone to Richmond — and will probably wait until tomorrow, though I think it altogether wise to accept.

And now, so soon as thou receivest this greeting pray bestir thee, as follows. I wish thee to come here on the Limited Express train of Thursday, 28th, leaving Baltimore about 10.35 A. M. from Charles St. Station. I will be on the lookout for thee at Jersey City at the proper time for that train, and will bring thee across the ferry. Come prepared to stay four or five days. Thou canst run to Macy's — a short distance from here — on the very afternoon of thy arrival, and buy thee a presentable dress and bonnet, all ready to put on, in the same store. Order household supplies enough to last five days, and get Letty [Wrenschall], Mrs. Wm Hand Browne, and Mrs. Fulton,[26] to look in for an hour each day, – and our good Mrs. Hall. Indeed would not the latter take Sidney or Charley with Ingram for that time, and, if Col. Johnson has a cook, might you not arrange to board two of the boys there for a week? Take a carriage, and make such arrangements as thou mayst.

I find that I cannot possibly do my work without thine aid. To dress in the morning completely exhausts me before my day is begun; and I need some special cares which no one can render but thou. Commit all to God's hands therefore, and come, as appointed.

I have not let any know of my presence here, as yet, being too unwell to bear visits.

I enclose a further check — this one (observe) payable to thine *order*. The fare by the Lim. Exp. train is about $6.50 to $7.00 . Do not give trunk-check to any baggage-express man on the train, but keep it until thou seest me.

---

native South–. . . if *you* are disposed to entertain a proposition to aid me– I would be glad to meet you at an early day."

Lanier apparently expressed his interest in a lost letter, Mar. 24, 1881; and Pope wrote again, Mar. 25, saying that he hoped to see Lanier in Baltimore at an early date. On Apr. 19 he wrote to suggest that Lanier meet him in New York, Apr. 23– the expenses of the trip to be refunded by Pope.

[26] Harriet Freeman Fulton, an old Macon friend, seems to have come to Baltimore at least a year before this time to be with her daughter, Norah Freeman, who was teaching music there.

And now no more – for fatigue's sake. I shall long for thee in inverse geometrical ratio during each diminishing period of time until I see thee here by

me.

To Clifford A. Lanier

435 N. Calvert St.
Bº. May 5, 1881.

Dearest Clifford:

Mary and I returned from New York last night,[27] and I think I am a little less feverish this morning.

You will have received, I hope, a couple of days ago, my letter written you from New York. I send this scrawl merely to add that upon further thought it seems altogether more wise — instead of trying to make a horseback journey at once, which I do not at all see how I could do, in my present feebleness — to fit up a tent as soon as we get to Asheville and select some pleasant site near that place, (or some stream where we can fish, and on a mountain-side where we can get good protection against storms &c) with a view to my trying camp-life for several months. This is, indeed, what Dr. Loomis wants. Mary and the baby will come on as soon as necessary closing

---

[27] Mary Day Lanier had joined her husband in New York on April 28. Lanier's letter to his brother written from New York, mentioned in the following sentence, has not been found; but the important details of their week's stay are given in two letters from Mary Day Lanier to Sarah Farley. On May 1, 1881, she wrote: " Saw Dr. A. Loomis. He says the out-door life, on a *high* level, is the *one* hope, with no time to lose in trying it. Three months will decide the possibility, but not place out of danger. Heart trouble secondary, will lessen if lung heals. He has to-day fresh pleuritic inflammations & loses ground. Too much noise." On May 3 she added: " Sidney has been enough worse to see that *he* ought not to attempt one thing unnecessary. . . . We leave here at 3:40 P. M. tomorrow. The agreement with Mr. Pope is concluded to-day in a personal interview, and Clifford is just written to – summoned at once to Bº., to take S. to Asheville before *I* can close up all and leave. *Four books* sold to Scribner to-day: one to be made & delivered by June 15– the ' Boy's Percy '. The ' Girl's King Arthur ' is to follow. Of course 1 book and ¾ have been used up long ago! but 2¼ remain. *Won't* I have cutting & pasting for 12 months to come! " (The " Girl's King Arthur " is probably a reference to the *Mabinogion*– see note 24, above. The other two were presumably the *Monstrelet* and the *Paston Letters*.)

out arrangements can be made here, and if we should not find it possible, with our then experience of tent-life, to accommodate them there, I can lodge them pleasantly at Asheville, with daily seeing-distance. Our boys are to go back to their old quarters at Rapidan for the summer. I know so little of Wilsie's movements that I say nothing more thereof. If you could arrange to leave your little ones with Sissa, – provided she is well enough, – I think we could have a double wall-tent that would accommodate us four (you & Will, Maydie & me) and enable us to spend a royal summer. I hope to do some profitable study and to have your company therein. Perhaps I may start you in some branch of scholarship which will give you just the ballast and specific actual freightage of facts which every man needs, as against a certain vagueness of general culture that I do not doubt you have already felt the disadvantage of.

But I am overtaxing my arm, which is now as it were but a rope of sand. I intended to put herein a P. O. order for twenty five dollars, – to pay your expenses here, – but cannot now get it in time for the mail, and will hand you that amount when you come. God bless you, dear soul, and all yours, –

Bro.

S. L.

To Mary Day Lanier

Eagle Hotel, Asheville, N. C.
Saturday, May 21, 1881.

Dearest Soul,   I am somewhat rested today from the fatigues of our journey, which were somewhat trying to my small modicum of strength. I much desired to write thee yesterday: but our morning was spent in a horseback excursion to Richmond Hill, – otherwise known as " Pearson's View," – and when we returned I was too weary for anything but the lounge during the rest of the afternoon, and so begged Clifford to give you some account of us.

We have decided to pitch our tent at this Richmond Hill. It is about three miles from town; secluded enough, yet within

a short distance of Mr. Pearson's house, where we can get milk
and butter, and other occasional supplies; we have arranged for
communication with the city, so as to get fresh beef and mutton
and the like, – a " Market ", or butcher's shop, is just across
the street from this hotel; and I have the prospect of a saddle-
horse, to be hired by the month, and kept at Pearson's stable
near our camp.   I will not now descant upon the natural
beauties of our location.   In some particulars it is far from
being the ideal I had brought with me: but it combines so
many conveniences which we could not hope to find in any
other that we consider ourselves lucky in discovering it so soon.
The Mr. Pearson who owns the land is a young man, son of
Judge Pearson – a prominent lawyer of this state – who, after
having practised law a while and after travelling extensively in
Europe and in the West, has bought this beautiful tract of
land lying almost entirely enclosed by the Swannanoa and
French Broad Rivers, and is devoting much money – with which
he seems to be abundantly supplied – to making it a sort of
mountain Eden.

We have just engaged a cook, black as to the countenance
thereof like the blackness of Erebus, but an old hotel cook and
evidently used to taking care of people.   As good luck would
have it, young Penniman, – who very civilly called with his
father, Miss Carrington's relative, as soon as we arrived, and
has been unceasingly attentive since, – is in the hardware business, and by further good luck we found in his store, a second-
hand cooking-stove scarcely used.   This we have bought: the
whole affair, with outfit of cooking utensils, costing us only
nine dollars and some cents. You had better bring with you
knives, forks and spoons, and such little matters of table-ser-
vice as may occur to you: but, as to all cooking-things, we are
supplied.

Our tent-man was frightfully in error about the Express
charges, which we found to be four dollars a hundred instead
of one – as he assured us. We have just paid twelve dollars
express-charges on the tents &c. You had better, therefore, ship
any heavy goods you may have to bring as freight. The baby-
carriage you can send according to the result of the inquiries
you were to make; but, if brought along with the baggage, the
necessity of looking after it at each change would be very

onerous upon Father,[28] and, on the whole, perhaps you had better just send it by Express. Whatever you have to ship, I would ship it immediately so that it may be sure to arrive by the time you do, or soon after.

After looking all about, at boarding-houses &c, I found a room for Father at the Swannanoa Hotel – the finest house in the city, fitted out with electric bells in rooms, Telegraph Office in hotel, and the like, and just now getting on its finishing touches. This room commands such a ravishing prospect of mountains, is so bright, airy, and altogether delightful, that although its price is considerably higher than that Clifford wrote, I determined at once, upon seeing it, to beg Father to let me supply the difference and make him comfortable at least for a month, during which time he can look about and make such other selection as may seem desirable to him. It is truly a beautiful location, and I long to see Father installed there; I think he will bloom out in this delicious mountain-air so that he will soon be walking to our camp. The price of the room — from May 25 to July 1st — is forty dollars a month, and I have engaged it for that time.

I forgot my Gray's *Botany*: please bring that with you, and Wood's Botany, also, if room. They are in our book-case.[29]

You can have your baggage checked through to *Salisbury*: there it must be re-checked to Asheville. As the train arrives at Salisbury after eleven at night, and the stay is very short – for the Asheville train is allowed to wait but a few minutes – Father would do well to speak to the conductor about it before reaching Salisbury, and ask his help in rechecking. If your train should be late, and you should possibly have to spend the night in Salisbury, take it with equanimity, and telegraph me at Eagle Hotel, here.

I can think of nothing more to ease thy path. God come with thee – help and grace and love always *do*, for me – and

---

[28] Charles Day, who had been almost constantly with the Laniers since the autumn of 1877.

[29] These two books have survived in Lanier's Library (Charles D. Lanier Collection, Johns Hopkins University): Asa Gray, *Introduction to Structural and Systematic Botany* (New York and Chicago, 1878), and Alphonso Wood, *Class-book of Botany* (New York, 1867) – the former with annotations in Lanier's autograph.

have special charge and bring thee in peace and gravity to thine always

lover –

Early on Wednesday morning, after thou leavest " Henry's Station – the breakfast-house,– look out at the elaborate engineering wind-about whereby the train ascends the mountain for half an hour.

FROM MARY DAY LANIER TO CLIFFORD A. LANIER [30]

Asheville.   May 29th. 1881.

Dearest Clifford:

What a vast want is this – of thee ! It seemed as though I had never stood alone, in the trial & combat, nor could ever begin to fight this good fight without thee – when Sidney told me that thou must go from us in three quick hours. Well, I would that dear Wilsie could know — but she cannot — what was our need and what thine answer to it. Thou wast the only one on earth that might be *all* that was needed. And I knew that the very resting of eyes upon thee, the very sound of thy voice, would help him back to life. If only – without grieving her – our little Sissa's " violet eyes " could also look their great love into his ! But as we *must* wait for that we will try to have him more like his old self when she comes to him. We think of thee, dear brother, as almost in the haven of love and home this Sunday evening. It is now half-past six. May all be well with wife and children and affairs, and may good tidings from Verbena fill the measure. Since 4 o'clock Sidney has struck " an almost-easy position " – the

---

[30] Clifford Lanier left for Montgomery on May 27. Mary Day Lanier had reached Asheville on May 25 with her youngest son, the three older boys having been sent to Virginia in care of Mrs. S. M. Maxwell. On May 28 she wrote to Lawrence Turnbull: " Sidney has had to conquer a fresh pleuritic attack in the opening of his stay here, and his nights are– as he says– abnormally bad; yet he is confident that he has gained strength of limb and of lung– working in the face of this new inflammation, which must speak volumes for the fine air and for out-door exposure."

Awaiting the arrival of furnishings shipped from Baltimore, the Laniers remained at the Eagle Hotel in Asheville for about two weeks before removing to " Camp Robin."

first of such since our parting, for he has had two very distress-
ful nights — and tempted by this exquisite freedom from acute
pain he has fallen into a dozen placid naps upon his flowery
couch. He now audibly breathes his comfort & rest. Poor
fellow ! I am sure *he* misses you. I am so outrageously sleepy
and feeble that I forget all my habits of tendance. Yesterday
we moved one room: opposite to Baby. A crowd of doctors
is expected and two beds were wasted upon us. The new
room is large enough, & sunnier. To-day Sidney has sent on
his letter of introduction from Mr. Pope to Mr. [J. R.] Macmurdo, Gen. Pass. Agt. at Salisbury, with a request that he will
cause the freight to be looked up. Needham of Balt⁰ tranquilly replied that it " left B⁰· on the 21ˢᵗ," — and there ended.
We spent yesterday morning at Camp Robin and there entertained Mr. Pearson, Mr. Connally & the latter's two little
daughters, in their riding habits, who were presented by Mr.
Pearson as his little cousins & had been scouring the country on
horseback with him. On his side Mr. Pearson entertained *us*
with some fine buttermilk, besides offering us the use of 'most
everything about him, and specially of his two workmen, Lee
& Isaac. Sidney finds that Thomas and Harris work " mighty
easy " when *you* are not taking hold. It was lovely out there
on our porch and we grieved to come indoors. Mr. Pearson
was much taken with the porch & entrance. On our return,
over the long, narrow bridge, we narrowly escaped crossing
that other River – whence no traveller returns. A horseman
apparently drunk started to meet us when we were more than
half over: lost his head when near us & jumped off his horse,
attempting to draw her to one side, but resulting in tangling
her up *between* our pony and our shafts. The two struggled &
kicked, wedged in together, pony refused to back and the buggy
was forcibly driven against the slender rail of the bridge for
awhile. Before we had broken through it the man perceived
that he had to pull his horse to one side, which Sidney assisted
by a heavy cut of the whip, stinging her into motion. This
hurt our poor darling more than it did the dull brute. Coupled
with the long dragging at the reins, to back pony, it bore
heavily on the chest and heart and a severe palpitation followed. Perhaps his bad night was due to this misadventure.
We could get no horse this morning and so went to Mrs. Penni-

man's pleasant yard and sat down under the trees. A thunder-shower with hail came after dinner, so we will have our tents somewhat tested before we move in. Robin tumbled out of bed this morning — my fault ! – but I think he has escaped all but light bruises. He is as big and saucy and merry as can be.

When I look at Sidney I can hardly wait to get into tents – As for myself, this intermediate rest is not amiss. Certainly it was good to have this rain first.

God be with us – darling Clifford – and enfold our treasure in His tenderest providence. Won't you send on my letter to our sweet Sissa – for my pen has ten times as much as its slow work warrants – and let it be one more link in drawing *all* together. Give us every word of her. How about the health in Montgomery. Kisses to our dear little folks.

Your Mamie.

FROM MARY DAY LANIER TO CLIFFORD A. LANIER

Eagle Hotel [Asheville]. May 31st P. M. [1881]

Dear Brother:

    Sidney broke the seals of your love-letters to see if there were any enclosures that concerned him. Nothing from Mr. Macmurdo, & the Salisbury Agt. still replies "Nothing here for you." Have just sent a long telegram to Richmond. There are moments when I approach desperation, as I see him losing every day — as he has, since Friday. Only one morning outdoors in four days (for it has rained for three days, more or less,) and he has fresh cold, and no sleep comes except these nervous, fitful dozes. This morning he said – "If I do not get out there soon it will not be worth while." I think the strain & excitement of our adventure on the bridge (of which I wrote on Sunday) was very hurtful to him. O, dear Clifford – It *did* look as if God meant to spare him to us when the opportunity up here came. But now, as I watch his increasing distress & feebleness a positive physical sickness overwhelms me – There are two persons in me: *one* still talks laughs with Baby and talks to Papa of our happy plans — but all the time

the other soul is fainting with anguish — Dear Brother
send me one little word apart to help me. Pray God to help
me that I may help him.

What of the Scarlet fever?

Your Maydie.

To Daniel C. Gilman [81]

Asheville, N. C.   June 5th. 1881.

Dear Mr. Gilman:

The map will be of great service to me.
Please address it " P. O. Box 95. Asheville. N. C."; though, if
you should forget this number, " Asheville ", alone, will always
be sufficient.

Can you help me — or tell me how to help myself — in the
following matter? A few weeks from now I wish to study the
so-called no-frost belt on the side of Tryon Mountain; and in
order to test the popular account I propose to carry on two
simultaneous series of meteorological observations during a
fortnight or longer, — the one conducted by myself in the
middle of the belt, the other by a friend stationed well outside
its limits. For this purpose I need two small self-registering
thermometers, two aneroid thermometers and two hygrometers
of any make. It has occurred to me that since these observations will be conducted during the University recess I might —
always provided, of course, that there is any authority or pre-
cedent for such action — procure this apparatus from the University collection, especially as no instrument is included which
could not easily be replaced. Of course I would cheerfully
deposit a sum sufficient to cover the value of the whole outfit.

Should this arrangement be possible I merely ask that you
turn this letter over to Dr. Hastings [82] with the request that he
will have the apparatus packed at my expense and shipped by
express to me at this point immediately.

You will care to hear that I get stronger from day to day.
My tents are pitched in a pleasant nook, three miles from Ash-

[81] Previously published, Mims, p. 333. This letter was signed by Lanier but
dictated to his wife.

[82] Charles S. Hastings, Associate in Physics, Johns Hopkins University.

ville, and we move into them tomorrow, having been delayed by the annual May storm incident to these mountains.

With regards to M^rs. Gilman and with earnest acknowledgements of your continued goodness, I am

Faithfully yours,

Sidney Lanier.

To Charles Scribner's Sons [83]

Near Asheville, N.C.
June 14th, 1881.

Dear Sirs:

I send to-day by Express ten large envelopes containing *ms.* of *The Boy's Percy* ready for the printer. The Introduction will follow within the next five days.

I hope you will find the book as taking as it seems to me. The pleasure of placing so strong, genuine and fascinating an English classic in the hands of my own children (from whom I have been obliged to hide it heretofore) is so keen that I fancy a somewhat similar sensation on your part in laying it before young American readers generally.

The *ms.* will make a book about the size of the *King Arthur*, as nearly as I can calculate. Consisting as it does of detached pieces it can easily be shortened or lengthened, if it should fail either way.

On May 29th, (in order to reach you by June 1st as promised,) I sent you eight pages *ms.* containing some thirty odd subjects for illustration in the *Percy*; but having no acknowledgement from you fear they may have miscarried. Please let me know immediately.[34]

The Mabinogion Introduction will reach you on or before July 1st, according to agreement.

My address is "P.O. Box 95, Asheville, N. C.", though simple "Asheville N.C." will always reach me.

Very truly yours,

Sidney Lanier.

[83] This letter was signed by Lanier but dictated to his wife.
[34] Lanier's letter of May 29, 1881, has not been found. Charles Scribner's

To Edward L. Burlingame [85]

Near Asheville. June 17th, 1881

Dear Mr. Burlingame:

Shall I return proof to you or to Rand, Avery & Co., Boston? The package comes without any clue except that I think I recognize your handwriting on the wrapper.

I greatly regret a delay of two days which has been caused by circumstances quite beyond my control.

I think I shall be able to send proof by return mail, hereafter. Indeed, this is such plain matter that perhaps there will be no necessity to send me anything more than plate-proofs, after I have got the book fairly started.

Page 3 of the *ms.* is missing; the package was very insecurely arranged when it reached me, and seemed as if it might have been opened in transit.

On May 29th last I sent you the subjects for illustration in the PERCY; and on June 15th the *ms.* of the book, complete.

Sincerely yours,

Sidney Lanier.

To Edward L. Burlingame [86]

Near Asheville. June 24th. 1881

My dear Mr. Burlingame:

Herewith I send by express the Introduction to *The Boy's Percy*; which, with copy of the body of the book already sent, places the *ms.* in your hands complete and ready for the printer.

Sons replied, June 18, 1881, acknowledging receipt of the MS of *The Boy's Percy* and the list of suggestions for illustrations, and stating that sample proofs of the *Mabinogion* had been forwarded.

[85] This letter was signed by Lanier but dictated to his wife. The proof here referred to was that of the *Mabinogion*. Edward L. Burlingame was literary adviser of Charles Scribner's Sons. All of the letters from this firm to Lanier after Apr. 1879, are in his handwriting– except, of course, the personal letters from Charles Scribner.

[86] This letter was dictated to Mary Day Lanier. Burlingame replied, June 29, 1881, that he had copied in the passage from " Henry and Emma," and that there would be no charges.

The blank page 15 — in the *Percy* Introduction — is to be filled by a passage from Prior's *Henry and Emma.* For several days I have been scouring the town of Asheville — which boasts of a Female College and a Circulating Library — to find a collection of the Queen Anne poets, but without success. It is this indeed which has delayed me in forwarding the Introduction. Finally I have concluded to ask you, as a personal favor, to look up Matthew Prior's *Henry and Emma* ballad (which you will find in any one of half a dozen such anthologies as *Johnson's Poets*, or the like, doubtless at hand in your store), to select that portion of the poem which paraphrases the two stanzas of *The Nut-brown Maid* given in the Introduction (pages 12 and 13), to have it copied by a clerk (for which service I enclose $1.00) and to insert the extract at the proper point, pages 14 and 15.

I trust you will like the Introduction. To me it is altogether the most satisfactory one of the series. It seems to put the reader in possession of every substantial fact, connected with a number of somewhat complex subjects; and, — whilst it suggests some of that kind of thoughts which, though only partially understood, nevertheless take beneficial lodgment in youthful minds and at a later time grow all the more freely for having lain in the ground so long, — it appears, in general tone, to appeal more exactly to the stage of intelligence for which this series has been specially designed.

It will be helpful to me if you will examine the book for final acceptance at your earliest opportunity.

Yours acknowledging return of the first *Mabinogion* proofs has reached me; and according to instructions therein I forward second parcel, just received, to Rand, Avery & Co. Boston.

I am now at work on the *Mabinogion* Introduction. This will be very much shorter than any of the others, since I so completely covered the King Arthur ground in the Introduction to *The Boy's King Arthur* that nothing remains save to give some account of the origin of this special collection, and of the peculiar effect which Welsh literature has had upon our own.

Faithfully yours,

Sidney Lanier.

per M.D.L.

FROM MARY DAY LANIER TO CLIFFORD A. LANIER

Camp Robin.   June 26th, 1881.

My darling Clifford:

We are at the eighth page of the Mabino-
gion Introduction – the Percy and (later) its Introduction
having been sent off: the latter portion delayed by the over-
whelming distress of his increased fevers.   In the long pauses
between his weary, fragmentary dictation I have been writing
snatches of love and counsel to little Sidney whose last letter
spoke poorly for his health.   But on our eighth page the
mother's yearning has silenced me.   I leave that sheet and
come to you, who are only *less* dear than that slender, fragile
likeness of his father – whom your own Wilsie's care held in
life for us, five years ago.   Tuesday is Harry's birthday; birth-
days and Sundays are times meet for longing.   I read and re-
read your tender letter (my own) and draw various sorts of
help and comfort from it, even while too crushed by the burden
of his interminable pain and growing wearyness for that up-
springing of hope towards which you lead me.   His appetite
has generally been tolerably good, though less than during our
first week out here, when our fare was far more limited:
breakfast-bacon, corn bread & toast, hominy and eggs – serving
for all meals.   It is true, Thomas' cooking is variable and
" swept " better as " a new broom " – (he is a steady, sober
fellow, which is much; but *very* lazy, obstinate & self-indul-
gent) but with all allowance for his part in the matter it seems
that the extremity of the fevers would, in any case make eating
difficult.   Sidney's prostration is so great too that he cannot
exercise, to help the appetite.   Over twelve days ago a nice
saddle-horse was hired for a month and brought to Mr. Pearson's stable.   Sidney has mounted him for a half-hour, twice.

He has been very seriously annoyed (and not a little damaged, in pocket and strength) by some very strange conduct on
the part of Mr. Pope, who has made no payment of the salary
due on the 14th, and who will not even reply to messages either
epistolary or telegraphic.   I have written two long letters for
Sidney and he must have spent several dollars on the long telegrams sent.   The first one of these Mr. Pope answered, on the

17th promising to mail draft from Richmond on the 20th ! and
asking Sidney to write to him there, as he had not the first
letter. But here, on the evening of the 26th, Pope still "lies
perdu" — — — ——————— ———————
——— . ——————— (July 1st.) ——————
— — being found, in the desired way: by his drafts & vouchers, —
on the 29th.   The accompanying letter tries to slip easily out
of the question of his transgressions by some lofty-reproachful
allusions to "viewing him in the light of the past transactions"
between them — in which view "he", himself, "can afford to
disregard criticism". Sidney's very prompt reply presented
"the view" that *he* could not "afford to disregard" the need
of means to carry out existing arrangements based on the punc-
tual payment of his salary, as by agreement. What it will all
come to — in the future — I have my doubts, even if our dear one
strengthens enough for the work.[37]   At present — it is such a
relief to him to put the matter out of his mind that I shall help
him to forget it as much as may be. I notice that business tires
him painfully. We had too much of it yesterday: a new cook
to engage (Thomas having proven unsafe in a recent escapade)
and a vehicle to buy or engage. The cook was installed this
morning: a decorous, dignified man of family "William
Brown," or "Brown" — as he calls himself —,   and we hope
for better things. The vehicle could not be found — then.
Something deep, low & well-cushioned, like Col. Ray's little
sundown, (for which Col. R. might — *unwillingly* — take $85!)
is necessary for his comfort. It is very painful to him to climb
into the high ones, and they are the ones we have had for some
time — as they've sent us whatever they chose from the stable.
It is raining quite steadily and we will not make trial of a
vehicle which Mr. Van Gilder was offering. Our good old
"gospel tent" keeps us in considerable suspense during the
rainfalls — From the first one it has leaked a little and is developing a faculty of getting very wet underneath — all along
the ridge-pole & thence extending down in broad divisions;

[37] Since Lanier's letters to Pope have not been found, the exact causes of the
misunderstanding cannot be explained. On July 4 Pope explained about the
submission of vouchers for current expenses and wrote: "I am satisfied from
the perusal of your various letters that you are making excellent progress with
the work in hand." (Actually, the book was never begun — see Mary Day
Lanier's letter to Sarah Farley, July 30, 1881, below.)

sometimes the rain falls through in several places.   We have resolved repeatedly to order a new fly, but a general feeling of uncertainty and Sidney's unfitness to direct even a business note have delayed us.   The changes in temperature from mid-day to night (often 28° & 30°) are so great and the dampness and cold so severe between midnight & 7 A. M. that we often question whether it is the right place for him, and discuss places of steady warmth – for which his soul longs.   Then again we have a most lovely day or two – when the idea of *ever* leaving our forest nook is unendurable.

At Post-Office, July 4th. And the last two days have been of this heavenly quality, bringing some healing to the dear, suffering, almost-*exhausted* one.   From last Sunday to Thursday a slight improvement followed a very dreary long interval – Then, bad weather, and utter misery, day and night, until yesterday afternoon.   He is enough brighter to-day to have driven me in, hoping to receive Father & Mama – –   but this happiness is deferred.   Leaving Macon Saturday night they have probably been caught over Sunday –   No news of the cots !   A kind visit from Miss Norton whom I was fain to embrace when she said she had just talked with little Sissa and Wilsie.   Many, many thanks for the bright records of our dear little Willie – and a glimpse of the kind of music our little niece is growing up on.   Bring her to us and let us see the workings of that clear quick Spirit –   How *could* yours and Wilsie's children be anything but lovely !

Your   Maydie .

To Daniel C. Gilman [38]

Asheville.   N. C.   July 1st 1881.

D. C. Gilman.
President of The Johns Hopkins University.

Sir:

In response to your official communication of June 15th informing me of my appointment as lecturer on English Literature in the Johns Hopkins Univer-

---

[38] This letter was signed by Lanier but dictated to his wife. Gilman's letter

sity for the forthcoming year, allow me to signify herewith my acceptance of the position thus tendered and to add earnest acknowledgements of my personal pleasure in discharging duties so congenial to my own tastes.

Very respectfully,

Sidney Lanier.

To Lawrence Turnbull [39]

Camp Robin, near Asheville.
July 5th. 1881.

My dear Lawrence:

Will you do me the favor to inquire at the two places mentioned in the advertisements pinned hereto:

(1) what is the price of one of these secondhand Panel Pony Phaetons with Rumble;

of June 15 was an official announcement of Lanier's appointment as lecturer for a third year.

A memorandum has survived (MS, Johns Hopkins University) which probably accompanied Lanier's letter to Gilman. It is entitled: " Public and Class Lectures," offered by Sidney Lanier, for 1881-1882," and outlines his academic courses for the coming year as follows:

" I. *Theory of General Literature.* (The Doctrine of Personality, developed in public lectures of this year, applied as a Philosophy of Literature in general, and illustrated from the literary products of all nations). Minor Course: twelve lectures.

" II. *Historical Development of English Literature.* (Historic study of great English authors, with special reference to the rise of epochal ideas, movements, and forms, in our literature, and the absorption of Welsh, French, Italian, and other influences). Lectures throughout the first half-year. Text-book partly used: Bro. Azarias' *Hist. Dev. Eng. Lit.*

" III. *Current Literature.* (Class to meet once a week at my house, where the main current publications will be cited, and contemporary movements of thought noted)."

Another surviving memorandum (MS, Johns Hopkins University), dated Apr. 19, 1881, and hence probably sent earlier, outlines for 1881-1882 forty-eight public lectures, twelve on each of the following subjects: " The Faults of Shakspere," " Readings in the Less Familiar Plays of Shakspere," " The English Satirists," and " Shakspere's Sonnets."

The Johns Hopkins University Circulars, No. 11, p. 151 (July, 1881), announced simply that Lanier would give readings in the minor plays of Shakespeare early in the autumn of 1881.

[39] This letter was signed by Lanier but dictated to his wife.

(2) what would be the expense of sending one from Baltimore to Asheville by Express;

(3) also, what would be the price of a secondhand conveyance exactly like the one I have seen you driving your family in.

I am dictating this to my wife, being quite tired with correcting proofs of my Boy's *Mabinogion* which is now going through the press, and am just about to get me to my hammock under the trees for some rest; so that you will understand a note which is as full of love as it is brief.

Pray tell Mrs. Turnbull that my wife re-read to me the other day her charming verses, under the very trees whose good offices she so beautifully describes, and that I hope to put into form, some time, the thoughts which come to me from her tender and delicate fancies.

I have been quite hardworked in getting off the *Boy's Percy* which I had contracted to furnish just at this time; but that work is now done, everything has been sent in according to appointed dates, and I am free from extraordinary pressure for the next four weeks. This relaxation I am enjoying to the utmost.

I send you and your lovely wife the whole valley-full of green-leaf wishes and summer longings. What a delight if you two sat with us two this morning on the porch of my tent in the great woods upon the friendly breast of this great mountain that lifts us into the air, two thousand feet higher than the corner of McMechen St. and Park Avenue !.

Your friend,

Sidney L.

To RICHARD M. JOHNSTON [40]

Camp Robin, near Asheville.

July 5th 1881

My dear Colonel (but why should I not spell it *Kernel*,— as being one to whom other men are but as shells or husks?):

I was just beginning to dictate this to May when she was called

[40] Previously published, *Maryland Historical Magazine*, XXXIV, 322 (Dec.,

away, and so I scrawl on, as well as I can, to tell you that your sweet letter came in upon me through my circumjacent woods like a rose peeping through the leaves, and that I should long ago have sent you my love for it if either work or health had permitted. Our camp-outfit required endless small labors, and as soon as we moved into our tents — which was about five weeks ago— I had to set very hard to work at completing my *Boy's Percy* (a redaction of Percy's *Reliques*) which I had promised to furnish — along with the Introduction to my Mabinogion — by July 1st, complete and ready for the printer. Although in the greatest bodily distress I have ever known,— I managed to get through in time, and had the gratification of fulfilling my contract in spite of old Chang Lung, the tyrant.

I am sure you will be glad to know that I am now comparatively free from pressure of work, and will be so for four or five weeks to come. It is too glorious for any words to sit under my great trees, here, and fold my hands, and lie fallow to the thoughts that rain down from God and from the mountains.

I have improved a little, I think, in one or two particulars, and my appetite is better; though my leg is certainly the most ridiculous object I ever beheld, and as for the muscle of my arm, there is none. Nevertheless, I shall get well, and look for great things in the next four weeks.

Tell me how the novel fares,— for I shall brood anxiously over each character.

But here comes May; (who takes her rebel into custody, with a reprimand) and as this is the longest letter I have written in a great while I will allow her to close for me. Please give our love to Dr. & Mrs. Browne, and tell them how completely hard work has barred both May and myself from putting on paper the kindly thoughts of them that continually dwell with us.

With as many sweet wishes for you as there be leaves in all the valley betwixt this mountain that my tent is on and yonder

1939). The author of the article in which this letter is printed (F. T. Long, "The Life of Richard Malcolm Johnston in Maryland," p. 323) identifies the allusion in the fourth paragraph as being to *Old Mark Langston*, Johnston's first novel, which seems to have been prompted by Lanier; it was published in 1883.

blue range twenty miles away that I glimpse across many an intervening lesser hill whenever I lift my eyes,

Your friend

S. L.

(Our love to Lucian on his birthday.)

Dear friend:

I know that Mr. Tabb will receive our news and loving remembrance through you. There has not been much to aid my hope; his sufferings are almost intolerable; yet the last three days have been the best of any within a month. *Uniform* dry, warm weather needed— & lacking.

M.[41]

From Mary Day Lanier to Clifford A. Lanier

Camp Robin.   July 18th. 1881.

Clifford, darling, — he may still rally — he *may* recover – impossible as it now looks; and yet, your Mamie would not be faithful to hide from you that he is steadily sinking away from us; that he is certainly worse every fortnight — and to-day worse than yesterday which was alarming enough. He is so low that I can hardly bear to wait for a letter to travel to you. Having lost three or four pounds more since you left, and the fever having grown more uncontrollable, the ready relish for food seemed the one hope. He has been unable to sit on a horse for four weeks: many days unable to sit up in the buggy. Now, since July 7th, every mouthful of food brings instant distress of the stomach, (very few meals excepted), and frequent attacks of colic follow for hours, with an exhausting diarrhea every few days. This is now his state: he is almost in a collapse, and the leathery dryness of mouth forbids swallowing any food to-day. Milk is intolerable – so is an egg. Whiskey and beef juice can be forced in small quantities.

---

[41] Mary Day Lanier's postscript is amplified in a letter written to Sarah Farley on the same day (July 5, 1881). She reported that her husband had had two days during the past week when she was "not *driven* to feel half-willing to let his warfare cease." Now he had had another good day, in spite of bad weather. (Mr. and Mrs. R. S. Lanier, she added, arrived on July 5.)

I hope to see him rally, — yet I watch fearing any day may cut off that sweetest life that ever lit up heaven and earth for me.

Papa has been shutting his too-grieved eyes to the truth before them; but I see that he perceives the immediate danger to-day.

You may naturally feel, my darling, that with *him* here you are not needed, but this is a mistake. Dear father – with all his great, deep love, with all his keen sympathy, is still not the one to be sure of in these hours of need. His temperament is such that feeling quite overpowers reason in a trying moment, and even allows a haste of temper & word which – though far from representing his heart aright, is calculated to do mortal injury to one so nervous & exhausted as our poor darling. Possibly the wound may never be given again — since he begins to feel the awful shadow so near. Yet I found our precious one longing aloud for *you* – in whom to *repose*. He clings to dear father with a most touching, childlike fondness – with the holiest reverence –, yet that very intense reverence increases his susceptibility to pain at any want of the largeness & self-control which he exacts from himself. Clifford, dear, this is *all* " our own "; – and you will forgive me for even paining you, so unwillingly, for the sake of showing you exactly how all stands with him in his needs. He ought to be sheltered from *everything* like that. His own reflections upon the probabilities that no one of us can conquer are enough for him to make silent battle with. Yet it was not to say this that I wrote – and I beg you to *burn this leaf.*

I wrote to call out to you — " if you would surely see him, come soon – soon as possible." You might help to hold him – but I do not think long of that — I only know that you will want each other. To poor sweet Sissa, who cannot come, I cannot speak thus. You must write to her that he has been losing strength and suffering more since I wrote the bulk of the letter to her which I will mail with this. Repeatedly interrupted, it still lies unfinished: for my darling requires very close nursing now and I am not as strong as I ought to be. It is *very* beautiful here – and comfortable, even luxurious it would be with moderate health and freedom from great sorrow – As he lay out-doors in his invalid chair under the great trees on July

8th & 9th, laboring for every breath and too feeble to speak, yet facing the blue heavens and surrounded by all the " great companies of oaks " – I felt like praying that he might pass away in that spot and in that holy company, without too long a torture, or the bondage of the sick-room repeated, like last winter's.

And yet he *may* come back from the gate of death, for a while longer to bless us in the shape we know. I talk to you, brother, and I face it all, and yet I know that when that hour comes I shall be all incredulous of it, and all unprepared.

To see Wilsie and you beside him among his beloved trees – and to feel your tenderness enfolding him – this is all the solace my imagination offers as possible. Whether *here* or *there*, God bless and comfort you.

Your Mamie

Later.

Dr. Hardy is here.   From his private talk with me he fears [no] cause for immediate apprehension. On feeling Sidney's pulse he finds it much stronger than he expected –   & I infer that he thinks him able to hold out a while longer – even against such odds. —

I will communicate with you tomorrow –

M.

To Charles D. Lanier [42]

Asheville, N. C.
July 20, 1881.

My dear Son Charley:

I have been for several weeks lying at the very gates of death—so close that I could almost peep in upon the marvels of that mysterious country — and it has been long since I could write a letter with my own hand; but your mother has read me Mrs. Maxwell's report of your ever-increasing manfulness and of your gentle disposition toward your brothers, and this has brought me such deep gratification that I cannot

---

[42] This is one of only two letters during the summer of 1881 written entirely in Lanier's autograph. The other is to Charles Scribner, July 26, 1881, below.

help devoting a part of my very little strength this morning to the pleasant work of sending you this brief line of thanks and love which will enable you to share my pleasure with me. It would require a great many more pages than I can now write for me to tell you how earnestly I admire the sight of a man fighting his own small failings, as a good knight who never ceases to watch, and war against, the least blemish or evil: you may therefore fancy how my heart warms with loving pride in you and for you as I learn from Miss Mary the patience and generosity and large conduct which you daily exhibit towards your brothers, the gentlemanly thoughtfulness which you show for the comfort of all about you, and the general advance and growth which your whole nature appears to be achieving.

This makes me much more easy in mind when I think of the possibility that death may at any time compel me to leave my dear wife and my three beautiful boys (you should see Robin at this moment! with his great shining blue eyes and his milk-and-roses complexion, and magnificent limbs, he is like a young inhabitant of a morning-star just caught among the rhodo-dendrons of these mountains) in your charge as head of the family; for I well know that as long as you behave like a man you will never lack men for your friends.

But, – over and above all this, – I take the gravest pleasure in seeing you unfold what I know to be your natural qualities; I have always known that your character is strong and fine, but I have feared that your beautifully-sympathetic disposition would sometimes be apt to persuade you that you liked people or things which were really unworthy of you, and that you might have trouble with entanglements or stains thus arising, even after you had yourself perceived the unworthiness: but I rejoice to find in you a reasonableness and good judgment which I think will always bring you out safely at the end.

This is but a dry and didactic letter: nor will you know how much pleasure, how much hope, and how much affection go with it, until you yourself, my dear, dear boy, shall have a son who seems as fine as my Charley and whom you love as loves

your own

father.

From Robert S. Lanier to Clifford A. Lanier

In Camp, Near Asheville N. C^a.
July 24/81.

My dear son:

It is surprising to think how rapidly the Fates spin off the time in these mountain regions. I have only written you, and you me, once in the three weeks of my tabernacling here. I am sure this is not so much from indolence, & certainly not from disinclination, on my part. Camp duties, in non-recorded and almost non-recordable, ways have occupied, if not amused me. Shortly after I came Sidney bought a very handsome mare & harness & hired a buggy. For some days after he seemed able to ride with me to town & back—once or twice he drove there & back, but under protest from me. For the last week he has not been able to ride, tho' for the last three days he has felt better & has sat at table with us, having some appetite. Has also read some proofs which he deems necessary to get off for his book. I have a pleasant ride to town every day to get Camp supplies & the mail. It has been quite hot in the day here. Occasional rains however lower the heat & we generally sleep under blankets.

The Doctor thinks Sidney able, & recommends him, to take a trip to Wayneville, about 30 miles from here, where there are fine Sulphur Waters, &c. He thinks of trying it in a day or so going in an easy, large carriage, with Mary. Should he prefer to remain there the Camp will be moved. I should like to go up there & have a taste of the mineral waters & the fine *speckele trout* that abound in Pigeon river & its creeks. It is hardly probable we shall move the camp, however.

Whilst as you well know I am ready to do, & am doing, everything I can for Sidney, it is very important for me to be in Atlanta in two weeks from now in special matters. Besides there are matters there needing my attention at home. Can't you & Willie come up here two weeks from now & take my tent & place for a month, or say three weeks? I will come back then, if necessary, & relieve you in turn. As the change has been good for wife & I surely we may believe it will be good for Willie & you & pay you for coming. See what you can do

& let me know in the course of a week or ten days. Can you not come shortly after the 1st Augt. & return by 1st Sept.? But for business engagements I should *prefer* to stay here. The mare Nellie is one of the finest buggy nags I ever drove, & we have a new saddle that she paced under as finely as she trots in harness. (She costs $125⁰⁰)

We drove out to the Sulphur Spring, wife & I, & had a glorious drink of the mineral water & brought home a gallon in a jug, which kept well in the spring house several days. The Camp is enlivened with chickens, one or more of which delights the table every day. We are beginning to have corn & tomatoes, okra &c.

Will write you again in a few days. Love to Willie and the children. Your aff. father,

R. S. Lanier

FROM MARY DAY LANIER TO CLIFFORD A. LANIER

Camp Robin.   July 24th [1881.]

Confidential.

Clifford A. Lanier.

My darling brother:

During our dear one's alarming attack of last Sunday, Monday & Tuesday, I wrote for advice (more especially regarding the trouble with stomach and bowels) to Dr. [Marbury] Brewer, the physician called in three times by Dr. [Thomas] Shearer, last December & January. I sketched the outline of Sidney's progress for six months and gave as exact a description as I could of his present & recent condition. From the most immediately alarming symptoms he is now free, and perhaps Dr. Brewer would have the same change of view as that which Dr. Hardy, of Asheville underwent after his Monday visit. Dr. H. then feared the worst must come speedily – though he told *me* he had known some to endure several weeks in our darling's then condition. When he saw Sidney on *Friday* and marked the great advance in digestion he told *him* that "he saw no reason now why he should not regain strength", & encouraged him to go to Waynesville. But he

seemed not to wish to speak plainly to me, again, and he
evinced so much pain & tenderness the first day that I would
not seek the occasion, there being no certainty & no more *to do*
than we already know.   I think he was less frank to Papa: –
poor Papa ! We all instinctively feel that he cannot endure,
without too much strain to look at these possibilities.   And I
have *not* shown him Dr. Brewer's letter.   He is here –   I will
not torture him needlessly, & there is *no such thing as preparation.*

But you, beloved, are *not* here; and the light that I can
get I must *share* with you – altho' it falls on a thorny road.   It
seems too cruel that perhaps you *cannot* come !   But God cannot be cruel !   And we know that only necessity will hold you
back.   I tell Sidney nothing that will lessen his hope.   I understand that if he ceases to hope he will go quickly.   He is eager
to live and to work. –   And oh, what a tender tone in his voice,
what a soft light in his eye, when he wonders " if Cliffie *will*
come on ! "

Bless you –

Maydie.

To Charles Scribner

Asheville, N. C.

July 26, 1881.

My dear Mr. Scribner:
               Can you without inconvenience order a
couple of galley-proofs of the Introduction to our Mabinogion
to be immediately printed off and sent me, here?   I wish to
submit a point, therein made, to a friend in Baltimore, and to
send a copy down while there is time to receive his answer and
make any amendment that might appear desirable.

I am going to beg, too, that you will show that part of the
Introduction which concerns the pronunciation of Welsh letters
&c. to some intelligent Welshman, or person familiar with that
language, and let me know if the hints I have given are in any
the least particular subject to objection.   These directions are so
perfunctory, and they are made so purely upon the basis of the
impression which an English ear receives from rapid Welsh
pronunciation, that I am a little nervous lest some one should

attack them, — and I want these books to be above all chance of opposition.

It is a real grief to me that you have not been able to see your way to print *the Boy's Percy* along with *the Mabinogion.* The relations between the Percy and the preceding series are very close and instructive: and the Percy is the first out-and-out pure English classic of the lot, — for the *Froissart* is a *translation* from the French, The *King Arthur* is partly at least a compilation from French sources, and the *Mabinogion* is from the Welsh, while the Percy ballads present the workings of English genius pure and simple, in English forms.

But of course you know best the limitations of " business." [43]

I have sent forward page-proofs of the Mabinogion up to p. 150, — from which I judge that book to be going forward well.

With cordial wishes for a pleasant and unfatiguing summer,

Sincerely yrs.

Sidney Lanier.

P.S. I believe I have not acknowledged your check for the *Percy,* and hereby send you my acknowledgments for your promptness in sending same.

Pray read the Mabinogion Introduction, — either you or Mr. Burlingame, — and give me without hesitation any suggestions which may occur to you looking towards the betterment thereof.

S. L.

From Mary Day Lanier to Sarah J. Farley

Camp Robin.   July 30th. 1881.

— Almost July 31st " – for it is nearly midnight and I have just finished the preparations for his hard night, after an unusually ill day. He seldom calls me up between the late hour of my retiring and half-past five in the morning, and I

---

[43] Scribner had written, July 11, 1881 (in answer to a lost letter by Lanier of June 28, 1881), saying that he already had on hand for publication an unusually large number of juveniles and dared not add *The Boy's Percy* to his lists for 1881.

try to have everything that could possibly be needed within his reach, after rubbing the dear wasted form with that oil which is to keep in it a little longer the laboring breath. At times when I am so exhausted that I am tempted to heed him and give it up " that one time " – I now brace myself by the thought " this may keep him with me two – three – four hours longer ". But, O, darling Sarah! is it the part of love to try to keep him? How he suffers – I would not try to hint to you; I have to dull my own sense of it in order to hold up. But he keenly desires life and while almost physically crushed (and even the mind too feeble to make any expression oft-times) his same brave hopefulness remains with him.

" Mc Aboy's ", near Tryon.

Spartanburg & Hendersonville R. R.

N. Carolina –

August 9th 1881.

I write with *her* pencil and fan Sidney with the other hand while he seeks afternoon sleep in *her* chair.[44] Unless I neglect him, or take time absolutely needful for restoring (by rest) my waning powers this seems to be almost my only opportunity for scrawling a note. In this same chair – which seems an embodiment of her farewell tone & look of love to us – he has for weeks found all his rest, only three times sleeping in a bed. This is our second excursion among the mountains, in easy carriage, – and the chair is folded and shares the driver's seat. On July 17th, 18th & 19th he was alarmingly ill – one of many attacks of the bowels supplemented by an overdose of Quinine; pulse 149, temp. 103½. Soon as digestion and strength warranted the attending physician sent him to a wonderfully beautiful region " Waynesville White Sulphur Spgs." 33 miles distant.[45] We made it in one day and the carriage motion in the perfect fresh air was a change for the better with him. Made

[44] The reference is to gifts from Sarah Farley's mother, who had died in Dec., 1880.

[45] Lanier and his wife went from Camp Robin to Waynesville on Tuesday, July 26 (see R. S. Lanier's letter to his son Clifford, July 28, 1881).

the journey home on 29th with equal success. Found Robin ill from teeth; not in danger, but sadly changed in three days. On the 4th we left him again (thinner but well), driving first 13 miles to the *earthly*-paradise home of some friends of my child-hood who moved to these mountains ten years ago — Mr. & Mrs. Westfeldt. They hail from Mobile but have lived much in New York & more in England & Dresden whence they have brought back much that is lovely – nothing to be regretted. They educated their boys at Rugby and knew intimately George Eliot's last husband, Mr. Cross. He was indeed in Mr. West-feldt's English business house. Under this roof, with the vast foreground of mountain valley sweeping for miles from east to west, forever within sight, my darling seemed to me to be in his right place.[46] I wish we had there remained – he might not have been so ill since if continuously ministered to in soul & body with such skill. But we were in search of a softer cli-mate than Asheville's for our camp, and bound for this edge of the " no-frost " belt of Tryon Mt., where a house of enter-tainment has long been kept by Dr. Mc Aboy D.D. – of Pa. & of the Presbyterian Church. Sidney finds this climate perfectly delightful and has telegraphed for Clifford to come help move our bulky camp & equipage. For one of us must stay with Sidney, who is too weak to return to A– needlessly.
The last & severest attack upon the bowels culminated on Saturday & Sunday after arriving here. I thought he could hardly lose more flesh, but so it is. The lung is almost easy in this air and the cough much lighter. I suspect at times that it is partly because of the disease tending in the other direction. Yet I see that he ought to have come *here* at first. If we had only known ! Asheville nights were too cold. This country is rarely beautiful, fruit in profusion, abundant table with many good points & kind people. It might shock you insufferably to meet the crudeness, the disorder, the slap & dash absence of method & scarcity of appointments — but if it did not – if it

[46] A note in *Poems* (New York, 1899, *et seq.*), p. 2, probably prepared by Mary Day Lanier, reads: "' Sunrise ' . . . was dedicated through his latest request to that friend who indeed came into his life only near its close, yet was at first meeting recognized by the poet as ' the father of his spirit,' GEORGE WEST-FELDT. When words were very few and the poem was unread, even by any friend, the earnest bidding came: ' Send him my " Sunrise ", that he may know how entirely we are one in thought.' "

did not ! you could so enjoy the mountains and the air — — —
with us — —— And board is $25. pr. month; the house 2
miles from Tryon Station, a point 28 miles from Spartanburg
by R. Rd.   We sat on the piazza at our cottage, last eve'g, at
sunset, and wished for you. " It would be perfect " ——*he*
answered to my wish. Whether you could bear to see him I
do not know. But to think how the Dryden [47] Climate is worst-
ing you – and how this one would renew you and how we long
for you —— all this forces me to say so much.   I think he
would rather see you than anyone else in the world –   But he
is very low, dear. I can hardly bear to tell *you* the truth about
him — And be careful when you reply – if you desire to say
anything that would lessen his hope – to place it on a separate
leaf. He does hope, far more than I do. I have coaxed myself
into a dream of hope again, because I have not strength to face
the facts & not be harmful to him, but I see no *reason* in my
hope. I constantly repeat to myself yr. words " you can do the
impossible." If this be so (and *you* said it !) I may still hope.
There is no longer power to dictate to me, & Mr. Pope's work
is not begun altho' we are living on his salary. A month hence
we are to be preparing dear, blessed Charley for boarding
school at Williston Seminary, Mass. –   there to prepare, during 4 years, for the Hoboken Stevens' Institute of Technology.
But what are we to look forward to? what, venture on!

Dear, I ought not to write to you. I *don't* write to anyone
else, except on business. What I have to say I have no words
for. God restore your strength for

One who needs you.[48]

[47] Sarah Farley was at Dryden Springs, N. Y.
[48] In an undated MS entitled " Recollections " (Charles D. Lanier Collection, Johns Hopkins University) Mary Day Lanier recorded an episode of
this summer which is not mentioned in the letters. A clergyman of the neighborhood, an " entire stranger," walked briskly into Lanier's tent one day, made
a brief expression of interest, and gave ghostly counsel which Lanier acknowledged with courteous deference. " Then he proceeded to apply the creed test
to that subtle reverent Soul, scarcely veiled by the fading flesh. The beautiful
Soul, mindful of good intention, & ever aflame with the passion of the love of
God, replied gently & fervently, yet contrived to parry the thrust and leave himself upon the broader ground where many baffling questions are not defined. But
the visitor must define and that rigidly, and after another unsuccessful attempt to
probe the sensitive spirit he became aggressive & loud as he put his ultimatum
forward– Then, like lightning from summer cloud the white face flashed back

To Robert S. Lanier [49]

("McAboy's.") Lynn. Polk Co. N.C.
August 15th 1881.

My dear Father:

On my way through Asheville, the other day,[50]
finding myself rather short of funds I drew a check on my Baltimore bank for $30.00 and got it cashed at the Bank of Ashe-
ville. A letter just rec'd. from the Baltimore bank informs me
this was an overdraw and had been refused. I am confident
the book-keeper there is mistaken, and will have my book made
up immediately, to show it; meantime you will of course realize
the pain & distress I am in until you see Mr. Waddell, Cashier
of the Bank of Asheville, and explain to him that my check
book shows still a considerable balance in my favor against the
Balto bank. Furthermore, before Clifford left, I gave him a
check, blank as to amount, on Bank of Asheville, so that he
might collect a small balance of account there and close it up.
You will remember that your $100.00 in gold had been de-
posited here; and I had intended to continue the account a little
longer by depositing $150. out of the Pope fund due Aug. 1st,
—in order to cover your amount and to pay off small out-
standing bills in Asheville.

Under these circumstances I write to ask that you will come
immediately into town, as soon as Lanier Eason[51] hands you
this, and attend to the following matters for me.

(1) Open the Pope package, sign the draft (which you
will therein find all made out with the exception of my signa-

---

defiance through those unclouded eyes, and the voice that often failed to reach
us rang out like a clarion 'No! no! I do not! I do not!'" The clergyman left
shortly, and Lanier dismissed the episode with a remark to his wife about the
"debt of conscience" his visitor had discharged. "Briefly recalling the scene
later in the eve'g for his father's benefit, a humorous twinkle of eye attested his
sense of having 'held the fort.'"

[49] This letter was dictated to Mary Day Lanier.

[50] The reference is, presumably, to Lanier's trip from Camp Robin to Tryon,
Aug. 4.

[51] Lanier Eason, son of Lanier's aunt Mrs. T. D. Eason of Charleston, had
joined the camp party at Tryon. Clifford Lanier had also arrived by this time,
but on Aug. 21 he was on his way back to Montgomery. Mr. and Mrs. R. S.
Lanier left Asheville about Aug. 29.

ture), using the form "Sidney Lanier, by R. S. Lanier," and attach the authorization, which I herein enclose, to the draft with a pin. Present the draft to M^r. Waddell, Cashier of the Bank of Asheville, and ask him to cash it as follows:

$100.^{00} to my credit in his own bank, and to this end Lanier will hand you my bank book with the Asheville bank, in which W. can enter the amount & hand same back to you;

$50.^{00} in cash (and let a good deal of it be small money) which bring to me;

The check of the Bank of Asheville on New York in favor of *The National Bank of Baltimore* for $300.^{00}, balance of the Pope fund after the above $150.^{00} is taken out;

(2) This being done please mail the last-mentioned check to "Cashier of The National Bank of Baltimore, Balt^o. Md.", enclosed in a note asking him to place this $300.^{00} to my credit;

(3) Sign the vouchers and receipt exactly like the draft, attaching by a pin the duplicate authorization, for which purpose I send two. Mail the signed vouchers and receipt to such person as you will probably find named in a penciled slip which usually comes attached to the blanks. Fill out dates, &c. in vouchers & receipts wherever left blank.

(4) The check refused was dated August 4th, for $30.^{00} I have received notice of protest, which I enclose. I do not know whether the amount should be sent to the Balt^o bank that presented it (which the protest states to be the "Farmer's & Merchant's National") or to the Bank of Asheville. Please ask Waddell and settle with him. I may state that I had left more than enough to my credit with him to pay the amount;

(5) Furnish Lanier with any additional funds he may need for his expenses on this business, out of the proceeds of the Pope draft;

(6) I do not know whether I distinctly mentioned to you that I wish to retain Brown as a body-servant. Perhaps it might be convenient for him to ride Nelly horseback, along with the waggons; but this arrange as you and Clifford judge proper.

(7) Ask Col. Ray to forward his entire bill to me at this point; also, Kepler, and leave all other large matters to be settled by me from this point. My arrangement for horse feed was $10. a month, besides which Jules was to be paid for

attending to Nelly. *I settled with Isaac* up to the 13th July—this being the 1st month.

There—that is all; I am very tired, though certainly better in lung than when I saw you last.

Lovingly –

S. L.

FROM VIRGINIA HANKINS

Alleghany Springs.
Virginia.
Aug. 24, 1881.

I stand upon the topmost of these " heaven-kissing hills " and long to pierce the distance and catch a glimpse of you, dear Friend, who stand upon other mountain heights, but my human gaze cannot see what the summer-tide has brought to you. – Ah! we climb fast up to the heights of Life, shall not our two souls, some time, see each other and know that " all is well "?

You, the Poet, must perforce *know* all things, and teach them to the world. – I, the Teacher, must in some guise, be a poet, else all my teaching would be in vain – empty words to fill out the blustering cheeks of the world's vapidity.

I wish the winds that blow Southward could carry to you some of the thoughts that are stirring up in my heart as I beg them to carry you health and strength. I remember you were here once [52] and perhaps, from this very spot, wrote me those letters beautiful in hopefulness of life, joyousness in nature and unchangeableness in friendship.

May I not hope to hear that you are growing stronger and that you do not forget your Friend?

Ginna – [53]

Address
  Petersburg.
    Va.

[52] Lanier had spent the summer of 1872 at Alleghany Springs.

[53] On the envelope of this letter Mary Day Lanier wrote: " The last letter ever read by the eyes of Sidney Lanier."

To Charles Scribner [54]

Lynn. Polk Co. N.C.
Sept. 3rd, 1881.

My dear Mr. Scribner:

About four weeks ago a desperate attack of illness suddenly rendered me unable even to correct proof. In the hope that abatement would come I held over from day to day such parcels of proof as arrived from Boston; but I find that this may involve more delay, as well as a constant burden of responsibility which works against the speediness of my recovery. I write therefore to say: (1) that I yesterday managed by pure *tour de force* to revise the proof of the Introduction, (which you had kindly sent at my request, and which I found greatly disfigured by printers, and proof-readers' errors), and to send same to Boston with a marginal note explaining cause of delay; (2) that I send you, at New York, all the other proof which has reached me up to date, asking that you will have it read by some person competent in the premises, and will charge expenses of same to my account. I had hoped, indeed, that by the time we should have reached the point where I stopped four weeks ago — I had then corrected about 150 *pp.* of page-proof — the proof-readers would have caught my very simple system of punctuation so clearly as to make any further supervision by me unnecessary; but I find them still sprinkling commas over the page as these country cooks in North Carolina sprinkle black pepper over their unspeakable chicken-pies, out of pepper-boxes whose holes have run together by liberal use and wont until they often give down three grains for one.

I am entirely ignorant, however, of dates, of necessity for haste, &c, in your plans for the book; and if such farther proof-reading as I suggest involves delay or inconvenience I beg you to disregard all said in that connection and to go forward as seems best to you.

Your little check for balance due on account copyright *Science of Verse* was received with joy and merrymaking by my little circle who are about me here in the mountains. You will

[54] This letter was dictated to Mary Day Lanier.

observe that my P.O. address is " Lynn, Polk Co. N.C." This will continue for at least a month. I shall pull through the present crisis and write many another book, whereof the germs have already been born in this strange and beautiful Tryon Valley.

With earnest thanks for the inquiries as to my health which I find in your last letters, I am always

Sincerely yours,

Sidney Lanier.

by M.D.L.[55]

---

[55] Scribner replied, Sept. 5, assuring Lanier that he need give himself no further anxiety about the proofs, which would be corrected by Mr. Burlingame without charge, and that *The Boy's Mabinogion* would be published at the end of October, as planned. But his letter probably reached Tryon too late. Lanier died on Sept. 7, 1881.

Numerous additional details concerning the last three months of Lanier's life can be found in the collateral correspondence listed in part three of the Calendar at the end of the present volume, especially in the letters written by his wife and his father to Clifford Lanier and in the following: Clifford Lanier to Virginia Hankins, Oct. 14, 1881; G. A. Westfeldt to J. A. Fisher, July 19, 1884; Mary Day Lanier to Anna Blauvelt, Feb. 26, 1898.

The funeral ceremony was performed by the Rev. William Kirkus at the Episcopal Church of Saint Michael and All Angels, Baltimore, at 5 P. M., Sept. 9, 1881. The pall bearers were T. W. Baxter, W. H. Browne, W. Hall, R. M. Johnston, Innes Randolph, and J. C. Wrenshall. The interment was in the Lawrence Turnbull lot, Greenmount Cemetery, Baltimore. In the interests of science Lanier had requested an autopsy, but for some reason none took place.

APPENDICES

A. LETTERS TO HURD & HOUGHTON [1]

195 Dean St
Brooklyn, N.Y.
Sep. 24, 1874

Messrs Hurd & Houghton:

Gentlemen:

Will you do me the favor of transmitting the enclosed to the Editor of the Atlantic Monthly?

It is the poem of which I spoke to you some days ago. It will sell several hundred copies of the Magazine in the South: I will myself be answerable for two hundred copies; and when it is thus introduced, I will have it published in book-form in the mode alluded to in our conversation. This method of publication — first in Magazine, then in book-form — has been suggested to me by a person prominent in letters in New York, as the proper method of getting the work before the public. For my object is not alone to sell the poem in the South — in which there will be no difficulty, since my own personal acquaintance, and the deep interest now felt by the people in those topics which the poem discussess, will secure a ready sale — but I desire also to get a hearing before the culture of the North and East, which when " Tiger Lilies " was published greeted it with many kindly prophecies of its author's fortune, and equally kindly criticism of his faults. It is natural that I should wish to know how far the prophecies have been fulfilled and the faults amended.

Any expedition which may secure in getting the poem read by Mr. Howells will be considered a favor by me.

---

[1] These two letters, concerned with Lanier's efforts to secure the publication of " Corn " and " In Absence " in the *Atlantic Monthly*, were discovered too late to be printed in proper sequence in vol. IX, which had already been set up. They are therefore given here, from transcripts courteously furnished to the present editors by William Charvat (Ohio State University), who found them in the store-room of the Riverside Press among the Hurd & Houghton papers, now the property of Houghton Mifflin & Co. (Three earlier letters from Lanier to Hurd & Houghton are printed in vol. VII of the present edition.)

Pray address me, as soon as you have heard from him, as at head of this letter.

Very Truly Yrs.

Sidney Lanier [2]

––––––––––

195 Dean St
Brooklyn, N.Y.
Oct. 7, 1874

Messrs. Hurd and Houghton,
New York

Gentlemen:

Pray allow me to thank you for your efforts in my behalf.

How the critics differ! — but having laid seige to Mr. Howells, I'm determined to conquer him: — so, will you do me the favor to examine the address of the enclosed letter, (I don't know whether it should be *Boston* or *Cambridge*) and, if you find it right, transmit to that gentleman. It contains a couple of short poems. [3]

I will call as soon as I can get time, — probably on Monday — and talk with you about publishing the poem. Please retain the ms. [4] until then.

Very truly Yrs.

Sidney Lanier

[2] In the upper left corner of this letter appears the notation in pencil in an unidentified hand: "Oct 7 Mr. Howells will please return letter after reading to M by mail." For Howells's opinion of "Corn," see his letter to Hurd, Oct. 3, 1874 (vol. IX, 96, and note 112, of the present edition).

[3] Two sonnets, obviously the first two in the "In Absence" sequence but called by the early title "Laus Mariae" (see Lanier's letters to his wife, Oct. 7, 1874, and to Taylor, Feb. 25, 1877).

[4] The MS of "Corn."

B. REMINISCENCES OF SIDNEY LANIER [1]

FROM ROBERT S. LANIER TO J. A. FISHER

Macon, Ga., Sept. 25th 1883

Revd J. A. Fisher.

Balt Md

Dear sir: Your letter of the 17th inst. was duly recd. & I have been trying to take a day from business engagements to make some proper response to it. But I fear that without more time than I could now well allow to make references to family correspondence, & other memoranda to revive recollections &c. the response will be meagre enough.

Whilst a student at Randolph Macon College Va I became acquainted with Mary Jane Anderson, of Nottoway Co. Va some 60 miles from the college.[2] Upon leaving the College shortly thereafter and returning to Macon, where I studied law for some months, I returned to Nottoway Co. & was married to Mary Jane A. by Revd Dr Pryor (father of Genl. Roget A. Pryor now of N. Y.) came home and was admitted to practice of law in the spring of 1841. About 1850 Clifford Anderson

---

[1] Among the many letters concerning Lanier in the several collections at Johns Hopkins University, the following seven are printed here because of the important biographical material they contain. Three of them (two by Lanier's father and one by his sister) were addressed to the Rev. John A. Fisher, a graduate student at Hopkins in the 1880's, whose plans for a full-length biography of Lanier (the first projected) were interrupted by ill-health and subsequent death. Another (by Lanier's wife) was addressed to F. A. King, who also at one time entertained plans for a biography; the first part of this letter is missing. A fifth (by Lanier's boyhood friend Charles E. Campbell) was written to Henry W. Lanier when the latter was gathering material for a biography of his father. The other two (by Lanier's wife and by James Woodrow, his teacher at Oglethorpe University) were written for Edwin Mims, Lanier's first biographer, who used them in part in his volume issued in 1905. None of these letters, with their recollections of Lanier by people who had known him intimately, have been previously published or even known to later students. (R. S. Lanier's careless use of parentheses has been corrected in four places.)

[2] Robert Sampson Lanier was born in Clarke County, Ga., Sept. 22, 1819. Mary Jane Anderson was born in Nottoway County, Va., Dec. 14, 1822. They met in July, 1840, at the Commencement exercises, Randolph-Macon College, and were married Oct. 27, 1840. After the death of his first wife in 1865, R. S. Lanier married a widow, Mrs. Morgan, in Jan., 1873.

343

youngest of wife's brothers then a youth, came to Ga. from V[a] & being admitted to the practice of law (having studied in my office) became my partner in the practice & we have been in partnership ever since. He is at present Attorney Genl. of the state, being now in his second term.

My son Sidney was born in Macon on the 3[d] day of February 1842.[3] (The house in which he was born has been remodeled) When our children (two sons & a daughter, the only children) were born we resolved to teach them, as far as we could, at home before sending them off to " school." Thro' the firmness of their mother this resolve was adhered to: and Sidney was well advanced in the rudiments & he had got beyond the home teaching when he started to " school." I think he must have been a " bright boy " because he seemed to learn his lessons with less effort than a majority of boys. He never had to be " made to study." For scholarship & deportment at home & at " school " he stood well, never rec[d] punishment at home or by his teachers. (It so happened that I never " whipped " one of my children & I think if their mother ever did it was of the slightest) I think he was not over four or five years old when he had a taste for certainly the habit of, reading. Among our " Christmas " presents select books to the children were the chief. I remember, among others, to have given Sidney as a Christmas present fine old Froissart in two big vol[s] illustrated, when Sidney was about 8 years old, supposing that in a year or so he would dip into it occasionally; but he did not wait & found it a source of great interest, & within 12 mos, had grown familiar with its contents. He was more or less fond of boyish sports, but was ready at any time to drop them for his reading. As he grew from boyhood to youth he seemed less inclined to engage in " play-ground " sports, – rather prefering to sit aside, with book at hand & watch the boys play. His boyhood *physique* was about equal to the average. Whilst never aggressive (never could have been one of a " *hazing* " party) he was never the subject of imposition from his school fellows. In the matter of school plays & sports he was much

---

[3] Clifford Anderson Lanier was born Apr. 24, 1844, in Griffin, Ga., where R. S. Lanier was associated in the practice of law with David Clopton and Samuel G. Jones. Gertrude Lanier was born Nov. 20, 1845, also in Griffin.

more likely to be found looking on & enjoying them than in participating in them. He was neither forward nor shy; modest, quiet, reflecting. There was however something about him that made him a leader among his fellows. For instance, when he was about 12 years old a " Military Company " of boys of like age was organized, they made him captain, were uniformed & drilled, well drilled by him with wooden guns for arms. At a " turn out " of the Military Co^s on a *Fourth* of *July* his Co. turned out too, & just before the Battalion was ready to be dismissed for " dinner " suddenly *his* Company was found *formed* on the *left*. The joke took & he & his Co. were invited to the " dinner." Being present & being called on for a toast he responded handsomely & with unexpected success (eclat)

When about 9 years old he rec^d –, as a Christmas present, a small plain flute, which he tried to play or blow from time to time & not making progress to himself laid it aside; but in a year or so took it up again & was encouraged to make new efforts. His mother then taught him the rudiments of music. (She played well on the piano forte) He was an apt pupil & soon learned all she could teach him, & pursued the study of his own inclination from such initial point – meantime getting a larger flute with a key or two to it. When about 12 years old there were some bright *colored* barbers, John Booker & others here who were ambitious to emulate the " Campbells' Minstrels." They got him to teach them the notes &C. Many a moonlight night I have heard him teaching & practicing with them in the yard, & John Booker & his Co. became such experts in negro Minstrelsy that they went to Europe & attracted attention there.

When, at this age, 12 year, when about home, Sidney was generally found with a book in hand, & apt to be abstracted & well absorbed therein, no matter what was going on round about. I have often seen him sitting in a chair tilted on *one* hind leg of it, closely studying a book in one hand with a half tasted but neglected cake in the other, & making an occasional half turn on the pivot as the study or reflection went on. Speaking of the Cake reminds me: From the time he was eight to fifteen years of age I was in the habit of taking my family to Montvale Springs Ten^e. (a fine property of my father, Sterling

Lanier) for part of the summer. When Sidney was about 12 years old there was a family servant of about his age who usually waited on & about him named John. Sidney had a mahogany " Secretary " in his room on which he did his writing. One day Sidney had been sitting writing & meditating before the open secretary for some time, while John was standing by, looking over his shoulder into the Secretary, when he spied some cake which Sidney had in there. Finally John exclaimed, " Mas Sid! Mas Sid! Ef you *guine* to eat dat cake *les'* eat it now ! " The point of the " *les'* eat it now " could not be mistaken. There was no one more genial or more quick to see or give the true point of a joke than Sidney, even then, & his manner of telling *this* in the family made a good joke for the season.

Whilst at Montvale we used to go out on camp hunts on Chilhowee, & the high ridges of old " Ball Mountain (on line between Ten. & N. Ca.) with a number of friends, including some of the " natives " from the coves, for a week at a time. It was out of material Sidney thus picked up that he essayed " Tiger Lillies," part of which he wrote whilst in service during the late war, & which novel he published shortly thereafter, – the first of his publications.

I cannot say what were Sidney's favorite studies as boy or youth. As to his textbooks he seemed to get on equally well in all, whilst, as to general reading, he took up & read most of what fell in his way. Chambers Miscellany, Harper's Monthly, Froissart, Milton, Shakespeare, (we had a large 7 vol. edition of the latter) & other English as well as modern American writers.

He was about 14 years old when he entered Oglethorpe University, (at Midway, about one mile from Milledgeville, then the Capitol of Ga., a fine village of wealthy planters & others, forming excellent society, scattered on healthy, rolling hills covered with great oaks.) Entering the Sophomore class half advanced & being quick to learn, & having acquired some skill on the flute & organized a quartette band among his fellow students, his social relations in town & village became extended & their claims upon him such that for the first 12 or 18 months he found himself not making a special point of close text studies. Tho' he kept up his general reading, & had good reports; but after that, & during the last year he made close application & " shared the First Honor " with a much older student who had been a close student all the time. To show the appreciation of the Trustees & Faculty of Sidney: they elected him Tutor of the College on the same day he graduated: and he was such Tutor when the war took him to the " field " – then between 17 & 18 years of age.

I reckon there never was a man or boy who made fewer enemies: but he had one affair of some moment during his first year at College. He, with a number of the students being at their boarding house one morning before breakfast, & whilst awaiting it, the joke running round as was frequent, some jousts of wit passed between Sidney & one of them, a very excitable person, who was touched perhaps too tenderly, who returned an insulting remark which brought a slap in his face, whereupon he whipped out his knife & cut Sidney badly in the back. They were soon parted, Sidney bedded & doctored, the young man begged forgiveness, which was readily granted, & *he* was *his best nurse*. Tho' unprovoked & the cutting serious no forgiveness could have been more thorough or injury sooner forgotten. Sidney had his digusts of vulgar – men & things, & contempts for the mean & small, but he had no malice or revenges. He hated to hate & loved to love all.

In youth & College days, he probably saw more of society than the average Southern boy. He was not boisterous or demonstrative in manner, but whilst of quiet manners, was genial & bright and whether as boy, youth, man, made ' troops of friends.' But he never mixed freely with the people at home or elsewhere generally; the " people he met " in social or business relations became his friends. (An illustrative incident occurred to me *last night*: A fine looking man, well dressed & of good address, knocked at my dwelling, asking for me. I was told a gentleman wished to see me. I went to the door & invited the " gentleman " into the parlor. " No ", he said, he ventured to call on me a moment to ask me something about my son Sidney, who he had heard was dead, whom he had known at " Montvale " & of whom he had since heard much &c. I asked him to step in my sitting room, where there was more light than in the hall. He did so. I then discovered he was a very bright *colored* man, evidently well educated, some 45 years of age. He stated he was a minister of the Gospel had recently been appointed " Presiding Elder " in the Macon Dist. whither he had just come, & was very desirous of knowing something more of my son, & his family & apologising for the intrusion &c.) (He had known Sidney at Montvale in boyhood & had thought a great deal of him, but had never met him afterwards.)

I cannot say if Sidney had a " passion " for " writing " in his youth. I rather think (tho' he exercised that way more or less) that he had a fondness for studying general literature. The teachings of physical nature, –mountains, hills, valleys, the sea &c. of studying natures in the crowd of men & women as they passed, – he standing apart – of reflecting on the lessons so studied, holding their suggestions in mind until these formulated into convictions. He was a " student of nature ", as well as of art.

The newspaper slip I herewith send you, contributed by a Mr Tabb of V^a (taken from the " Independent " I believe, sent me by a friend) tells in some eloquent words much of the man. It was in Point Lookout prison during a very cold winter (of 1864-65) when even the " magic flute " could not call up fire & fuel & blankets, that I think Sidney rec^d the seeds of his fatal, & hard fought, disease. He got back home, after discharge from prison, just as the war was closing. He was subjected to great hardships in getting home, & a few days thereafter he had a fearful attack of Erysipelas in the head, which affected the brain, as he was " out of his head " for about a week, (during which time he talked much of the beauties of the Seminole Indian language. He discoursed about it as tho' he had before studied it: but on his recovery upon being questioned he said he never had.) The Physician then told me that unless Sidney took great care of himself he would have consumption. Tho' there are some grounds to think his disease may have been hereditary on his mothers' side there is so much room to doubt it that I have no fixed opinion.

Before Sidney commenced the study & practice of the *law* his tastes disinclined him thereto. He seemed to think that its tenets and principles were so rigid & inflexible as to deprive it of its true soul and spirit. Having been the principal of a fine Academy at Prattville Ala. & finding the work overtaxing his strength he came to Macon with his young wife & commenced the study of the *law* in L & A's office. In its prosecution his prepossessions gave way & he soon became fond of it. He remained with us about 3 years, continuing his studies, after admission to the Bar in Macon and doing much work. Being the Solicitors of several Building & Loan Associations, which advanced money on real estate we had much to do, in connection with our general business, with real estate law, trust estates &c. involving intricate questions, Sidney showed such quickness in his work that we soon entrusted a large portion of it to him. Just as he became useful & took rank as a lawyer his failing health brought him to a pause, & whilst reflecting what change might better his health, he concluded that the northern air was more bracing, and less hurtful than ours here, that he felt he could do better in " literature " and " Music "; (which had continued to occupy him all along), that he desired to have access to the great libraries in Balto Phila & New York, & the advantages he would thus have in these fields of labor, – feeling, as he said, that they were the fields in which he could do most as better suited to his tastes & allowing greater latitudes in controlling his time &c. Thus he was forced by disease to leave the law wherein he soon would have become, no doubt, a successful advocate, & one of its most conscientious & distinguished expounders. (Thus into the great, expensive Cities, without means, he went with his family, to work in bad health, as an " author "! It is amazing to me how much this poor, feeble man, racked by disease, actually accomplished!)

It would be easy to infer from his writings, Music &c. that Sidney was a *mere poet* & *musician*. Such may be the general impression. But nothing was farther from the fact. He was very practical. He had that fine, catholic common sense that enabled him to adopt business methods where necessary, to understand business transactions of the most complicated sort, among business men. He was a fine mathematician, & illustrated his business aptitudes in our law affairs and in his own. In matters of mechanics, carpentry, as occasion required, he showed like aptitudes. There was no awkwardness; but quickness to seize & adjust means to ends. He had the insight of a bird in building its nest.

Whilst practicing law with us a youngish fat, well to do looking farmer came in the office to collect, from M͏ʳ A[nderson] the price of some mutton the farmer man had left at A's residence. Mr. A. stepped from the office into the street to get some " change " leaving Sidney & the farmer man in the office, when the latter told Sidney how, a year or two before, he had bought an adjoining " worn out " farm from a neighbor who took the purchase money & himself & family to newer lands in Texas, & how that, a few days before, this neighbor came back from Texas to his house while he was at breakfast without money, in rags–: came back to see this farm renewed, & *thrift* all around, &C, &C. Shortly after the farmer got his " change " & left the office, when Sidney turned to his desk and composed the poem, ' There's more in the man than there is in the land," – a poem that was then published in The Daily T & M.ʳ here & republished all over the country: – This poem illustrates two traits: not only the fine sense of humor, but a sense of the practical in the farmer's life, *thrift*. His treatment of his subject, " The New South," in Scribner's some two years ago, also shows the *practical*, I think. Take his book on Florida: There are few works ever gotten thru' the American Press which from conception to execution & publication occupied so short a time. He engaged to have the work ready in a given time. " The world (of Florida) was before him where to choose." Yet in a *few months* he visited that State, gathered his material, prepared his matter, read his " proofs " & the work was published. Under the circumstances of the undertaking he might have taken 12 months instead of the few: – In all his engagements (with publishers & otherwise) he made *promptness* a special point. The intensity of the labor in producing his " Florida " no doubt made serious inroads on his feeble body.

My dear sir: Exceeding nervousness & pressure of restraint in writing this about my so-much valued son unfit me for the work. Heretofore under other invitations I have not dared to do anything of the sort, and only do so now at the request of a *post graduate of* " Johns Hopkins," for which Institution I have the highest regard.

Sidney's mother died [May 22,] 1865, just at the close of the War & just after Sidney & Clifford had come up out of the vicissitudes & storms thereof to gladden her departing. We have no picture or photograph of her worthy the virtuous woman & noble mother she was. (It was she who so taught those children as to need no punishment. It was she (Roman matron she was), who so instilled in them true principles, and elevated sentiments of manhood & womanhood that the lessons of early years have been illustrated in their after lives. I esteem Clifford Anderson Lanier as one of the most perfect, symmetrical men I ever knew, and I would like to speak of his sister Gertrude – but – pardon me ! I see I wander ! –)[4]

If your " sketch " shall need a photograph of myself it will be sent you; but I shall be well content if you dispense with it.

I should like for you to see my son Cliffords' & daughter Gertrude's whether you use them or not. Clifford & I both have copies of M[r] Keysers' bust of Sidney, & we have very fine photographs of him.

Pardon my nervousness, apparent all thro' these pages (which I should like to transcribe) and believe me to be, very trl. yr &c.

R. S. Lanier.

[4] Clifford Lanier died Nov. 3, 1908; Gertrude Lanier (Mrs. J. C. Gibson), on Nov. 18, 1889.

From Robert S. Lanier to J. A. Fisher

Macon, Ga., Oct. 11th, 1883.

Revd. J. A. Fisher,
  Dear Sir:

Your letter of the 29th ulto. duly rec'd. Business engagements prevented an earlier response. I have written to son, Clifford, to inform you what Sidney taught when tutor at Midway. I do not recollect & the Faculty are all dead or so scattered as to be out of the way.

Sterling Lanier, my father, was born in Brunswick County, Va., but was " raised " and rec'd a good academic education in Rockingham Co., N. Ca, where his father Sampson Lanier, raised a large family of children, & was a well-to-do farmer, a country gentleman, fond of good horses & fox hounds. (We trace our Lanier ancestry back from the south of France to England and thence to Va.). My father's mother had Scotch-Irish blood, as I have been told. My father came to Georgia in 1817, and married my mother, Sarah Vivian Fullwood, daughter of Robert F. in Clarke Co. near Athens, Ga. She was one of five beautiful daughters. There was also a son *Dr.* Edward Fullwood who died whilst a surgeon in U. S. Army. My mother's father was also a well-to-do farmer, living on the east side of Apalachee River and fond of the excitement of frontier life. I understood he was of English descent, but married a Miss Hunter, Scotch-Irish, whose brother Mr. ——— Hunter resided in Washington City, & who had several daughters distinguished for their beauty, one of whom married Gen'l. Buell, U. S. A. and who met my mother in Montgomery, Ala. some ten years ago.

I should have stated before that our family have copies of an auto-biography of J. F. D. Lanier, a New York banker, lately dec'd, to which Sidney appended a letter relating to the Lanier family. If Dr. [W. H.] Brown or Mrs. Sidney Lanier cannot furnish you a copy I can do so. Much of the material of Sidney's letter (in appendix) was furnished me by Judge Iverson L. Harris, late a Judge of our State Supreme Ct. Bench & Judge Nichols, Judge of U. S. Circuit & District Courts for

Southern District of Ga. (Savannah) — both of whom are dead
& whose mothers were Laniers.

The father of Sidney's mother was Hezekiah Anderson, who
represented Nottoway Co., Va. many years in the State Legislature. He was a large man, of symmetrical physique, elegant
in person and manners, having a mind characterized by fine
sense, & who wielded considerable influence in political circles.
He had an elegant home near the court-house site, where distinguished men of the state often met, & where he dispensed a
liberal hospitality. His public life brought him in contact with
many persons, among whom were those who got his name on
their bonds as surety. In the " hard times " that came between
1836-42, this surety-ship took a large portion of his property
and he died a few years after my marriage in embarassed
circumstances. His father was an Episcopalian minister who
was a cultivated man, independent in circumstances, I have
been informed. (His oldest son Wm. Henry A. was a graduate
of Hampden Sidney College at 16, was a speaker in the hustings at 17, was in the Va. Legislature one session, got in bad
health, came to Ga. & after giving the highest promise of
distinguished usefulness, died when only about 26 years of
age.)

Toward the close of my former letter I referred to my son
Clifford in parenthesis: — I fear the context was hardly enough
to show you that I referred to the *intellectual* & *moral* make
up of the man & not the physical (tho' I might well have
included the latter) in using the term " symmetrical."

I should have been glad to have been able to furnish you
with a more satisfactory sketch of the early life of Sidney than
that sent. I could only give you a few imperfect hints, from
which you might get useful impressions in the preparation of
your proposed sketch.

Very t'y yrs. &c.

R. S. Lanier.[5]

---

[5] R. S. Lanier died Oct. 20, 1893.

FROM MARY DAY LANIER TO FRED A. KING

[Lynn, N. C., Autumn, 1891]

x   x   x   x   x   x   x

Long as was my letter of a week ago, I lacked time to complete it, and so, inadvertently passed over your question concerning Mr. Lanier's mother. When he first spoke of her to me, he called her – " a dear good common-sense mother " — with a reserve born of his sacred love and worship for her. Common-sense she had, richly: that miscalled, uncommon gift. But he well knew then what I only learned later, and imperfectly, that she was an unconscious, heroic soul, given to patient devotion, to silent endurance such as spring of the love akin to God's. She was a consecrated soul, drawing her daily and hourly life from Christ her Master. Her love of righteousness, of truth, of holiness she bequeathed to her son: nay he received it with his life and inbreathed it with all his first knowledge of her. She was his first teacher in music (on the piano) as in English. A good judge described her to me — in my girlhood — as a woman of large intellectual endowment and noble principle, but so simple and self-oblivious that she had been undervalued by her inferiors around her, just for lack of self-assertion. Her personality was, however, a well defined one in the family and influential in blessing to her children. She taught her two sons and one daughter to choose always the thing that was *right*, to suffer cheerfully, to regard all men with charity and to love one another with exquisite tenderness. During the first months of our married life we had in our little cottage-home in Prattville, Ala. an old " Mammy " for our cook who had filled the same office for Mr. Lanier's parents when they were young people.[6] She told me once: " I lived with them people eleven years, and I never had a cross word or a quick one spoke to me all that time, and I never heard such a word, nor seen an unkind look between any of them, children or parents."

I was with Mrs. Lanier only four times and always in her

---

[6] See Sidney Lanier's letter to Mary Day, Sept. 25, 1867.

sick room, – and under some little embarrassment: for it was before I believed I might accept the treasure of her child's love.

The father's companionship with his son was an uncommon one, stimulating to the intellect and fine in example of fidelity to duty and in quiet benevolence; while as to the sportiveness and hilarity and zest in life that answer a young boy's need, the father had retained his uncommon youthful share after the son had grown very grave and careworn. The father was known among his colleagues as "the most industrious lawyer in Georgia," and only a stroke of paralysis at seventy has abated his work and his buoyancy. He has had a keen and delicate appreciation of the best in literature and was a successful friend and guide to his young sons in this path. I imagine that Mr. Lanier's mother had an unusual share of the quality for which her brother Judge Clifford Anderson has long been noted: the judicial cast of mind.

Mary Day Lanier

FROM GERTRUDE L. GIBSON TO J. A. FISHER

Verbena, Ala. Oct. 1883-

Rev. J. A. Fisher.
    Dear Sir.

I can not tell you how gladly I take up this labor of love responding to your call to aid in this work – I fear me though you have chosen one, who can only speak his praise – for so beautiful was his life to me, and so far removed from an ordinary life, that I can scarcely think of plain facts. All that I can I will do most cheerfully– And my heart is full of earnest gratitude, when I realize that he may yet be known to the world.

I can look back now through a vista of years, and see his genius budding forth, and have watched the blossoming, and doubted not the fruition – had God seen fit to keep him at his work here –

As far back as I can remember, this brother was a hero in my estimation. Ever kind ever tender to us younger ones. Always considerate and forbearing. I can not recall a single harsh utterance toward me – If ever reproof were given it was always in gentleness, and with brotherly interest.

He would enter into our games, and often be the prime actor. Well do I remember a little amateur minstrel performance in which he was conspicuous as " Bones." And again after we had enjoyed a visit to the Circus, where sometimes we were allowed to go to witness the tumbling &c– he got us up a minature one, and delighted us with his wit and acting. Actuated by boyish impulse and instincts – he generally joined in the games and pleasures of his school fellows and companions – I do not remember any great intimacy with any – but he was friendly to all. I think in the pride of my heart, that he was generally looked up to, as above the common average – At 14 years of age he was captain of a boy Military company, and held in high esteem. One fourth of July – this young company in neat and bright uniforms – marched proudly forth and joined the Companies of our city – and took part in the exercises of the day.

When very young he gave evidence of a far reaching mind – He was studious and thoughtful reading much of History – He delighted greatly in the works of Sir Walter Scott. And I have heard our mother say – that even at the tender age of 8 or 9 – he would pour over Froizzarts Chronicles, and other books of that sort. Later on he studied for knowledge – and sifted in his own mind each fact – and accepted it only after deep reasoning and untiring study. He was always making observations of things, and drew his own conclusions on every subject. He was steadfast in his opinions, and would argue a question interminably.

He gave evidence of musical talent when not more than 10 or 12 years old. A small flute found among his Santa Claus gifts one Christmas morning, was joyfully welcomed and kept as a treasure – And I think then he first began to give vent to the soul thoughts stirring within him. Soon, our father who took exceeding pride in this music promise, presented him with a new and more complete instrument – And without instruction he learned to delight us with the sweet flute notes. He could perform on other instruments but the flute and organ were his own special delights. In later years I have seen him sit at the organ and pour forth his soul in its deep toned notes, and rise from his seat finally with a look on his face, as of inspiration. I do not know that he had written any thing in prose or poetry up to this time. His letters to family and friends were gems of thought. One of us would say: " he never writes us anything about himself " ! His letters were full of flowery descriptions and beautiful imaginings.

He entered Oglethorpe College, at Midway Georgia, near Milledgeville, the capital then of the State, when 16 years of age.

I think he went through the first year of College. Mechanically with no very great heart in it – His mind was so full of the Poetry of life – it was a difficult task for him to settle down to its practicalities. I remember his telling me that he was once taking a horse back ride for recreation, and losing himself so utterly in deep thought, as to forget where he was, and being rudely brought back, on finding himself lying prone upon the ground. The second year he studied with diligence and energy, seeming to realize its importance. And graduated at 18, sharing the First honor in his class – I do not think any who listened to his graduating speech can ever forget it.

Being brought up a Presbyterian, his proclivities were in that direction. And wishing to unite with the church he chose that, and became a member of the Macon church, while at home visiting, during his college life. Up to the time of his leaving home, he was a constant attendant at Sabbath School. Among my treasures now, I have a little Hymn book, (sent recently by my sister, Mrs. Lanier, to my little baby boy, my brothers' name sake)– which was given him, as a reward of diligence – when he was quite young.

The war came on not long after he graduated, and filled with patriotic enthusiasm he joined the Southern soldiers, serving until he became a prisoner, while acting as Signal Officer on a vessel running the Blockade for amunition &c. His letters during this time, many of which we have kept, and treasured, were very beautiful. He indulged in much dreaming then – Everything in life, was beautiful to him. Rocks – Trees – Hills, Water, Night, Day, all things to him had a personality, and a beauty, which filled his soul, and ever longed for expression.

There was much of suffering at the close of the war – for him. The loss of the cause – for which he had had such bright hopes, much sickness, brought on by Prison life, and war hardships. And finally the death of our good mother, who seemed to only just wait for the return of her soldier boys, before she left us forever.

He studied Law, and tried the practice of it long enough to realize that his tastes and aspirations led in a different channel– His choice was a Literary career, but his health was such for a long time as to preclude any possibility of a settled purpose and much of his time was spent in travelling from one place to another in search of health and strength. In these travels he began to write a great deal. Florida our beautiful land of flowers, furnished scope for his poetic mind.

He was married in 1867, to one whose soul was akin to his – one who understood him – and who was ever a treasure to him. He lived some time in Macon – then removing to Baltimore, most of the rest of his life was spent there among those true & good people who appreciated him –

P. S. Writing thus far – I left my letter open – (as I was just on the eve of making my brother Clifford a visit, thinking – he might furnish me with a complete list of dates of the writings – He advises me however, to refer you to our sister now in Baltimore – who can furnish you with a more complete list than either he or I have – With regret at having kept your letter so long unanswered, and with the sincere hope that I may have given you some aid. I am

Very Respectfully

Mrs. J. C. Gibson –

FROM CHARLES E. CAMPBELL TO HENRY W. LANIER

> Macon Ga. March 31st 1903
> #817 Mulberry St.

Dear Mr. Lanier:

In accordance with your request, I give notes of my long friendship and association with your father; which, while probably valueless as assistants to your proposed biography, may be pleasant to his loved ones to hear and are certainly a delight to me to record.

Our first acquaintance began at school when he was about 11 years old and I three years his senior and I very distinctly remember that he was at that time in class with myself and others of equal age, – and his proficiency in the language and mathematics were so marked as sometimes to have me wonder if I were below the average in intellect – a discomfort that was, however, fully relieved in after days, when I discovered that I had been measuring myself with an extraordinary genius. This association continued for about 2 years when I was sent elsewhere to school, and from that time until he went to College our comradeship was maintained through our musical practice.

At the opening of the war, he, [C. K.] Emmell & myself all became members of the same Company and on going to Virginia took our flutes with us. For 11 months we were stationed in the neighborhood of Norfolk, and we soon gathered about us others of the Battalion who were musical, resulting in the formation of an orchestra, with Lanier as Conductor – He wrote the parts for all the other performers in music, which was not already arranged for orchestra and devised an unique system of notation for the use of our guitarist who was ignorant of written music but played delightfully by ear.

This orchestra comprised 3 flutes 2 violins 1 cello 1 cornet & 1 guitar, a motley combination tis true, but was greatly enjoyed by us & our fellow soldiers – & was effective in passing us thro' the lines to go serenading in Norfolk & Portsmouth, frequently at the request of some of the officers who wished to honor their lady acquaintances with a serenade.

Our greatest enjoyment however was with our 3 flutes for which we had many delightful compositions and which music is now my own, but has been silent since the death of your father, Mr. Emmell.

In March 1862 we were moved to Goldsboro, N. C. in expectation of immediate battle, but that danger checked and quart. in tents we waited the expiration of our enlistment one month later. When the Batt. was moved all of our little musical club except Lanier & Emmell sent our instruments home, but while in camp near Goldboro, our 1st violin stated that he had a cousin in Goldsboro who sold musical instruments & suggested we might borrow to fill of him & so continue our pleasant practice – Acting on this we were graciously equipped by Mr. Freeman the jeweler, and thereby added another month of pleasure before we were separated –

One incident connected with the Goldsboro experience I must give –

After selecting the necessary instruments at Mr. Freeman's store he suggested we go to his home for a preliminary tuning up &c. Arriving there we were invited to a lunch – after discussing which we played a few concerted pieces which seemed to please our little audience greatly , – Seated at the table was an old gentleman, a portrait painter, named Wilson, as I now think, who on Lanier' playing a solo, " La Melancholie," rose from his chair, standing thro the performance, the tears rolling down his withered cheeks – and as the music ceased stretched his hand across the table saying " Young man, I ask to take your hand; I ve travelled pretty much over this world, but have never heard the flute so played before, nor approached in but one instance "

Remember Lanier was only about 19 years old –

Another incident –

While at Fort Norfolk, we planned a serenade to our Portsmouth lady friends – Crossing the river in open boats in bright moonlight – & stopping in mid-river to see what our music might be on water – we landed at Portsmouth ferry, Passing up the main street we were attracted by music of some club on an upper floor.

We listened to the close of the number, and I requested L – to play " La Melancholie " & surprise them.

He complied and soon all sounds above ceased except a rush to the window– then a rush down the stairway and the inquiry " who are you, anyway " – We introduced ourselves – which became an introduction to everything musical & social in P – so far as we were, as soldiers, permitted to [illegible] That party followed up the whole night on our pilgrimage thro' P – but Lanier's solo " broke up the meeting " of the Harmonic Society for that evening.

Another incident here in Macon.

Emmell – L. & I used to practice quite regularly in Emmells room – I had frequently noted a gentleman who quite as regularly stationed himself on the sidewalk below. – I became interested in his evident devotion to music, so on passing up to the room for practice one evening I approached him, saying that if he cared to hear it I would be pleased to have him come up with us. – He joyfully thanked me,– After many concerted numbers I asked L. to give us a solo – This ended, our visitor exclaimed " throw away that flute young man, & get a cornet-a-pist & your fortune is made " – He proved to be a French professor which accounts somewhat for his love of the Cornets.

After L's return from prison we 3 renewed our musical which was never interrupted until he left the city. When he went to N. Y. intending to take lessons of Theo' Thomas flutist, he wrote me of his experience –
After some playing for his teacher, using his 8 keyed flute, the teacher complimented him highly, but taking up his own Boehm flute executed some difficult pyrotechnics – saying " when you can do that, you'll pass " – or similar words. Lanier repeated his preceptors work so faithfully – on his 8 keys – that the latter said, " give up that flute & take this Boehm, – aside from correcting some errors, there's nothing I can teach you " Lanier immediately wrote me to get a Boehm by all means – and I acted on his suggestion.
I jointed him in Marietta the day after he received his silver flute [7] & we tried it together – but he decided that his old wooden one was better – If he had known that the simple substitution of a rubber or wooden head for the silver first joint, he would have had a perfect instrument. I have two heads to mine – one silver & one wood – and always used the wood in solo playing.
I simply believe your father was the greatest flutist that ever lived – To play with him was an education – and your errors were so skilfully covered by his work, that it gave one great confidence.
I will add to my recollections of him, musically speaking –

[7] In July, 1873.

When I was married, as I left the alter I heard for the first time Mendelsohn Wedding March, *on the organ* – looking up to the loft, I saw Lanier at the organ – an accomplishment of which I was ignorant – and you can imagine my delight at commencing 'my wedding' march thro life to his dear accompaniment.

From June '62 to the close of the war, I was in another Command but L & Emmell were together, in the Signal service until near the close – – Emmell was slightly wounded & lost his flute to the Federals dropping it in the fall of his horse.

As to his literary ability –

I have said to him in walking in the woods of Virginia that he was living and thinking in a different plane from the rest of us,– one denied to most of us – and he heard music where mortals are almost invariably deaf.

My first real attraction to his work was on reading " Corn " – since when his development has always been a joy and a marvel to me – Justice will yet be done him – and some of our New England poets of latitude & [*illegible*] only, when measured by the true poetry that Lanier breathed – that was his very life –

Added to all he was the purest associate I have ever known – as boy and man – and I cannot recall an indelicate speech or action in all our long companionship.

A knightly soul and I loved him – is about the only excuse I can offer for this long and carelessly written reply to your request.

I shall not attempt to rewrite, – I've used a stenog – so long I've almost lost the use of a pen .–

My regards to your Mother – and to any member of his household who cares to number among their friends one to whom Sidney Lanier was so dear,

Very sincer'ly yours

Chas. E. Campbell

I greatly regret that I have none of his letters – only a note jointly to myself & wife the night of our marriage.

I did have letters from N. Y. & San Antonio – but they are lost with all of my correspondence which disappeared during my absence from Macon.

To Henry W. Lanier
    34 Union Sq. East
        New York City

FROM JAMES WOODROW TO EDWIN MIMS [8]

Columbia, South Carolina
May 21st. 1904.

Dr. Edwin Mims,
    Professor in Trinity College, N. C.

My dear Sir:

I received your letter as to Sidney Lanier long ago, but I have been too feeble to answer it in addition to work that must be done.

I have often heard that I had a decided influence over him when we were together at Oglethorpe University just before the war, but I have never been able to understand in what directions. He was a faithful student, of good disposition, so that I became very much attached to him. When he graduated I caused him to be appointed Tutor in the University, so that I became better acquainted with him, and liked him better and better. I was Professor of Natural Science, and I often took him to ramble with me, observing and studying whatever we saw, but also talking about everything either of us cared for. About the same time I was licensed to preach, and spent my Saturdays and Sundays in preaching to feeble churches, and in school-houses, Court-houses, & private-houses, within forty or more miles of the College; trying to make my Sunday night services come within twenty-five miles of home, so that I could drive to the College in time for my Monday morning sunrise lecture. Every now and then I would invite Lanier to go with me. During such drives we were constantly engaged without

[8] Previously published in part, Mims, pp. 29-30.

interruption in our conversations. In these ways, and in listening frequently to his marvellous flute-playing, you see we were much together. We were both young, and fond of study; I had just been spending two years or so in studying and wandering in various countries in Europe; so we did not lack for topics.

You ask me to tell you something of myself, my views, etc., This I find it very hard to do. I found constant delight in the study of God's works, and also in his Word — this Word to me being the Bible fairly and honestly construed. I think I know more now than I did forty-five years ago; but I can perceive no change in my fundamental views. What these are, and what I think they have always been, you may see pretty fully in the pamphlets I send you, if you care to wade through them.

So far as I know, my attitude has not changed: my mind and heart have always been wide open to give hearty welcome to all that I could recognise as *truth*; ready to exclude and sternly reject whatever offered itself under a false guise, however specious the mark; willing fairly and without prejudice or partiality to examine the claims of the remaining mixed multitude.

As to German literature and philosophy, I have some acquaintance with the former; less with the latter. I never found the philosophy attractive, either as studied in books, or listened to in German University lecture rooms. Perhaps because I knew too little about it. German theology, so far as it is characteristic, I reject, as I am, unwilling to receive my theology from any source except the Bible fairly construed, and from reasonable interpretations of the thoughts of God presented in His works.

After we parted at Oglethorpe, I saw my dear friend but once. He spent a few hours with me here at my house, when he was on his way homeward after the war.

I am afraid I have given you very little of value to you in the performance of your task – but this is all I can do.

I think you were a Vanderbilt student. If so, there is a connecting link between us in J. M. Safford, under whom I studied Mathematics fifty-eight years ago at Athens, Ohio. I was warmly attached to him. At that time his eyes had not been opened to the glories of natural science.

Regretting my long (unavoidable) delay in answering your letter,

> I am
> > Yours very truly,

> > James Woodrow.

FROM MARY DAY LANIER TO EDWIN MIMS

> 20 W. Elm St., Greenwich, Conn.
> July 31st, 1905

My dear Mr. Mims:

It is probably too late for you to use the promised memoranda autobiographical that I mislaid, unfinished; yet I will send this as a pledge of good intention, and you can return the few pages – if it will not trouble you – when more pressing matters are disposed of.

My mother, Mary Jane Crocker, was born in Hartford: her grandparents of English birth. When she was fourteen she left a simple country home and her younger sisters and widowed mother in New England, to enter the family of the eldest sister (mother of Mr. A. Foster Higgins of Greenwich) who had married in Savannah and made a home in Macon, Ga. There my mother and father met, and were married when she was nineteen. There she lived, much beloved for her personal charm and gentle womanly sympathies, for seventeen years of married life, spending the summers at the North, and generally at Saratoga (for health) and West Point. Her failing health carried us to New York when I was almost six years old,[9] and there I grew up, until the age of sixteen.

As it influenced my husband, I cannot discern any helpful outcome of my brief and desultory education beyond a fair amount of painstaking accuracy, (here I had my mother's teaching and example), a distinct hand-writing, —— to serve his need, — a little more school French than he had, a dawning

---

[9] Mary Day (Lanier) was born June 10, 1844; she died Dec. 29, 1931.

sense (no more) of literary quality, the fruits of a good education in piano-playing from seven to fifteen, and some familiarity with the music popular in New York among music-lovers in the fifties. There were a few Italian operas, and Philharmonic rehearsals, a taste of oratorio and the church music; and through the summers, fine bands were daily playing at our hotels at Saratoga and West Point.

I grew up among well-bred, well-to-do people: for over five years in one New York boarding-house, and for shorter periods in apartments and hotels; my teachers were intelligent, conscientious, well-drilled and Christian men and women; but among them all I recall no one who suggested the art-atmosphere or liberal thought, until I come to my last winter of study, 1860-1861, as a boarding-pupil for seven months in Poughkeepsie, N. Y., at the school of Rev. George J. Rider, of the Episcopal Church. He was the first person who taught me to think, at-all: to do any more than recite faithfully by rote,— and his care of me lasted for only seven months. Then, at sixteen, I was hurried to Georgia by my brother, lest the gathering war-cloud should break and separate us from our father who was then in Macon: The dear father had taken me from school early in the previous year, because I was much out of health.

Two years earlier, at the age of thirteen, the same thing had been done to give me the privilege of waiting on my ill mother, who died in July following. At no time had I strength to undertake the regular school course. I chose my favorite studies each fall, and coaxed a reluctant permission from the doctor— "just to give me playmates and interests." Arrived at womanhood, I had but the slightest literary culture, no breadth of view, little general information, no interest in current affairs. And as my own feeble health and my environment hindered me along intellectual lines, so my mother's long years of painful decline forbade me any wholesome domestic training. I brought my husband no home-making faculty, no habit of quick observation and judicious command, no housewifely experience and skill. After I was five years old we had a home once, for seven months – the limit of my ill mother's possible effort.

All this lack in me my husband had to supply, — and he did it. No one could imagine what he was in symmetry of endowment and of character without first knowing my exceptional deficiencies. And I could not often " drive through by main force." I was physically very weak from infancy, and nine years within city walls did not favor growth in vitality.

On the other hand: he found in me the accord of the musical temperament, – vastly inferior, it is true, to his own. Music was for me the first, the compelling influence. And I was very responsive to art, especially sculpture. All imaginative expression appealed to me; also I found a keen – different – delight in the sure logic of mathematics.

So, we had many of the same loves; and we loved *love*: each of us felt it the all-in-all.

To some expression of my hopelessness in face of my ineffectiveness, he has replied: " Any one who loves as much as you love can do anything."

I suppose he loved my possibilities that only he apprehended – or believed he did.

Finally: from the hour of our meeting I was conscious of all beauty; of all worshipfulness in him; and ever afterward I knew him for the poet of Music, the voice of the Spirit.

And his flight was checked by no measuring line of my smallness; I never limited him by one thought. I believed – and believe – in him, always.

Mary Day Lanier

C. SIDNEY LANIER'S IMPRISONMENT,
1864–1865 [1]

During the last part of his career in the Confederate Army Lanier served as signal officer on the blockade runner *Lucy* (an English steamer), as his brother Clifford served on the *Talisman*. The *Lucy*, laden with 414 bales of cotton and 25 tons of tobacco, and bound from Wilmington, N. C., to New Providence, Nassau, had been captured after a chase of two hours, at 11 A. M., Nov. 2, 1864, Lat. 32° 40′ North, Longitude 77° 48′ West, by the U. S. S. *Santiago de Cuba*. After the prisoners were removed, the ship was sent on to Boston, where it was libelled on Nov. 19 and condemned on Dec. 30. The prisoners were landed at Norfolk, Va., on Nov. 3, and examined at Fort Lafayette. All were released except Lanier and seven others. Lanier described himself, upon interrogation, as a Signal Officer, born in Macon, Ga., a minor and a student, and on his first trip. His personal effects were confiscated but returned to him later, upon his exchange.[2]

From Norfolk Lanier was taken to Fortress Monroe, where he probably spent only one night, then to Camp Hamilton from which place he addressed the letter of Nov. 11, 1864, to his uncle, Clifford Anderson, requesting that he arrange a " *special exchange*." Finally, Lanier was taken to Point Lookout, a prison tent camp situated on a high bluff at the confluence of Chesapeake Bay and the Potomac River, in St. Mary's County, Md. He probably had not reached Point Lookout when his brother Clifford wrote, on Nov. 12, 1864, to his mother from Columbia, S. C., that he had returned on the *Talisman* " last Sunday night " and gave the first news in the Lanier family letters of his brother's capture:

[1] The following account of Lanier's capture, imprisonment, and release has been prepared by Aubrey H. Starke from the most reliable available sources, cited in the text and notes. Numerous other accounts survive, but they are too inaccurate or inconsistent to be cited here; nor is there a clear and detailed record of these events in Lanier's own letters.

[2] Information in this paragraph is taken with the author's permission from an unpublished article by John S. Mayfield, " The Capture and Exchange of Sidney Lanier," based upon contemporary newspaper accounts, the *Official Records of the . . . War of the Rebellion* (Washington, 1900), unpublished documents in the Naval Records and Library, Navy Department, Washington, D. C., and other sources.

Brother Sid sailed on the " Lucy " Nov. 1st. That vessel is reported captured. Do not distress yourself about this, my darling, for we have a thousand causes of congratulations. When I think of the numerous dangers through which we have gone unscathed, I am filled with gratitude to an Infinite God who has thus guarded us.

What is a few weeks or months captivity compared with the terrible fatigue which a soldier in Hood's or Lee's army will undergo this winter?

I believe that the exchange of invalids, now going on, will lead to an exchange of all prisoners and that Brother Sid, if he is caught, will soon be restored to us.

On Nov. 15, 1864, Robert S. Lanier wrote from Camp Cooper, Macon, Ga., to his son Clifford what is hardly an answer to the letter quoted, but refers apparently to an earlier " dispatch " (*i. e.* telegram)[3] that Clifford Lanier had sent:

What is done with blockade runners when captured? Where sent? Let me know. I have written to your Uncle C. at Richmond [4] to try to communicate through Mr. Ould, with Sidney, & gave the names of some old family friends at New York who may be of service to him.

On Nov. 29, 1864, Robert S. Lanier wrote again to Clifford:

I wrote to your Uncle C. at Richmond to try to communicate by Flag of truce with your dear brother, & enclosed a letter to him. Have not heard from him since. To-day I have written another to Sidney to be taken by a lady going tomorrow to Kentucky, and have also written to an old friend North to assist him &c.

Clifford, once more in Bermuda on further assignment to his blockade-runner, wrote to his father from St. George, Dec. 1, 1864:

I have seen a man captured on the "Lucie." Brother Sid and a passenger were the only persons detained. Those of her officers and crew, who were not Englishmen, said they were and were released. Brother Sid made no effort to deceive them and was sent to Fort LaFay-

---

[3] R. S. Lanier's letter of Nov. 29, 1864, quoted below, indicates that such a telegram was sent.

[4] Lanier's uncle Clifford Anderson was in Richmond as a member of the Confederate Congress. To him Lanier himself had addressed a letter of Nov. 11, 1864, written after his capture but before his imprisonment. It is possible that Lanier's letter did not reach his uncle until some time after Lanier had been transferred to Point Lookout. For Judge Ould see VII, 183, note 55.

ette. I have written to him, reminding him of Judge Russel [5] and giving him the address of another party, one of Mamie Day's friends and one who will do everything in her power for him, I am certain.

The reference to Mary Day's friend is probably to the same person referred to by Mary Day herself in a letter of Nov. 22, 1864, to her friend Georgia (Shackleford?), of which only the following fragment has been brought to the attention of the present editors:

My loved friend, Sid, is a prisoner, captured the first of the month, as Signal Officer on board of the Lucy, which ran the blockade from Wilmington. It was his first trip out. We can hear nothing more of him. I wrote yesterday, by flag of truce, at this point to a dear lady-friend now at the North entreating her to seek and relieve him. He is rather delicate, and has gone at this trying season to that colder climate before he had received any warm clothing from home.

The friend may have been the Mrs. Du Barry of whom Mary Day wrote in a letter of May 15, 1865, asking Lanier if he had "heard from Mrs. Du Barry while in prison," and may likewise have been the Mrs. Carrie H. D. B. of New York, to whom one of the newspaper notices quoted below (Dec. 24) was addressed.

Back in Wilmington, Clifford Lanier repeated, in a letter of Dec. 10, 1864, to his parents most of the information he had already sent from Bermuda, but indicated later efforts to get in touch with his brother and to effect his release:

I saw a fellow captured on the "Lucy"—Brother Sid & a passenger were the only ones on her detained—These were sent to Fort Lafay-ette—an indication, you see that they are to be treated with some more consideration than ordinary prisoners of war. I wrote to him from Bermuda asking many of the questions contained in your letter to me, received here just as the Talisman got under way to start down the river—viz. about his flute &c & giving him an address at New York that he might use & reminding him of Judge Russel, Barnard Smythe &c. He was dressed in Citizens clothing when taken and had 5$ gold. I trust he will soon be restored to us. I understand that Maj Norris, whom we met once and became known to through our music, told a friend here that he should make an effort with Hatch, the Agent Ex-change to obtain his release.

[5] Judge Russell, about whom no further information is available, was the father-in-law of Sidney Lanier's uncle Sidney Lanier.

The efforts of friend and family to establish contact with Lanier led to the publication of the following items in the " personals " column of the Richmond *Enquirer* later in the month (Dec. 20, 21, 24):

Richmond, Dec. 16, 1864.

To Sidney C. Lanier, captured on the blockade runner Lucy, about the 3rd of November, and supposed to be at Fort LaFayette.

Your mother's health has somewhat improved. Your father, brother and sister are well. All feel much anxiety to hear from you.

Answer through New York Daily News.

C. Anderson.

Petersburg, Dec. 19, 1864.

To Cobinus:

My beloved friend, S. C. Lanier, was taken prisoner on the steamer Lucy, off Wilmington; he is probably in Fort Lafayette. Find him, if possible, for my sake; he is everything you could desire in a friend and companion.

Yours, as ever,

Oldem.

N. Y. News please reply.

Wilmington, N. C. Dec. 12.

Mrs. Carrie H. D. B., New York:

Mr. Lanier, of Macon, is in Fort Lafayette. Do what you can for him. W. D. D.

Yours, etc.,

Clifford A. Lanier

New York News please reply.

Efforts to effect Lanier's release failed, and if he received any of the letters and messages addressed to him by relatives and friends, no record has been preserved of that fact. No letters by him have been found between Nov. 11, 1864, when he wrote to his uncle Clifford Anderson the letter printed in the present work,[6] and Mar. 18, 1865, when he addressed a letter to Mary Day, from Macon. A draft of a letter of later

[6] VII, 183.

date, to an unnamed person,[7] does however suggest that Lanier had some contact, while in prison, with influential people outside.

Of the unhealthy conditions at Point Lookout, and of Lanier's life there, a good deal has been written by his several biographers, much of it based on the recollections of John B. Tabb,[8] who had entered Point Lookout Prison some time before Lanier, and who there formed the friendship which, renewed later in Baltimore, was to last until the end of Lanier's life.

At Point Lookout Lanier wrote two verses, "Translation from the German of Heine," dated Dec. 11, 1864, and "Spring Greeting." Of more comfort to him than poetic composition, however, was the playing of his flute. This he is said to have concealed in his sleeve when other personal effects were confiscated, and he used it not only to give pleasure to himself and to his fellow prisoners, but also for their advantage. One of the officers of the fort, "fascinated" by the flute, wished to have lessons, and to pay for them: "Lanier gave the lessons, but declined the money, and the Lieut. remembered to improve the prison fare by slices of beef from his own table, and other helps in the way of diet."[9] One fellow prisoner, W. H. Mims, of Laredo, Texas, stated in later years that Lanier organized a minstrel troup among the prisoners, and directed it in entertainments which "all the federal officers" attended.[10]

Besides John B. Tabb and W. H. Mims, Lanier's fellow prisoners remained silent concerning his and their experiences. In a letter of Jan. 27, 1868, Virginia Hankins wrote: "I saw a few days past your old prison comrades, Dr. Jones, Mr. Wrenn & Mr. Jordan." But these have not been further identified.

Father Tabb's statement "we lived as fellow prisoners for more than six months, and at the end of that time were exchanged together"[11] is not altogether correct. Records in the United States War Department indicate that on Feb. 15, 1865, after hardly more than three months at Point Lookout, Lanier

[7] VII, 213-214.
[8] See Mims, pp. 59-60, and an undated clipping from the *Independent* (1883?) in the Lanier Room, Johns Hopkins University.
[9] Letter from Sarah J. Farley to W. F. Ward, Jan. 9, 1884.
[10] W. H. Mims to Henry W. Lanier, Dec. 24, 1902.
[11] See note 8, above (*Independent*).

was paroled and exchanged.[12] The voyage from Fortress Monroe, if not from Point Lookout itself, to Varina, Va., on the James River, was made on the flag of truce steamer *New York*, of which Col. John Elmer Mulford was the officer in charge. There were some 1,100 Confederate prisoners who were marched from Varina a mile or so westward to Cox's Landing, in Henrico County, Va., where the actual exchange of Confederate and Federal prisoners took place. Presumably the released Confederates were conveyed from Cox's Landing to Richmond on the Confederate steamer that had carried Federal prisoners to Cox's Landing.

Of the boat trip to Varina a full though highly colored and sentimental account has been given by Alfred Allen, whose information was derived from Mrs. Mattie Montgomery, the mother of " Little Ella," an Alabama lady who returned from New York to the South on the same flag of truce ship that carried the prisoners.[13] On a copy of the Allen article now in the Charles Day Lanier Collection, Johns Hopkins University, Mrs. Lanier made manuscript notations that correct somewhat the bias of Allen's article but that also emphasize the suffering of the trip. She wrote:

Father Tabb said they did *not* come away in rags, but that their better clothing had been saved and was restored to them. The illness and suffering and danger were all there; but the boat trip was much shorter than this lady's memory preserved it.

Mr. Lanier replied to my inquiry of " the worst physical suffering he had ever known ": " *the cold* upon that boat " that brought him away from prison.

Father Tabb, who was Sidney Lanier's companion on this journey from prison, declared the narrative to be exaggerated to inaccuracy; the long time interval no doubt responsible for this. One feature, however, remains the same.

The " one feature " referred to and marked by Mrs. Lanier was the account of the suffering from intense cold. But one

[12] Discovered by John S. Mayfield, who published them in " Sidney Lanier's Civil War Experiences," Macon (Ga.). *Telegraph*, Jan. 31, 1937. Lanier's reminiscent account of the " mode of my release " is given in his letter to Northrup, June 11, 1866.

[13] Alfred Allen, " Reminiscences of Sidney Lanier," *Mid-Continent*, VI, 81-86 (May, 1895); see also Boston *Evening Transcript*, Apr. 13, 1895.

more episode also claimed her attention — the account of the actual debarkation when Lanier, fearful that his name, added to the original list, might be omitted from the debarkation roster, gave his flute to Mrs. Montgomery, to take to his brother Clifford. From this episode Mrs. Lanier struck out the description of Lanier's "old slouch hat" as "battered, torn and faded," and one other line: "his feet sticking bare through tattered shoes."

From Cox's Landing, or from Richmond, Lanier made his way home. There is some evidence that he stopped by Columbia, S. C., to see his former teacher, James Woodrow.[14] Somewhere on the road he encountered another released prisoner, and near relative, T. D. Dotterer, who was a nephew of T. D. Eason, the husband of Lanier's aunt, Wilhelmina Lanier Eason. The Easons, though residents of Charleston, S. C., had been refugeeing at Cokesbury, S. C., where Lanier's mother and sister Gertrude had visited them in the fall of the previous year. Dotterer wrote to Mary Day Lanier, March 28, 1884:

Many years have passed since Sidney and myself tramped across this state. It was a few days after the burning of Columbia by Sherman's army, when I had to travel around the country through Greenville, S. C. and it was on that road that Sidney and I met. He had been released . . . from prison but a few days before, and looked thin and care worn, wearing his hair long, falling upon his shoulders, and carrying a blanket, and satchel, and his flute which he had saved. We were both bound for our aunts, Mrs. T D Eason who lived at Cokesbury S. C. where we arrived and [were] received with great kindness. After a rest there of two days, we started on foot for Georgia. . . . My weariness of travel was lessened by my agreeable companion, whose delightful conversation assisted in passing away the time.

I recollect one morning that we came up to a farmer who with his team was hauling off cotton to hide away from the enemy. We had a chat & asked for assistance along our journey, but was refused. He however asked us up to his house to get refreshments & while there Sidney took out his flute & began playing. The music was very sweet indeed and so charmed the farmer & wife that he at once hitched up a team and sent us on towards Edgefield S. C. where we met up with a few of Georgia Cavalry Sidney knowing one of them who loaned us a horse.

[14] James Woodrow to Edwin Mims, May 21, 1904. (Letter printed in this volume, Appendix B.)

After reaching Edgefield & a short rest we made a last start for
Augusta, Ga. arriving at the hospitable home of Mr Senby on Green
St 'twas about 8 o'clock at night when we announced ourselves as
confederate soldiers begging shelter &c. It was not long however before
we were recognized by Mr. Senby & a hearty welcome given us.

Sidney remained there that night & left the next day on the Rent
Road for his father's home Macon.

When Lanier reached Macon is not known, but there is in
the files of the United States War Department a Confederate
" Medical Certificate for Extension of Furlough," dated March
29, 1865, in which Lanier is described as suffering from " Bronchitis, with great debility." Presumably the original furlough,
like the extension, had been for thirty days.

D. THE MENTAL PHOTOGRAPH OF
SIDNEY LANIER [1]

WHAT IS —

1. YOUR FAVORITE COLOR? The opal-grey which one sees on the horizon just after a gorgeous sunset.

2. FLOWER? The Tube-rose.

3. TREE? The Mimosa.

4. OBJECT IN NATURE? A certain glen in the heart of the Smoky Mountains.

5. HOUR IN THE DAY? The two twilights — of morning and evening.

6. SEASON OF THE YEAR? The last half of spring and the first half of summer.

7. PERFUME? The combination of heliotrope and violet.

8. GEM? The Opal.

9. STYLE OF BEAUTY? Oval face, large gray eyes, slender figure.

10. NAMES, MALE AND FEMALE? Clifford and Mary.

11. PAINTERS? Raphael, Titian, Guido, Salvator Rosa, Ary Scheffer.

12. MUSICIANS? Schumann, Wagner, Beethoven, Chopin.

13. PIECE OF SCULPTURE? A Mercury in the act of flying. (Author unknown.)

14. POETS? Shakspere, Chaucer, Lucretius, Robert Browning.

---

[1] In Baltimore, during the winter of 1874, Lanier acceded to the request of a Miss Anne Perot and made a "mental photograph" of himself by writing answers to certain printed questions in her album. These answers are interesting not only because they reveal Lanier to an extent equalled only by certain of his letters, but because the idea of making a "mental photograph" impressed him sufficiently to bring out a reference to the fad in his Peabody lectures on Shakespeare (III, 170, of the present edition). They are printed here from a MS copy in the handwriting of Mary Day Lanier, Charles D. Lanier Collection, Johns Hopkins University. (Previously published by J. S. Short in "Sidney Lanier, 'Familiar Citizen of the Town,'" *Maryland Historical Magazine*, XXXV, 134-135, June, 1940, from a copy owned by Miss Eleanor Turnbull.)

15. POETESSES? Elizabeth Browning, George Eliot.

16. PROSE AUTHORS? Sir Wm. Hamilton, Sir Thomas Browne, Carlyle, Richter.

17. CHARACTER IN ROMANCE? Equally fond of Chaucer's *Persone*, Dumas' *Athos* & Scott's *Richard Coeur de Lion*.

18. CHARACTER IN HISTORY? Sir Philip Sidney.

19. BOOK TO TAKE UP FOR AN HOUR? *Hood's Own*, or Dumas' *Three Guardsmen*.

20. WHAT BOOK (NOT RELIGIOUS) WOULD YOU PART WITH LAST? My Chaucer.

21. WHAT EPOCH WOULD YOU CHOOSE TO HAVE LIVED IN? The present.

22. WHERE WOULD YOU LIKE TO LIVE? Somewhere where lungs are not necessary to life.

23. WHAT IS YOUR FAVORITE AMUSEMENT? To be on a springy horse in a hilly country.

24. WHAT IS YR. FAVORITE OCCUPATION? Teaching: either by poems, by music, or by lectures.

25. WHAT TRAIT OF CHARACTER DO YOU MOST ADMIRE IN MAN? Knightly magnanimity.

26. WHAT TRAIT DO YOU MOST ADMIRE IN WOMAN? The power of implicitly trusting.

27. WHAT TRAITS OF CHARACTER DO YOU MOST DETEST IN EACH? The opposites of these: Littleness & Suspicion.

28. IF NOT YOURSELF WHO WD. YOU RATHER BE? If *I* were *not* I, what choice *could* I have?

29. WHAT IS YR. IDEA OF HAPPINESS? A table with pen, ink & paper, under a big oak, in early summer: wife seated where I can see her every second: three boys rolling on the grass: a mountain in the distance and a certainty that my article won't be declined.

30. WHAT IS YR. IDEA OF MISERY? To find the flute too sharp for the oboe, after we've commenced the *Andante* of the Fifth *Symphony*.

31. WHAT IS YOUR BÊTE NOIR? A certain moustache hair that will get across the embouchure when I play for company.

32. WHAT IS YOUR DREAM? To study the highest civilization of the world — i. e. of London.

33. WHAT IS YR. FAVORITE GAME? Chess.

34. WHAT DO YOU BELIEVE TO BE YOUR DISTINGUISHING CHARACTERISTICS? Suppose *you* answer this question for me!

35. IF MARRIED, WHAT DO YOU BELIEVE TO BE THE DISTINGUISHING CHARACTERISTICS OF YR. BETTER HALF? A passionate love for art: a heavenly combination of romantic spirituality with practical judgment: and an intense desire to take all the suffering people of the world into her heart.

36. WHAT IS THE SUBLIMEST PASSION OF WHICH HUMAN NATURE IS CAPABLE? Necessarily Love — for it includes all other passions.

37. WHAT ARE THE SWEETEST WORDS IN THE WORLD? " My dear Sweetheart " (in the beginning of a certain lady's letters).

38. WHAT ARE THE SADDEST WORDS? *Vater rufe dein kind zuruck!* — in Thekla's song.[2]

39. WHAT IS YOUR AIM IN LIFE? *Aimer, toujours aimer, et toujours être aimé!*

40. WHAT IS YOUR MOTTO. *Ich Dien.*

---

[2] Misquoted from Schiller's *Wallenstein*; the line should read " Du Heilige " instead of " Vater."

CALENDAR OF LETTERS

KEY TO SYMBOLS

GA   Gellert Spencer Alleman, Wallingford, Pa.
HA   Huntington Library and Art Gallery, San Marino, Calif.
NA   National Archives, Washington, D. C.
RA   R. L. Anderson, Macon, Ga.
GB   Gordon Blair, Richmond, Va.
BC   Mrs. B. B. Comer, Verbena, Ala.
HC   Harvard College, Cambridge, Mass.
LC   Library of Congress, Washington, D. C.
WC   Wesleyan College, Macon, Ga.
HF   Hankins Family Collection, Johns Hopkins University, Baltimore, Md.
NF   Northrup Family Collection, Johns Hopkins University, Baltimore, Md.
HG   H. S. Gulliver, Valdosta, Ga.
CH   Craigie House, Cambridge, Mass.
FH   Family of Mrs. C. N. Hawkins, Brooklyn, N. Y.
PH   Pennsylvania Historical Society, Philadelphia, Pa.
SH   Mrs. S. J. Hinsdale, Burlington, N. C.
PI   Peabody Institute Library, Baltimore, Md.
CL   Charles D. Lanier Collection, Johns Hopkins University, Baltimore, Md.
HL   Henry W. Lanier Collection, Johns Hopkins University, Baltimore, Md.
ML   H. M. Lovett, Delhi, N. Y.
PL   Enoch Pratt Free Library, Baltimore, Md.
SL   Mrs. Sidney Lanier, Jr., Collection, Johns Hopkins University, Baltimore.
AM   Aldrich Memorial Museum, Portland, Me.
BM   British Museum, London.
EM   Edwin Mims Collection, Johns Hopkins University, Baltimore, Md.
HM   Houghton Mifflin, Boston, Mass.
JM   John S. Mayfield, Washington, D. C.
WM   Washington Memorial Library, Macon, Ga.
CN   Columbia University, New York, N. Y.
EP   Miss Elizabeth Price, Nashville, Tenn.
AS   Aubrey H. Starke, Centralia, Ill.
CS   Charles Scribner's Sons, New York.
MS   Mont de Sales Academy, Sisters of Mercy, Macon, Ga.
PS   Philip G. Straus, Baltimore, Md.
ET   Miss Eleanor Turnbull, Baltimore, Md.
JT   Clifford Lanier Collection, owned by Mrs. John Tilley, Montgomery, Ala.
UT   University of Texas, Austin, Texas.
BU   Brown University, Providence, R. I.
CU   Cornell University, Ithaca, N. Y.
DU   Duke University, Durham, N. C.
EU   Emory University, Atlanta, Ga.
JU   Johns Hopkins University, Baltimore, Md.
YU   Yale University, New Haven, Conn.
  o   Indicates that the letter has survived in fragmentary form.
  †   Indicates that the MS is a copy of a lost original.
 **   Indicates publication prior to appearance in the Centennial Edition.
  *   Indicates that the letter is here published for the first time.

A. LETTERS BY LANIER [1]

			1857					1862	
**	Jan.	6	R. S. Lanier	CL	*	Jan.	18	C. A. Lanier	JT
*	Apr.	21	R. S. Lanier	JT	*	Feb.	19	R. S. Lanier	CL
**	Apr.	26	R. S. Lanier	JT	*	[May ?]		Augusta Lamar	JT
*	May	26	R. S. Lanier	JT	*	Sept.	10	R. S. Lanier	CL
**	Oct.	8	R. S. Lanier	JT	*	Oct.	5	R. S. Lanier	CL
					*	Dec.	15	Anna L. Anderson	RA
			1858 [?]					1863	
**	Feb.	22	Anna L. Anderson	RA					
					*	Feb.	26	R. S. Lanier	JT
			1859		*	Mar.	30	Mary Day	CL
						Apr.	3	Mary Day	JT
*	Feb.	25	I. L. Harris	JM	**	Apr.	6	Virginia and Celeste Clay	DU°
*	[Oct.?]	8	R. S. Lanier	JT	*	Apr.	6	Mary Day	CL
*	Oct.	11	C. A. Lanier	CL	*	Apr.	10	Harriet B. Freeman	HL†
*	Nov.	14	R. S. Lanier	JT	*	Apr.	21–23	Mary Day	CL
					*	Apr.	23	Mary Day	CL
			1860		*	Apr.	24	Mary Day	CL
					*	May	5	Mary Day	CL
*	Feb.	3	R. S. Lanier	JT	*	May	12	R. S. Lanier	CL
*	May	7	R. S. Lanier	JT	*	May	19	Mary Day	CL
**	[Summer]		S. L. Knox	—[2]	**	[May	30?]	Virginia Hankins	—[3]
*	Oct.	8	R. S. Lanier	CL	*	June	13	Mary Day	CL°
*	Dec.	6	R. S. Lanier	HL	*	July	9	R. S. Lanier	JT
					*	[July ?]		Virginia Hankins	HF
			1861		*	[Aug.	5]	Virginia Hankins	HF
					**	[Sept.	15]	W. A. Hopson	—°[4]
*	Feb.	5	An editor	CL	*	Sept.	18	Virginia Hankins	HF
*	Feb.	12	R. S. Lanier	JT	*	Oct.	1	Virginia Hankins	HF
*	Mar.	1	R. S. Lanier	JT					
*	[July ?]		C. A. Lanier	JT					
*	Dec.	4	C. A. Lanier	JT					

[1] This list includes all letters written by Lanier that have been located by the present editors. Conjectural dates are bracketed; then follow the names of the addressees and the initials of the owners of the MSS, which have been located for all but 16 letters. For these the text has been taken from the most reliable printed sources, referred to in footnotes by a key word: Clifford Lanier, "Reminiscences of Sidney Lanier," *Chautauquan*, XXI, 403-409 (July, 1895); G. H. Clarke, *Some Reminiscences and Early Letters of Sidney Lanier* (Macon, Ga., 1907); *Letters of Sidney Lanier* (New York, 1899); Edwin Mims, *Sidney Lanier* (Boston, 1905); Virginia Hankins, "Some Memories of Lanier," *Southern Bivouac*, II [n. s.], 760-761 (May, 1887); Horace Traubel, *With Walt Whitman in Camden* (New York, 1906). A number of other letters known to have been written by Lanier but not found are mentioned in the notes to vols. VII-X.

[2] MS not found; *Chautauquan*, 406.

[3] MS not found; *Bivouac*, 760.

[4] MS not found; Clarke, 19-20.

*	Oct.	1	Mary Day	CL
*	Oct.	4	Harriet B. Freeman	HL
*	Oct.	14	Virginia Hankins	HF
*[	Oct.	?]	Mary Day	CL
*	Nov.	5	R. S. Lanier	CL
*	Nov.	16	Gertrude Lanier	JT
*[	Dec.	?]	Virginia Hankins	HF
*	Dec.	7	R. S. Lanier	CL

1864

*	Jan.	4	R. S. Lanier	CL
**[	Jan.	?]	Rebecca Alexander	SH
**	Jan.	18	R. S. Lanier	CL
*	Feb.	28	Mary Day	CL
**	Mar.	14	R. S. Lanier	CL
*	Apr.	9	R. S. Lanier	CL
*	Apr.	12	Mary Day	CL
*	May	7	R. S. Lanier	JT
*	May	28	R. S. Lanier	JT
*	July	1	Mary Day	CL
*	July	28	Virginia Hankins	HF
*	Aug.	1	Virginia Hankins	HF
*	Aug.	2	R. S. Lanier	JT
**[	Aug	?]	Virginia Hankins	—5
*	Aug.	11	R. S. Lanier	CL
*	Aug.	16–24	Virginia Hankins	HF°†
**	Aug.	24	W. A. Hopson	—6
*	Sept.	13	R. S. Lanier	CL
*	Sept.	24	Virginia Hankins	HF
*	Oct.	1	Mary Day	CL
*	Oct.	6	R. S. Lanier	CL
*	Oct.	14	R. S. Lanier	CL
**[	Oct.	21]	W. A. Hopson	—7
*	Nov.	11	Clifford Anderson	HL†

1865

*	Mar.	18	Mary Day	CL
*	May	8	Mary Day	CL
*[	June	?]	Mary Day	CL
*[	July	?]	Mary Day	CL
*	July	24	C. A. Lanier	JT
*[Summer]			Mary Day	CL
[Summer]			Mary Day	CL
*	Sept.	1	Mary Day	CL
*	Sept.	1	C. A. Lanier	JT
*	Sept.	16	C. A. Lanier	JT
*	Sept.	16	Mary Day	HL

**	Sept.	30	C. A. Lanier	JT
*	Oct.	15	Mary Day	CL
*	Oct.	25	Mary Day	CL
*	Nov.	15	Virginia Hankins	HF
*	Nov.	25	C. A. Lanier	JT

1866

*	Jan.	14	Virginia Hankins	HF
*	Jan.	22	Harriet (Freeman) Fulton	HL†
*[	Feb.	?]	[——— ?]	JT
*	Mar.	21	R. S. Lanier	CL
*	Mar.	24	R. S. Lanier	CL
*	Mar.	26	R. S. Lanier	CL
*	Mar.	30	R. S. Lanier	CL
	Apr.	4	Virginia Hankins	HF
*	May	4	Gertrude Lanier	JT
**	May	12	M. H. Northrup	NF
*	May	13	Virginia Hankins	HF
*	June	9	Virginia Hankins	HF
**	June	11	M. H. Northrup	NF
[	June	?]	Virginia Hankins	HF†
**	June	29	M. H. Northrup	NF†
*	July	1	R. S. Lanier	CL
**	July	13	R. S. Lanier	CL
**	July	28	M. H. Northrup	NF
*	Aug.	10	R. S. Lanier	CL
*	Sept.	25	Virginia Hankins	HF
**	Sept.	26	Gertrude Lanier	EM†
	Oct.	1	R. S. Lanier	JT
*[	Oct.	6?]	R. S. Lanier	CL
*	Oct.	6	Mary Day	HL
*	Oct	14	Virginia Hankins	HF
*	Oct.	14	R. S. Lanier	CL
[	Oct.	27?]	Mary Day	CL
	Oct.	31	Mary Day	CL
	Nov.	1	Mary Day	CL
*	Nov.	3	R. S. Lanier	CL
[	Nov.	?]	Virginia Hankins	HF
*	Nov.	5	R. S. Lanier	CL
*	Nov.	5	Virginia Hankins	HF
	Nov.	13	Mary Day	CL
[	Nov.	16?]	Mary Day	CL
**[	Dec.	9–15?]	Mary Day	CL
[	Dec.	25–31?]	Mary Day	CL

1867

*	Jan.	20	J. B. Tabb	JT

---

5 MS not found; *Bivouac*, 760.
6 MS not found; Clarke, 21-22.
7 MS not found; Clarke, 22-23.

	Date	Recipient	Code
*	Jan. 30	Gertrude Lanier	JT
*[	c. Feb. 15]	Mary Day	CL
*[	Feb. 23?]	Mary Day	HL
*	Mar. 3	R. S. Lanier	JT
*	Mar. 14	Jane Watt	JT
**	Mar. 15	M. H. Northrup	EM†
*	Mar. 16	Mary Day	HL
*	Mar. 19	C. A. Lanier	JT
*	Mar. 21	C. A. Lanier	JT
*	Mar. 22	C. A. Lanier	JT
*	Mar. 30	C. A. Lanier	JT
**	Apr. 11	M. H. Northrup	NF
[	Apr. ?]	Gertrude Lanier	JT°
**	Apr. 16	R. S. Lanier	CL
[	Apr. 16?]	Mary Day	CL
*[	Apr. ?]	C. A. Lanier	JT°
*	May 7	R. S. Lanier	CL
*	May 8	Mary Day	CL
**	May 17	Gertrude Lanier	EM†
*	June 9	R. S. Lanier	CL
*	June 15	Virginia Hankins	HF
*	June 15	John Hankins	HF
*	June 15	C. A. Lanier	JT
*	June 16	Gertrude L. Shannon	JT
*[	June 19?]	Mary Day	CL
*	July 1	C. A. Lanier	JT
*	July 2	C. A. Lanier	JT
*[	July 5?]	Mary Day	CL
*[	July 6?]	Mary Day	CL
*[	July 7?]	Mary Day	HL
[	July ?]	Mary Day	HL
[	July ?]	Mary Day	HL
[	July ?]	Mary Day	HL
[	July ?]	Mary Day	CL
[	July ?]	Mary Day	CL
*	July 12	C. A. Lanier	JT
*	July 16	Virginia Hankins	HF
*	July 22	Hurd & Houghton	HM
*	Aug. 6	Virginia Clay	DU
	Aug. 7	A. G. Houghton	HM
*	Aug. 10	Mary Day	CL
[	Aug. 12]	Mary Day	HL
[	Aug. 14]	Mary Day	HL
*	Aug. 15	Mary Day	**HL**
*	Aug. 17	Mary Day	HL
[	Aug. 18?]	Mary Day	HL
[	Aug. 19]	Mary Day	HL
**	Aug. 21	Hurd & Houghton	BM
*	Aug. 23	Virginia Hankins	HF
[	Aug. 25]	Mary Day	HL
*	Aug. 25	R. S. Lanier	CL
*	Sept. 5	C. A. Lanier	JT
*[	Sept. 6?]	Mary Day	HL
[	Sept. 8?]	Mary Day	HL
*[	Sept. 10?]	Mary Day	HL
[	Sept. 11?]	Mary Day	HL
*[	Sept. 12?]	Mary Day	HL
*[	Sept. 13?]	Mary Day	HL
*[	Sept. 15?]	Mary Day	HL
*[	Sept. 16?]	Mary Day	HL
*[	Sept. 17?]	Mary Day	HL
*[	Sept. 18?]	Mary Day	HL
*[	Sept. 20?]	Mary Day	HL
*[	Sept. 22?]	Mary Day	HL
*[	Sept. 24?]	Mary Day	HL
*[	Sept. 25?]	Mary Day	HL
*	Sept. 26	C. A. Lanier	JT
*[	Sept. 29]	Mary Day	HL
*	Sept. 29	R. S. Lanier	CL
[	Oct.] 10	Mary Day	HL
*	Oct. 10	R. S. Lanier	CL
*[	Oct.] 18	Mary Day	HL
*[	Oct. 20]	Mary Day	HL
*[	Oct. 23]	Mary Day	HL
*	Oct. 24	Mary Day	HL
	Oct. 26	Salem Dutcher	JM
*	Oct. 28	Mary Day	HL
*[	Nov. 1]	Mary Day	HL
*	Nov. 3	Mary Day	HL
*	Nov. 3	Virginia Hankins	HF
*	Nov. 3	C. A. Lanier	JT
*	Nov. 7	C. A. Lanier	JT
*[	Nov. 11?]	Mary Day	HL
	Nov. 13	Mary Day	HL
	Nov. 15	C. A. Lanier	JT
*	Nov. 15	Mary Day	HL
**	Nov. 15	R. S. Lanier	CL
	Nov. 18	Mary Day	HL
*	Nov. 19	C. A. Lanier	JT
*	Nov. 27	Mary Day	HL
*	Nov. 28	C. A. Lanier	JT
*	Nov. 28	Mary Day	HL
	Dec. 5	Mary Day	HL
*	Dec. 9	Mary Day	CL
	Dec. 11	C. A. Lanier	JT
**	Dec. 16	M. H. Northrup	NF
*	Dec. 16	C. A. Lanier	JT
*[	Dec. 17?]	Mary Day	HL
*[	Dec. 19]	Mary Day	HL
*	Dec. 31	C. A. Lanier	JT

1868

* Jan.	7	C. A. Lanier	JT
* Jan.	12	Jane L. Watt	JT
* Jan.	14	Virginia Hankins	HF
* Jan.	14	C. A. Lanier	JT
* Jan.	17	C. A. Lanier	JT
* Jan.	20	C. A. Lanier	JT
* Jan.	21	C. A. Lanier	JT
** Jan.	21	R. S. Lanier	CL
* Jan.	24	C. A. Lanier	JT
* Jan.	24	R. S. Lanier	CL
[Jan. ?]		C. A. Lanier	JT
[Jan. ?]		Mary D. Lanier	CL
[Jan. ?]		Mary D. Lanier	CL
[Jan. ?]		Mary D. Lanier	CL
[Jan. ?]		Mary D. Lanier	CL
[Jan. ?]		Mary D. Lanier	CL
[Jan. ?]		Mary D. Lanier	CL
[Jan. ?]		Mary D. Lanier	CL
* Feb.	10	R. S. Lanier	CL
* Feb.	14	Mary D. Lanier	HL
* Mar.	3	C. A. Lanier	JT
* Mar.	8	C. A. Lanier	JT
** Mar.	8	M. H. Northrup	NF
* Mar.	16	R. S. Lanier	CL
* Apr.	7	R. S. Lanier	CL
Apr.	10	C. A. Lanier	JT
* Apr.	12	Virginia Hankins	HF
Apr.	17	R. S. Lanier	CL
* May	20	R. S. Lanier	CL
** May	28	R. S. Lanier	CL
* May	28	Hurd & Houghton	HM
** June	1	R. S. Lanier	CL
June	2	W. C. Howell	CL
June	3	Lilla Hazlehurst	HL†
*[Summer ?]		A publisher	CL
*[July	17?]	Mary D. Lanier	HL
* July	20	Mary D. Lanier	HL
* Oct.	1	C. A. Lanier	JT
* Nov.	4	C. A. Lanier	JT
** Nov.	9	Virginia Hankins	HF
*[Dec.	2]	Charles and Caroline Campbell	WC

1869

**[Feb. ?]		Virginia Hankins	HF
* Feb.	22	C. A. Lanier	JT
*[Mar.	7?]	Virginia Hankins	HF°
** Mar.	9	Virginia Hankins	HF
** Mar.	15	M. H. Northrup	NF
** Mar.	15	P. H. Hayne	DU
*[Mar.]	24	Mary D. Lanier	CL
* Mar.	27	Mary D. Lanier	CL
*[Apr. ?]		Virginia Hankins	HF°
* Apr.	13	C. A. Lanier	JT
Apr.	20	Mary D. Lanier	CL
Apr.	27	Mary D. Lanier	CL
** Apr.	28	Mary D. Lanier	—8
* Apr.	29	Charles Day	CL
Apr.	29	M. H. Northrup	NF
* May	1	Mary D. Lanier	CL
May	1	Mary D. Lanier	CL
* May	4	R. S. Lanier	CL
May	4	Mary D. Lanier	HL
[May ?]		Mary D. Lanier	CL
[May ?]		Mary D. Lanier	CL
** May	4	Virginia Hankins	HF
* May	6	Mary D. Lanier	CL
May	8	Mary D. Lanier	HL
* May	9	Mary D. Lanier	HL
* May	10	R. S. Lanier	CL
May	13	Mary D. Lanier	CL
[May	14?]	Mary D. Lanier	CL
[May	14?]	Mary D. Lanier	CL
** May	15	R. S. Lanier	CL
May	15	Mary D. Lanier	HL
[May	15?]	Mary D. Lanier	CL
May	15	Mary D. Lanier	CL
*[May	16]	Mary D. Lanier	CL
May	17	Mary D. Lanier	CL
* May	17	Mary D. Lanier	HL
* May	17	Virginia Hankins	HF
* May	18	Mary D. Lanier	HL
* May	20	Mary D. Lanier	CL
May	22	Mary D. Lanier	HL
May	25	Mary D. Lanier	HL
* May	26	R. S. Lanier	HL
May	26	Mary D. Lanier	HL
* May	28	Mary D. Lanier	HL
*[July	7?]	Virginia Hankins	HF
* Aug.	18	R. S. Lanier	CL
* Sept.	19	Virginia Hankins	HF
* Nov.	6	Mary D. Lanier	HL
* Nov.	10	Mary D. Lanier	CL
** Nov.	19	C. A. Lanier	JT
* Nov.	30	Virginia Hankins	HF
* Dec.	23	Mary D. Lanier	CL

8 MS not found; *Letters,* 67.

[1869?] — Three undated notes to Mary D. Lanier — CL

1870

	Date	Recipient	
*	Jan. 7	Virginia Hankins	HF
*	Feb. 10	Charles Day	MS
*	Feb. 15	Mary D. Lanier	CL
	Feb. 16	Mary D. Lanier	CL
*	Feb. 17	Mary D. Lanier	CL
	Feb. 19	Mary D. Lanier	CL
*	Feb. 21	Mary D. Lanier	HL
**	Feb. 22	Mary D. Lanier	CL
	Feb. 23	Mary D. Lanier	CL
*	Feb. 25	Mary D. Lanier	HL
*	Feb. 28	Mary D. Lanier	HL
	[Mar. 1]	Mary D. Lanier	CL
*	Mar. 2	Mary D. Lanier	HL
**	[Mar. 3?]	Mary D. Lanier	CL
*	Mar. 4	Mary D. Lanier	ET
*	Mar. 4	Virginia Hankins	HF
	Mar. 4	C. A. Lanier	JT
	Mar. 5	Mary D. Lanier	CL
**	Mar. 5	P. H. Hayne	AS
	Mar. 7	Mary D. Lanier	HL
*	Mar. 8	Mary D. Lanier	CL
**	Mar. 21	P. H. Hayne	DU
*	[Mar. 23?]	Mary D. Lanier	HL
*	Mar. 25	Mary D. Lanier	HL
	Mar. 30	Mary D. Lanier	HL
*	[Apr. ?]	Virginia Hankins	HF
**	Apr. 13	P. H. Hayne	DU
*	May 18	Jane L. Watt	JT
*	May 20	Virginia Hankins	HF
*	June 15	Lilla Hazlehurst	JT†
**	[ante June 20]	Virginia Hankins	HF
*	July 7	R. S. Lanier	CL
*	July 11	R. S. Lanier	CL
*	July 28	R. S. Lanier	CL
*	July 31	Mary D. Lanier	CL
*	Aug. 2	R. S. Lanier	CL
	Aug. 2	Mary D. Lanier	HL
	Aug. 3	Mary D. Lanier	HL
*	Aug. 4	Mary D. Lanier	HL
*	Aug. 5	Mary D. Lanier	CL
*	Aug. 7	Mary D. Lanier	CL
**	[Aug. 8?]	Mary D. Lanier	CL
*	Aug. 9	Mary D. Lanier	CL
**	Aug. 9	P. H. Hayne	DU
*	Aug. 11	Mary D. Lanier	HL
	Aug. 12	Charles Day	CL
*	Aug. 12	Mary D. Lanier	CL
**	Aug. 13	Mary D. Lanier	CL
	Aug. 15	R. S. Lanier	CL
**	Aug. 15	Mary D. Lanier	CL
	Aug. 16	Mary D. Lanier	CL
	Aug. 17	Mary D. Lanier	CL
	Aug. 18	Mary D. Lanier	CL
*	Aug. 19	R. S. Lanier	CL
	Aug. 19	Mary D. Lanier	CL
	Aug. 20	Mary D. Lanier	CL
*	Aug. 22	R. S. Lanier	CL
	Aug. 22	Mary D. Lanier	CL
	Aug. 23	Mary D. Lanier	HL
*	Aug. 24	Mary D. Lanier	HL
	Aug. 25	Mary D. Lanier	HL
*	Aug. 26	Mary D. Lanier	HL
*	Aug. 26	Virginia Hankins	HF
*	Aug. 29	Mary D. Lanier	HL
	Aug. 30	Mary D. Lanier	CL
*	Aug. 31	Mary D. Lanier	CL
*	Sept. 1	Mary D. Lanier	HL
	[Sept. 2]	Mary D. Lanier	HL
*	Sept. 4	Mary D. Lanier	HL
	Sept. 5	Mary D. Lanier	CL
*	Sept. 7	Mary D. Lanier	CL
	Sept. 8	Mary D. Lanier	HL
	Sept. 9	Mary D. Lanier	CL
*	Sept. 12	Mary D. Lanier	CL
	Sept. 13	Mary D. Lanier	HL
*	Sept. 14	Mary D. Lanier	CL
*	Sept. 16	Mary D. Lanier	HL
*	Sept. 16	C. A. Lanier	JT
	Sept. 17	Mary D. Lanier	HL
	Sept. 17	Mary D. Lanier	CL†
	Sept. 17	Mary D. Lanier	CL
	Sept. 18	Mary D. Lanier	CL
*	Sept. 19	Mary D. Lanier	CL
*	Sept. 20	Mary D. Lanier	HL
*	Sept. 21	R. S. Lanier	CL
	Sept. 21	Mary D. Lanier	HL
	Sept. 22	Mary D. Lanier	CL
**	Sept. 24	Mary D. Lanier	CL
	Sept. 25	Mary D. Lanier	HL
*	Sept. 26	Mary D. Lanier	CL
	Sept. 29	Mary D. Lanier	HL
*	Sept. 30	R. S. Lanier	CL
	Sept. 30	Mary D. Lanier	HL
	Oct. 1	Mary D. Lanier	HL
	Oct. 2	Mary D. Lanier	CL
*	Oct. 4	Mary D. Lanier	CL
*	Oct. 5	Virginia Hankins	HF
*	Oct. 5	Mary D. Lanier	CL

* Oct.	22	C. A. Lanier	JT
*[Nov.	9?]	Virginia Hankins	HF
[Nov.–Dec.]		Virginia Hankins	HF
*[Dec.	3?]	Virginia Hankins	HF
* Dec.	7	P. H. Hayne	DU

1871

* Jan.	7	Virginia Hankins	HF
* Feb.	28	Mary D. Lanier	CL
*[Feb.–Mar.?]		Virginia Hankins	HF
* Mar.	7	Mary D. Lanier	CL
* Mar.	8	Mary D. Lanier	CL
* Mar.	11	R. S. Lanier	CL
*[Mar.	11?]	Mary D. Lanier	CL
Mar.	14	Mary D. Lanier	CL
*[Mar.	15?]	Mary D. Lanier	CL
** Mar.	20	P. H. Hayne	DU
* Apr.	3	Mary D. Lanier	HL
Apr.	6	Mary D. Lanier	CL
* Apr.	6	Virginia Hankins	HF
* Apr.	28	Mary D. Lanier	CL
*[Apr.	30?]	Mary D. Lanier	CL
* May	3	Mary D. Lanier	HL
* May	4	Mary D. Lanier	CL
* May	22	Virginia Hankins	HF
* June	4	Mary D. Lanier	CL
* June	6	Mary D. Lanier	CL
[June]	10	Mary D. Lanier	CL
* June	10	Mary D. Lanier	HL
June	12	Mary D. Lanier	CL
June	13	Mary D. Lanier	CL
* June	14	Mary D. Lanier	CL
June	19	Mary D. Lanier	CL
* June	19	Mary D. Lanier	CL
* June	26	Mary D. Lanier	HL
* July	10	C. A. Lanier	JT
*[July	20?]	Mary D. Lanier	CL
* July	21	R. S. Lanier	CL
* July	23	Mary D. Lanier	CL
July	27	Mary D. Lanier	CL
* July	31	Virginia Hankins	HF
* Aug.	2	R. S. Lanier	CL
* Aug.	13	R. S. Lanier	JT
Aug.	16	Charles Day	CL
* Aug.	19	R. S. Lanier	CL
* Aug.	28	R. S. Lanier	CL
* Aug.	28	Virginia Hankins	HF
* Sept.	8	Charles Day	CL
** Sept.	13	P. H. Hayne	DU
Sept.	13	R. S. Lanier	CL
* Sept.	21	Mary D. Lanier	HL
Sept.	23	C. A. Lanier	JT

*[Sept.	23?]	Mary D. Lanier	HL
[Sept.	24]	Mary D. Lanier	HL
* Sept.	26	Mary D. Lanier	HL
[Sept.	27?]	Mary D. Lanier	CL
* Sept.	27	Virginia Hankins	HF
**[Sept.]	28	Mary D. Lanier	CL
* Sept.	29	Mary D. Lanier	CL
[Sept.	30?]	Mary D. Lanier	HL
* Oct.	1	Mary D. Lanier	CL
* Oct.	2	Mary D. Lanier	CL
Oct.	3	Mary D. Lanier	HL
* Oct.	4	R. S. Lanier	CL
Oct.	5	Mary D. Lanier	HL
Oct.	6	Mary D. Lanier	CL
* Oct.	7	Mary D. Lanier	HL
Oct.	8	Mary D. Lanier	HL°
* Oct.	9	Mary D. Lanier	CL
Oct.	10	Mary D. Lanier	CL
Oct.	11	Mary D. Lanier	HL
* Oct.	12	Mary D. Lanier	CL
* Oct.	13	Mary D. Lanier	HL
* Oct.	14	Mary D. Lanier	CL
Oct.	15	Mary D. Lanier	CL
Oct.	16	Mary D. Lanier	CL
* Oct.	17	Mary D. Lanier	HL
* Oct.	18	Mary D. Lanier	HL
Oct.	19	Mary D. Lanier	CL
Oct.	20	Mary D. Lanier	CL
* Oct.	21	Mary D. Lanier	CL
Oct.	22	Mary D. Lanier	HL
Oct.	23	Mary D. Lanier	HL
* Oct.	24	C. A. Lanier	JT
* Oct.	24	Mary D. Lanier	CL
Oct.	25	Mary D. Lanier	CL
Oct.	26	Mary D. Lanier	HL
Oct.	27	Mary D. Lanier	CL
* Oct.	28	Mary D. Lanier	HL
Oct.	29	Mary D. Lanier	CL
* Oct.	31	Mary D. Lanier	HL
* Nov.	1	Mary D. Lanier	CL
** Nov.	2	R. S. Lanier	CL
* Nov.	2	Mary D. Lanier	CL
Nov.	3	Mary D. Lanier	CL
* Nov.	4	Mary D. Lanier	CL
* Nov.	4	Virginia Hankins	HF
Nov.	5	Mary D. Lanier	CL
* Nov.	5	C. A. Lanier	JT
* Nov.	6	Mary D. Lanier	HL
* Nov.	7	Mary D. Lanier	CL
Nov.	8	Mary D. Lanier	CL
* Nov.	8	R. S. Lanier	CL
* Nov.	9	Mary D. Lanier	HL

	Nov.	11	Mary D. Lanier	HL
*	Nov.	13	Mary D. Lanier	HL
*	Nov.	14	Mary D. Lanier	CL
*	Nov.	14	Virginia Hankins	HF
*	Dec.	2	C. A. Lanier	JT
*	Dec.	6	Virginia Hankins	HF
	Dec.	12	Mary D. Lanier	CL
	[Dec. ?]		Mary D. Lanier	CL
	[Dec. ?]		Mary D. Lanier	CL
*	Dec.	28	J. C. Harris	EU

1872

*	Feb.	12	Virginia Hankins	HF
*	Mar.	2	P. H. Hayne	AS
**	Apr.	17	P. H. Hayne	AS
*	May	1	Virginia Hankins	HF
*	June	18	Virginia Hankins	HF
**	July	2	Virginia Hankins	HF
*	July	8	Mary D. Lanier	HL
*	July	9	Mary D. Lanier	CL
*	July	11	R. S. Lanier	CL
*	July	11	Mary D. Lanier	CL
**	July	12	Mary D. Lanier	CL
	July	12	R. S. Lanier	CL
*	July	13	Mary D. Lanier	HL
	July	14	Mary D. Lanier	HL
	July	14	Virginia Hankins	HF
*	July	14	Charles Day	CL
*	July	15	Virginia Hankins	HF
*	July	16	Mary D. Lanier	HL
	July	16	Mary D. Lanier	CL
*	July	18	Mary D. Lanier	HL
*	July	18	Virginia Hankins	HF
*	July	19	Mary D. Lanier	CL
*	July	22	Mary D. Lanier	CL
*	July	23	Mary D. Lanier	CL
	July	24	Mary D. Lanier	CL
*	July	25	Mary D. Lanier	CL
*	July	26	Virginia Hankins	HF
*	July	26	Mary D. Lanier	CL
	July	27	Mary D. Lanier	CL
*	Sept.	18	R. S. Lanier	CL
*	Oct.	16	Mary D. Lanier	CL
	Oct.	17	Mary D. Lanier	HL
*	Oct.	18	Mary D. Lanier	CL
*	Oct.	20	Mary D. Lanier	CL
*	Oct.	21	Mary D. Lanier	CL°
	Oct.	22	Mary D. Lanier	CL
*	Oct.	23	Mary D. Lanier	CL
	Oct.	24	Mary D. Lanier	CL
*	Oct.	28	R. S. Lanier	CL

*	Nov.	9	Virginia Hankins	HF
	Nov.	12	Mary D. Lanier	CL
*	Nov.	14	Mary D. Lanier	CL
*	Nov.	15	Mary D. Lanier	CL
*	Nov.	17	Mary D. Lanier	CL
*	Nov.	18	Mary D. Lanier	CL
*	Nov.	22	Mary D. Lanier	CL
*	Nov.	23	R. S. Lanier	CL
	Nov.	23	Mary D. Lanier	CL
*	Nov.	25	Mary D. Lanier	CL
	Nov.	25	C. A. Lanier	JT
*	Nov.	26	Mary D. Lanier	CL
*	Nov.	27	Mary D. Lanier	CL
*	Nov.	28	Mary D. Lanier	CL
	Nov.	29	Mary D. Lanier	CL
**	Nov.	30	Gertrude L. Shannon	DU† & EM†
	Nov.	30	Mary D. Lanier	CL
	Dec.	1	Mary D. Lanier	CL
	Dec.	2	Mary D. Lanier	CL
	Dec.	4	Charles Day	CL
	Dec.	4	Mary D. Lanier	CL
	Dec.	5	Mary D. Lanier	CL
**	Dec.	6	R. S. Lanier	CL
	Dec.	6	Mary D. Lanier	CL°
	Dec.	7	Mary D. Lanier	CL
	Dec.	8	Mary D. Lanier	CL
*	Dec.	9	Mary D. Lanier	HL
	Dec.	11	Mary D. Lanier	HL
	Dec.	11	Mary D. Lanier	CL
*	Dec.	11	R. S. Lanier	CL
	Dec.	13	Mary D. Lanier	CL
*	Dec.	14	Mary D. Lanier	CL
	Dec.	19	Mary D. Lanier	CL
*	Dec.	20	Mary D. Lanier	JT
	Dec.	21	Mary D. Lanier	CL
*	Dec.	22	R. S. Lanier	CL
	Dec.	22	Mary D. Lanier	CL
*	Dec.	23	Mary D. Lanier	CL
*	Dec.	24	Mary D. Lanier	CL
*	Dec.	25	Mary D. Lanier	CL
**	Dec.	26	R. S. Lanier	CL
	Dec.	27	Mary D. Lanier	CL
	Dec.	29	Mary D. Lanier	CL
*	Dec.	30	Mary D. Lanier	CL
*	Dec.	31	Mary D. Lanier	CL

1873

*	Jan.	1	Mary D. Lanier	CL
*	Jan.	1	R. S. Lanier	CL
*	Jan.	2	Mary D. Lanier	CL

	Month	Day		
	Jan.	3	Mary D. Lanier	CL
	Jan.	4	Mary D. Lanier	CL
*	Jan.	5	Mary D. Lanier	CL
*	Jan.	6	Mary D. Lanier	CL
*	Jan.	7	Mary D. Lanier	CL
*	Jan.	7	R. S. Lanier	CL
	Jan.	7	Wilhelmina L. Eason	JM
	Jan.	8	Mary D. Lanier	CL
	Jan.	10	Mary D. Lanier	CL
	Jan.	11	Mary D. Lanier	CL
*	Jan.	12	Mary D. Lanier	CL
	Jan.	13	Mary D. Lanier	CL
	Jan.	14	Mary D. Lanier	CL
*	Jan.	15	Mary D. Lanier	CL
*	Jan.	15	R. S. Lanier	CL
*	Jan.	16	Mary D. Lanier	CL
	Jan.	17	Mary D. Lanier	CL
[Jan.	18?]		Mary D. Lanier	CL°
	Jan.	19	Mary D. Lanier	CL°
	Jan.	20	Mary D. Lanier	CL
	Jan.	22	Mary D. Lanier	CL
	Jan.	23	Mary D. Lanier	CL
*	Jan.	27	Mary D. Lanier	CL
**	Jan.	30	Mary D. Lanier	CL
	Jan.	30	Mary D. Lanier	CL
*	Feb.	1	R. S. Lanier	JT
	Feb.	1	Mary D. Lanier	CL°
*	Feb.	2	Mary D. Lanier	CL°
	Feb.	4	Mary D. Lanier	CL
	Feb.	6	Mary D. Lanier	CL
	Feb.	7	Mary D. Lanier	CL
*	Feb.	8	C. A. Lanier	JT
	Feb.	8	Mary D. Lanier	CL
	Feb.	9	Mary D. Lanier	CL
	Feb.	10	Mary D. Lanier	CL
	Feb.	11	Mary D. Lanier	CL
*	Feb.	12	Mary D. Lanier	CL
*	Feb.	13	Mary D. Lanier	CL
*	Feb.	14	Mary D. Lanier	CL
	Feb.	15	Mary D. Lanier	CL
*	Feb.	16	Mary D. Lanier	CL
	Feb.	17	Mary D. Lanier	CL
*	Feb.	20	Mary D. Lanier	CL
	Feb.	22	Mary D. Lanier	CL
	Feb.	23	Mary D. Lanier	CL
**	Feb.	24	Mary D. Lanier	CL
*	Feb.	25	Mary D. Lanier	HL
*	Feb.	26	Mary D. Lanier	CL
[Feb.	27?]		Mary D. Lanier	CL°
**	Feb.	28	Mary D. Lanier	CL
*	Mar.	1	Mary D. Lanier	CL
*	Mar.	8	Mary D. Lanier	HL
*	Apr.	16	Mary D. Lanier	HL
	Apr.	17	Mary D. Lanier	HL
*	Apr.	18	Mary D. Lanier	HL
[Apr.	?]		Mary D. Lanier	HL
	Apr.	21	Mary D. Lanier	CL
*	Apr.	22	Mary D. Lanier	HL
	Apr.	23	Mary D. Lanier	CL
*	May	15	Charles Day	CL
	May	17	R. S. Lanier	CL
*	May	19	Charles Day	CL
*	May	19	R. S. Lanier	CL
*	May	24	C. A. Lanier	JT
**	May	26	P. H. Hayne	DU
*	May	27	Virginia Hankins	HF
*	May	29	Charles Day	CL
	June	9	R. S. Lanier	CL
**	June	10	P. H. Hayne	AS
*	June	13	R. S. Lanier	CL
*	June	17	Charles Day	CL
*	June	28	Charles Day	CL
	June	28	C. A. Lanier	JT
*	July	1	Charles Day	CL
*	July	4	R. S. Lanier	HL†
	July	4	Charles Day	CL
	July	10	Charles Day	CL
	July	15	Charles Day	CL
	July	15	R. S. Lanier	CL
*	July	17	Virginia Hankins	HF
*	July	20	Charles Day	CL
	July	21	R. S. Lanier	CL
**	July	21	C. A. Lanier	JT
	July	29	R. S. Lanier	CL
	Aug.	2 [4?]	Charles Day	CL
*	Aug.	6	Mary D. Lanier	CL
*	Aug.	13	R. S. Lanier	CL
*	Aug.	19	Virginia Hankins	HF
*	Aug.	21	Charles Day	CL
	Aug.	21	R. S. Lanier	CL
*	Aug.	26	H. C. Day	HL†
*	Aug.	30	Virginia Hankins	HF
	Sept.	1	Gertrude L. Gibson	BC
	Sept.	1	R. S. Lanier	CL
*	Sept.	3	Charles Day	CL
	Sept.	8	M. H. Northrup	NF
*	Sept.	14	Mary D. Lanier	HL
	Sept.	14	R. S. Lanier	CL
	[Sept.	15]	Virginia Hankins	HF
*	Sept.	19	Mary D. Lanier	CL
*	Sept.	20	Mary D. Lanier	CL
*	Sept.	22	Mary D. Lanier	HL

	Date	Recipient	Code
*	Sept. 24	R. S. Lanier	BC
**	Sept. 24	Mary D. Lanier	CL
*	Sept. 25	Mary D. Lanier	HL
*	Sept. 26	Virginia Hankins	HF
*	Sept. 26	Mary D. Lanier	HL
	Sept. 27	Mary D. Lanier	CL
	Sept. 27	C. A. Lanier	JT
*	Sept. 29	Mary D. Lanier	HL
	Oct. 1	Mary D. Lanier	HL
*	Oct. 4	Mary D. Lanier	HL
**	Oct. 6	Mary D. Lanier	CL
	Oct. 7	Mary D. Lanier	HL
*	Oct. 8	Mary D. Lanier	HL
**	Oct. 10	Mary D. Lanier	CL
	Oct. 12	Mary D. Lanier	HL
*	Oct. 13	Mary D. Lanier	CL
*	Oct. 14	Mary D. Lanier	HL
**	Oct. 15	Mary D. Lanier	CL
**	Oct. 17	Mary D. Lanier	CL
*	Oct. 19	Mary D. Lanier	CL
*	Oct. 21	Mary D. Lanier	HL†
	Oct. 25	Mary D. Lanier	HL
**	Oct. 26	Mary D. Lanier	CL
*	Oct. 26	Virginia Hankins	HF
	Oct. 29	Mary D. Lanier	HL
	Oct. 30	Mary D. Lanier	CL
	Nov. 1	Mary D. Lanier	HL
*	Nov. 3	Mary D. Lanier	CL
*	Nov. 5	Mary D. Lanier	CL
*	Nov. 6	Mary D. Lanier	CL
*	Nov. 7	Mary D. Lanier	CL
	Nov. 11	Mary D. Lanier	HL
**	Nov. 16	Mary D. Lanier	CL
**	Nov. 17 [18]	Mary D. Lanier	CL
**	Nov. 21	Mary D. Lanier	CL°
	Nov. 22	Mary D. Lanier	CL
	Nov. 23	Mary D. Lanier	HL
**	Nov. 23	M. H. Northrup	NF
*	Nov. 29	Mary D. Lanier	CL
**	Nov. 29	R. S. Lanier	CL
**	Dec. 2	Mary D. Lanier	HL†
*	Dec. 9	Mary D. Lanier	HL
**	Dec. 11	Mary D. Lanier	CL
	Dec. 11	Mary D. Lanier	CL
*	Dec. 12	Mary D. Lanier	HL
*	Dec. 16	C. A. Lanier	JT
*	Dec. 17	Mary D. Lanier	HL
*	Dec. 18	Mary D. Lanier	HL
**	Dec. 20	Mary D. Lanier	CL
**	Dec. 21	Mary D. Lanier	CL
*	Dec. [22?]	His sons	SL
*	Dec. 23	R. S. Lanier	CL

	Date	Recipient	Code
**	Dec. 23	Virginia Hankins	HF
**	Dec. 25	Mary D. Lanier	CL
	Dec. 26	Mary D. Lanier	HL

1874

	Date	Recipient	Code
**	Jan. 3	Mary D. Lanier	CL
*	Jan. 4	Mary D. Lanier	HL
*	Jan. 4	R. S. Lanier	CL
*	Jan. 4	C. A. Lanier	JT
*	Jan. 8	G. W. F. Price	EP
	Jan. 8	Mary D. Lanier	CL
**	[Jan. 10?]	Mary D. Lanier	CL & HL
	Jan. 18	Mary D. Lanier	CL
*	[Jan. 20?]	Mary D. Lanier	CL & HL†
*	Jan. 22	Mary D. Lanier	CL
**	Jan. 23	Mary D. Lanier	HL
	Jan. 26	R. S. Lanier	CL
	[Jan. 26?]	Mary D. Lanier	CL
*	Jan. 28	Mary D. Lanier	HL
	Jan. 31	C. A. Lanier	JT°
*	Jan. 31	Mary D. Lanier	HL
**	Feb. 3	Mary D. Lanier	CL
**	Feb. 7	Mary D. Lanier	CL
**	Feb. 7	Mary D. Lanier	CL
	Feb. 7	R. S. Lanier	CL
**	Feb. 8	Mary D. Lanier	CL
**	Feb. 12	Mary D. Lanier	CL
*	Feb. 16	Mary D. Lanier	HL
	Feb. 20	Mary D. Lanier	HL
*	Feb. 21	Mary D. Lanier	CL
	Feb. 23	Mary D. Lanier	CL
	Feb. 26	Mary D. Lanier	HL
	Feb. 28	Mary D. Lanier	CL
	[Mar. 2?]	Mary D. Lanier	CL
	Mar. 4	Mary D. Lanier	HL
*	Mar. 5	Mary D. Lanier	CL
*	Mar. 8	Mary D. Lanier	CL
*	Mar. 11	R. S. Lanier	CL
*	Mar. 11	Mary D. Lanier	HL
	Mar. 12	Mary D. Lanier	HL
**	Mar. 15	Mary D. Lanier	CL
	Mar. 20	Mary D. Lanier	CL
*	Mar. 21	Mary D. Lanier	CL
*	Mar. 21	R. S. Lanier	CL
*	Mar. 25	Mary D. Lanier	HL
	[Mar. 29]	Mary D. Lanier	CL
*	[Mar. 31]	Mary D. Lanier	CL
	Apr. 1	Mary D. Lanier	HL
**	Apr. 3	Mary D. Lanier	CL

	Date		Correspondent	Code
**	Apr.	9	Mary D. Lanier	CL
*	Apr.	11	Mary D. Lanier	HL
*[	Apr.	14?]	Mary D. Lanier	CL
*	Apr.	16	Mary D. Lanier	CL
*	Apr.	19	Mary D. Lanier	CL
	Apr.	24	Mary D. Lanier	HL
*	Apr.	26	Mary D. Lanier	CL
*	May	11	C. A. Lanier	JT
**	May	23	P. H. Hayne	DU
*	May	26	Virginia Hankins	HF
[	May	27?]	Mary D. Lanier	CL
[	May	28?]	Mary D. Lanier	CL
*	May	28	C. A. Lanier	CL
	June	3	Mary D. Lanier	CL°
*	June	9	R. S. Lanier	CL
*	June	12	Mary D. Lanier	CL
*	June	15	Mary D. Lanier	CL
*	June	16	Mary D. Lanier	HL
*[	June	17?]	Mary D. Lanier	CL
	June	18	Mary D. Lanier	CL
	June	19	Mary D. Lanier	CL
*	June	25 [26]	Mary D. Lanier	HL
*	Aug.	7	C. A. Lanier	JT
*	Aug.	20	Mary D. Lanier	CL
	Aug.	21	Mary D. Lanier	CL
*	Aug.	22	Mary D. Lanier	CL
	Aug.	23	Mary D. Lanier	HL
*	Aug.	25	Mary D. Lanier	CL
*	Aug.	26	Mary D. Lanier	HL
	Aug.	27	Mary D. Lanier	HL
	Aug.	28	Mary D. Lanier	HL
*	Aug.	29	Mary D. Lanier	HL
*	Aug.	30	Mary D. Lanier	CL
	Aug.	31	Mary D. Lanier	HL
**	Sept.	1	M. H. Northrup	NF
	Sept.	1	Mary D. Lanier	HL
*	Sept.	2	C. A. Lanier	JT
**	Sept.	3	Mary D. Lanier	CL
*	Sept.	4–5	Mary D. Lanier	HL
	Sept.	5	C. A. Lanier	JT
	Sept.	6	Mary D. Lanier	HL
**	Sept.	7	Mary D. Lanier	CL
	Sept.	8	Mary D. Lanier	CL
*	Sept.	8	R. S. Lanier	CL
	Sept.	10	Mary D. Lanier	CL
	Sept.	11	Mary D. Lanier	HL
*	Sept.	12	Mary D. Lanier	HL
*	Sept.	13	Mary D. Lanier	CL
	Sept.	14	Mary D. Lanier	HL
	Sept.	15	Mary D. Lanier	HL
	Sept.	17	R. S. Lanier	CL
**	Sept.	17	Mary D. Lanier	CL
*	Sept.	19	Mary D. Lanier	HL
	Sept.	20	Mary D. Lanier	CL
**	Sept.	21	Mary D. Lanier	CL
*	Sept.	24	Mary D. Lanier	CL
*	Sept.	24	R. S. Lanier	CL
*	Sept.	24	Hurd & Houghton	HM
**	Sept.	25	Mary D. Lanier	CL
	Sept.	27	Mary D. Lanier	HL
*	Sept.	28	Mary D. Lanier	CL
**	Oct.	1	Mary D. Lanier	HL
	Oct.	2	R. S. Lanier	CL
**	Oct.	2	Mary D. Lanier	CL
*	Oct.	7	Mary D. Lanier	CL
*	Oct.	7	Hurd & Houghton	HM
**	Oct.	9	L. E. Bleckley	HL†
	Oct.	13	Mary D. Lanier	CL
*	Oct.	14	C. A. Lanier	JT
**	Oct.	18	Mary D. Lanier	CL
*	Oct.	21	Mary D. Lanier	CL
**	Oct.	23	Mary D. Lanier	HL
*	Oct.	25	Mary D. Lanier	CL
*	Oct.	28	Mary D. Lanier	CL
	Oct.	28	R. S. Lanier	CL
**	Oct.	29	Mary D. Lanier	CL
*	Nov.	1	Mary D. Lanier	CL
*	Nov.	2	C. A. Lanier	JT
*	Nov.	3	Mary D. Lanier	HL
*	Nov.	5	E. C. Stedman	HA
*	Nov.	6	Mary D. Lanier	HL
**	Nov.	8	Mary D. Lanier	CL
	Nov.	8	R. S. Lanier	CL
*	Nov.	11	Mary D. Lanier	HL
**	Nov.	15	L. E. Bleckley	HL†
*	Nov.	16	Mary D. Lanier	CL
*	Nov.	21	R. S. Lanier	CL
*	Dec.	1	C. A. Lanier	CL
[	Dec.	2?]	Mary D. Lanier	HL
*[	Dec.	3?]	Mary D. Lanier	HL
*[	Dec.	4?]	Mary D. Lanier	HL
	Dec.	7	Mary D. Lanier	CL°
*	Dec.	8	Mary D. Lanier	CL
*	Dec.	17	C. A. Lanier	JT
*[	Dec.	24?]	Mary D. Lanier	HL
*	Dec.	26	Mary D. Lanier	CL
*	Dec.	29 [28?]	Mary D. Lanier	CL
*	Dec.	29	Mary D. Lanier	CL
*	Dec.	30	Mary D. Lanier	HL
	Dec.	31	Mary D. Lanier	CL

1875

**	Jan.	1	Mary D. Lanier	CL
**	Jan.	3	Mary D. Lanier	CL
**	Jan.	3	Laura N. Boykin	WM
**	Jan.	6	Mary D. Lanier	CL
**	Jan.	9	Mary D. Lanier	CL
**	Jan.	12	Mary D. Lanier	CL
*	Jan.	13	Mary D. Lanier	CL
	Jan.	14	Mary D. Lanier	CL
*	Jan.	17	Mary D. Lanier	HL
*	Jan.	18	Mary D. Lanier	CL
**	Jan.	20	Mary D. Lanier	CL
**	Jan.	21	M. H. Northrup	NF
	Jan.	22	Mary D. Lanier	HL
*	Jan.	22	Mary D. Lanier	CL
*	Jan.	23	L. E. Bleckley	HL†
	Jan.	24	C. A. Lanier	JT
**	Jan.	24	Mary D. Lanier	CL
*	Jan.	26	Mary D. Lanier	CL
**	Jan.	26	Gibson Peacock	HC
*	Jan.	26	R. S. Lanier	CL
*	Jan.	28	Virginia Hankins	HF
*	Jan.	31	Mary D. Lanier	CL
	Feb.	3	Mary D. Lanier	CL
*	Feb.	3	Virginia Hankins	HF
*	Feb.	5	Mary D. Lanier	HL
[Feb. ?]			Mary D. Lanier	CL°
**	Feb.	7	Mary D. Lanier	CL
*	Feb.	8	C. A. Lanier	JT
**	Feb.	11	Mary D. Lanier	HL
	Feb.	14	Mary D. Lanier	HL
*	Feb.	17	Mary D. Lanier	CL
*	Feb.	24	Mary D. Lanier	CL
**	Feb.	26	Mary D. Lanier	CL
**	Feb.	26	Edward Spencer	GA
**	Feb.	28	Mary D. Lanier	CL
**	Mar.	2	Gibson Peacock	HC
*	Mar.	3	Mary D. Lanier	CL
*	Mar.	7	Mary D. Lanier	HL
	Mar.	9	Mary D. Lanier	HL
	Mar.	11	Mary D. Lanier	CL
*	Mar.	12	Mary D. Lanier	CL
*	Mar.	14	C. A. Lanier	JT
	Mar.	16	Mary D. Lanier	HL°
*	Mar.	16 [17?]	Mary D. Lanier	HL
	Mar.	18	Mary D. Lanier	HL
*	Mar.	21	Mary D. Lanier	HL
	Mar.	22	L. E. Bleckley	HL
*	Mar.	23	Mary D. Lanier	HL
**	Mar.	24	Gibson Peacock	HC
*	Mar.	24	Mary D. Lanier	CL
*	Mar.	28	Mary D. Lanier	CL
*	Mar.	31	Mary D. Lanier	CL
**	Apr.	1	Edward Spencer	GA
*	Apr.	7	Mary D. Lanier	CL
*	Apr.	10	Mary D. Lanier	CL
	Apr.	12	Mary D. Lanier	HL
	Apr.	12	C. A. Lanier	JT°
**	Apr.	18	Mariquita Peacock	HC
*	Apr.	21	C. A. Lanier	JT
*	Apr.	27	Mary D. Lanier	HL
*	May	11	Mary D. Lanier	CL
*	May	13	Mary D. Lanier	HL
*	May	14	Mary D. Lanier	HL
*	May	19	Mary D. Lanier	HL
*	May	22	Mary D. Lanier	CL
*	May	27	C. A. Lanier	CL
*	May	27	Mary D. Lanier	HL
*[June 4]			R. S. Lanier	JT
*	June	15	Virginia Hankins	HF
*	June	16	Edward Spencer	GA
**	June	16	Gibson Peacock	HG
**	June	17	Charlotte Cushman	EM
*	June	19	Mary D. Lanier	HL
**	June	22	Mary D. Lanier	HL
*	June	23	Mary D. Lanier	CL
	June	23	C. A. Lanier	JT
*	June	24	Mary D. Lanier	HL
*	June	27	Mary D. Lanier	HL
*	June	29	Mary D. Lanier	HL
*	July	3	Virginia Hankins	HF
*	July	10	Gibson Peacock	EM
*	July	13	Mary D. Lanier	HL
*	July	18	Mary D. Lanier	HL
	July	19	Mary D. Lanier	CL
*	July	22	Mary D. Lanier	CL
	July	23	Mary D. Lanier	CL
*	July	26	Mary D. Lanier	HL
*	July	30	Mary D. Lanier	CL
**	July	31	Gibson Peacock	HC
**	July	31	Charlotte Cushman	EM
*	Aug.	3	Mary D. Lanier	CL
**	Aug.	7	Bayard Taylor	CL
**	Aug.	10	Gibson Peacock	HC
	Aug.	10	Mary D. Lanier	HL
**	Aug.	15	Charlotte Cushman	—°
*	Aug.	15	Virginia Hankins	HF

⁹ MS not found; Mims, 189-90.

	Month	Day	Name	Source
	Aug.	15	Mary D. Lanier	HL
**	Aug.	19	Bayard Taylor	CL
*	Aug.	19	R. S. Lanier	CL
	Aug.	19	Mary D. Lanier	CL
*	Aug.	24	Mary D. Lanier	CL
*	Aug.	28 [29?]	Mary D. Lanier	CL
**	Aug.	30	Bayard Taylor	CL
	Aug.	31	Mary D. Lanier	HL
*	Sept.	4	Mary D. Lanier	HL
*	Sept.	5	Mary D. Lanier	CL
	Sept.	7	Mary D. Lanier	HL
	Sept.	8	Mary D. Lanier	CL
*	Sept.	9	Mary D. Lanier	HL
**	Sept.	9	Gibson Peacock	HC
*	Sept.	10	Mary D. Lanier	HL
	Sept.	11	Mary D. Lanier	HL
*	Sept.	12	Mary D. Lanier	CL
	Sept.	12	R. S. Lanier	CL
*	Sept.	15	R. S. Lanier	CL
	Sept.	15	Mary D. Lanier	HL
	Sept.	15	Mary D. Lanier	HL
*	Sept.	17	Sarah C. Bird	HL†
	Sept.	19	Mary D. Lanier	CL
**	Sept.	24	Gibson Peacock	HC
**	Sept.	25	Bayard Taylor	CL
*	Sept.	26	Mary D. Lanier	CL
*	Sept.	26	C. A. Lanier	JT
**	Sept.	29	Bayard Taylor	CL
**	[Oct.	2?]	Bayard Taylor	CL
*	Oct.	2	R. S. Lanier	CL
**	[Oct.	3?]	Bayard Taylor	CL
**	Oct.	4	Mary D. Lanier	HL
**	Oct.	5	E. C. Stedman	YU
	Oct.	9	R. S. Lanier	CL
	Oct.	9	Mary D. Lanier	HL
*	Oct.	12	Mary D. Lanier	CL
	Oct.	14	C. A. Lanier	JT
**	Oct.	15	Bayard Taylor	CL
**	Oct.	16	P. H. Hayne	DU
*	Oct.	16	C. A. Lanier	JT
	Oct.	16	R. S. Lanier	CL
	Oct.	21	Mary D. Lanier	CL
*	Oct.	29	Charlotte Cushman	EM
	Oct.	29	Mary D. Lanier	HL
**	Oct.	29	Bayard Taylor	CL
*	Nov.	2	Mary D. Lanier	CL
	Nov.	3	Mary D. Lanier	HL
**	Nov.	4	Gibson Peacock	HC
*	Nov.	5	H. W. Longfellow	CH
*	Nov.	5	T. B. Aldrich	AM
**	Nov.	10	Gibson Peacock	HC
**	Nov.	24	Bayard Taylor	—10
*	Nov.	29	Mary D. Lanier	CL
*	Dec.	2	Mary D. Lanier	CL
*	Dec.	4	Mary D. Lanier	CL
*	Dec.	5	Mary D. Lanier	CL
	Dec.	7	Mary D. Lanier	CL
	Dec.	7	Mary D. Lanier	CL
*	Dec.	8	Mary D. Lanier	CL
*	Dec.	15	Mary D. Lanier	CL
**	Dec.	16	Gibson Peacock	HC
**	Dec.	17	H. W. Longfellow	CH
*	Dec.	19	Mary D. Lanier	CL
*	Dec.	21	C. A. Lanier	JT
	Dec.	21	Mary D. Lanier	CL
*	Dec.	22	Mary D. Lanier	HL° & CL†
*	Dec.	26	Mary D. Lanier	CL
**	Dec.	29	Bayard Taylor	CL
**	Dec.	30	Charlotte Cushman	—11

1876

	Month	Day	Name	Source
*	Jan.	1	Mary D. Lanier	CL
**	Jan.	4	Bayard Taylor	CL
*	Jan.	4	Dudley Buck	DU†
**	Jan.	8	Mary D. Lanier	CL
**	Jan.	9	Bayard Taylor	CL
**	Jan.	12	Bayard Taylor	CL
**	Jan.	13	Bayard Taylor	CL
**	Jan.	15	Bayard Taylor	CL
**	Jan.	15	Dudley Buck	DU†
	Jan.	15	Mary D. Lanier	CL
**	Jan.	18	Gibson Peacock	HC
*	Jan.	19	Dudley Buck	DU†
	Jan.	20	Mary D. Lanier	HL
*	Jan.	22	Dudley Buck	DU†
*	[Jan.	22]	Mary D. Lanier	CL•
	Jan.	23	Mary D. Lanier	HL
*	Jan.	25	Dudley Buck	DU†
	Jan.	25	Mary D. Lanier	HL
**	Jan.	25	Gibson Peacock	HC
	Jan.	26	Mary D. Lanier	CL
*	Jan.	29	Dudley Buck	DU†
**	Feb.	1	Dudley Buck	DU†
*	Feb.	7	Mary D. Lanier	CL
	Feb.	9	Mary D. Lanier	HL

---

10 MS not found; *Letters*, 133-135.
11 MS not found; facsimile, Mims, opp. 190.

	Date		Recipient	
*	Feb.	11	Dudley Buck	DU†
*	Feb.	12	Mary D. Lanier	CL
**	Feb.	12	Laura N. Boykin	WM
**	Feb.	12	Edward Spencer	GA
*	Feb.	13	Mary D. Lanier	CL
*	Feb.	14	Dudley Buck	DU†
*	Feb.	16	Mary D. Lanier	CL
*	Feb.	21	Mary D. Lanier	CL
*	Feb.	23	Mary D. Lanier	HL
	Feb.	23	C. A. Lanier	JT
*	Feb.	26	R. S. Lanier	CL
*	Feb.	26	Mary D. Lanier	CL
**	Feb.	27	Bayard Taylor	CL
	Feb.	27	Mary D. Lanier	CL
	Mar.	2	Mary D. Lanier	HL
*	Mar.	5	Mary D. Lanier	CL
*	[Mar.	9?]	Mary D. Lanier	HL
*	Mar.	10	Mary D. Lanier	HL
**	Mar.	11	Bayard Taylor	CL
*	Mar.	11	C. A. Lanier	JT
	Mar.	11	Mary D. Lanier	CL
*	Mar.	14	Mary D. Lanier	HL
**	Mar.	18	Mary D. Lanier	CL
	Mar.	20	Mrs. [Carter?] Edmunds	HC
**	Mar.	20	L. E. Bleckley	HL†
**	Mar.	24	Bayard Taylor	CL
*	Mar.	26	Dudley Buck	DU†
*	Mar.	26	Mary D. Lanier	CL
*	Mar.	30	Mary D. Lanier	CL
**	Apr.	1	Bayard Taylor	CL
**	Apr.	4	Bayard Taylor	CL
*	Apr.	4	R. S. Lanier	CL
	Apr.	4	Mary D. Lanier	CL
**	Apr.	8	Bayard Taylor	CL
*	Apr.	9	Mary D. Lanier	CL
**	Apr.	11	Gibson Peacock	HC
*	Apr.	13	R. S. Lanier	CL
*	[Apr.	13?]	Virginia Hankins	HF
**	Apr.	27	Gibson Peacock	HC
*	May	8	Mary D. Lanier	HL
*	May	12	R. S. Lanier	CL
	May	12	Mary D. Lanier	CL
*	May	15	Mary D. Lanier	CL
	May	16	Mary D. Lanier	HL
**	May	18	R. S. Lanier	CL
*	May	18	Mary D. Lanier	HL
*	May	21	Mary D. Lanier	HL
**	May	23	C. A. Lanier	JT
**	May	27	Mary D. Lanier	CL
**	May	28	Mary D. Lanier	CL
*	May	31	Mary D. Lanier	HL
	June	2	R. S. Lanier	CL
	June	4	Mary D. Lanier	HL
*	June	8	Mary D. Lanier	CL
*	June	12	R. S. Lanier	CL
	June	12	C. A. Lanier	JT
	June	15	Mary D. Lanier	CL
*	June	26	R. S. Lanier	CL
*	June	28	Mary D. Lanier	CL
*	June	29	C. A. Lanier	JT
**	July	19	Bayard Taylor	CL
*	July	24	R. S. Lanier	CL
*	[Aug.	7?]	R. S. Lanier	CL
	Aug.	15	A. H. Dooley	AS
**	Aug.	15	Edward Spencer	GA
*	Aug.	22	R. S. Lanier	CL
*	Sept.	3	Mary D. Lanier	HL
	Sept.	6	Mary D. Lanier	HL
*	Sept.	7	Mary D. Lanier	CL
*	Sept.	18	D. C. Gilman	JU
**	Sept.	21	Bayard Taylor	CL
	[Sept.	28?]	D. C. Gilman	JU
	Oct.	1	R. S. Lanier	CL
	Oct.	4	C. A. Lanier	JT
**	Oct.	4	Gibson Peacock	HC
**	Oct.	6	Bayard Taylor	CL
*	Oct.	10	R. S. Lanier	CL
	Oct.	11	Charles Day	CL
	Oct.	17	Gibson Peacock	HC
*	Oct.	22	R. S. Lanier	CL
**	Oct.	22	Bayard Taylor	CL
*	Oct.	22	D. C. Gilman	JU
	Oct.	25	Charles Day	CL
*	Nov.	12	C. A. Lanier	JT°
**	[Nov.	13?]	Bayard Taylor	CL
**	Nov.	24	Bayard Taylor	CL
	Nov.	28	Mary D. Lanier	CL
**	Nov.	29	Bayard Taylor	CL
*	[Nov.	29?]	Mary D. Lanier	CL
**	Dec.	6	Bayard Taylor	CL
*	Dec.	6	Mary D. Lanier	CL
*	Dec.	10	Mary D. Lanier	CL
**	Dec.	20	Gibson Peacock	HC
*	Dec.	27	C. D. Lanier	CL
**	Dec.	27	Gibson Peacock	HC
**	Dec.	31	Gibson Peacock	HC

1877

	Date		Recipient	
*	Jan.	10	Sarah C. Bird	HL†
**	Jan.	11	Bayard Taylor	—¹²

¹² MS not found; *Letters*, 180-181.

Mark	Month	Day	Name	Code
**	Jan.	17	Gibson Peacock	HC
**[	Feb.	4?]	C. N. Hawkins	FH
**	Feb.	7	Bayard Taylor	CL°
**	Feb.	11	Bayard Taylor	CL
**	Feb.	25	Bayard Taylor	CL
**	Mar.	4	Bayard Taylor	CL
*	Mar.	15	R. S. Lanier	BC
**	Mar.	25	Mariquita Peacock	HC
**	Mar.	29	Bayard Taylor	CL
*	Apr.	18	R. S. Lanier	CL
**	Apr.	26	Bayard Taylor	CL
**	Apr.	26	Gibson Peacock	HC
**	May	25	Bayard Taylor	CL
**	May	26	Gibson Peacock	HC
*	June	13	R. S. Lanier	CL
**	June	13	Gibson Peacock	HC
	June	16	R. S. Lanier	CL
*	June	27	Mary D. Lanier	CL
*	June	28	R. S. Lanier	CL
*	July	3	R. S. Lanier	CL
**	July	9	Bayard Taylor	CL
*	July	12	R. S. Lanier	CL
*	July	16	R. S. Lanier	CL
*	July	23	R. S. Lanier	CL
	July	23	C. A. Lanier	JT°
**	July	28	Bayard Taylor	CL
*	Aug.	1	R. S. Lanier	CL
**	Aug.	7	Gibson Peacock	HC
	Aug.	8	R. S. Lanier	CL
*	Aug.	11	Sarah J. Farley	HL
*	Aug.	16	Mary D. Lanier	CL
	Aug.	19	Mary D. Lanier	CL
*	Aug.	25	J. B. Tabb	BU
**	Aug.	26	Bayard Taylor	—13
*	Aug.	26	R. S. Lanier	CL
**	Sept.	8	Gibson Peacock	HC
**	Sept.	11	J. B. Tabb	GB
*	Sept.	11	R. S. Lanier	CL
*	Sept.	20	Mary D. Lanier	HL
	Sept.	21	Mary D. Lanier	HL
*	Sept.	25	Mary D. Lanier	HL
**	Sept.	26	D. C. Gilman	JU
**	Sept.	27	Gibson Peacock	HC
*	Sept.	27	Mary D. Lanier	HL
*	Sept.	28	Mary D. Lanier	CL
	Sept.	29	C. A. Lanier	JT
*	Sept.	30	Mary D. Lanier	HL
	Oct.	1	R. S. Lanier	CL
	Oct.	2	Mary D. Lanier	CL
[	Oct.	3?]	Mary D. Lanier	HL
*	Oct.	4	Mary D. Lanier	CL
* [	Oct.	5?]	D. C. Gilman	HL
*	Oct.	8	Mary D. Lanier	CL
*	Oct.	8	C. A. Lanier	JT
**	Oct.	8	Bayard Taylor	CL
	Oct.	13	Mary D. Lanier	CL
*	Oct.	14	R. S. Lanier	CL
**	Oct.	19	J. B. Tabb	GB
*	Oct.	21	R. S. Lanier	CL
	Oct.	23	Mary D. Lanier	CL
*	Oct.	26	R. S. Lanier	CL
**	Nov.	3	Gibson Peacock	HC
**	Nov.	6	R. M. Johnston	—14
*	Nov.	8	Mary D. Lanier	CL
*	Nov.	9	Mary D. Lanier	CL
*	Nov.	14	R. S. Lanier	JT
[	Nov.	14?]	C. A. Lanier	JT
	Nov.	21	R. S. Lanier	CL
**	Nov.	22	J. B. Tabb	GB
*	Nov.	25	Sarah J. Farley	HL
**	Nov.	27	R. M. Johnston	EP
*	Nov.	30	R. S. Lanier	CL
**	Dec.	3	Gibson Peacock	HC
**	Dec.	6	J. B. Tabb	GB
	Dec.	11	R. S. Lanier	CL
*	Dec.	18	C. A. Lanier	JT
*	Dec.	19	J. B. Tabb	GB
*	Dec.	19	R. S. Lanier	CL
*	Dec.	25	R. S. Lanier	CL
	Dec.	30	C. N. Hawkins	FH

1878

Mark	Month	Day	Name	Code
**	Jan.	6	Bayard Taylor	CL
**	Jan.	6	Gibson Peacock	HC
	Jan.	10	R. S. Lanier	CL
**	Jan.	11	Gibson Peacock	HC
*	Jan.	15	L. E. Bleckley	HL†
*	Jan.	15	C. A. Lanier	JT
**	Jan.	20	J. G. James	UT
**[	Jan.	23?]	Bayard Taylor	CL
*	Jan.	26	R. S. Lanier	CL
**	Jan.	30	J. B. Tabb	GB
**	Jan.	30	Gibson Peacock	HC
*	Jan.	30	R. S. Lanier	CL
**	Feb.	3	Bayard Taylor	CL
**	Feb.	11	Bayard Taylor	CL
	Feb.	19	C. A. Lanier	JT

---

13 MS not found; *Letters*, 200-201.
14 MS not found; Mims, 295-297.

	Date		Recipient	Code
*	Feb.	24	R. S. Lanier	CL
*	Mar.	3	C. A. Lanier	JT
**	Mar.	4	Bayard Taylor	CL
*	Mar.	10	R. S. Lanier	CL
**	Mar.	11	J. B. Tabb	GB
**	Mar.	25	Bayard Taylor	CL
**	Apr.	2	J. B. Tabb	GB
	[Apr.	5?]	[D. C. Gilman?]	JU
*	Apr.	15	L. E. Bleckley	HL†
*	Apr.	21	C. A. Lanier	JT
*	Apr.	28	R. S. Lanier	JT
*	Apr.	28	J. R. Tait	PS
*	Apr.	30	J. F. D. Lanier	JT
	[Apr.–May]		D. C. Gilman	JU
**	May	5	Walt Whitman	—15
**	May	5	J. G. James	UT
**	May	12	J. B. Tabb	GB
*	May	13	R. S. Lanier	CL
**	May	21	R. M. Johnston	PL
*	May	28	R. S. Lanier	JT
*	June	1	Charles Day	CL
*	June	15	R. S. Lanier	CL
*	July	9	R. S. Lanier	CL
*	July	13	R. S. Lanier	CL
*	July	28	D. C. Gilman	JU
	July	28	R. S. Lanier	CL
*	[Aug.	3?]	R. M. Johnston	PL
*	[Aug.	11?]	R. M. Johnston	EM†
*	Aug.	16	R. S. Lanier	CL
*	Aug.	16	Mary D. Lanier	CL
*	Aug.	18	Mary D. Lanier	CL
	Aug.	19	Mary D. Lanier	CL
	Aug.	20	Mary D. Lanier	CL
	Aug.	21	Mary D. Lanier	CL
**	Aug.	24	J. F. Kirk	HC†
*	Aug.	24	R. S. Lanier	CL
	Aug.	26	Mary D. Lanier	HL
	Aug.	30	Mary D. Lanier	CL
*	Sept.	1	Charles Scribner's Sons	CS
*	Sept.	3	Mary D. Lanier	CL
	Sept.	9	Mary D. Lanier	CL
	Sept.	13	Charles Scribner's Sons	CS
*	Sept.	13	R. S. Lanier	CL
*	Sept.	29	D. C. Gilman	JU
*	Oct.	4	R. S. Lanier	CL
	[Oct. ?]		D. C. Gilman	JU
**	Oct.	20	Bayard Taylor	CL
*	Oct.	27	Sarah J. Farley	HL
*	Nov.	1	Edward Spencer	GA
**	Nov.	5	Gibson Peacock	HC
*	Nov.	6	R. S. Lanier	CL
	Nov.	6	C. A. Lanier	JT
*	Nov.	12	C. A. Lanier	JT
	Nov.	21	C. A. Lanier	JT
*	Nov.	25	D. C. Gilman	JU
	Nov.	27	Mrs. C. N. Hawkins	JM
*	Nov.	28	Mary D. Lanier	CL
	Dec.	14	C. A. Lanier	JT
*	Dec.	17	J. B. Scribner	CS
	[Dec.	18?]	D. C. Gilman	JU
	Dec.	21	C. A. Lanier	JT
*	Dec.	21	R. S. Lanier	JT
**	Dec.	21	Gibson Peacock	HC
*	Dec.	22	Charles Scribner's Sons	CS
*	Dec.	29	R. S. Lanier	CL

1879

	Date		Recipient	Code
*	Jan.	1	C. A. Lanier	JT°
	Jan.	2	C. A. Lanier	JT
	Jan.	2	N. H. Morrison	PI
*	[Jan.	5]	Edward Spencer	GA
*	Jan.	8	C. A. Lanier	JT
**	Jan.	8	H. W. Longfellow	CH
	Jan.	8	R. S. Lanier	CL
	Jan.	13	R. S. Lanier	CL
*	Feb.	1	R. S. Lanier	CL
	Feb.	2	N. H. Morrison	PI
*	Feb.	5	R. S. Lanier	CL
*	Feb.	5	D. C. Gilman	JU
*	Feb.	17	R. S. Lanier	CL
*	Feb.	17	Charles Scribner	CS
	Mar.	5	R. S. Lanier	CL
	Mar.	8	Charles Scribner	CS
*	Mar.	10	R. S. Lanier	CL
*	Mar.	13	R. S. Lanier	CL
	[Spring?]		D. C. Gilman	JU
*	Apr.	7	C. A. Lanier	CL
**	Apr.	12	J. G. James	UT
*	Apr.	29	C. A. Lanier	JT
	Apr.	29	R. S. Lanier	CL
*	May	3	Charles Scribner	CS
*	May	6	R. S. Lanier	CL
*	May	7	R. S. Lanier	CL
*	May	16	R. S. Lanier	CL

15 MS not found; facsimile, Traubel, opp. 208.

*[May	16]	Mary D. Lanier	CL			**1880**		
May	17	R. S. Lanier	CL	*	[Jan.	9?]	Frances L.	
* May	22	Charles Scribner	CS				Turnbull	ET
* May	27	C. A. Lanier	JT	*	[Jan.	17?]	Lawrence Turnbull	ET
May	30	R. S. Lanier	CL	*	Jan.	22	Charles Scribner	CS
* June	4	Mary D. Lanier	CL	*	Jan.	25	C. A. Lanier	JT
*[June	4?]	H. W. Long-			Jan.	25	R. S. Lanier	CL
		fellow	CH	*	Jan.	27	R. S. Lanier	CL
** June	8	C. A. Lanier	JT		Jan.		[Charles Talia-	
[June	12?]	R. M. Johnston	PL				ferro?]	CL°
* June	13	Charles Scribner	CS		Feb.	10	[Lippincott &	
June	15	C. A. Lanier	JT				Co.?]	PH
** June	15	J. G. James	UT	*[Feb.]		17	D. C. Gilman	JU
* June	17	E. C. Stedman	YU	*	Feb.	25	R. S. Lanier	CL
* June	25	R. S. Lanier	CL		Feb.	25	Rossiter Johnson	JM
* June	25	J. F. Kirk	EM°	*	Mar.	1	R. S. Lanier	CL
June	30	D. C. Gilman	JU		Mar.	11	R. S. Lanier	CL
** July	13	D. C. Gilman	JU	*	Mar. 16 [17?]		D. C. Gilman	JU
* July	16	R. S. Lanier	CL		Mar.	18	A. B. Turnure	JM
* July	22	R. S. Lanier	CL	*	Mar.	26	Charles Scribner	CS
* July	22	C. A. Lanier	JT	*	Mar.	26	R. S. Lanier	CL
* July	28	J. R. Tait	PS		Mar.	28	Rossiter Johnson	JM
* Aug.	5	J. R. Tait	PS		Mar.	30	Charles Scribner	CS
* Aug.	25	R. S. Lanier	CL	**	Apr.	5	Virginia Hankins	HF
** Sept.	15	J. G. James	UT		Apr.	5	R. S. Lanier	CL
* Sept.	22	D. C. Gilman	JU		Apr.	5	C. A. Lanier	JT°
* Sept.	25	C. A. Lanier	JT°	*	Apr.	6	Mary D. Lanier	HL
Sept.	26	R. S. Lanier	CL		Apr.	7	Mary D. Lanier	CL
Oct.	4	C. A. Lanier	JT	*	Apr.	21	Charles Scribner	CS
* Oct.	9	C. A. Lanier	JT	*	Apr.	22	R. S. Lanier	CL
Oct.	16	C. A. Lanier	JT°	*	May	1	R. S. Lanier	CL
** Oct.	16	J. G. James	UT	*	May	1	C. A. Lanier	JT
* Oct.	29	R. S. Lanier	CL		May	3	C. A. Lanier	JT
Nov.	1	R. S. Lanier	CL		May	5	Charles Scribner	CS
* Nov.	12	R. S. Lanier	CL	*	May	6	Charles Scribner	CS
* Nov.	15	Charles Scribner	CS	*	May	11	Charles Scribner	CS
* Nov.	16	R. S. Lanier	CL	**	May	14	E. C. Stedman	CU†
Nov.	23	R. S. Lanier	CL		May	15	R. S. Lanier	CL
* Nov.	23	*Scribner's Monthly*	JM	*	May	16	Charles Scribner	CS
* Dec.	4	Charles Scribner	CS	*	May	18	Charles Scribner	CS
* Dec.	6	Charles Scribner	CS	*	May	18	T. R. Lounsbury	YU
* Dec.	10	Charles Scribner	CS	*	May	20	Charles Scribner	CS
[Dec.	14?]	D. C. Gilman	JU		May	20	C. A. Lanier	JT
** Dec.	17	D. C. Gilman	JU		May	21	R. S. Lanier	CL
Dec.	17	R. S. Lanier	CL		[May	25?]	Lawrence Turnbull	ET
* Dec.	21	C. A. Lanier	JT	*	May	30	Charles Scribner	CS
* Dec.	21	Charles Scribner	CS	**	May	30	Annie A. Fields	HA
* Dec.	29	Charles Scribner	CS	**	June	1	Gibson Peacock	HC
					June	12	R. S. Lanier	CL

	Date	Recipient	
**	[June 15]	J. F. Kirk	—16
	June 15	Charles Scribner	CS
*	June 19	R. S. Lanier	CL
	[June 24?]	Mary D. Lanier	CL
*	June 26	Charles Scribner	CS
*	June 29	R. S. Lanier	CL
*	[July 3?]	Ephraim Keyser	JU
*	July 15	Charles Scribner	CS
*	July 17	C. A. Lanier	JT†
*	July 17	D. Appleton & Co.	CL
**	July 19	W. S. Pratt	HG
	July 29	Charles Scribner's Sons	CS
**	July 31	F. F. Browne	JU
	Aug. 3	O. W. Holmes	LC
*	Aug 10	R. S. Lanier	CL
*	Aug. 11	Lawrence Turnbull	ET
*	Aug. 13	Charles Scribner	CS
*	Aug. 14	R. S. Lanier	CL
	Aug. 14	Gertrude L. Gibson	JT
	[Aug. 14]	Sarah J. Farley	HL
*	Aug. 15	Charles D. Lanier	CL
	Aug. 18	Sarah C. Bird	HL†
**	Aug. 18	Isabel L. Dobbin	HL†
*	Aug. 19	Epes Sargent	JM
*	Aug. 26	Epes Sargent	JM
*	Aug. 27	H. W. Lanier	HL†
**	Aug. 28	F. F. Browne	JU
**	Aug. 28	R. M. Johnston	—17
	Aug. 28	R. S. Lanier	CL
*	Sept. 2	Mary D. Lanier	CL
	Sept. 3	Mary D. Lanier	CL
	Sept. 5	E. L. Burlingame	JU
**	Sept. 5	W. S. Pratt	HG
*	Sept. 7	Ephraim Keyser	JU
*	Sept. 10	Mary D. Lanier	CL
*	Sept. 12	Mary D. Lanier	CL
*	Sept. 14	Mary D. Lanier	CL
*	Sept. 15	Mary D. Lanier	CL
*	Sept. 16	Mary D. Lanier	HL
*	Sept. 17	Mary D. Lanier	CL
	Sept. 19	Mary D. Lanier	CL
*	Sept. 20	Mary D. Lanier	CL
*	[Sept. 22]	Mary D. Lanier	CL
**	Sept. 24	C. A. Lanier	JT
*	Sept. 24	Mary D. Lanier	CL
*	Sept. 26	Mary D. Lanier	CL
	Sept. 27	Charles Scribner's Sons	CS
*	Sept. 28	D. C. Gilman	JU
*	Sept. 29	Mary D. Lanier	CL
*	Sept. 30	Mary D. Lanier	CL
	Oct. 2	Mary D. Lanier	CL
*	Oct. 4	Mary D. Lanier	CL
	Oct. 5	Mary D. Lanier	CL
*	Oct. 5	Ephraim Keyser	JU
*	Oct. 29	Charles Scribner	CS
*	Oct. 30	C. A. Lanier	JT
	Oct. 30	F. F. Browne	JU
*	[Oct. 30?]	D. C. Gilman	JU
	Nov. 3	S. M. Maxwell	HL°
*	Nov. 5	D. C. Gilman	JU
**	Nov. 6	D. C. Gilman	JU
	Nov. 7	O. W. Holmes	LC
	Nov. 8	D. C. Gilman	JU
*	Nov. 12	Sidney Lanier, Jr.	SL
*	Nov. 12	A publisher	CL
	Nov. 12	Nicholas Murray	JU
**	Nov. 12	Charles Scribner	CS
**	Nov. 14	Editors, St. Nicholas	JM
*	[Nov. 15?]	D. C. Gilman	JU
*	Nov. 17	Charles Scribner	CS
	Nov. 18	G. E. Dorsey	JU
**	Nov. 19	P. H. Hayne	DU
	[Nov. 22]	G. E. Dorsey	JU
	Dec. 2	[Nicholas Murray?]	JU
*	Dec. 6	W. H. Ward	HA
	Dec. 7	G. E. Dorsey	JU
	[Dec. 9]	Sarah J. Farley	HL
*	Dec. 10	[Nicholas Murray?]	JU
	Dec. 11	C. J. Meyer	JU
*	Dec. 13	F. F. Browne	JU
	Dec. 15	Sarah J. Farley	HL
*	Dec. 18	Frances L. Turnbull	ET
*	Dec. 31	Sarah J. Farley	HL

1881

	Date	Recipient	
*	Jan. 7	Charles Scribner	CS
*	Jan. 7	D. C. Gilman	JU

16 MS not found; Mims, 316-317.
17 MS not found; Mims, 322-325.

* Jan.	19	D. C. Gilman	HL†
* Jan.	28	Sarah J. Farley	HL
Feb.	12	[——— ?]	JU
** Feb.	12	Sarah J. Farley	JT
*[Feb.	21?]	Lawrence Turnbull	ET
*[Feb.–Mar.?]		Sarah C. Bird	HL†
* Mar.	7	C. A. Lanier	JT
* Mar.	15	Lawrence Turnbull	CL
** Mar.	19	J. B. Tabb	GB
*[Mar.	19?]	C. A. Lanier	JT
* Apr.	8	C. A. Lanier	JT
* Apr.	15	Sarah J. Farley	HL
[Apr.	17?]	Lawrence Turnbull	ET
* Apr.	19	Charles Scribner	CS

* Apr.	26	Mary D. Lanier	CL
* May	5	C. A. Lanier	JT
* May	21	Mary D. Lanier	HL
** June	5	D. C. Gilman	JU
* June	14	Charles Scribner's Sons	CS
* June	17	E. L. Burlingame	CS
* June	24	E. L. Burlingame	CS
* July	1	D. C. Gilman	JU
* July	5	Lawrence Turnbull	ET
* July	5	R. M. Johnston	PL
* July	20	C. D. Lanier	CL
* July	26	Charles Scribner	CS
* Aug.	15	R. S. Lanier	JT
* Sept.	3	Charles Scribner	CS

B. LETTERS TO LANIER [1]

Adams, C. B.: Oct. 9, 1858 (JT)
Aldrich, T. B.: Nov. 8, 1875 (CL)
Armstrong, J. S.: Feb. 22, 1870 (CL)
Badger, A. G.: Dec. 8, 1874 (CL)
Ballini, Vittaria: May 16, 1866 (CL)
Barnett, Col.: Sept. 13, 1873 (CL)
Bass, W. C.: Mar. 5, 1880 (CL)
Beaumont, S.: Oct. 20, 1880 (CL)
Bleckley, L. E.: Oct. 14,[2] Nov. 27, 1874; Jan. 17, 1875; Jan. 18, 1878 (CL)
Bowen, Mary: Feb. 9, 1877 (CL)
Boykin, Laura W.: *ante* Apr. 26, 1870 (CL)
Boynton, Henry: Nov. 22, 1880 (CL)
Brady, Sarita M.: Aug. 2, 1877 (CL)
Brainerd, Erastus: Dec. 2, 1879 (CL)
Brown, J. E.: May 28, 1873 (CL)
Browne, F. F.: Nov. 18, Dec. 9, 1880 (CL)
Browne, W. H.: Mar. 29,[3] Dec. 21, 1870; Jan. 10, Feb. 17, Mar. 15, *Apr. 20,
    May 26, Aug. 22, Dec. 18, Dec. 30, 1871; Feb. 26, Dec. 11, 1872; June
    20, 1873; Aug. 29, Oct. 23, Nov. 9, Nov. 30, 1874; Nov. 29, Dec. 11,
    Dec. 19, Dec. 27, ——, [1878]; ——, ——, 1880; ——, 188–; Aug. 8,
    1881 (CL)
Browne, Violet: Jan. 10, Feb. 14, 1880 (CL)
Bryant, W. C.: Jan. 24, 1878 (CL)

---

[1] This list includes all letters to Lanier known to the present editors. They
are arranged alphabetically according to correspondents and chronologically
within the divisions. Square brackets indicate that the month or day or both,
are conjectural; a bracketed query indicates that the year is conjectural. Following the date, in parentheses, are the initials of the owners of the MSS. A
symbol of ownership should always be read as referring to all letters preceding
it, after the last such symbol. If a sequence of letters belongs entirely to one
owner, the symbol is given only after the last.
    Some of these letters to Lanier have been published in the following works,
cited in the notes by a key word: Morgan Callaway, Jr., *Select Poems of Sidney
Lanier* (New York, 1895); Fabian Franklin, *Life of Daniel Coit Gilman* (New
York, 1910); Laura Stedman and G. M. Gould, *Life and Letters of Edmund
Clarence Stedman* (New York, 1910); *Letters of Sidney Lanier* (New York,
1899).
    Letters from Bayard Taylor to Sidney Lanier were originally published in
part in *Life and Letters of Bayard Taylor* (Boston, 1884), edited by Marie
Hansen-Taylor and Horace E. Scudder. A more complete selection of Taylor's
letters was published in "Letters Between Two Poets," by Henry Wysham
Lanier, *Atlantic Monthly*, LXXXIII, 791-807 (June, 1899); LXXXIV, 127-141
(July, 1899). The text of this article, with additional letters, was reprinted
in the volume of *Letters of Sidney Lanier*, cited above. This latter gives the
best and most complete text at present available of Taylor's letters to Lanier.
    [2] Published in part, Callaway, 61.
    [3] Signed: " Turnbull & Murdoch, per B."

Buck, Dudley: Jan. 5, Jan. 11 [21?], Jan. 17, Jan. 19, Jan. 27, Jan. [30?],
Jan. 31, Feb. 2, Feb. 12, Mar. 14, Apr. 1, Apr. 4 (copy),[4] Apr. 12, May
29, Aug. 21, Nov. 7, 1876; Jan. 8, Jan. 29, 1877 (CL)
Bunce, O. B.: Mar. 15, 1878 (CL)
Burlingame, E. L. (see also Charles Scribner's Sons): Sept. 24, 1879; June 20,
June 29, Sept. 2, 1881 (CL)
Burroughs, Mrs. W. B. (see Hazlehurst, Lilla)
Butts, A. G.: Nov. 13, 1880 (CL)
Butts, A. K.: Feb. 15, 1879 (CL)[5]
Calhoun, Mrs.: June 17, [1878?] (CL)
Calvert, G. H.: Oct. 23, 1875; Mar. 22, Oct. 28, Nov. 26, 1879; May 29,
Oct. 13, Nov. 21, 1880 (CL)
Campbell, C. E.: Nov. 26, 1867 (CL)
Clay, Virginia T.: Aug. 21, 1867, Aug. 4, 1870 (CL)
Cluskey, Kate: Jan. 30, 1880 (CL)
Cozby, J. S.: Dec. 6, 1860 (JT); Mar. 20, 1872 (CL)
Cushman, Charlotte: Jan. 3, June 23, Aug. 3, Oct. 21, Dec. 12, 1875; Jan. 11,
Feb. 3-4, Feb. 6, 1876 (CL)
Cushman, E. C.: July 2, 1876 (CL)
Daves, E. G.: Oct. 6, [1879?] (CL)
Day, Charles: Aug. 15, 1868; July 3-4, July 10-11, 1870 (CL)
Day, H. C.: Sept. 27, Nov. 27, Dec. 3, Dec. 7, Dec. 22, 1867; May 10, June 1,
July 10, 1868; May 5, May 10-13, Sept. 16, 1869; July 19, 1870; June 29,
July 3, Aug. 1, Oct. 26, Nov. 19, Nov. 23, Dec. 7-10, 1873; Jan. 24,
Feb. 23, Sept. 19, 1875 (CL)
Day, Mary (see Lanier, Mary D.)
DeMotte, J. B.: May 22, 1880 (HL)
Dobbin, Isabel L.: Mar. 31, 1878; May 12, [1878?]; Aug. 20, [1880?] (CL)
Dodge, Mary M. (see also *St. Nicholas Magazine*): Sept. 17, Oct. 6, 1880 (CL)
Dooley, A. H.: July 10, 1876 (CL)
Dorsey, G. E.: Nov. 11, Nov. 13, Nov. 24, Dec. 7, 1880 (CL)
Dunn, W. M.: July 24, 1877 (CL)
Dunwoody, W. E.: Dec. 16, 1873 (CL)
Dutcher, Salem: *Jan. 5, *Mar. 13, Mar. 15-16, Mar. 20, Mar. 27, Apr. 1 [?],
Apr. 9, May 4, May 17, June 2, June 5, June 17, July 2, July 12, July 30,
Aug. 28, Nov. 4, Dec. 26, 1867 (CL); Jan.. 5, 1868 (JT): Jan. 8, [Jan.?]
Jan. 22, Jan. 27, Mar. 10, July 19, Oct. 8, 1868; Mar. 1, May 6, May 16,
[May 24?], July 1, [July 21?], Sept. 24, 1869; Mar. 22, May 24, July 24,
1870: Jan. 15, Apr. 23, Nov. 7, 1871; Apr. 23, 1873; Oct. 30, 1874;
June 11, 1875 (CL)
Edmonds, W. D.: Apr. 12, 1879 (CL)
Eve, Philoclea [?] E.: May 31, [1876?] (CL)
Farley, Sarah J.: Sept. 8, Sept. 15, Sept. 23, Oct. 9, 1880; Feb. 23, Apr. 19,
1881 (CL)
Field, S. M.: ——, 188– (telegram) (CL)
Fields, Annie A.: Mar. 9, June 10, 1880 (CL)
Fletcher, Alice C.: Nov. 14, 1873 [6] (CL)
Foxcroft, F.: July 28, 1877 (CL)

---

[4] Published, *Letters*, 165-166, note 1.
[5] Signed: " E., The Evolution."
[6] Published, *Letters*, 79-80, note 1.

Francis, D. G.: Nov. 20, 1880 (CL)
Fraser, Daniel: July 11, 1866 (JT)
Furness, H. H.: Oct. 20, 1878 (CL)
Garrett, F. M.: Aug. 26, 1881 (CL)
Gibson, Mrs. J. C. (see Lanier, Gertrude)
Gilder, R. W. (see also *Scribner's Monthly*): July 2, 1875; Sept. 10, 1878 (CL)
Gilman, D. C.: Sept. 21, Oct. 9, 1876 (CL); Feb. 4,[7] July 3 (CL), July 16,[8]
    1879; Nov. 15, 1880;[9] June 15, 1881 (CL)
Graffenreid, de, M. Clare: Dec. 8, 1875; Jan. 11, Jan. 26, May 29, July 3,
    1876 (CL)
Hamerik, Asger: Oct. 23, 1875; Nov. 1, Dec. 2, 1876; [Nov. 12?], 1877 (CL)
Hankins, Virginia W.: *[May ?], 1864;[10] Oct. 24, 1867 (JT); Jan. 27, Dec.
    10, 1868; Feb. 17, Mar. [23], Apr. [13?], May [13] (CL), *May 22
    (HL), May 28 [?], Nov., 1869; Jan. [2], Jan. 19, Mar. [?], [June 20?],
    [Sept. 15?], [Dec. ?], 1870; Jan. 9-12, Apr. 15, June 28, Aug. 6, Nov.
    17, *Dec. 13, 1871; Jan. 12, Apr. 6, July 10, Oct. 13, 1872; May 3, June
    2-4 [Sept. 15], [Sept. 19], Oct. 5-13, Nov. 1, Dec. 31, 1873; Jan. 30, Feb.
    27, Aug. 5, Sept. 22 (CL), Oct. 10 (JT), 1875; *Aug. 24, 1881 (CL)
Harris, J. C.: June 29, 1868 (CL)
Hawkins, C. N. (and wife): Feb. 4, 1877 (CL)
Hawley, J. R.: Dec. 31, 1875; May 7, 1876 (CL)
Hayne, P. H.: *Sept. 7, Dec. 5, 1868; Jan. 14, Feb. 23, *Oct. 30, Dec. 11,
    1869; Mar. 7, Mar. 10, Mar. 12, May 12, July 16, 1870; Jan. 10, Feb. 25,
    Mar. 6, Mar. 23, May 6, May 24, Aug. 30, Aug. 31, Sept. 8, Sept. 27,
    Oct. 16, Oct. 24, 1871; Feb. 15, Feb. 25, Mar. 6, 1872; Feb. 27, Mar. 27,
    Mar. 29; May 2, May 31, 1873; Mar. 21, June 1, July 30, Oct. 10, 1874;
    Jan. 19, Jan. 21, Apr. 7, Oct. 23, 1875 (CL); June 13 (HL), June 29,
    July 3, 1876; Mar. 16, July 19, July 25, 1877; Jan. 5, 1878; Oct. 19,
    1880 (CL)
Hazlehurst, Lilla (later Mrs. W. B. Burroughs): Sept. 19, 1868; [post]
    1868 (CL)
Heckel, G. B.: July 22, 1876 (CL)
Herrick, Sophie B.: [Aug. ?, 1878] (CL)
Herring, Elbert: Jan. 27, 1868 (CL)
Hilliard, H. W.: Aug. 12, 1875 (CL)
Hoge, E. F.: Oct. 8, 1874 (CL)
Holland, J. G. (see also *Scribner's Monthly*): Oct. 18, 1876 (CL)
Holmes, O. W.: *July 24, *Aug. 11, Aug. 20, 1880 (CL)
Hopkins, G. T.: July 4, 1879 (CL)
Hopkins, E. B.: July 8, 1879 (CL)
Hunt, Mrs. William: [1876?] (CL)
Hurd & Houghton: July 20, July 24, July 29, Aug. 7, Aug. 13, Aug. 29, Sept.
    2, Nov. 4, Dec. 10, 1867; Jan. 14, Jan. 29,[11] Feb. 4, Feb. 27, June 3,
    1868; Apr. 10, Aug. 10, 1869 (CL)
Houghton, H. O., & Co.: Apr. 10, 1875 (CL)

---

[7] MS not found; published in part, Franklin, 241.
[8] MS not found; published in part, Franklin, 241-243.
[9] MS not found; published in part, Franklin, 243-244.
[10] MS not found; an extract from Miss Hankins' letter was copied by Lanier
in the *Ledger* (HL) and from that source published, Clarke, 17.
[11] Signed by A. G. Houghton.

Hyman, F. M.: Aug. 14, 1865 (CL)
Innes & Co.: July 12, 1879 (CL)
Johnston, R. M.: May 9, 1878 (CL)
Johnson, Reverdy, Jr.: Feb. 27, [1875] (CL)
Keyser, Ephraim: [Oct. ?] 1880 (CL)
King, M. E. & A. M.: Oct. 15, 1888 (CL)
James, J. G.: Dec. 6, 1877; Apr. 26, May 14, 1878; May 7, 1879 (CL)
Kirk, J. F. (see also *Lippincott's Magazine*): *Jan. 16, Mar. 20, 1875; June
    16, 1879 (CL)
Lamar, Augusta (later Mrs. J. M. Ogden): Nov. 27, 1861; June 21, 1864.
Lamar, L. Q. C.: Mar. 1, 1878 (HL)
Lanier, A. B.: Mar. 4, 1880 (CL)
Lanier, Charles: May 17, 1870; Apr. 26, Aug. 1, 1876; Aug. 23, Dec. 12,
    1879; Mar. 18, 1881 (CL)
Lanier, C. D. (son): Dec. 14, 1879 (JT); Sept. 4, 1881 (CL)
Lanier, C. A.: May 3, 1858 (JT); Sept. 6 (CL), Dec. 3, 1865 (JT); Mar. 22,
    Mar. 24, Apr. 16, Apr. 23, May 22, July 10, Sept. 8, Nov. 30, Dec. 3,
    1867; Jan. 2, Jan. 21, Jan. 28, May 20, June 2, Aug. 9, Aug. 15, Sept. 3,
    Sept. 6, Sept. 16, Nov. 1, Dec. 10, 1868; June 25, July 11, Aug. 29 (CL),
    Sept. 12, 1869 (JT); Jan. 4, Feb. 27, Aug. 17, 1870; Jan. 11, Apr. 20,
    May 20, July 9, Aug. 27, Oct. 3, 1871; May 22, 1873; May 13, Aug. 28,
    1874; Jan. 28, Apr. 15, May 31, Aug. 22, Dec. 28, 1875; May 20, Oct.
    20, 1876; Dec. 16, 1878; Mar. 15, 1879; Nov. 28, 1880; Aug. 21, 1881
Lanier, Gertrude (married E. B. Shannon May 21, 1867; married J. C. Gibson
    Jan. 14, 1873): [Mar. 24?], July 14, Oct. 19, 1861; Feb. 26, Mar. 18,
    June 12, July 26, Nov. 4, 1864; July 26, [Aug. 7?], Aug. 21, [Sept. 6?],
    1865; Jan. 27, Jan. 29, July 25, Aug. 14, Aug. 21 [?], Sept. 8, Oct. 30,
    Oct. 30, Nov. 21, Dec. 12, Dec. 25, 1866; Jan. 12, Feb. 5 (JT), June 10,
    Aug. 29, Sept. 9-10, 1867; Jan. [28], 1868; Feb. 4, 1871 (CL)
Lanier H. W.: Aug. 16 (JT), Sept. 4, 1880; Sept. 3, 1881 (CL)
Lanier, J. F. D.: Oct. 14, 1868 (CL); Feb. 4, 1869 (CL)
Lanier, Mary A.: *May 13, 1857 (JT); *May 20, 1858; Apr. 24, 1860 (CL);
    Dec. 29, 1861; Mar. 9, 1862 (JT)
Lanier, Mary Day: *Apr. 3, 1864; May 15, [June 29?], [July?], [July?],
    [July?], Aug. 7, *Nov. 1, 1865; *Aug. 5, Sept. 10-12, Oct. 8-12, *Oct. 11,
    Oct. 16, Oct. 29, Nov. 2-4, Nov. 13, Nov. 16, Nov. 20, Nov. 28-Dec. 1, Dec.
    8, Dec. 9, Dec. 15, Dec. 17-21, Dec. 25, 1866; Jan. 2, Jan. 16-18, Jan. 20,
    Feb. 2-3, [Feb ?], [Feb. 21?], Feb. 24-26, Mar. 1 (JT), *June 16, Aug. 12,
    Sept. 12, Sept. 16, Sept. 23, Sept. 25, Oct. 4, Oct. 30°, Nov. 1, Nov. 21, Nov.
    25, Nov. 27, Dec. 9, 1867; Apr. 24, Apr. 30, May 7, May 9, May 13, May 15,
    May 21, Nov. 5, 1869; Feb. 18, Feb. 25, Mar. 6, [Mar?], July 30, Aug.
    19, [Aug. 23]°, Aug. 26, Aug. 30, Sept. 5, [Sept. 10-13]°, [Sept. ?]°
    Sept. 25, Sept. 26, Oct. 1, 1870; Mar. 6, Mar. 9, Mar. 16, June [7], June
    8, June 13, June 15, Sept. 20, Sept. 26, Sept. 30, Oct. 3, Oct. 4, Oct. 5,
    Oct. 13-14, Oct. 17-18, Oct. 23, Oct. 26-28, Nov. 1, Nov. 8, Nov. 8, 1871;
    July 12, July 15, July 16, July 18, July 22°, July 23, July [24]°, Oct. 15,
    Oct. 17, Oct. 19, Oct. 21, Oct. 23, Oct. 24, Nov. 14, Nov. 16, Nov. 24,
    Nov. 28, Dec. 4, Dec. 8-9, Dec. 11, Dec. 13, Dec. 16, Dec. 24-28, Dec.
    25, Dec. 30, Dec. 31, 1872; Jan. 1, Jan. 3-5°, Jan. 5, Jan. 14-22, Jan. 20-
    22, Feb. 2, Feb. 3, Feb. 12, Feb. 22, Feb. 24, Feb. 27, Sept. 16, Sept. 22,
    Sept. 24, Sept. 27, Sept. 29, Oct. 3, Oct. 4, Oct. 7, Oct. 13, Oct. 15, Oct.
    18, Oct. 21, Oct. 25, Oct. 31, Nov. 8, Nov. 15, Nov. 17, Nov. 30, Dec. 5,

Dec. 10, Dec. 12, Dec. 19, Dec. 22, Dec. 25, (CL), Dec. 28 1873 (HL);
Jan. 4, Jan. 16, Jan. 20°, Jan. 22, Jan. 26, Jan. 30, Feb. 2, Feb. 5, Feb.
13, Feb. 19-20, Feb. 22, Feb. 27, Mar. 8, Mar. 9, Mar. 22, Mar. 23, Mar.
27, Mar. 30, Apr. 1, Apr. 29, June 3, June 12, June 14, June 15, June 18,
Aug. 21, Aug. 26, Aug. 28, Sept. 1, Sept. 2, Sept. 4, Sept. 5, Sept. 7,
Sept. 8, Sept. 9, Sept. 12, Sept. 17, Sept. 18, Sept. 19, Sept. 21, Sept. 22,
Sept. 24, Sept. 26, Sept. 30, Oct. 2, Oct. 3, Oct. 7, Oct. 12, Oct. 13, Oct.
15, Oct. 19, Oct. 19, Oct. 21, Oct. 24, Oct. 27, Oct. 28, Nov. 2, Nov. 4,
Nov. 6, Nov. 10, Nov. 10, Dec. 1, Dec. 2, Dec. 3, Dec. 4, Dec. 24, Dec.
27, Dec. 31, 1874; Jan. 4, Jan. 6, Jan. 10, Jan. 12, Jan. 15, Jan. 20, Jan.
22, Jan. 25, Jan. 27, Jan. 29, Feb. 3, Feb. 9, Feb. 14, Feb. 16, Feb. 19,
Mar. 1, Mar. 5, Mar. 8, [Mar. 9], Mar. 10, Mar. 14, Mar. 23, Mar. 27,
Apr. 14, Apr. 23, Apr. 25, May 16, May 19, May 21, May 23, May 26,
May 28, June 20, June 22, June 24, June 25, June 27, June 30, July
14, July 15, July 18, July 25, July 27, Aug. 11, Aug. 13, Aug. 21,
Aug. 25, Sept. 2, Sept. 10, Sept. 11, Sept. 14, Sept. 19, Sept. 24, Sept. 24,
Sept. 28, Oct. 1, Oct. [5?], Oct. 10, Oct. 15, Oct. 26, Oct. 28 (CL), Oct.
31 (HL), Nov. 2, Nov. 5, Dec. 3, Dec. 5, Dec. 12, Dec. 12, Dec. 17, Dec.
19, Dec. 22, Dec. 27, 1875; Jan. 3, Jan. 12, Jan. 19, Jan. 26, Jan. 30,
Feb. 3, Feb. 5, Feb. 11, Feb. 15°, Feb. 16, Feb. 19, Feb. 26, Mar. 1, Mar.
5, Mar 5 [6?], Mar. 8, Mar. 14, Mar. 20, Mar. 26, Mar. 29, Apr. 2, Apr.
5, [May 7?], May 10, May 12, May 12, May 14, May 15, May 16, May 29,
June 6, June 11, June 13, Nov. 19, 1876; Aug. 16, Sept. 28, 1877 (CL)
Lanier, R. S.: *May 20, 1858; *Feb. 21 (CL), *[Apr. 21?] (JT), *May 16
(CL), *Sept. 23, Dec. 28, 1861; Apr. 25, *May 7, June 25, 1863; July 25,
Aug. 6, 1864; [July?], Nov. 7, Nov. 15, Nov. 29, Dec. 13, 1865; Jan. 10,
Jan. 16, *Apr. 11, June 6, June —, July 4, Aug. 15, (JT), Dec. 2, 1866
(EM); Jan. 29 (CL), Feb. 17, Apr. 4 (JT), Apr. 17, Apr. 27, May 29
(CL), Sept. 24, 1867 (JT); Jan. 9, Jan. 26, Jan. 29, May 23, May 25,
June 9, 1868; Apr. 24, Apr. 29, May 7, May 15, June 4, 1869; May
28 [?], July 4, July 13, July 16, [Aug. 1?], *Aug. 26 [?], 1870; Aug. 19,
1872; Jan. 30, July 1, Sept. 1, Sept. 3, 1873; Mar. 17, Aug. 15, Aug. 21,
1875; Nov. 11, Nov. 19, Nov. 30, 1880.
Lanier, Sidney, Jr.: Jan. 30, 1876 [12] (CL); Aug. 16, 1880 (JT); Sept. 3,
1881 (CL)
Lanier, Sterling: Jan. 26, 1868 (CL)
Lathrop, G. P.: Apr. 20, 1878 (CL)
LeConte, Joseph: Nov. 6, 1880 (CL)
Lippincott, J. B. & Co.: [Jan.], Apr. 4, 1875; Feb. 11, 1880; May 14, 1881.
Lippincott's Magazine(see also Kirk, J. F.): Sept. 12, 1873; Dec. 6, 1875;
Sept. 26, 1877 (CL)
Little, George: Mar. 8, 1869 (CL)
Locke, M. Florence: Sept. 1, [1876?] (CL)
Lodeman, A.: Nov. 13, 1880 (CL)
Longfellow, H. W.: Nov. 6, 1875; Jan. 3, June 5, 1879; May 16, 1880 (CL)
Lounsbury, T. R.: May 29, 1880 (CL)
Lowell, J. R.: Nov. 6, 1875 (CL)
MacDonald, Ronald: Apr. 9, 1874 (CL)
Macmurdo, J. R.: July 6, 1881 (CL)
McCoy, J. W.: Dec. 8, 1879; Dec. 15, 1880 (CL)
Mason, Percy: Dec. 20, 1878 (CL)

---

[12] Written by Mary Day Lanier.

Seaton, Josephine: [Mar. 11?], [Mar. 17?], [1874]; [Jan. 22?], [Feb. 16?],
[Mar. 27-28], Nov., 1875: [Jan. 9?, 1876]; Feb. 28, [1879?], Apr. 3,
1880 (CL)
Shannon, Mrs. E. B. (see Lanier, Gertrude)
Shearer, Dr. Thomas: Sept. 6, 1881 (CL)
Singleton, Mrs. M. C.: Sept. 27, 1879 (CL)
Smith, F. E., & Co.: Dec. 30, 1868 (CL)
Smith, F. H.: Jan. 21, 1875 (CL)[13]
Smith, R. A.: Sept. 9, 1861 (JT)
Smith, W. B.: Dec. 4, 1867 (CL)
Spedding, James: Aug. 24 (HL†), Dec. 17, 1880 (CL)
Spencer, Edward: Feb. 22, [Mar. 31?]°, 1875 (CL)
Spencer, Herbert: Nov. 29, 1880 (CL)
Stebbins, Emma: May 2, June 22, Aug. 17, Sept. 10, Sept. 21, Oct. 7, Nov. 27,
1875; Jan. 11, [Mar. 1], Mar 27, Apr. 11, May 11, May 27, June 6,
[June 27], June 29, July 6, July 8, July 14, July 27, Sept. 4, Sept. 23,
Oct. 14, 1876; Feb. 18, Apr. 13, June 1, Aug. 10, Nov. 29, 1877; Apr. 10,
1878; Dec. 21, 1880 (CL)
Stedman, E. C.: Nov. 6, 1874; May 17, 1880[14] (CL)
Tabb, J. B.: Oct. 4, 1877 (CL); Mar. 26, 1878 (HL)
Taylor, Bayard: Aug. 17[15] Aug. 23, Aug. 26, Sept. 2, Sept. 28 (CU), [Oct. 9]
(CL),[16] Oct. 16, Nov. 1, Dec. 13, Dec. 28, 1875: Jan. 7, Jan. 12, Jan. 13,
Jan. 20 (CU) [Feb. 25?] (CL),[17] Mar. 4, [Mar. 17], Mar. 23, Mar. 26,
Apr. 3, Apr. 11, July 21 (CU), Aug. 16 (CL), Sept. 23, Nov. 15, 1876;
Jan. 27, Feb. 5, Mar. 12, Apr. 15, May 9, [June], July 11, Aug. 11, Sept.
6, Oct. 13, 1877; Jan. 20, Feb. 19, Mar. 6, Apr. 1, 1878 (CU)
Taylor, Marie H.: Apr. 21, 1878 (CL)
Tucker, H. H.: Feb. 25, 1875 (CL)
Turnbull, Lawrence (see also Turnbull & Murdoch and Turnbull Brothers):
July 13, 1870 (CL)
Turnbull Brothers (see also Turnbull & Murdoch, Turnbull, Lawrence, and
Browne, W. H.): Aug. 9, 1873 (CL)
Turnbull & Murdoch (see also Browne, W. H.): Aug. 28, 1869; Mar. 29,
1880 (CL)
Wallen, Mary: May 7, Dec. 23, 1876; Nov. 19, 1880 (CL)
Ward, W. H.: Mar. 10, 1878; Aug. 19 [1879]: July 23, Dec. 7, Dec. 24,
1880 (CL)
Whitman, Walt: May 27, [1878] (CL)
Willmarth, A. F.: Nov. 30, 1880 (CL)
Wilson, Mrs. M. P. (later Mrs. Price, James): Nov. 6, 1864 (JT)
Wysham, H. C.: [Mar. 24?], 1877 (CL)

---

[13] Published, *Letters*, 110-111.
[14] Published, *Stedman*, II, 154.
[15] MS not found; *Letters*, 122-123.
[16] Note accompanying guest card to the Century Club (CL).
[17] Note on a calling card (CL).

C. LETTERS ABOUT LANIER [1]

Anderson, Clifford: to L. Q. C. Lamar, Aug. 9, 1867 (CL); to Mary Day Lanier, Mar. 5, 1875 (CL)

Bleckley, L. E.: to Clifford Anderson, Apr. 22, 1877 (NA)

Brady, Sarita M.: to W. M. Dunn, July 20, 1877 (CL)

Brewer, Marbury: to Mary Day Lanier, July 21, 1881 (JT)

Browne, W. H.: to C. A. Lanier, Nov. 11, 1882 (JT); to H. W. Lanier, Feb. 19, 1903 (HL); to Mary Day Lanier, Dec. 24, 1906 (CL)

Cable, G. W.: to J. A. Fisher, Sept. 8, 1883 (HL)

Calvert, G. H.: to Gibson Peacock, May 25, 1875 (CL)

Campbell, C. E.: to H. W. Lanier, *Mar. 31, 1903 (HL)

Century Magazine, Editor of: to Mary Day Lanier, Mar. 23, 1882 (CL)

Day, Charles :to Mary Day Lanier, Aug. 9-10-12, 1868; Oct. 3, 1873; Nov. 9, 1881 (CL)

Dotterer, T. D.: to Mary Day Lanier, *Mar. 28, 1884 (HL†)

Duncan, Mrs. Wm.: to Mary Day Lanier, May 8, 1869 (CL)

Dunn, W. M.: to W. N. Evarts, Aug. 11, 1877 (NA)

Dutcher, Salem: to Anna Marie Dutcher, Nov. 13, 1867 (HL); to C. A. Lanier, Mar. 22, 1868 (JT)

Eggleston, G. C.: to J. B. Tabb, Dec. 5, 1877 (HL†)

Farley, Sarah J.: to W. H. Ward, Jan. 9, 1884 (JT)

Fettinger, Katherine: to H. W. Lanier, Aug. 6, 1934 (HL)

Graffenried, de, M. Clare: to Mary Day Lanier, Sept. 30, [1873?] (CL)

Gottlieb, F. H.: to Edwin Mims, Jan. 21, 1904 (EM)

Hamerik, Asger: to Mary Day Lanier, Sept. 29, 1884 (CL)

Hankins, Virginia: to C. A. Lanier, Aug. 14, 1865 (CL); June, 1884 (JT); to Mary Day Lanier, Jan. 27, 1868 (CL)

Hayne, P. H.: to J. R. Thompson, Sept. 27, 1871 (CL); to A. O. Bunce, Oct. 16, 1871 (CL)

Herrick, Sophie B.: to Edwin Mims, [1904?] (EM)

Hill, W. B.: to J. A. Fisher, Jan. 19, 1884 (HL)

Howells, W. D.: to M. M. Hurd, *Oct. 3, 1874 (CL)

Hyman, F. W.: to Mary A. Lanier, *Nov. 4, 1864 (CL)

Keyser, Ephraim: to J. A. Fisher, Sept. 13, 1883 (HL)

King, Henry C.: to Mary Day Lanier, Nov. 15, 1872 (CL)

Kirkus, William: to J. A. Fisher, Sept. 20, 1883 (HL)

Lamar, Augusta: to C. A. Lanier, Aug. [28?], 1865 (JT); to Mary Day, Sept. 1, 1865 (CL)

Lanier, C. D.: to Mary Day Lanier, Jan. 22, 1880 (JT); to W. M. Baskervill, Sept. 21, 1896; Feb. 8, 1897 (DU)

Lanier, C. A.: to W. M. Baskervill, Sept. 21, 1896; Feb. 8, 1897 (DU); to W. H. Browne, Sept. 26, 1881 (HL); to Virginia T. Clay, Apr. 17, 1863 [2]

---

[1] This is a selected list of the known letters concerning Lanier. Discovered too late to be itemized in this calendar are 65 letters from Mary Day Lanier (Sept. 20, 1881–Mar. 15, 1906), 18 letters from Henry W. Lanier (1898-1900), and 19 letters from W. H. Browne (1882-1883), all to Charles Scribner's Sons. the present owner of the MSS.

[2] Published, *A Belle of the Fifties, Memoirs of Mrs. Clay, of Alabama* (New York, 1905), 198-99.

(DU); to ———, July 4, 1895 (DU); to J. A. Fisher Sept. 13, 1883; Sept. 27, 1883 (HL); to Harriet B. Fulton, Sept. 5, 1864 (JT); to Virginia Hankins, [Aug. 7?, 1863], Jan. 2, Jan. 22, June 10, Sept. 16, Nov. 17, 1864; July 3, 1866; Oct. 14, 1881 (HF); to Gertrude Lanier, June 8, *July 27, Aug. 10, Aug. 25, 1864; May 27, 1866 (JT); to H. W. Lanier, Jan. 27 1899 (CL); ———, 1900 (HL); to Mary A. Lanier, Oct. 21, Nov. 6?, 1860; Sept. 24, Oct. 31, Nov. 29, 1862; Mar. 4, May 10, *Nov. 1, 1863; *Jan. 7, Aug. 31, Oct. 10, Nov. 12, 1864 (JT); to Mary Day Lanier, June 24 (HL†), Sept. 10, 1866; Feb. 7, 1869 (CL); Dec. 27, 1876 (JT); Aug. 21, 1882 (CL); to R. S. Lanier, July 1, Oct. 7, 1860; Oct. 19, *Dec. 30, 1862; *May 5, *June 4, *Aug. 3, *Sept. 26, Nov. 13, Dec. 23, *Dec. 30, 1863; *Feb. 6, May 14, Dec. 1, Dec. 10, 1864; Aug. 13, 1865; Nov. 29, 1867 (JT); to Edwin Mims, Mar. 7, 1904 (EM)

Lanier, Gertrude (later Mrs. Gibson): to C. A. Lanier, Nov. 29, 1861; July 12, Aug. 24, Oct. 15, Nov. 12, Nov. 25, Dec. 1, 1865; Jan. 25, May 22, Sept. 1, 1866; Apr. 24, 1867; July 9, 1868 (JT); to J. A. Fisher, *Oct., 1883 (HL)

Lanier, J. F. D.: to R. S. Lanier May 18, 1877 (CL); to John Sherman, May 18, 1877 (NA)

Lanier, Mary Day: to W. H. Browne, Nov. 28, 1882; Jan. 29, [Aug.], 1883; Sept. 4, 1894 (LB); to Anna Blauvelt, Feb. 26, 1898 (JT†); to Charles Day, Dec. 29, 1867; June 24, 1873; Sept. 20-21, 1875 (CL); to Sarah Farley, Jan. 8, Aug. 5, 1877; Feb. 26, Apr. 1, 1878; [Sept. 4, 1880]; May 1, May 3, July 4-5, *July 30–Aug. 9, Sept. 7, Sept. 10, 1881 (HL); to Mrs. S. E. Farley, Apr. 11, 1879 (HL); to Gertrude Lanier Gibson, Oct. 9, Dec. 31°, 1876; Feb. 4, 1877 (BC); to Mrs. C. N. Hawkins, Apr. 22, 1877 (FH); to R. M. Johnston, [Jan. 9?, 1880] (EP); to F. A. King, *[Autumn], 1891° (CL†); to C. D. Lanier, May 31, 1872, Oct. 11, Dec. 25, 1876; Jan. 11, [Apr. 15?], May 4, May 29, 1877 (CL); to C. A. Lanier, Apr. 21, Apr. 22, 1866; Jan. 26-30, Sept. 23, 1867; Jan. 17, Feb. 7, 1868; [June 9?], Sept. 4, 1870; Apr. 24, 1871; Aug. 7, 1874; May 28, June 29, Nov. 11-15, Nov. 16, Dec. 6, 1875; May 29, June 8, July 19, Aug. 11, Aug. 17, Oct. 6, *Nov. 8, Dec. 19, 1876: Jan. 3, Jan. 20, Feb. 14, Mar. 15, 1877; Jan. 1-Apr. 22, *Dec. 10, 1880; *May 29, *May 31, *June 26, *July 18, July 23, *July 24, July 31, Aug. 2, Sept. 2, Sept. 6, Oct. 7?, 1881; Feb. 1, 1886; Feb. 16, 1901; May 2, 1903 (JT); to R. S. Lanier, Jan. 21, 1868 (CL); Sept. 25, 1873 (BC), Dec. 29, 1876; Apr. 15, 1878, Dec. 18, 1880 (JT); to Sidney Lanier, Jr., Nov. 18, 1874 (HL); to Wilhelmina C. Lanier *May 26, 1868; Mar. 6-8-21°, Mar. 23°, 1871; Jan. 3, 1874; Apr. 29–May 1, 1876; Jan. 7, Feb. 10, Feb. 14, Mar. 19, May 21, 1877; Feb. 19, Sept. 10, 1878 (JT); to her sons, Dec. 18, 1880 (CL); to Edwin Mims, *July 31, 1905 (EM); to Gibson Peacock, Dec. 27, 1876 (HC); to W. S. Pratt, Aug. 31, 1880; Feb. 3, 1882 (HG); to Georgia [Shackleford?], *Nov. 22, 1864 (AS†); to Mrs. Cosby Smith, Oct. 4, Nov. 25,³ 1867; Jan. 10, Apr. 2, June 6, [June 6?], June 10, [c. June 14], [Summer?], 1868 (ML); to E. C. Stedman, Aug. 14, Sept. 20, 1882; Mar. 27, 1895 (CN); to J. B. Tabb, *Nov. 5, 1880; Mar. 19, 1881 (GB); Mar. 15, 1915;⁴ to Lawrence Turnbull, *Feb. 2,

---

³ Published in part, *Confederate Veteran*, XXXII, 98.
⁴ MS not found; published, Jennie Masters Tabb, *Father Tabb* (Boston, 1922), 6-7.

May 28, 1881 (ET): to Frances L. Turnbull, Dec. 21, Dec. 22, 1879; Aug. 26-27, Sept. 7, Sept. 15, 1880; Jan. 10, [Jan. 31?], Feb. 23, Sept. 6, 1881; Apr. 7, 1900; Aug. 30, 1903 (ET); to Mrs. Charlotte Ware, Sept. 13, 1910 (SL); to Jane L. Watt, Jan. 12, 1868 (JT)

Lanier, R. S.: to J. A. Fisher, *Sept. 25, *Oct. 11, 1883 (HL); to C. A. Lanier, Apr. 26, 1861; Mar. 10, 1862; May 12, 1863; Jan. 20, Sept. 9, Sept 28, Oct. 9, Nov. 8, Nov. 9, Nov. 15, Nov. 18, Nov. 29, Dec. 9, 1864; July 5, Aug. 21, Sept. 24, Oct. 6, Nov. 2, Dec. 5, 1865; Feb. 23, Mar. 10, June 22, July 26, Oct. 9, 1866; Jan. 12, Mar. 7, Apr. 8, Apr. 10, May 9, May 10, May 17, May 29, June 3, Sept. 21, Sept. 23, Sept. 28, Oct. 13, Oct. 18, Oct. 30, Nov. 7, Nov. 15, Nov. 21, Dec. 3, 1867; Feb. 14, Apr. 5, Apr. 6, Apr. 14, 1868; May 3, 1869; *Apr. 28, 1870; [Nov.?] 23, 1873; May 5, 1874; Jan. 8, June 8, Sept. 9, Dec. 24, 1875; Jan. 8, Feb. 14, Mar. 26, Apr. 4, 1877; Dec. 26, 1878; Dec. 27, 1879; Apr. 4, May 18, Aug. 19, Sept. 30, Dec. 5, Dec. 24, 1880; Jan. 10, Jan. 16, May 22, June 3, July 2, *July 24, July 28, Sept. 2, Sept. 7, Sept. 13, Sept. 23, Oct. 15, 1881; May 14, 1882; Mar. 30, 1883; Nov. 21, 1884; May 23, 1886 (JT); to Gertrude Lanier (later Mrs. Gibson) Nov. 13, 1865 (JT); Mar. 5, 1877 (BC); to Mary A. Lanier, Aug. 17, 1864 (CL); to Mary Day Lanier, Nov. 15, 1873: Apr. 22, Sept. 9, Oct. 5, 1875 (CL) to Sterling Lanier, July 10, 1865 (JT); to Bayard Taylor, Apr. 21, 1877 (CU); to Editor, Syracuse (N. Y.) *Daily Courier*, Sept. 14, 1881 (CU)[5]

Lanier, Sterling: to R. S. Lanier, Sept. 18, 1865 (CL)

Lanier, Wilhelmina C.: to C. A. Lanier, June 9, 1870 (JT)

LeConte, W. L.: to H. W. Lanier, Feb. 28, 1903 (HL)

Ligon, Carrie: to Jane L. Watt, Mar. 22, 1866 (JT)

Lowell, J. R.: to D. C. Gilman, Jan. 28, 1888[6]

Mims, W. H.: to H. W. Lanier, Dec. 24, 1902 (HL)

Morgan, J. T.: to John Sherman, Apr. 23, 1877 (NA)

Peacock, Gibson: to Mary Day Lanier, May 28, 1875 (CL); Mar. 20, 1884 (JT); to R. S. Lanier, Apr. 27, 1877 (CL); to Bayard Taylor, May 21, June 6, 1875 (CU)

Scribner, Charles: to Mary Day Lanier, Sept. 28, 1881 (CL)

Shearer, Thomas: to Mary Day Lanier, Sept. 6, 1881 (CL)

Smith, Mrs. G. L.: to Mary Day Lanier, Dec. 30, 1902 (HL)

Smith, R. A.: to General Withers, Aug. 24, 1861 (JT)

Tabb, J. B.: to C. D. Lanier, Feb. 16, 1884 (JT†);[7] to Holly Tabb, Nov. 28, 1877 (GB)

Taliaferro, Charles: to H. C. Day, Sept. 9, 1875 (CL)

Taylor, Bayard: to H. M. Alden, Dec. 2, 1876 (HA);[8] to T. B. Aldrich, Nov. 1, 1875 (CL); to J. R. G. Hassard, Sept. 1, 1875 (CL); to R. S. Lanier, Apr. 28, 1877 (CL); to J. R. Lowell, Nov. 1, 1875 (HC); to Gibson Peacock, June 3, 1875 (CL); to John Sherman, Apr. 28, 1877 (NA)

Taylor, Marie H.: to Mary Day Lanier, Mar. 12, 1877; Aug. 28, 1882 (CL)

---

[5] Published in part, *Lippincott's*, LXXV, 315.

[6] MS not found; published, *46th Birthday of Sidney Lanier* (Baltimore, 1888), 25.

[7] Published, Mims, 59-60.

[8] Published, *Unpublished Letters of Bayard Taylor in the Huntington Library* (San Marino, Cal., 1937), 196, ed. by J. R. Schultz.

Turnbull, Lawrence: to Mary Day Lanier, Oct. 13, 1881 (CL)
Walker, Florida: to Mary Day Lanier, June 21, 1875 (CL)
Westfeldt, G. R.: to J. A. Fisher, July 19, 1885 (HL)
Woodrow, James: to H. W. Lanier, Jan. 14, 1904 (HL); to Edwin Mims
      *May 21, 1904 (EM)
Wysham, H. C.: to ———— Weber, Sept. [22?], 1873 (CL†)

Manuscript Reminiscences

Mrs. Edgeworth Bird (HL†)   Mrs. Arthur Machen (JT)
Mrs. G. L. Dobbin (HL)   Mary Day Lanier (JT)
Mrs. Arthur Machen (EM)

GENERAL INDEX
VOLUMES I–X

GENERAL INDEX

Abbot, E. A., II: 78

Abbreviations, and symbols, I: 286; X: 380

Abel, Thomas, III: 205

Abernethy, Cecil E., I: xi; V: xxxiii, lx

About, Edmund, X: 35

" Abused Lover Seeth His Folly . . ." (Wyatt), text, III: 108

Academy of Music, Baltimore, VII: xvii, xxvi*n*

Accelerando, II: 55*n*

Accent, L's theory appraised, II: xlii, xxii; Coleridge's conception, 6, 11, 77; antiquity, 11; inexact ideas about, 26, 78, 111; nature of, 53, 60, 111; function, 53, 78ff.; recurrence in bar, 66, 93; logical (intensity-and-pitch) accent, 68, 94, 95, 183; distinction between rhythmic and logical, 69, 96; not the basis of rhythm, 78; bearing upon music, 79; true relation to rhythm in verse, 81, 93-109; discrimination and functions of rhythmic, pronunciation, and logical, accents, 94ff.; III: 353f.; in Anglo-Saxon poetry, II: 111; relation of rests to, 147, 149; Shakspere's use of the rhythmic, 166-75; III: 352-55, 405; IV: 325; his three methods of varying, II: 170; on bar, in 4-rhythm, 178ff.; antithetic, IV: 19; in old ballads, 398

" Acknowledgment " (L.), I: l*n*, lii, lxvii; IX: 239*n*, 251*n*, 405; text, I: 56; reprint, note, 342; first printing, VI: 383

Acknowledgments, editor's, I: xiif.

Acoustic construction of music halls, VII: lx

Acta Sanctorum, II: 247*n*

Acte Concernyng Fermes and Shepe, An, V: 354f.

Acts of the Apostles, versification, excerpt, III: 223

Adagio, II: 82

Adam Bede (Eliot), IV: 14, 15, 60, 137, 139, 169, 170, 183f., 186, 232,

249; authorship disputed, 138; not an immediate popular success, 188

Adams, Misses, school, X: 117, 147, 247

Adams, Annie, IX: 216

Adams, Herbert B., III: x, xi, 415; VII: xliii, xliv*n*, xlvii, xlix; X: 70

Adams, John, VI: 29

Addison, Joseph, IX: 83

" Address, An, . . ." (L.), V: 265*n*; *see* " Confederate Memorial Address "

Address of the Soul to the Dead Body, The, with excerpts, III: xvi, xxi, 11-17, 89; X: 94

" Address to Workmen " (Eliot), IV: 249

Adelaide (Beethoven), II: 323; IV: 52

Adult education, *see* Education

Adventures of an Atom (Smollett), IV: 155

Adventures of Ferdinand Count Fathom (Smollett), IV: 155

Adventures of Joseph Andrews, The . . . (Fielding), IV: 152

Advertiser, Montgomery, VII: viii*n*

Ælfric's Homilies, IV: 11

Æneas, IV: 356

Æneid (Virgil), II: 182; V: 128*n*, 200*n*, 309, 318; Surrey's translation, 130, 143; excerpts, V: 314

Æschylus, IV: 74, 95, 108; progress from time of, 5, 7, 9, 21, 144f., 189; *Prometheus Bound,* 66, 79, 82, 85, 87, 88, 100; V: 310; X: 293*n*; excerpts, IV: 68-74, 77; failure to conceive personality, 79

Æsop's Fables, excerpt, V: 35

Aetas Prima (Chaucer), text, IV: 81

" Aëthra " (Hayne), V: 333; VIII: 12

Agassiz, J. L. R., I: lxxiv; VI: 159

" Agatha " (Eliot), IV: 249

" Agincourt, Ballad of . . . ," II: 137, text, 140

Agnew, J. L. and F. D. Lee, VI: xv; quoted, 162-64, 167

Agra (Akbarabad), India, VI: 295, 305

Agricultural College of Florida, VI: 84

413

Critics, follies committed by, in all ages, III: 131, 132; IX: 369; judgment upon great literary artists reversed in succeeding ages, III: 165, 166; lack of factual basis, 314; VI: 333; thinly disguised scolding of, xxii; L's sensitiveness to, xxv; fable of the critics of society and how to deal with them, 333ff.; their war against Genius, 336; treatment of Centennial Cantata and L's reaction, IX: 348ff. *passim*; why he was badly treated, 507; his wide experience of "newspaper follies," X: 270; *see also* Reviews

Crocker, Mary Jane, early life: marriage to Charles Day: death, X: 365f.

Crockett, David, VI: 227, 229, 230; VIII: 277

Cross, Professor, III: 415

Cross, J. W., IV: 132, X: 332; marriage to George Eliot, IV: 247

Cross of Christ, poems about, III: 57, 58-61, 88

Crouch, H. V., VI: 33

Crowley, Robert, V: 356*n*

Crozat, Anthony, VI: 203

Cruger, Colonel, VI: 171

Cryptology, VII: 299

"Crystal, The" (L.), I: lxviii, lxxi, lxxii; X: 224*n*, 292, 297; text, I: 136-139; textual vraiants, 321; reprint: note, 363; first printing, VI: 383

"Cubbie," *see* Day, Henry Coit

"Cuckoo and the Nightingale, The" (Chaucer?), III: xix, 55; IV: 335

"Cuckoo-Song," II: 121*n*, 209; III: 89, 212; rhythmic scheme, with excerpts, II: 125-27; III: 217ff., 225

Cudworth, Benjamin, VI: 33

Cumberland Route to Florida, IX: 440

Cunliffe, J. W., III: 258*n*

Current Literature, I: 236

Cursor Mundi, MS, III: 60*n,* 71, 72

Cushings and Bailey, I: lxxii

Cushion-dance, III: 232

Cushman, Charlotte S., I: xliv; II:203; IV: 31, 209; IX: 190, 191, 217, 248, 327*n*; L's four poems to, I: 342 (*see* "At First"; "Dedication"; "To Charlotte Cushman"; "To Miss Charlotte Cushman"); greatness in:

appreciation of Mazzini, III: 314f.; L's introduction to, IX: 148; their friendship, 149, 160, 181, 187, 188, 305; her request for a poem to be recited, 149; X: 12; his grief and poem about, IX: 328; her companion, 118*n,* 194; L's letters to, 206, 226, 231, 262, 289; his visit during her illness, 264-72; physician, 267; death, 323, 326; project for a "Life" of, 348, 356, 371, 372, 384, 385, 387*n*, 388, 390, 421; memorial volume substituted, 421 503

Cushman, Edwin, IX: 323, 348*n*

Custis, George Washington Parke, VI: 353, 357

Custom of the Country (Fletcher), III: 349

Cutler, Elizabeth Pettit, VIII: 135*n*

Cuttle, Captain, a Dickens character, VI: 190

Cyclopaedia of . . . Poetry, Sargent's *see Harper's Cyclopaedia*

Cymbal, II: 303, 304

Cymbeline (Shakespeare), II: 160, 166, 170; III: 193, 238, 292; chronology and metrical tests, III: 329, 334, 341, 348; IV: 320

Cymric (Cymry) Kelts, IV: 380

Cynewulf, II: 7, 130; IV: 295; author of *The Phœnix?* III: 42, spelled in Runic letters, 69

Czurda, Vincent, IX: 45*n*

Dabney, Julia P., II: xxxii

Dactyl, classic, I: lxi; II: 9, 88, 174, 176, 177; in English verse: the logaœdic, I: lxii; II: 176; III: 46; IV: 24; example of, 55

Dade, Francis L., and troops massacred, VI: 92, 136

Daily Graphic, New York, IX: 382*n*; excerpt, 432

Daily Herald, Atlanta, IX: 69*n*

Daily Telegraph, Macon, VI: 381, 386, 387; *see also Telegraph*

Daisy Miller (James), excerpts, IV: 198-200

"Dakota Wheat fields" (Coffin), V: lviii

Damon and Pythias (Edwards), III: 216

marriage to Gertrude Lanier Shannon, VIII: 297n
Gifford, Robert S., IX: 392
Gifford, Sanford R., IX: 392
Gilbert, Senator, VI: 28
Gilded Age, The (Mark Twain), a L. poem compared with episode in, I: 384
Gilder, Richard Watson, I: 331, 360, 361, 385; IX: 305, 421, 493n
Gildersleeve, Basil, III: x, 415; VI: xix; VII: xlivn, xlvii, 29n; X: 44, 45, 54, 70; career: research and publication at Johns Hopkins, VII: xlii, xliv, li; relations with L., li
Giles, J. A., editor, III: 310n
Gill, Alexander, III: 180
Gillett, Miss, singer, II: 324
Gillis, Judge, quoted, VI: 91
Gilman, Daniel Coit, II: 247n; III: viii, ix; IV: 105; VII: xxxn; IX: 389; X: 176, 256, 276; articles by, I: xlviiin; VI: 396; VII: viin, xlin, xlv, xlvi, xlix; X: 408n; elected president of Johns Hopkins University: his few but revolutionary principles, III: 412; VII: xli; Franklin's *Life of*, xli-liii *passim*, X: 132n, 272n, 399; building of a true university and its staff, VII: xliiff.; efforts to connect L. with the University, xlivff.; IX: 399, 407, 474, 479; references to him in published articles, VII: xlv, xlvi, xlix; motto for his memorial tablet, lxii; on his Cantata and theory of verse, IX: 363n; L's letters to, 397, 406, 474, 479; X: 54, 68, 82, 98, 128, 129, 144, 159, 175, 178, 254, 261, 263, 264, 271, 285, 313, 319; reception: wife, X: 21; on L's lectures, 26, 33; cooperation with his plans, 44, 149; on his " Boy's " books and his valiant fight, 272
Gilpin, Bernard, V: 356
Giraud, Mayor of San Antonio, VI: 214
Girls, projected books for, IV: 256; X: 284, 302, 304, 306; *see also Arcadia* (Sidney); *Mabinogion*; *Paston Letters*
Gita-Govinda, V: 309; excerpts, 313
Gittern, III: 201

Given, Mr., VIII: 83, 195
Given, Sallie E., poem to, I: 9, 331; VI: 381; VII: 241
Gladstone, William E., V: 250; utterances relating to U. S., 345n; to small farming for England, 345n, 357
" Glaucus " (Hayne), V: 332
Glaze, M. A., IX: 21
Gleason, W., VI: 99
" Glimpses of Texas " (King), VI: viii
Gluck, C. W. von, II: 268
Glynn County, marshes, I: 358; *see also* " Marshes of Glynn, The "
" Gnats " (L.), *see* " Danse des Moucherons "
" Gnomic Verses " of the *Exeter Book*, III: 58
God (the Unknown), evidences of L's belief in, I: lxv, lxviii, lxix; VIII: 283, 326, 366; IX: 21, 175n, 184, 265, 338; poem outlines concerned with, I: 238, 267-71 *passim*; man's effort to relate himself to, II: 286, 292; relation shown in Anglo-Saxon poem, III: 11f.; in three Shakspearean plays, 13-16, 368-78; the above-direction toward which man looks, 18; Constable's sonnets to, 139; music the form expressing relation to, IV: 129, 130, 145
Godwin, Eddie and Leroy, VII: 181
Godwin, William, IV: 159
Goetchius brothers, VII: 30n
Goethe, Johann Wolfgang von, III: 132; IV: 34, 158, 240; V: xx, xxiv, 263, 297; VII: 84, 89, 160; VIII: 31, 80
Goethe Festival, IX: 234n, 237
" Goethe's Words " (Clifford A. Lanier), VII: 139, 145
Gohdes, Clarence, I: xi; ed., *The English Novel* (*q. v.*), IV: vii-xi, 3-251
Gold, identified with death, IV: 211-14
Gold-embroidered cloths, VI: 299f.
Golden Age, I: xliv, 343; IX: 212
Golden Age in history, IV: 81
" Golden Wedding of Sterling and Sarah Lanier, The " (L.), VII: 396, 398; text, I: 17; note, 334; first printing, VI: 381
Goldingham and Ferrers, III: 258

Harvard Musical Association, VII: xi

Harvey, Gabriel, II: 6, 177, 226; III: 173n; IV: 272; quarrel with Greene and Nash, III: 381, 383ff.; IV: 330

Harvey, John, IV: 272

Harvey, William, doctrine of circulation of blood, IV: 271f.

Haslam, IX: 95

Hassard, J. R. G., IX: 247; criticism of Centennial Cantata, 348n (*see also Tribune,* New York)

Hastings, Doctor, III: 415

Hastings, Charles S., VII: 1; X: 313

Hathaway, Anne, III: 239, 253, 292, 335

Hathaway, Richard, III: 239

Hau Kiou Chooan (tr. by Percy), IV: 389.

Hautboy, *see* Oboe

Havana, ceded to Spain, VI: 128

" Have you forgot how through the April weather' (L.), text (untitled), I: 199; note, 378

Havens and Brown, VII: 311n, 358n, 364, 369

Hawkeye, Burlington, excerpt, IX: 382

Hawkins, Charles N., IX: 429

Hawkins, Mrs. Charles N., I: 379; IX: 429, 430n; X: 78n

Hawkins, Sir John, VI: 36, 366, 371; quoted, 364, 365

Hawley, J. R., IX: 288n, 315, 387; invitation to L. to write Cantata, 294; approval of it, 308n, 364

Hawthorne, Nathaniel, VII: 168, 185, 298; X: 35

Hay, John, IX: 115n

Haydn, Franz Josef, II: 147, 149, 210, 254; III: 234

Hayes, Rutherford B., IX: 386, 409; X: 25

Haygood, Confederate officer, V: 132, 133

Hayne, Paul Hamilton, I: xxxiii, 335, 338, 340; IV: ix$n$; VII: xxxv; IX: 204n; friendship, literary compatibility and mutual encouragement between L. and, I: xxii; IV: 400; V: x, lif.; VI: 176n; VII: 394; VIII: 175, 185; IX: 260, 476n; X: 274; helpful criticisms and comments by, I: 293, 297, 341, 375; VIII: 3, 137n; IX: 108, 159; economic and health

difficulties, V: li; VIII: 42; wrote for periodicals: volumes of poetry published, V: li; supplanted by L. as foremost Southern poet, lii; influenced by William Morris? liii, 325f.; VII: 395; VIII: 43; IX: 145; titles of poems, V: 322-33 *passim*; VI: 177; VII: 395; VIII: 12, 43, 64, 71n, 94n, 133, 145ff., 175, 222, 224, 330, 347, 352; IX: 55, 261n; X: 273; rebuke of L. for criticism of Timrod: high praise of the latter, VI: xix; L's correspondence with, 92n; VII: 394; VIII: 3n, 10, 42, 50n, 64, 66, 71, 94, 133, 137n, 145, 174, 222, 223, 337n, 347, 352; IX: 55, 260; X: 272; photograph, VIII: facing 10; L's epistolary scrutiny, or comments on poems by, 64, 133, 145, 224, 347, 352; cured of consumption, 175n; wanted L. to. edit his literary remains but outlived him, IX: 261n; *Poems . . . ,* X: 125n; L's efforts to help in its publication, 142; for review of poetry by, and reactions to it, *see Legends and Lyrics* (Hayne); " Paul H. Hayne's Poetry " (Lanier)

Hays, Colonel, VI: 232, 233

Hazard, Apthorpe & Co., VIII: 84

Hazelhurst, Lilla, VII: 245, 266n, 323n, 326, 362; VIII: 16, 76, 203; marriage, 290; *see also* Burroughs, Lilla H.

Heabani, quoted, VI: 78

" Heart Hungry," VIII: 348

Heat, effect upon water, VI: 104, 105

" Heathen Chinee " (Harte), IX: 115

Hebrew poetry, *see* Psalms

Heenan, John C., V: 22n, 218; VII: 288n

Heidelberg, plan to study at, VII: 359n

Heilbron, Mlle, II: 328

" Heimweh Polka," composition by L., VI: 390; IX: 74n

Heindel, Edward, VII: xvi$n$; X: 112

Heine, Heinrich, I: xxix; IX: 204, 319; translations from, *see* " Spring Greeting "; " Translations. . ."

Heinin Vardd, IV: 378

Heinrich von Ofterdingen (Hardenberg), V: xx, xxi, xxv

Heintzelman, Major, VI: 199

363, 431; IX: 7, 53, 59, 67, 75, 99, 113, 123, 128, 161, 176, 192, 200, 248, 262, 283, 336, 373, 385, 409, 480, 504; X: 8, 22, 32, 81, 93, 95, 103, 107, 117, 120, 135, 145f., 164, 171, 187, 212, 250, 259, 293, 297f., 306; student at Oglethorpe, VII: 26, 30, 36, 39, 41; hotel positions, 46n; IX: 108; writings and literary style criticized or guided by L., VII: 47, 201, 252; IX: 55, 67, 113, 115, 161, 192, 249; correspondence with father, VII: 66n, 67, 90, 107, 113, 117, 123, 129, 138, 209n; VIII: 74; X: 327; account of a military engagement, VII: 78n; gallantry in service, 152; business opportunities, 209n; VIII: 46; L's confidence in literary future of, VII: 291; engagement to Wilhelmina Clopton, 296; marriage, 351n, 355; biographical sketch of L. and, in *Living Writers . . . ,* 376n; IX: 407; X: 276, 310ff., 317, 323, 328; study of law, VIII: 5, 47; birth of daughter, 6n (*see* Lanier, Wilhelmina); of son, 119; financial troubles, 431, 441; IX: 262; address delivered by, IX: 54, 60; hope of finding another hotel to manage, 108, 114, 278, 478, 480; X: 81, 123; convinced that L. had inspired all he had accomplished, IX: 161n; invitation to L's family to spend winter with, 271n; appreciation of *Florida,* 290; purchase of L's silver flute, 336; yearnings toward poetic expression, X: 22; photographs, facing X: 104; (references to them, VII: 215n; X: 103f.); L's desire that he become a publisher: preparation leading to it, X: 120f., 150; summoned to take L. to mountains, 306; L's great need of, in last illness, 324, 329; birth place and date, 344n; intellectual and moral symmetry, 351, 353; death, 351; letters re brother's capture and imprisonment, 369, 370, 371
—— writings: " Notes Biographical of Sidney Lanier . . ." MS, V: xxxn; " Reminiscences of Sidney Lanier,"

I: xxiii, 374; VII: 17n; X: 381
novels: *Carpet-baggery . . . ,* V: xlii; VII: 377; IX: 112n, 113, 306, 313; X: 9; *Thorn-Fruit,* I: xxx, 329; V: viiin, ix, xi, xxiin; VII: 92n, 145n, 222, 303n, 364, 373
poems, I: lxxxix, 331, 384; VII: 139, 145, 241; IX: 176; X: 104; sonnets to his brother, IX: 176, 180, 192, 249; poems by L. and, I: xlix, 384, 385; texts, 213-17 (*see* " Power of Prayer "); "A Sea-Shore Grave "; "A Song—(' Day is a silver veil ')"; " To —— (' 'Twas winter when I met you first ') "; "Uncle Jim's Baptist Revival Hymn "
short story: " The Doctor's Legend," IX: 161n
Lanier, Clifford Anderson, Jr., VIII: 119n
Lanier, D. G., VI: 360
Lanier, Edmund, VI: 360
Lanier, Elizabeth, VI: 357
Lanier, Elizabeth C. (Mrs. Sampson), VI: 357
Lanier, Elizabeth Washington (Mrs. Thomas), VI: 354; descendants, 357ff.
Lanier, Gertrude (" Sissa "), V: xlii; VII: viin, 30n, 99, 219, 329, 342, 362n; IX: 314, 321; X: 374; Sidney's letters to, VII: 124, 219, 239, 263, 285, 294; VIII: 286; Clifford's, VII: 157; earliest love affair, 124, 143; engagement and marriage to Edward B. Shannon, 283, 285; yellow fever: death of husband, 333; birth of son, 380; Vineville house, 398n.; VIII: 285n; X: 48n; New Orleans property, VIII: 101n, 142; marriage to Joseph Carr Gibson, 297n, 318n; birth place and date, X: 344n; death, 351; reminiscences of L. in letter to J. A. Fisher, 355-58
Lanier, Henry Wysham (Harry), V: xxxiii, lx; IX: 408; collection of Lanieriana, I: v; works of L. edited by, 236, 366; III: xvii; V: xxvii; VI: 202n, 324n, 340n, 380; VII: lxii; poem in which referred to, I: 355; on L's most ambitious prose work, III: xvii; birth, VIII: 358; naming of, 397, 407, 416; photo-

tion, 248, 249, 259; engagement, 305n; wedding, honeymoon, 362; VIII: 23n; letters to Clifford Lanier, VII: 385; IX: 407; X: 276, 310ff., 317, 323, 328; living in home of sister-in-law, VII: 398n; VIII: 126n, 285n; letter from L., facsimile, VIII: facing 56; appearance, 125; IX: 23; problem of finding new home, VIII: 285n, 322, 324; L's eulogy: preferred one of her charm and gifts to one more industrious and economical, 304; Higgins relatives, 395, 401 (*see entries under* Higgins); care of brother's baby, 397; notes in French, IX: 88n; gift for letter writing, 111, 197, 247; spent winter of 1875 with the Clifford Laniers, 271n; appreciation of the artistic, 326; cultural life repressed, 327; L's efforts to sell her lots, 407; eye trouble, 407, 422; X: 126, 165, 166; ability to do home work, 9, 294; letters to friends, 261, 287, 296, 330; problem of godfather for baby, 287-89; called to New York to aid L., 305; excerpt from her MS "Recollections," 333; reminiscences re L. in letter to F. A. King, 354f.; to Edwin Mims, 365-67; birth: death, 365n; ancestry, childhood, education, 365f.; on L's capture and imprisonment, 370, 373; *for references to their companionship and life together see entries under* Lanier: biography

Lanier, Mary Jane Anderson (Mrs. Robert S., first), character: personality, I: lix, X: 351, 354, 355; sons' poem in memory of, I: 214 (*see* "A Sea-Shore Grave"); ill health, VI: xxiv, VII: 188; relatives, VII: 3n, 4n; IX: 414n; X: 374; correspondence with sons, VII: 8, 15, 34n, 53, 121, 133; home, 110n; death, 188; X: 351; resemblance between her portrait and Mary Day's, VIII: 125; where and when born: meeting with, and marriage to, R. S. Lanier, X: 343

Lanier, Mary Russell (Mrs. Sidney C.), VII: 15n, 229, 280n; VIII: 199, 200n; IX: 235n

Lanier, Nancy (Mrs. Vaughn), VI: 357
Lanier, Nicholas, first, II: 210; VI: xxiii, 361, 363-68, 369, 370, 372, 373; X: 37-39; masque by Jonson and, III: 231; VI: 363; X: 38; portrait, VI: 365; X: 37, 99
Lanier, Nicholas, second, VI: 361, 362, 363, 366, 369-73
Lanier, Nicholas, of Virginia, X: 111
Lanier, Rebecca (Mrs. Walton Harris), VI :357
Lanier, Richard, VI: 357
Lanier, Robert Sampson, V: 197n, 277n; VI: 357, 360; VII: 190n; advice and encouragement re sons' literary endeavors, I: xxiv, xxv, xxxin; VII: 209n, 230n; approval of L's *Poems*, I: lii; generous financial aid to son, lxxxiii (*see also L's appeals for help in his letters*); quoted, 336; suggestions by, the possible genesis of sons' literary work, V: vii, xli; VII: 92n, 230n, 377; comments on *Tiger-Lilies*, V: x, xiv, xviin, xxiv, xxxv; resemblance of fictional characters to, xxv, xxvii, xlii; first wife and her family, VII: 3n; X: 343; law partner and firm, VII: 3n; VIII: 10; X: 343, 344n (*see also* Anderson; Clifford; Lanier and Anderson); L's letters to, VII: 3ff., 9f., 18, 21-37, 39, 51, 60ff., 69, 99, 110, 123, 127, 131, 135, 141, 147, 151f., 161, 166, 171, 177ff., 214ff., 230f., 237, 241, 250, 252f., 267, 278, 282, 287, 313, 339f., 353, 371, 373f., 380f., 383, 387, 389; VIII: 20, 24ff., 33, 39, 80ff., 87, 100f., 122, 126, 141, 165, 168ff., 185, 204, 211, 231, 254, 260, 287, 290, 296, 301, 306, 312, 316, 321, 342, 353, 360, 368, 384, 423, 440; IX: 6, 36, 42, 61, 89, 123, 152, 201, 234, 244, 251, 325, 351, 357, 362, 366, 381, 383, 388f., 393, 402ff., 437, 440, 447, 451f., 455ff., 461, 467, 471, 483, 486, 489, 495, 501, 508f.; X: 13, 16, 20, 26, 35, 44, 47, 51f., 58, 63, 68, 80, 84, 89, 96f., 99, 101f., 110ff., 126, 133f., 141, 151f., 155, 173, 176f., 180, 185f., 206, 209, 220, 226, 334; opinion about letter writ-

Lecturer, Writer, Scholar

469, 475, 491, 502; X: 4, 6, 15, 76,
87, 203; editor of *Evening Bulletin*
(*q. v.*), 149*n*; relatives in Georgia,
150*n*; L. at home of, 174, 188, 244,
257*n*, 408, 417, 418*n*; probable
donor of five hundred dollar bill,
417*n*, 502; interest in government
post for L., 445, 449
Peacock, Mariquita da G. A. de la F.
(Mrs. Gibson), IX: 163, 174, 180,
188, 190, 408, 438; L's poem to,
I: 82 (see " To —, with a Rose ");
friendship with Dom Pedro, IX:
364*n*; L's appreciation of her kind-
nesses, 423
Peacock throne, VI: 298
" Pearl dissolved in wine," L's use of
phrase, I: 351; VII: 90
Pearl mosques, VI: 287, 295, 305, 306
Pearson, C. H., II: 129*n*
Pearsons of North Carolina, X: 308,
311
Peck, Edward (Ned), VII: 313*n*, 314,
322
Peck, Edward B., V: x, xii; quoted,
xxxii*n*
Pedro II, of Brazil, IX: 363
Peirce, Charles S., *see* Noyes, John B.,
and Peirce
Peishwa Mahadeo, suicide, VI: 273
Pelham (Bulwer), IV: 162
Pembroke, Countess, *Arcadia* written
for, III: 384
Pendleton, William N., V: 274; VII:
164
Penfield, Chester N., VI: 85
Pen Lucy school, VII: xxxviii; VIII:
430*n*; IX: 24*n*; X: 5, 20, 28, 147*n*
Penniman, X: 308
Pennsylvania Board of Pardons, poem
addressed to, I: 206, 381
Pensacola, Fla., VI: 64f., 123, 125,
132, 133
Pensacola and Louisville Railroad, VI:
57, 65, 95
Pepys, Samuel, *Diary*, VI: 368, 370;
excerpts, IV: 121; collection of bal-
lads, 394; *Diary* references to Nicholas Lanier, VI: 366, 369-72 *passim*
Percussion, instruments of, II: 192,
303
Percy, Thomas, Bp., *Reliques of Ancient English Poetry* . . . , II: 5; IV:

382ff.; Hales and Furnivall's edition
of Percy's MS, II: 12, 78*n*, 99, 140*n*;
IV: 353, 390; X: 302; influence of
the *Reliques*, IV: 383, 385; its
origin, 388; authenticity challenged,
389ff.; Percy's education, 389; other
literary work, 389, 394; literary
conscience, 392; success: money and
preferment, 393; later life: qualities,
395; three fascinating essays by, 399
—— " Introduction to *The Boy's
Percy* " (L.), I. vii*n*; IV: 256; VI:
379, 410; X: 302, 304, 314, 315,
321, 330; text, IV: 382-400
Percy Society's reprints, IV: 260, 261*n*;
VII: lvii
Percymmon, in *Tiger-Lilies*, V: xvi,
xix, xxii, 8
Perdido Railroad, VI: 65
Peredur, a Mabinogi, IV: 378
Peregrine Pickle (Smollett), IV: 155
Pericles (Shakespeare), III: 329, 334,
390f.; IV: 259
Periodicals and newspapers, reviews
following publication of *Poems*
(1877 and 1884), I: liiff., lxxxivff.;
VI: 411; magazines to which L.
shifted from *Lippincott's*, I: lxvii;
theory and content of newspaper,
IV: 176-78; those in which poems
first printed, VI: 381-85; short prose
printed, 386f.; list of selected re-
views of all published volumes,
409-12
Periods, past: provincialism: relation to
our time, III: 135, 171; IV: 273
Perot family, VIII: 383, 430, 446; IX:
166, 291
Perot, Anne, X: 376*n*
Perrine, Rebecca, IX: 167
Perrine of Baltimore, VIII: 383, 430
Perry, Captain, VI: 219
Persian proverb, VI: 330
" Personal Recollections of Sidney
Lanier " (Gilman), VII: xlv*n*
Personality, doctrines of Emerson, I:
lxxi; and L., lxxi, lxxiv*n*; relation-
ship of " The Cloud " to theme of,
364; idea of the individual embodied in music, II: 309f., 311;
importance of L's demonstration
about psychology of, IV: x; defined
as spontaneous variation between

blank verse, II: 145ff.; use of the rest, 145-52; metrical tests for ascertaining chronology and authenticity of plays, 145ff.; III: 316, 328-67; IV: 316-26; method for determining doubtful lines of, II: 148f.; old and new criticism and methods of inquiry, 156; III: 316; scholars associated with metrical-test research, II: 164, 228; III: 336, 347, 366; IV: 312n, 320n; use of weak-ending and light-ending lines, II: 165f.; III: 345-47, 405; IV: 321, 322ff.; use of the rhythmic accent, II: 166-75; III: 352-55, 405; IV: 325; transference into verse, of rhythms of common speech, II: 166, 168, 172; speech-tunes, 200, 201, 204, 210, 216; relations of Robert Greene and, 227; III: 283, 381ff.; IV: 330; rhyme, II: 227; III: 336-38, 405; IV: 321ff.; use of alliteration, II: 243; L's methods of presenting S. in the several lectures, III: xxff.; music of the time of: references to, in plays, xxii, 196-238 passim; X: 117; domestic life of time of, III: xxii, 239-99; relation to nature compared with that of earlier poets, 35-39; complex ideas in bird-poem, 56; attitude toward own work, 156, 170; use of a term in double sense, 159; failure of his own time to recognize his true value, 165; pronunciation in time of, 168-95; fondness for puns and other word-tricks, 176, 177, 180; effects arising from archaic sounds of words used, 183; moral teaching: why his plays are powerful sermons, 185ff.; why both the truest and the most unreal of writers, 188ff.; great adoration for music, 196, 209f., 235; three periods of career, and plays of each period, 237, 328ff.; IV: 309-15, 326; list of world-events preceding and during life of, III: 243-48; tobacco never mentioned by, 246; IV: 224, 269; drew sustenance from *Gorboduc*, III: 294; a reformer of English life, 317; two old plays giving moral atmosphere of his boyhood, 321; entire process of artistic and moral develop-

ment so revealed by chronology of plays, 328, 329, 334, 356ff.; 402ff.; IV: 243, 307-28 passim; Marlowe's influence, III: 331; self-control, 349, 350, 357; plays-within-plays, or anti-masks, 380ff.; IV: 330; three plays showing the three great relations of man: to God, III: 368-78; to man, 379-91; IV: 328; to nature, III: 392-410; IV: 328; Jonson's eulogy of, IV: 32; regret vs. repentance in works of, 181-83, 217-20, 222f.; growth of man from time of, to George Eliot: limitations of his time, 222-24; forgiveness and reconciliation group of plays, 243, 314; comparative study of three plays each, by Chaucer and, 255, 304-45 passim; III: xiv; VI: 387; X: 166n, 200, 208, 213, 266; doctors in time of, IV: 255, 258-72; in works of S., 259, 264, 266; L's readings, and class for study of Chaucer and, 256; interrelations of the three plays, 307-28; normal spiritual growth as explanation of the astonishing universality of his appeal, 312; art in play construction equal to verse-art, 326n; generalization of the three works each by Chaucer and, 329; slightly sketched anatomy of the special forms assumed in each, 329-34; inspired by, and borrowed from, Chaucer, 345; verbal echoes of, in *Tiger-Lilies*, V: 10, 21-191 passim; language difference at time of Chaucer and, 325; Furness editing *variorum* edition, IX: 174; projected textbook on modern study of, X: 143; *see also the plays, e. g., Hamlet*
—— personal and family life: pictures of his environment and early life, drawn from facts and suppositions, III: xxii, 239-99 passim; cloud over life, 162, 164, 237, 332; contributions towards mental and physical photographs of, 170f.; parents, 239, 250, 331; becomes "Gentleman" and a man of substance, 240, 406; wife, 253, 335; children, 332, 390; IV: 259; probable return to Stratford: relic preserved there, III: 335;